EAST ASIA IMPERILLED
Transnational Challenges to Security

Security issues have traditionally been defined in military terms, yet the post-Cold War security landscape contains numerous non-military challenges to security. In this pathbreaking analysis, Alan Dupont argues that an emerging new class of non-military threats has the potential to destabilise East Asia and reverse decades of hard-won economic and social development. He shows that these transnational shifts must be grasped and dealt with by governments and non-government organizations both regionally, and internationally, if conflict is to be avoided. Transnational threats stem from overpopulation, deforestation and pollution, global warming, unregulated population movements, transnational crime, virulent new strains of infectious diseases and a host of other issues not previously associated with international security. Collectively they represent a new agenda that stretches our understanding of security and pose novel challenges for foreign and defence policy. This highly informative, compelling and authoritative book is essential reading for East Asia specialists and makes a significant and timely contribution to international security debates.

Alan Dupont is a former army officer, intelligence analyst, journalist and diplomat who has worked on East Asian security issues for over 25 years and is now a prominent academic at the Australian National University. He has served in the Australian embassies in Seoul (1984–87) and Jakarta (1991–94), and has written over fifty articles and book chapters on defence and international security, including an Adelphi Paper for the International Institute for Strategic Studies on the environment and security in Pacific Asia. He is also a well-known commentator on political and strategic developments in East Asia.

For the three women in my life – Rosemary, Clair and Pia.

CAMBRIDGE ASIA–PACIFIC STUDIES

Cambridge Asia–Pacific Studies aims to provide a focus and forum for scholarly work on the Asia–Pacific region as a whole, and its component sub-regions, namely Northeast Asia, Southeast Asia and the Pacific Islands. The series is produced in association with the Research School of Pacific and Asian Studies at the Australian National University and the Australian Institute of International Affairs.

R. Gerard Ward and Elizabeth Kingdon (eds) *Land, Custom and Practice in the South Pacific*
0 521 47289 X hardback

Stephanie Lawson *Tradition Versus Democracy in the South Pacific*
0 521 49638 1 hardback

Walter Hatch and Kozo Yamamura *Asia in Japan's Embrace*
0 521 56176 0 hardback 0 521 56515 4 paperback

Alasdair Bowie and Daniel Unger *The Politics of Open Economies: Indonesia, Malaysia, the Philippines and Thailand*
0 521 58343 8 hardback 0 521 58683 6 paperback

David Kelly and Anthony Reid (eds) *Asian Freedoms*
0 521 62035 X hardback 0 521 63757 0 paperback

Danny Unger *Building Social Capital in Thailand*
0 521 63058 4 hardback 0 521 63931 X paperback

Yongnian Zheng *Discovering Chinese Nationalism in China: Modernization, Identity, and International Relations*
0 521 64180 2 hardback 0 521 64590 5 paperback

Doh C. Shin *Mass Politics and Culture in Democratizing Korea*
0 521 65146 8 hardback 0 521 65823 3 paperback

John A. Mathews and Dong-Sung Cho *Tiger Technology: The Creation of a Semiconductor Industry in East Asia*
0 521 66269 9 hardback

Samuel S. Kim (ed.) *Korea's Globalization*
0 521 77272 9 hardback 0 521 77559 0 paperback

Gregory W. Noble and John Ravenhill (eds) *The Asian Financial Crisis and the Architecture of Global Finance*
0 521 79091 3 hardback 0 521 79422 6 paperback

Peter Dauvergne *Loggers and Degradation in the Asia-Pacific: Corporations and Environmental Management*
0 521 80661 5 hardback 0 521 00134 X paperback

Anthony J. Langlois *The Politics of Justice and Human Rights: Southeast Asia and Universalist Theory*
0 521 80785 9 hardback 0 521 00347 4 paperback

EAST ASIA IMPERILLED

Transnational Challenges to Security

ALAN DUPONT
Australian National University

CAMBRIDGE
UNIVERSITY PRESS

PUBLISHED BY THE PRESS SYNDICATE OF THE UNIVERSITY OF CAMBRIDGE
The Pitt Building, Trumpington Street, Cambridge, United Kingdom

CAMBRIDGE UNIVERSITY PRESS
The Edinburgh Building, Cambridge CB2 2RU, UK
40 West 20th Street, New York, NY 10011–4211, USA
10 Stamford Road, Oakleigh, VIC 3166, Australia
Ruiz de Alarcón 13, 28014 Madrid, Spain
Dock House, The Waterfront, Cape Town 8001, South Africa

http://www.cambridge.org

First published 2001

Printed in China by Everbest Printing Co.

Typeface New Baskerville (*Adobe*) 10/12 pt.   *System* QuarkXPress®   [PK]

A catalogue record for this book is available from the British Library

National Library of Australia Cataloguing in Publication data
Dupont, Alan, 1950– .
East Asia imperilled: transnational challenges to security.
Includes index.
ISBN 0 521 81153 8.
ISBN 0 521 01015 2. (pbk)
1. Environmental degradation – Social aspects.
2. National security – East Asia.
3. Environmental degradation – Political aspects.
I. Title.
354.3095

ISBN 0 521 81153 8 hardback
ISBN 0 521 01015 2 paperback

Contents

Tables, Figures and Maps

Tables

Figures

Maps

Acknowledgments

In the early 1990s, when I first began seriously to contemplate the likely sources of insecurity in the post-Cold War world, the transnational issues which are the subject of this book were generally regarded by the strategic and foreign policy community to be of marginal significance for international security. Traditionalists argued that the environment and other non-military security issues had no real place in the study of war and conflict. Defence planners and senior military officers were concerned that too broad an interpretation of security could distract them from their core business, thereby running the risk of 'dulling the sword', as my colleague Lorraine Elliott has written.

Coming as I did from a traditional security background as a former military officer, intelligence analyst, diplomat and strategist, these criticisms and anxieties initially struck a sympathetic chord in me. However, as a result of the experiences and insights gained while working on East Asian security issues during the 1980s and 1990s, I gradually came to the view that the salience of transnational forces had been seriously underestimated by scholars and policy-makers. There were clearly important, if still poorly perceived, connections between East Asia's deteriorating physical environment and the capacity to govern, feed and provide for the region's burgeoning populations. Growing numbers of people were on the move outside the control of governments, and the activities of organised crime were increasingly traversing the grey area between law and order and security. More fundamentally, the realist security framework seemed in need of substantial revision if not major renovation. Its familiar and once reassuring verities no longer seemed capable of providing a reliable guide for making sense of a world in transition or illuminating the dynamics of a rapidly evolving international security environment. In short, there was a worrying disconnection between theory and the practice. Not all will be convinced by the arguments in this book but there will, I hope, be some enlightenment even for the most committed and unrepentant of traditionalists.

My first attempt to come to grips with the theoretical concepts explored in the Introduction and Chapter 1 of this book appeared as 'New Dimensions of Security', in Denny Roy (ed.), *The New Security Agenda in the Asia-Pacific Region* (Macmillan Press, Hampshire, 1997). An article in *Pacifica Review* entitled 'Unregulated Population Flows in East Asia: A New Security Dilemma?' contains some initial thoughts on the subject of unregulated population movements. Chapter 10, which deals with drug-trafficking, was first published in *Asian Survey* as 'Transnational Crime, Drugs and Security in East Asia' and is used here with the permission of the regents of the University of California, Berkeley. Peter Gleick very kindly consented to the use of several of his excellent tables on water availability. I am particularly indebted to the International Institute for Strategic Studies and Oxford University Press for permission to draw on the material from my Adelphi Paper 'The Environment and Security in Pacific Asia'. In virtually all cases, the material in these earlier publications has been substantially rewritten, revised and updated for this book.

Finally, I would like to thank my colleagues Des Ball and Denny Roy for their early words of encouragement in pursuing this project, Pauline Kerr for her valuable comments and advice on the conceptual chapters, the late Gerry Segal for his critique of the section dealing with environmental security, and two anonymous reviewers. This book would not have been possible without the industry of my research assistant, Jena Hamilton, and her unique ability to unearth useful references from the most unlikely sources. Having suffered through five years of distracted husband syndrome, I owe a special debt of gratitude to my wife Rosemary for her understanding and forbearance.

Abbreviations

ADB   Asian Development Bank
AIDS   Acquired Immune Deficiency Syndrome
ARF   ASEAN Regional Forum
ASEAN   Association of South East Asian Nations
ATS   amphetamine-type stimulant
BBM   Bugis, Buton and Makassarese
BCP   Burma Communist Party
bpd   barrels per day
BTK   Born To Kill (Vietnam)
CFCs   chlorofluorocarbons
CIA   Central Intelligence Agency (USA)
CIS   Commonwealth of Independent States
CSCAP   Council for Security Cooperation in the Asia Pacific
EEZ   Exclusive Economic Zone
FAO   UN Food and Agriculture Organisation
FARC   Revolutionary Armed Forces of Colombia
FBI   Federal Bureau of Investigation (USA)
G7   Group of Seven
GDP   gross domestic product
GM   genetically modified
GMO   genetically modified organism
GNP   Grand National Party (South Korea)
HIV   Human Immunodeficiency Virus
IDU   injecting drug-user
IEA   International Energy Agency
IISS   International Institute for Strategic Studies
IMF   International Monetary Fund
IPCC   Intergovernmental Panel on Climate Change

IUU	illegal, unreported and unregulated (fishing)
KEDO	Korean Peninsula Energy Development Organisation
LDP	Liberal-Democratic Party (Japan)
LWR	light-water reactor
MIED	Maritime Information Exchange Directory
MITI	Ministry of International Trade and Industry
NGO	non-government organisation
NPA	New People's Army (Philippines)
OECD	Organisation for Economic Cooperation and Development
OPEC	Organisation of Petroleum Exporting Countries
OPM	Free Papua Movement
ODA	Overseas Development Assistance
PLA	People's Liberation Army (China)
PUB	Public Utilities Board (Singapore)
SPDC	State Peace and Development Council (Burma)
TCO	transnational criminal organisation
TFR	total fertility rates
UMNO	United Malays National Organisation
UNAIDS	Joint United Nations Programme on HIV/AIDS
UNCLOS	United Nations Convention on the Law of the Sea
UNDP	United Nations Development Programme
UNEP	United Nations Environment Programme
UNHCR	United Nations High Commissioner for Refugees
UPMs	unregulated population movements
USCR	US Committee for Refugees
UWSA	United Wa State Army (Burma)
WFP	World Food Programme
WHO	World Health Organisation

Introduction

A familiar brown haze settles over the verdant jungles of Kalimantan, dissipating the last moisture-laden clouds of the departing rainy season. Fuelled by countless fires lit by human hands, the haze intensifies as the dry season takes hold, blanketing the island and spreading into nearby Malaysia and Singapore. Factories are forced to close, tourism plummets and affected locals pack into overwhelmed hospital casualty wards complaining of respiratory problems caused by the acrid smoke. The muted response of the Association of South East Asian Nations (ASEAN) belies the region's frustration and anger that Jakarta has failed to prevent the wanton acts of environmental vandalism that are destroying the remnants of Indonesia's once pristine forests and levying significant human and economic costs on neighbouring states.

Two thousand four hundred kilometres to the northwest, the skies are clear as a caravan of heavily laden mules carefully picks their way down a boulder-strewn gorge abutting Burma's border with Thailand. A heavily armed ethnic Wa tribesman smiles in anticipation as he calculates his profit from the heroin destined for the affluent and captive markets of North America, Europe and East Asia. This brief moment of satisfaction is his last. A bullet from a Thai border patrol policeman eviscerates his brain and a salvo of mortar rounds brackets the panicked mules, decimating their guards. As the Wa draw their last breath, security officials meeting in Seoul and Beijing peer out at the receding snows of an unusually warm Northeast Asian winter and dust off their contingency plans for North Korea. There is little discussion of North Korea's military and ballistic missile capabilities. These are relatively known quantities. Of more immediate concern to the South Korean and Chinese officials is how they should handle the anticipated inflow of millions of refugees from a famine-stricken North Korea.

1

In a windowless, electronically screened room, Singapore's political leaders ponder the implications of a secret intelligence assessment on the island state's strategic vulnerabilities. At the top of the list is water. Reliant on Malaysia for 50 per cent of its fresh water and mindful of past threats by Kuala Lumpur to turn off the tap, Singapore's leaders are being forced to consider alternative sources of fresh water. There are, however, few viable options and all are expensive. Meanwhile, in distant, cosmopolitan Geneva, an impeccably attired United Nations official briefs a jostling crowd of unruly reporters. He warns that Asia is about to overtake sub-Saharan Africa as the region most affected by AIDS and that some Southeast Asian countries are already in the throes of an explosive epidemic. Earlier, the Security Council had convened for its first ever session on AIDS at the behest of US Ambassador Richard Holbrooke, who argued that the disease has metamorphosed from a public health issue to one of international security.

Transnational Threats

Although partly imagined, these scenarios suggest that the 'drivers' of East Asia's future security environment will be substantially different from those of the past.[1] A new class of threats is emerging which is stretching the boundaries of conventional thinking about security. Some of these threats are economic; others relate to the earth's physical environment; many are contemporary manifestations of age-old afflictions.[2] They stem from demographic pressures, resource depletion, global warming, unregulated population movements (UPMs), transnational crime, virulent new strains of infectious diseases and a host of other issues not previously associated with international security. Complex, interconnected and multidimensional, these non-military, transnational issues are moving from the periphery to the centre of the security concerns of both states and people. Collectively they represent a new security agenda that will increasingly demand the attention of policy-makers everywhere.[3]

This new agenda has important implications for international relations theory as well as for the conduct of foreign and defence policy. Many of the emerging transnational causes of conflict are the result of forces outside the traditional framework of strategic analysis that have little to do with the exercise of coercive power by competing nation-states but everything to do with the stability of states and human survival. Transnational phenomena are likely to become more prominent causes of conflict and insecurity, particularly in the developing world, as pressure on natural resources increases, people become more mobile, and non-state actors compete with states for money, influence and power. Environmental degradation intensifies the problems of governance and development in poorer countries and precipitates trans-border and internal migration. The very existence of some states may be threatened by sea-level rise resulting from human-induced climate change. Access to food, energy and water is dependent on preserving and sustaining the earth's natural resource base. Drug-trafficking distorts economic development and promotes the spread of AIDS, a disease that is destroying the social fabric of many communities and causing millions of preventible deaths.

These are all problems that fall squarely within the realm of international security, yet paradoxically they have been largely excluded from the mainstream academic discourse on security. As a result, policy-makers are struggling to locate transnational threats conceptually and to comprehend their causes and strategic significance. The main reason for the intellectual inertia and policy confusion about the place and importance of transnational threats is that they do not fit comfortably within the worldview of realism, which is the leading theoretical paradigm in international relations and the conceptual frame of reference for most policy-makers and scholars working on international security issues.[4] To understand why realism has been unable to accommodate the transnational agenda, which is a central task of this introductory section, it is necessary to appreciate the theory's historical roots, its defining beliefs and the reason for its waning explanatory power. A second task is to sketch out an alternative framework for thinking about security that encompasses the transnational agenda.

Realism's Limitations

Realism, in its many forms, has dominated European and by extension Western thinking about security since the Treaty of Westphalia in 1648, which is generally accepted as having laid down the foundations of the contemporary state system. Europe's ruling classes were conditioned by centuries of internecine warfare, dynastic competition and colonial expansionism to seek security through military strength and alliance-building rather than cooperation. The consequences for Western security thinking were profound and enduring. Since force seemed a more effective means of maximising strategic influence and protecting vital interests, especially for the larger states, cooperative impulses were often short-lived and expedient. In order to maintain the equilibrium of the system and to preserve their own independence and interests, states frequently sought to maintain a balance of power, either by reducing the strategic weight of potential hegemons or by increasing their own.[5]

Security was thus associated in the minds of Europeans with the protection or acquisition of territory. The most serious and frequent challenges to state sovereignty invariably originated in the actions of other states seeking to enhance their power or wealth by increasing their control of territory. European nations had good cause to fear the territorial encroachments and ambitions of others. Richard Rosencrance estimates that 95 per cent of the states that existed in 1500 have since been 'obliterated, subdivided, or combined into other countries'.[6] The Cold War subsequently imbued a generation of American scholars and policy-makers with the tenets of realism, and these were subsumed and internalised in the idea of national security.[7] As the United States assumed the role of standard-bearer and protector of the West's political and spiritual heritage, American academic thinking on security became the accepted Western orthodoxy, and it was the orthodoxy of realism that prevailed. The Cold War also encouraged the development of a subdiscipline of international relations known as strategic studies. Strategic studies reinforced the realist bias towards the military aspects of national security, producing, as Barry Buzan has noted, a large volume of empirical literature on the problems of military policy but giving little attention to alternative approaches or interpretations of security.[8]

For these reasons, both classical realists and contemporary neo-realists are primarily concerned with the balance of power between states and how best to deal with the security dilemma that arises from the structural tensions inherent in a system of independent states when there is no supranational authority to maintain order.[9] Realists consider anarchy to be the ordering principle of the international system and independent, sovereign states the principal actors, engaged in an unending and brutal struggle for survival. However, anarchy does not presuppose the total absence of rules or norms, nor does it mandate conflict. Rather it denotes the absence of an overarching authority or 'government of governments' that can impose its will over the state.[10] Uncertainty over neighbours' intentions or actions creates a mutual security dilemma: feeling threatened by others, states may feel compelled to attack first or run the risk of being destroyed.[11] From a realist perspective, military threats are therefore paramount. Defending national sovereignty and territory from the hostile or predatory intentions of others is a fundamental responsibility of government, and survival of the state as a distinct political, cultural and social entity is the primary objective of security.[12] Economic vulnerabilities and strengths figure prominently in traditional security thinking but usually only as elements of military power and important measures of a state's strategic weight and war-fighting potential.[13]

I argue that this characterisation of the security problematique is too narrowly conceived and Western-centred to encompass and make sense of the transnational challenge to global security, especially in East Asia. My reasons are fourfold. First, realism's concentration on state power and the use of force to achieve political and strategic goals allows little scope for considering the new salience of non-state actors and the non-military dimension of security. Transnational criminal organisations (TCOs) demonstrably threaten international security, even by the parsimonious standards of realism, through their involvement in drug-trafficking, 'people-smuggling' and other illicit practices that compromise the authority of governments, weaken the economic foundations of the state, and accentuate the permeability of national borders.

More fundamentally, transnational forces are recasting notions of power and sovereignty away from their traditional rootedness in the territorially bounded state.[14] It is this detachment from territory that distinguishes economic and political activity in the twenty-first century. To paraphrase Jessica Matthews, many resources and threats that matter, be they money, information, infectious diseases or environmental degradation, circulate and shape lives and economies with little regard for political boundaries.[15] In the 1980s, the American liberals Joseph Nye and Robert Keohane recognised that the channels connecting societies were increasingly outside the prerogative of national governments and that states had to deal with a multitude of non-military security issues.[16] This trend is even more evident in today's globalised world where the density of networks of interdependence has thickened immeasurably and institutional velocity (how rapidly a system and the units within it change) has accelerated.[17] There is no preordained hierarchy which mandates the preeminence of the military over other dimensions of security policy, and military force may not be the most effective instrument for achieving security in a world increasingly characterised by widening circles of interlocking economic, political, social and environmental interests.[18] Even committed realists like Henry Kissinger acknowledge that the balance of power and the idea of national security 'no longer [define] our perils or our possibilities'.[19]

Second, realists tend to be dismissive, or at least highly sceptical, of the security-degrading effects of transnational issues, mainly because these are not seen as significant causes of interstate conflict.[20] On the contrary, as I will show, many transnational phenomena have the potential to generate significant political and military tensions between states. Moreover, there is a complex but clearly discernible nexus between the transnational and traditional causes of interstate conflict which is not well understood. Ecological stress heightens competition for scarce resources, compounds sovereignty disputes and deepens ethno-political cleavages. Maritime conflict may be driven by the desire to harvest marine living resources as well as to defend territory and protect vital sea-lines of communication, as the 1972–73 'Cod War' between the United Kingdom and Iceland illustrates.[21] The unregulated movement of people across borders can trigger or worsen hostilities between states, as has been demonstrated in virtually every major region of the world over the past few decades.

Third, the focus of realists on conflict between states blinds them to the destabilising effects of transnational phenomena on the internal stability of states. AIDS, for example, has strategic implications because it destabilises countries politically, fractures the social glue that binds communities together, reduces state capacity by siphoning off scarce economic resources, and hollows out military forces in poorer countries that cannot afford high standards of health care. More generally, the bloody internal conflicts that raged across Bosnia, Kosovo, Rwanda, Afghanistan and East Timor in the 1990s illustrate the essential meaningless of defining security for any of the protagonists and their innocent victims purely, or even primarily, in terms of defence from the aggression of other states.[22] Separatism, ethnic struggles, guerrilla insurgencies and armed criminal challenges to the state are today more frequent than interstate war, and the security consequences are just as severe.[23] On the other hand, major wars between states over territory, ideology and power-balancing are declining in frequency and magnitude. Of the 120 armed conflicts fought during the Cold War, most were between states and eleven accounted for more than 200 000 casualties each. By contrast, the great bulk of those recorded since 1989 have been internal. In effect, there is a disjuncture between realism's fixation with war between states and the rise in intrastate conflict.[24] Most significant armed conflicts of the past decade, including those in East Asia, have been internal rather than international. Population pressures, resource scarcity and organised crime are some of the transnational factors that have the potential to aggravate intrastate conflicts and occasionally be their primary cause.

Fourth, there are reasons to question realism's portrayal of a determining natural order based on the balance of power between states. The West's strategic preoccupation with the balance of power is not shared to the same degree by developing nations in East Asia, reflecting their different historical experiences and post-independence focus on nation-building. As Robert Gilpin observes, post-Westphalian Europe is 'unique in the systemic character of its balancing mechanism'.[25] There are few examples of European-style balancing in pre-colonial East Asia because for more than a millennium, the East Asian state system was essentially hegemonic or imperial.[26] Smaller states acknowledged the power of the major hegemon by paying tribute and acts of symbolic obeisance in exchange for a relatively high level of autonomy and independence.[27] While some might aspire to be the new hegemon, all accepted a system of interstate relations in which the rules and conventions were determined by the hegemon.[28]

Threats to social order and stability from within the national polity are accorded a far higher priority in developing East Asia than in Europe or

North America, and providing sufficient food, water and energy to sustain burgeoning populations is regarded as a critical security issue for the region. Even as a global power, China is deeply concerned with maintaining the internal stability of the state, preserving social cohesion and feeding its people to a far greater extent than its Western counterparts.[29] This is not to argue that the balance of power and other realist considerations have no relevance at all for East Asia or are without influence on Asian security thinking – strategic competition between states and disputes over territory and resources are important underlying causes of friction. Realism still captures much of the region's security dynamics, particularly in Northeast Asia, where there are closer parallels with Europe and where two of the four major actors, Russia and the United States, are European as well as Asian powers. Even in Southeast Asia, balancing behaviour is not uncommon. Although ASEAN adheres to a declaratory policy opposing intervention by external powers in the affairs of the region, most of its member states are quite willing to accommodate, and even encourage, a countervailing US presence to Chinese power.[30]

However, there is no strict hierarchy among security issues in East Asia such as realists assume. States are not the only arbiters of their citizens' security and not the only players on the international relations board, and the desire to protect material interests is not always the decisive determinant of state behaviour. Interdependence and cooperation characterise the region's geopolitics as much as self-help and competition.[31] Moreover, as constructivists point out, the security dilemma is not structurally predetermined or the inevitable result of anarchy. Threat perceptions and the construction of vulnerabilities are also socially contingent since they reflect different cultural, perceptual and historical experiences.[32] These factors are, as Muthiah Alagappa contends, 'crucial to the security thinking and behaviour of Asian governments and must therefore feature in their explanation'.[33]

Extended Security

The key conclusion to be drawn from this analysis of realism's limitations is that a more comprehensive concept of security is required that embraces the transnational agenda. This I will call *extended security* because its conceptual boundaries stretch beyond the traditionally accepted causes of interstate war and the use of organised violence by states, to include non-military threats to survival and the destabilising activities of non-state actors. However, extended security acknowledges that the old drivers of conflict have not been displaced or rendered suddenly impotent. They coexist in the same space as the new transnational forces and may be influenced or intensified by them. Thus, scarcity of fresh water sharpens interstate rivalries and complicates border and sovereignty disputes as well as raising wider regional and global concerns about food security.

Extended security accepts the realist proposition that maintaining the territorial integrity, political sovereignty, economic viability and social cohesion of the state are key measures of security. Unlike realism, however, it recognises that many threats which matter are not immutably linked to the exercise of state power, or the survival of the state. The concept of security must be extended upward, to incorporate the biosphere which sustains all life, and be detached from the structures that define and give meaning to our existence as political beings. Environmental threats stem not from competition between states or shifts in the balance of power, but from human-induced disturbances to the fragile balance of nature, the consequences of which may be just as injurious to the integrity and functioning of the state as those resulting from military conflict. They may also be more difficult to reverse or repair, as global warming and the depletion of the ozone layer illustrate. Security also needs to be extended outward to include those non-state actors that challenge the state's traditional monopoly over taxation and organised violence.[34]

The idea of extended security is best characterised as a shift in the security paradigm rather than a transformation, since important elements of the old paradigm remain. Nonetheless, the shift is significant because extended security accepts that abuse of the environment and scarcity of resources can be broadly destabilising and detrimental to human survival and represent the collective deprivation of all people and states. From the perspective of extended security, deforestation results not only in the loss of a valuable resource for a local community or particular state. It can also trigger catastrophic flooding across national borders and contribute to widespread pollution and climate change that, in turn, may cause food shortages, population displacement, economic damage and death. Another important conceptual departure is the change to a circular mode of thinking which recognises that many of the security problems of the modern era do not have a distinct beginning, middle and end.[35] Conceived in this way, ecological breakdown is a root cause of migration, but the large-scale unregulated movement of people contributes, in turn, to environmental degradation.[36] Both can cause conflict. The linear thinking and zero-sum calculations of realism, on the other hand, in which security is measured according to the relative losses and gains by competing nation-states, are of little use in understanding or assessing the threat from environmental degradation, unregulated population movements or violence perpetrated by transnational criminal organisations.

Of course, threats comprise only part of the security problematique. There is also the question of the appropriate referent or object of security. Simply stated, who or what is to be protected? The state, the individual, or humanity at large? Realist notions of security assume that the security of the state is coterminous with that of the individual. This may be so in the world's genuine democracies but it is rarely the case in authoritarian or weak states, where governments may be responsible for violating or diminishing the security of their people. In many parts of the world, ruling elites have consciously pursued policies such as ethnic cleansing and the forced displacement of targeted minorities that are deliberately harmful to sections of their own population. Far from being the ultimate guarantor of their security, the state may actually be the principal threat to the life and liberty of its own citizens. The disconnection between the security of the state and the individual is illuminated by the transnational agenda. North Korea's devastating famine in the late 1990s which claimed at least 2 million lives was largely the result of ill-conceived government policies and a manifest disregard for the well-being and security of the North Korean people. The object of extended security must therefore be people as well as states, and people ahead of the state, when governments abrogate their responsibility for security through volition or inaction.[37]

There is increasing recognition of the need to distinguish between national security and individual, or human, security where the two clearly conflict. Advocates of human security go further and argue that the *who* or *what* of security should be the individual, as a rights-bearing person, or humanity in general, rather than the state.[38] There are several permutations of this school of thought. The UN defines human security as safety from chronic threats such as hunger, disease and repression and 'protection from sudden and hurtful disruptions in the patterns of daily life'.[39] Lloyd Axworthy, a former Canadian Foreign Minister, conceived human security as a 'condition, or state of being characterized by freedom from pervasive threats to people's rights, their safety or even their lives'.[40] Others define the concept more broadly, maintaining that anything which reduces people's quality of life also diminishes their security, just as anything that improves quality of life is an enhancement of human security.[41] This alternative view of security is not entirely new, since liberals have always considered the individual to be a central referent of security. There are, however, significant points of departure from classical liberalism as well as from realism. Crucially, preserving the political sovereignty of the state is subordinated to protecting human rights and guaranteeing the safety and well-being of the individual.[42] In effect, human security decouples security from national identity and the survival of the state.

Human security as a concept is not without its own failings. Its advocates need to explain better who is going to provide for 'the security of humankind' and how the concept can be effectively made operational.[43] There may be no clear answer to this particular dilemma because human security is more a statement of principle than a guide for action in areas such as defence and foreign policy. Protecting people from the manifold hurtful disruptions to daily life is a worthy societal goal, but giving meaningful effect to it may be problematic. Nevertheless, the concept of human security underlines the inefficacy of enshrining the state as the exclusive object of security and serves a useful purpose in providing an alternative criterion for evaluating the harmful effects of transnational threats.

The need for a broader conceptualisation of security to take account of transnational threats has already won endorsement from influential epistemic communities in East Asia. In a highly significant but little noted shift, the 'second track'[44] Council for Security Cooperation in the Asia Pacific (CSCAP) has explicitly rejected the balance of power as an appropriate organising principle for the region, maintaining that the security of vital interests and core values extends 'beyond the military sphere'.[45] Instead, East Asians have embraced the notion of comprehensive security, defined as 'the pursuit of sustainable security in all fields (personal, political, economic, social, cultural, military, environmental) in both the domestic and external spheres, essentially through cooperative means'.[46]

Recognition of the need for a more comprehensive approach to security is not confined to East Asia, nor is it a recent phenomenon. In the 1970s, the Brandt Commission called for a redefinition of security that would incorporate the non-military agenda of complex interdependence.[47] A decade later, Richard Ullman asserted that the needs and concerns of the state must be balanced against those of the individual and take greater account of non-government entities.[48] Neither the Brandt Commission nor Ullman was able to elicit much change in the mindset of the defence and foreign policy establishment of the time, which was still preoccupied with the Cold War security agenda. However, their ideas have since germinated in more fertile policy soil. In a major departure from Cold War thinking, the UN Security Council declared in January 1992 that 'the non-military sources of instability in the economic, social, humanitarian and ecological fields have become threats to peace and security'.[49] Eight years later, during the first ever debate on AIDS in the UN Security Council, US Vice President Al Gore called on UN member states to 'see security through a new and wider prism'. In a significant departure from conventional thinking, Gore urged the council to adopt a more expansive definition of world security that would include issues like AIDS because 'the heart of the security agenda is protecting lives'.[50]

Many states have begun to redefine security and adjust their policy settings to take account of transnational forces. The US is illustrative. National Security Council document 68 was the seminal statement of US national security policy at the height of the Cold War.[51] Written in 1950 for President Truman, NSC 68 described the international security milieu of that time in classical balance-of-power terms, focusing on the Soviet Union's challenge to US values and interests. In contrast, the national security policy enunciated by another Democratic President, Bill Clinton, almost five decades later was concerned with a far wider range of threats and conceptualises security in a way that the authors of NSC 68 would have found difficult to comprehend. The Clinton national security strategy devoted considerable space to detailing the challenges posed by transnational threats, which were regarded as having moved 'to center stage with the Cold War's end'.[52] Highlighted were drugs, organised crime, smuggling, money-laundering, corruption and weapons of mass destruction. Environmental damage and high population growth were recognised as having the capacity to undermine 'economic prosperity and political stability in many countries'.[53] As a result, the US National Intelligence Council now closely monitors the availability of fresh water in China, recognising the close connection between water, China's grain harvests and Beijing's ability to feed its 1.3 billion people.[54]

The Structure of this Book

Nevertheless, a great deal more research is needed to establish convincingly the causal connections between transnational phenomena and conflict. On this point supporters and detractors agree.[55] There are relatively few detailed case studies and of these only a handful concentrate on East Asia, a surprising lacuna given that East Asia is home to a third of the world's population and is overwhelmingly comprised of developing states, precisely the kind of states that are most vulnerable to transnational threats.[56] The main task of this book is to cast some much needed empirical light on the importance and relevance of these threats to the security of East Asia by examining the impact of environmental degradation, UPMs and transnational crime. Aggregated under these broad headings are critical issues of resource scarcity, population growth, climate change, refugees, undocumented labour migration, drug-trafficking and AIDS. These subjects have been selected from among the multitude of transnational threats competing for the attention of policy-makers for two main reasons.[57] First, they are among the most serious of the transnational threats to East Asia's security because they affect the region's common security interests rather than those of any one state. Second, individually and collectively, they provide clear evidence of the paradigm shift that is now under way. Their dynamics are circular rather than linear, their security effects cannot be properly evaluated through the lens of realism, and they present novel problems of response as well as of analysis.

The book is divided into three parts, preceded by an overarching chapter which surveys the existing literature, introduces the major theoretical debates and draws out the connections between environmental degradation, UPMs, transnational crime and security. Part I comprises four chapters dealing with the major drivers of environmentally generated

insecurity and conflict. Chapters 2 and 3 explore the effects of population
growth, pollution, deforestation and climate change and makes the case
for their inclusion in the policy calculations of East Asia's security planners. Chapters 4–6 consider how environmental degradation is contributing to three potential resource scarcities – of energy, food and water
– and demonstrate that the perception, as well as the reality, of shortages
can create insecurity.

Part II is concerned with the link between security and unregulated
population movements. Chapter 7 explains the reasons for the upsurge
in UPMs and shows how ethnic conflict and government policies can
stimulate them. Chapter 8 analyses three new catalysts of East Asia's escalating UPM problem – people-smuggling by transnational criminal
groups, undocumented labour migration and environmental degradation which is creating a new class of 'environmental refugees'.

The three chapters in Part III provide insights into the growing threat
from organised criminal groups in East Asia and their role in the illicit
trade in drugs, sex and the spread of AIDS. Chapter 9 explores the organisation and characteristics of these groups and evaluates the criminal
threat to global and regional security. Chapter 10 appraises the security
implications of narcotics-trafficking in East Asia, while chapter 11 analyses the reasons for the rapid growth in HIV/AIDS infection throughout
the region and the pandemic's likely consequences for security. Each of
the transnational issues discussed is situated in a global context so that
the reader gains a sense of perspective and has a benchmark for measuring their significance for East Asia.[58] The book is firmly focused on the
big picture and has no aspirations to being a detailed country-by-country
study. Its primary aim is to facilitate understanding among scholars, policy-makers and the interested public of how transnational forces are
reshaping East Asia's security landscape.

Although primarily concerned with East Asia, many of this book's
judgements will have wider import, conceptually and in policy terms. East
Asia's transnational problems are replicated in other developing regions
and are also affecting the affluent West, as evidenced by the high proportion of Asians among the illegal migrants entering Europe, the US,
Canada and Australia and the global market that now exists for Southeast
Asia's heroin. The book's main conclusion is that transnational forces will
play a seminal role in determining East Asia's future security environment
and for this reason they must be factored into an extended security paradigm that includes people as well as states, and incorporates non-military
threats to both. Better theory does not guarantee good policy. But without it, East Asians will struggle to comprehend and meet the transnational
security challenges of the twenty-first century.

CHAPTER 1

Transnational Issues and Security

This chapter serves as a conceptual foundation for the empirical chapters on East Asia that follow. Here I survey the literature on environmental degradation, unregulated population movements and transnational crime, clarify some definitional issues and locate the key theoretical debates. I also address the question of why transnational issues ought to be included in an extended security praxis and identify their distinguishing characteristics.

The Environment and Security

Although the term 'environmental security' has firmly entrenched itself in the lexicon of international relations, there is considerable disagreement about its meaning and significance. In common with advocates of human security, many 'environmentalists' accept that security ought to extend beyond the boundaries of the state to include the individual as well as humanity in general, but others believe that environmental decline has an important security dimension mainly because it reduces state capacity (a measure of the ability of states to meet the basic nutritional, welfare and security requirements of their people).[1] Realists are less inclined to accept that there is a direct connection between the environment and security, or that the environment warrants inclusion on the core security agenda of the twenty-first century. If the definition of 'security' has been marked by controversy and contention, so too has that of the 'environment', which has been preceded by almost as many adjectives as 'security' and subject to a multitude of different interpretations. The definition of the environment used here embraces the concept of biosphere – 'that part of the planet where life exists, and upon which life depends for continued existence' – essentially the atmosphere, the surface and subsurface of the land and all bodies of water.[2]

Most of the contemporary literature on the environment does not deal explicitly with security. The writings of environmental luminaries such as Paul Ehrlich and Rachel Carson have an implicit security dimension, however, since they touch on fundamental questions of human survival, political sovereignty and economic well-being.[3] Some ecologists share common ground with traditional strategists in rejecting the notion of environmental security, fearing that linking the two may lead to 'either a militarisation of environmental politics or a demilitarisation of security thinking'.[4] Nevertheless, the use of the term 'environmental security' is now widely accepted and there is a significant body of cross-disciplinary research which explores the connections between environmental degradation, security and conflict. While this research is united around the core belief that environmental issues should form an integral part of a reconstructed security paradigm, there are two discernible schools of thought which privilege different security referents.

'Gaian' environmentalists draw their inspiration from the Gaia hypothesis advanced by the scientist James Lovelock.[5] According to Lovelock the earth must be seen as a single living organism of interconnected parts that includes the atmosphere, oceans and soils. Gaians regard environmental degradation as the ultimate security threat because it strikes at the foundations of the earth's life-support systems.[6] In the words of Robert Kaplan, it is '*the* national security issue of the early twenty first century'.[7] Since environmental degradation threatens the very survival of the planet, security ought to be redefined to include preserving and protecting the natural elements that sustain life. Michael Renner contends that 'a reasonable definition of security needs to encompass breathable air and potable water, safety from toxic and radioactive hazards, an intact atmospheric ozone layer, a stable climatic system, and protection against the loss of the topsoil that assures us of our daily bread'.[8]

'Statists', by definition, have a more restricted, state-centric view. Ecological threats are important, statists assert, because they can abrade national institutions and natural resources, leading to social and political instability and ultimately conflict – conflict that may be played out either between states or at the subnational level.[9] This particular conceptualisation of the link between the environment and conflict now seems to be dominant in the literature, although there are several iterations which privilege different causal factors. Some focus on environmental threats to sustained economic growth and the 'conflictual possibilities arising from a highly inter-dependent system in the throes of faltering or even declining real growth'.[10] Others emphasise distributional issues stemming from environmental pressures on already stretched natural resources.[11] Virtually all take the view that the strategic and foreign policy community needs to consider more seriously a range of non-military dangers to security arising from environmental disasters, population growth (threats from rising worldwide demand), and growing resource scarcity (threats from the supply side).[12]

How then should we think about the environment and security? As the protection of the global ecosystem since it is the basis of all life and has an intrinsic importance that transcends conventional notions of international security? Or more specifically, and prosaically, in terms of the conflict attributable to environmental degradation? Both are valid and clearly linked. The protection and preservation of the environment is a legitimate long-term objective of security policy since human survival is dependent on the health of the biosphere. However, a comprehensive discussion of the relationship between the health of the global environment and international security is beyond the scope of this book and, in any event, has been attempted elsewhere.[13] This analysis will concentrate on the capacity of environmental degradation to generate conflict within and between states, and to threaten human survival.[14]

Sceptics contest the arguments of environmentalists on three grounds. First, they argue that it is misleading to conceive of environmental degradation as a threat to security since the traditional focus of national security is interstate or organised violence, which has little to do with environmental problems. There is a misfit between environmental well-being and national security from violence because of the differing degrees of intention involved. Violence is normally a highly directed human activity and combating it has little in common with environmental degradation, which is largely unintentional and has multiple causes. Should environmental stress be seen as a security issue simply because people die or are dispossessed as a consequence of it? If so, then how can this view of the link between the environment and conflict be reconciled with disease and crime, which 'routinely destroy life' but are not considered security threats, just as natural disasters are not events that threaten national security.[15] Accordingly, attempts by environmentalists to redefine security more broadly only create conceptual muddle and 'sloppiness', resulting in a de-definition rather than a meaningful redefinition of security.[16] In the words of Lothar Brock, 'if everything is a security matter, then nothing is'.[17]

Second, critics of the environmental case assert that the nexus between resource scarcity and conflict is weakening because there has been considerable progress in developing substitutes for many essential raw materials;[18] the robust character of the world trade system is lessening the resource vulnerability of national economies; and acquiring resources through military force is less attractive than it once was due to changing norms of state behaviour.[19]

Third, there is a lack of hard evidence to support the thesis that environmental degradation causes significant conflict. The foundation on which much of the environmental case is built is made of sand – the 'evidence' is anecdotal, sparse or inconclusive.[20] Much of the literature on the environment and security focuses on global trends and outcomes. There is comparatively little information on the impact of environmental degradation on national and regional security.[21] A commonly cited example is climate change. Since the scientific evidence documenting climate change is contested, the security effects of global warming are uncertain. Conflict may not necessarily follow and some of the outcomes of climate change may actually be positive. While reductions in rainfall may lead to desertification or water shortages in some regions, others will benefit from increased rainfall and higher crop yields.[22] Even where the fabric of the state is torn by environmentally induced conflicts, in all likelihood they will be local and have negligible effects on world order – 'visions of starving millions from the "South" invading the "North" in search of food are far fetched …'[23]

The first of these criticisms – that environmental issues fall outside the traditional focus of national security – is unconvincing. Even though many environmental threats are unrelated to state-sponsored violence, they can nevertheless imperil the state as well as human survival. Environmentalists are not asserting that all ecological threats have implications for security, but only those that demonstrably reduce the productive capacities of the state or result in significant political, social or military conflict. In fact a great deal of the literature on environmental security is unashamedly state-centric, which suggests that the concerns of environmentalists are not as far removed from those of realists as their critics assert. Most environmentalists do not argue that ecological stress is a discrete or direct cause of conflict but rather that a deteriorating physical environment can aggravate interstate tensions and domestic instability by interacting with other causes of conflict.[24]

What of the contention that the nexus between resource scarcity and conflict is loosening, implying that the environmental case in this area is weak? It is certainly true that most of the world's non-renewable resources are already owned and protected under international law, which reduces the likelihood of conflict over them. There is also a greater range of substitutes for many strategically important metals and sources of energy, and a globalised economy can in theory deliver virtually any commodity or service for a price, or at least encourage a move to cheaper alternatives. What critics tend to ignore, however, is the changing nature of resource scarcity and the impact of environmental decline on the capacity of states to meet the steadily rising demand for energy, food and water.

Environmental damage is creating new kinds of resource scarcity. The critical scarcities of the twenty-first century will be in resources that were once considered to be 'renewable', for which there are few, if any, substitutes. Water, forests and fresh air, as well as many plant and animal species, are being exploited to such an extent that they are becoming 'functionally non-renewable'.[25] It is the assault on the planet's primary renewable resources, the abuse of the 'global commons', which differentiates the resource scarcity of this era from that of the past. These environmental scarcities do not mandate conflict nor, in most cases, will they become serious enough to jeopardise the survival of people or states. But they will add to the economic and resource pressures on governments in developing countries, heighten concerns about future food, water and energy security, and exacerbate disputes over contested river basins and areas that are rich in forests and fish.

Embedded in the discourse of mainstream political and social history are well-documented accounts of human-induced environmental change and scarcity that resulted in economic decay, societal dislocation and death. Nearly 3700 years ago, the ancient Sumerians were forced to abandon their cities after discovering that their elaborate irrigation systems brought short-term bounty but eventually environmental disaster from rising levels of soil salinity and waterlogged agricultural fields.[26] Overpopulation sowed the seeds of ultimate collapse for the tenth-century Mayan civilisation, while the demise of the old Norse settlement in Greenland at the end of the fifteenth century was in part due to significant climatic change. The decline of Greenland's sister colony in Iceland was a direct result of overgrazing and destruction of the forest cover, which allowed the harsh Icelandic weather to denude the island's fragile topsoil.[27]

However, it is the scale, gravity and interconnectedness of today's environmental ills that accounts for their new-found policy salience. At the beginning of the twenty-first century, the earth's physical environment is under unprecedented stress from the combined effects of reductions in arable land, soil fertility, potable water and critical natural resources due to overpopulation, pollution, deforestation and unsustainable development practices. Damage to the global maritime environment from overfishing, pollution, urbanisation and the degradation of ecologically sensitive marine coastal environments is already severe in many parts of the globe, particularly in Asia. Fishing disputes have become an increasingly frequent cause of naval clashes in the Pacific Ocean and the South China Sea. Climate change of the order predicted by scientists and climatologists, resulting from a build-up of greenhouse gases and atmospheric pollution, could place further pressure on the world's food and water resources.[28] Governments which routinely proclaimed the mantra that 'growth is good' now accept that there are finite limits to resources once considered inexhaustible and 'free'.

The third criticism concerning the relationship between the environment and security turns on the question of 'evidence'. Here the sceptics are on stronger ground. A great deal of the evidence is indeed anecdotal, sparse or inconclusive, with causality unproved. Environmental collapse leading to societal breakdown, anarchy and war has so far proved the exception rather than the rule. It is not always clear whether environmental degradation is a consequence or cause of conflict. Much existing casework concentrates on 'weak' states and regions that are particularly vulnerable to transnational threats because of institutional fragility and endemic ethnic or tribal conflicts. But since few East Asian countries fit the classical definition of weak states considerably more casework is required to establish the precise nature of the connections between environmental degradation, resource scarcity and conflict among the nations of this region.[29]

Unregulated Population Movements

The unregulated movement of people across the globe is a second transnational issue that has begun directly to engage the attention and interests of international security specialists. Sometimes referred to as illegal or undocumented migration and less accurately as the problem of refugees, UPMs may be defined as the forced or unsanctioned (by governments) movement of people across borders and within states for economic reasons, or as a consequence of war, persecution or environmental factors. Three distinct but related subcategories of people – refugees, displaced persons and undocumented labour migrants – are subsumed within this definition.[30] Although each has generated discrete literatures, this separation is largely artificial, concealing rather than illuminating their interconnectedness and salience for international security. As Barbara Harell-Bond observes, 'these literatures have not been "communicating" with one another'. The challenge is to bring them together by encouraging more interdisciplinary studies of UPMs.[31]

Labour and political economists, along with sociologists, historians and migration specialists, are responsible for most of the existing theory and case studies.[32] Neoclassical migration theory conceptualises migration as a mechanism for redistributing labour, while sociological approaches emphasise the need to flee life-threatening situations, the relative attractiveness of areas of origin versus intended destinations, and the role of the family.[33] Expanding populations, poverty and uneven economic development are regarded as prominent causes of UPMs along with wage differentials, employment opportunities and other market forces. Although abject poverty may cause people to move within states, contrary to popular belief it has rarely been responsible for the major international migration flows of the twentieth century. If a country is too poor, its people have neither the drive, nor the knowledge nor the resources to emigrate legally or illegally. Countries in the middle range of development account for most of the surge in migration because it is their upwardly mobile citizens who are motivated to seek out greener pastures. Nowhere is this more evident than in developing Asia where 2 billion people are fast approaching this 'middle range'.[34]

Aside from the mass population displacements of the early Cold War years in Europe and the large-scale migration of people that preceded and accompanied the de facto partitioning of Vietnam and Korea in the mid-1950s, the issue of migration rarely featured in the discourse on international security before 1989. None of the standard realist and liberal expositions of security give any significant space to UPMs and there has been little attempt to locate the issue conceptually.[35] The Western security policy community has generally considered UPMs to be a matter of 'low politics' (pertaining to the wealth and welfare of the citizens of the state) rather than 'high politics' (associated with security and the continued existence of the state).[36] Asians, on the other hand, have been more sensitive to the security ramifications of refugees and illegal migration for historical and cultural reasons – multi-ethnic Southeast Asia particularly so, because of endemic racial and religious tensions and the preoccupation of political elites with nation-building and the maintenance of regimes.

Analysis of the security impact of UPMs has been hindered by a lack of reliable quantitative data and the looseness with which terms like 'illegal' and 'undocumented' migrants are used. Many countries do not maintain continuous and authoritative statistical records on migration or do not publish the data they have because it is considered too politically sensitive. Even the material that is published varies in its accuracy, scope and usefulness.[37] Disagreement over exactly who should qualify as a refugee poses another set of problems underlining how political, rather than humanitarian, considerations generally determine refugee status.

While few would quibble with the proposition that UPMs have important implications for social and economic development, there are at least four grounds for scepticism about their significance for international security. First, nation-building is essentially a history of migration. Most states are melting pots of disparate religions, races and cultures and have benefited, as well as suffered, from the infusion of outside influences and people. The somewhat schizophrenic official attitude towards undocumented labour migration indicates that this is so, even today. Receiving states are inclined to turn a blind eye to undocumented labour migrants in boom times because of the contribution they make to economic development. Migrants compensate for domestic labour shortfalls and are typically employed in dirty or dangerous work that locals are not willing to do. Sending countries are enthusiastic because their expatriates acquire valuable skills and remit foreign currency. It is incumbent on those who maintain that UPMs are dangerously destabilising to articulate the circumstances in which they constitute a threat to security.

Second, judgements are also required about the seriousness of UPMs. Are they central to the security concerns of nation-states and their citizens or are they of a lesser order? Third, it is often asserted that labelling UPMs as a security threat diminishes the concept's usefulness and heuristic value. Moreover, the 'securitisation' of migration confers a significance that is not warranted and may result in inappropriate state-centric policy responses.[38] It is difficult, if not impossible, to differentiate between the security and non-security effects of UPMs, which in any event ought to be treated as the unintended consequences of military conflict or social breakdown rather than their root cause. There is insufficient evidence in the form of persuasive case studies to warrant the elevation of UPMs onto the already crowded international security agenda.

Finally, how tight and discernible are the connections between conflict and refugee movements, displaced persons and undocumented labour migration, and between UPMs and other transnational issues? Prima facie, the relationship between ecological stress and migration is a pertinent illustration of the causal circularity of many transnational issues. A deteriorating physical environment may be a key factor in forcing people to move, leading to social dislocation and attendant political and security problems. A sudden influx of refugees or transmigrants can add, in turn, to existing pressures on scarce natural resources, thereby perpetuating a cycle of migration, environmental degradation and conflict. While theoretically appealing, it could be argued that this kind of circular logic does little to help practitioners and policy-makers understand the precise links between UPMs, the environment and security. For instance, is the environment a major cause of migration or only one of a number of contextual variables 'that influences the economic, social and risk calculation of individuals and communities'?[39]

These arguments underscore the need for more empirical studies and a holistic framework of analysis that allows greater scope for exploring the connections between UPMs and security and the circumstances in which migration triggers conflict. Most existing studies concentrate on the economic causes of migration. Although economic and migration models help to explain the social and developmental dynamics of population movements, they tend to be reductionist and place too much emphasis on market mechanisms, neglecting other causes that have little to do with economics. Migration cannot be understood only, or even principally, in terms of calculated and rational decisions of economic self-interest.[40] Government policies have a large bearing on population flows, and national decisions to control entry and egress are influenced as much by political and security considerations as economic logic. The generally unsympathetic response by Southeast Asian governments to the unremitting stream of boat people leaving Vietnam in the two decades after 1975 largely reflected their fears that providing a permanent home for the Vietnamese could generate ethnic and political conflict in their own countries. Viewing UPMs through the prism of security throws additional analytical light on their multiple causes and effects. As the UN High Commissioner for Refugees (UNHCR) acknowledges, 'The subject of refugees and displaced people is high on the list of international concerns today not only because of its humanitarian significance, but also because of its impact on peace, security and stability'.[41]

Many economists and sociologists writing on UPMs assume that the state is of little importance in arbitrating and regulating population flows because they regard migration as primarily a function of economic forces and historical trends which are independent of the structure and norms of the state system.[42] However, if conceptually decoupled from the notion of state sovereignty, the commonly accepted definitions of a refugee and illegal migrant have little meaning.[43] Michael Teitelbaum correctly observes that international migration on a large scale could not have taken place without the development of the Westphalian state system and the growth of human population to very high levels.[44] Before the Treaty of Westphalia entrenched the idea that states are sovereign entities and the political embodiment of the citizens who live within their boundaries, international migration was largely unregulated in the sense that it was not controlled by national governments.[45] In establishing the modern state system, the Treaty of Westphalia arrogated to national governments the right to determine who is a migrant or refugee.

This is reflected in the highly political way in which refugees are defined in the 1951 Convention, which is specifically designed to provide refuge and protection for the millions of people fleeing from the advances of European and Asian communism in the late 1940s.[46] Members of this second great wave of post-Second World War migrants were virtually guaranteed refugee status because receiving Western states regarded them as victims of communist oppression and a living testimony to the moral and political superiority of liberal democracy.[47] By the time the 1967 Protocol was adopted, extending the geographical jurisdiction of the 1951 Convention to cover the globe, a third and altogether different wave of refugees from the poor South were finding it a far tougher proposition to find a new home. The same Western countries that had willingly opened their doors to European migrants two decades earlier were beginning to interpret the Convention much more narrowly.[48] Restrictions on refugees have subsequently increased to such an extent that relatively few are granted entry and then usually on the understanding that they will be repatriated once circumstances improve in their home countries.

The narrow UN definition, which is used by most countries to determine refugee status, has the unintended side-effect of obscuring the real causes and magnitude of UPMs.[49] The 1951 Convention does not include victims of deliberately divisive social policies or people who move internally and across state borders for environmental and economic reasons.[50] Nor does it account for the growing number of displaced victims of civil war who remain inside the borders of their home state. The Bosnian, Kosovo, Rwandan, Cambodian and East Timor conflicts all generated considerable numbers of displaced persons, none of whom qualified for refugee status under the 1951 Convention.[51] A significant number of states have not ratified or acceded to the 1951 Convention and its 1967 Protocol and do not necessarily abide by even the circumscribed UN definition of what constitutes a refugee.[52] Furthermore, the United Nations, in common with most academic studies of migration, does not include estimates of undocumented labour migrants in its statistics, even though they form an intrinsic element and rapidly growing proportion of UPMs.

These important definitional issues aside, UPMs and international security are linked in several ways. Uncontrolled migration, especially involving sudden large influxes of people who are ethnically or religiously different from the indigenous inhabitants of receiving countries, strikes at the whole notion of nationhood. As Barry Buzan observes, 'ethnic and cultural parochialism is everywhere a stronger political force than cosmopolitanism'.[53] When historical fears and insecurities colour the attitudes and responses of receiving states, the perception of threat is heightened. Americans worry about the inflow of illegal migrants from Mexico, Russians of being overwhelmed by ethnic Chinese in sparsely populated Siberia. Australians continue to show acute sensitivity to the arrival of boat people from Asia and the Middle East, while Japan still denies citizenship rights to second and third-generation Korean immigrants for fear of cultural dilution.[54]

Illegal migrants arriving by air and sea and people-smuggling by transnational criminal organisations are posing novel challenges to the state. Where ethnic minority groups straddle one or more land borders or congregate in sensitive frontier regions, as is the case with the Kurds in the Middle East and the Uighurs in Central Asia, cross-border UPMs can become a source of interstate tensions and a *casus belli*. Weak states are frequently more capable of mounting an effective defence against military attack than they are of coping with the security consequences of large-scale migration from neighbouring states.[55] Even developed states may experience considerable difficulty in maintaining the integrity of national borders and dealing with the formidable institutional and resource demands of managing large and sudden inflows of refugees and migrants. As a consequence, receiving countries are now more inclined to regard UPMs as a politico-security issue rather than a humanitarian or social concern – hence the inclusion of UPMs on national security agendas and the growing propensity to use military assets to stem the flow of illegal migrants.

From Europe to Africa, and from Asia to the Americas, defence forces and intelligence agencies are directly involved in the surveillance, arrest and repatriation of illegal migrants – tasks that are beginning to reshape military force structures and operational and intelligence priorities. In 1994, the United States deployed naval ships in support of the Coast Guard to deal with a sudden influx of people from Haiti. Italy has used its armed forces on several occasions to help control and manage refugees fleeing conflicts in Bosnia, Albania and Kosovo. South Africa has stationed troops on its borders with neighbouring Mozambique and Zimbabwe to control illegal migrants from these countries. The Malaysian navy repelled Indonesian boat people from the island of Sumatra at the height of the Asian economic crisis and Australia has used naval and air units to support police, customs and immigration operations against illegal migration rackets.[56]

The security effects of UPMs cannot be judged only in terms of their impact on interstate relations. They are also having a major impact on the internal stability of states, particularly in the developing world, threatening communal identity, intensifying existing social and cultural divisions, and weakening the political and social fabric of communities. Increasingly, the rights, welfare and security of refugees and illegal migrants are being ignored or subordinated to the perceived interests of the state. Ordinary people are commonly the targets and victims of state-sanctioned population displacements.[57] In multicultural states like Rwanda and Yugoslavia, politically dominant ethnic groups have persecuted minorities in the name of national security, creating the very insecurity they seek to guard against and stimulating waves of internal migration. Civil wars may also lead to the displacement of people on a large scale. As Africans and Turks have found in Europe, and Indonesians, Filipinos and Bangladeshis in Asia, the same undocumented labour migrants who are tolerated and tacitly encouraged when economies are booming may be suddenly branded as threats to national security and expelled or incarcerated when recession takes hold. Other causal factors seem neglected or poorly understood. They include the involvement of criminal groups in people-smuggling and worsening environmental degradation, which is creating a new class of environmental refugees.

Transnational Crime

Transnational crime is a third emerging security issue with credible claims for inclusion in the core security agenda of the twenty-first century.[58] Aggregated under the rubric of transnational crime is an extremely diverse and seemingly eclectic mix of subjects. They range from the illicit drug trade, arms-trafficking, environmental crime, terrorism, piracy, illegal gambling and crimes of violence (contract killings and bombings), to smuggling (of commodities and people), large-scale fraud and corruption, money-laundering, counterfeiting, and cyber-crime.[59] With the exception of terrorism, the arms trade and to a lesser extent drug-trafficking, these issues also barely rated a mention in the Cold War security discourse. However, the unprecedented power and influence exercised by modern organised criminal groups and the internationalisation of their networks are compelling a major reassessment of the links between crime and security.

As with the other concepts explored in this chapter, there is no unanimity of view on the meaning of the term 'transnational crime', or agreement about the extent to which crime impinges on security. One reason for the absence of consensus is that disciplines other than international relations have provided the theoretical models and cognitive frameworks for conceptualising the organisational and social dynamics that govern the activities of criminal groups. Social scientists regard crime as primarily a social phenomenon, economists emphasise organisational imperatives and structures, while anthropologists view crime through the lens of culture.[60]

A further complication and impediment to understanding are difficult jurisdictional and ethical conundrums concerning the nature of crime itself. What is considered a criminal act in one country may be legal in another. Even if certain acts are regarded by the state as illegal, unresolved moral dilemmas may attenuate their prosecution. For example, should prostitution be considered a crime? If so, who is the criminal? The provider of the service, or the client? In most societies white-collar and corporate crime tends to be ignored or treated more leniently than crimes of violence. Corruption is so widespread and ingrained in the national political and commercial culture of some states that it has effectively been decriminalised. As James White observes, 'the ethical and social frameworks of different cultures and societies result in different interpretations of the rules used to regulate society, making any universal definition of crime increasingly problematic.'[61]

If the definition of crime is contested, so is the idea of 'organised' crime.[62] Although a great deal has been written about the behavioural characteristics and operational modes of criminal groups, no single theoretical model has attained the same level of influence and acceptance among criminologists and the law enforcement community as realism has achieved among security professionals. Social scientists first became interested in the study of organised crime following a series of dramatic revelations in the United States during the 1960s which exposed the criminal activities and culture of La Cosa Nostra, later immortalised in films like *The Godfather* and *Bella Mafia*. Research on La Cosa Nostra gave rise to the archetypal bureaucratic/corporate model of organised crime, sometimes called the 'Godfather model', which theorises that criminal gangs operate in highly formalised, authoritarian and hierarchical structures akin to a bureaucracy or corporation.[63] The typical La Cosa Nostra family with its rules and regulations, bosses, *consiglieres* and soldiers is said to resemble the operations of its legitimate corporate counterparts in terms of leadership, management and professionalism.[64]

A second, entrepreneurial model focuses on how 'organized crime activities are organized' rather than 'how organized crime groups are organized', an important but often overlooked distinction.[65] According to the entrepreneurial model, the only appreciable difference between the operations of criminal and bona fide business organisations is that the criminals deal in illicit rather than licit products and services. Another way of putting it is that criminal enterprises specialise in providing legal goods and services in illegal ways.[66] Criminal and legitimate businesses are both motivated by the need to make money and expand market share while each responds to the needs and demands of suppliers, customers, regulators and competitors.[67] An alternative and later stream of scholarship disputed some of these findings. On closer examination, La Cosa Nostra was found to be far more loosely structured than had previously been thought and dependent on close ethnic and family ties for its coherence and effectiveness rather than on hierarchical structures. These findings gave rise to two other theories. The first, often described as the ethnic model, holds that organised crime is akin to an 'underworld corporate enterprise comprised of ethnically or culturally distinct alien groups that corrupt fundamentally sound political and economic units'.[68] The second, or flexible network model, emphasises the fragmented and ephemeral nature of criminal associations and alliances.[69]

Although these behavioural models provide useful insights into the way criminals organise and operate, their heuristic value is limited because there is no prototype criminal organisation or single mode of behaviour. Nor is there likely to be one given the range of the activities conducted by criminals and the multiplicity of forms they take.[70] The organisational dynamics, density of linkages and degree of hegemony and coherence varies enormously from one criminal group to another. The quasi-religious character of the Chinese triads, for example, contrasts with the secular functionality of the Russian mafiya and the tribalism of the groups that dominate the drug trade in Central and Southeast Asia.[71] Many groups display the organisational and operational characteristics of more than one of the models presented and most alliances are tactical rather than strategic. Furthermore, the existing models have almost nothing to say on the relationship between crime and international security.

Mainstream international relations theory is also unhelpful. This is hardly surprising since realists are concerned with state rather than non-state behaviour, and combating crime has historically been regarded as a

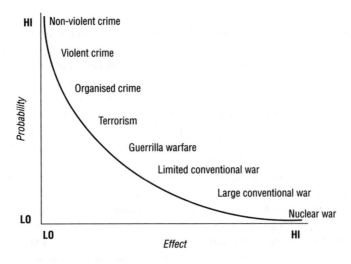

Figure 1.1 The Cold War national security continuum
Source: John Ciccarelli (ed.), *Transnational Crime: A New Security Threat* (Australian Defence Studies Centre, Australian Defence Force Academy, University of New South Wales, Canberra, 1996), p. 10.

law-and-order issue rather than one of international security. Such attitudes were understandable during the Cold War when a graphical representation of crime would have depicted it as a high-probability, low-impact security threat.

Since the end of the Cold War, however, criminal activities – particularly those that are conducted on a large scale and involve significant international cooperation – have moved along the threat continuum towards the traditional concerns of the national security apparatus. At the same time, the threat probability curve has extended outward, mirroring the accretion of political, economic and military power by transnational criminal organisations.[72] As a result, security planners have begun to take greater account of their activities although not always with a clear understanding of the threat that criminals pose, or their operational and organisational characteristics. Hence the need for more empirical, cross-disciplinary studies which can provide a clearer picture of the structure and activities of TCOs and enhance awareness, among policy-makers and international relations scholars, of their capacity to threaten states and human security.

Western interest in the links between transnational crime and international security was first awakened by the breakdown of social and political order in the former Soviet Union during the early 1990s, and the subsequent rise and spread of Russian and East European criminal gangs. Over the past decade, the Russian mafiya has internationalised its

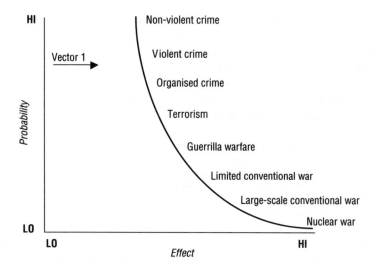

Figure 1.2 The post-Cold War national security continuum
Source: Cicarelli (ed.), *Transnational Crime*, p. 10.

activities well beyond the borders of the old Soviet empire, establishing new forms of criminal enterprise and strategic alliances with some of the largest and most notorious crime syndicates. These include La Cosa Nostra, the Colombian drug cartels, the Sicilian mafia, the Japanese boryokudan – or yakuza – and the Chinese triads. Unfortunately, the Russian mafiya has also inspired a great deal of sensationalist reporting about crime by the popular press and led to widespread misperception about their activities, which are typically portrayed in stark and apocryphal terms. According to one view, transnational crime, unless checked, will pose a threat to peace and stability that could rival or even surpass that of the Cold War.[73] Some maintain that organised crime, especially in Russia, is a 'new empire of evil',[74] a 'Pax Mafiosa' in which the threat of international communism embodied in the organisation and activities of the infamous 'Com-intern', is being supplanted by an equally insidious 'Crime-intern', global in its reach but driven by Mammon rather than ideology.[75] This multinational crime consortium is said to operate without regard for borders, sharing resources and intelligence in pursuit of profits and power.[76]

In fact there is very little evidence to support the notion of a monolithic criminal conspiracy or a transnational criminal consortium. No single organisation dominates the criminal world or has a monopoly over the supply of illicit commodities or services, which are subject to the competition of the marketplace. Depicting crime as a monolithic, global phenomenon is a form of threat 'inflation' which belies the complexity and diversity of transnational crime.[77] A related tendency is to conjure up the image of an alien conspiracy as the American Senator Joseph McCarthy did during his manipulation of the destructive anti-communist crusades of the 1950s in the United States. The xenophobic and racist overtones which once permeated the language of the Cold War have already featured in the rhetorical war against crime. Before the return of Hong Kong to China, one writer characterised the triad threat thus:

> Britain faces one of the most frightening and dangerous influxes of crime that it has ever encountered. Before Communist China takes over Hong Kong in 1997, the world's most ruthless criminal cartel will be stepping up its bid to take control of the underworld of Western society, and to spread within our culture like a criminal cancer. This cartel is the Chinese Triads – the yellow peril of the East, and now the West.[78]

This characterisation of crime is as flawed as the notion of a 'Pax Mafiosa', and for many of the same reasons. Ethnicity is only one of the elements that underpins criminal associations and organisations and it is by no means the crucial one. That distinction falls to the profit motive. Demonising putative foreign criminal threats obscures the real nature of organised crime, which today is overwhelmingly acultural and firmly rooted in a globalised society rather than a specific region or nation. The predisposition to blame others for local or international problems is, of course, not peculiar to the issue of organised crime or the current geopolitical milieu. Nor is the associated tendency to seek out new global security threats once others have lost their virulence or currency. Treating transnational crime as a global conspiracy – or an alien one for that matter – is appealing because it implies, as Phil Williams notes, that a 'threat to international security may be emerging that is a worthy successor to the challenge posed by the Soviet Union during the Cold War'.[79]

The argument that transnational crime has become a serious international security issue rests on less dramatic, more substantial, intellectual foundations. Criminal activities may pose a direct threat to national sovereignty by undermining and subverting the political authority and legitimacy of governments. In their search for illicit profits, criminals implicitly and explicitly challenge the monopoly over taxation and violence traditionally enjoyed by the state and work at cross-purposes to the aim of good government, which is to protect the rights, property, welfare and security of its citizens.[80] Where government control is weak, or contested, powerful criminal organisations have been known to co-opt or supplant the institutions of government to such an extent that they effectively form a state within a state. The Medellin drug cartel, for example, launched a direct assault on the Colombian state in 1989, murdering Luis Carlos Galan, the leading presidential candidate, and carrying out a series of bombings, kidnappings and other violent attacks against individuals and institutions in Colombia. The cartel's objective was to force the government into a *de facto* power-sharing arrangement.[81] Narcotics-traffickers have also achieved notoriety for their ability to 'pirate government functions or inherit them by default'.[82]

The political authority of the state has been further circumscribed by the growth in the coercive power of organised crime and the internationalisation of its activities. Drug-running, clandestine arms shipments and people-smuggling 'accentuate the permeability of national borders, fundamentally challenging the real and symbolic boundaries of state power'.[83] Ironically, while many modern criminal groups are what James Rosenau has termed 'sovereignty-free' actors, the forces of law and order are 'sovereignty bound' – constrained by the very nature of the polity they seek to defend and preserve.[84] In extreme cases weak states may suffer from a kind of criminal anarchy leading to a complete breakdown in government control and eventually the institutions and processes which define statehood.[85] The international drug and arms trade has contributed to the dissolution of states and destabilised whole regions, particularly in Central Asia, the Balkans and the Golden Triangle region of Southeast Asia. Colombia's difficulties with home-grown drug cartels eventually developed into a security issue for the wider American region in the same way that crime in Russia has gravitated from a local law-and-order problem to a European and global security issue.

Transnational crime also has a significant military dimension which can manifest itself in different and often surprising ways. Where governments are co-opted by organised crime, as the Noriega regime was in Panama during the 1980s, the armed forces and police may become the *de facto* military instruments of organised crime. Criminal groups can also develop their own military capabilities – independently or through tactical alliances with terrorist organisations or insurgent armies – sometimes to the point where they rival and even surpass those of the governments they confront, as occurred in Burma during the 1970s and 1980s.[86] A particularly graphic illustration of the military capabilities being sought and acquired by modern TCOs was the discovery of a 30 metre-long submarine under construction on the outskirts of Bogota in September 2000. Built according to a Russian design, the submarine was constructed so that it could have been disassembled into easily transportable components. When launched it would have been able to move around 150 tonnes of cocaine or heroin with little chance of detection by Colombian police.[87]

Drug-traffickers are increasingly willing to link with terrorist or separatist organisations in mutually beneficial collaborations. Virtually all terrorist/insurgent groups rely on drug-trafficking and other criminal activities to obtain guns and raise funds for their cause.[88] In countries as geographically and culturally diverse as Colombia, Russia and Thailand, the activities of organised crime have become the principal concern of the authorities responsible for national security. But the enemy is no longer another state. As non-state actors, some organised criminal groups use high levels of violence that are comparable in method and lethality to terrorist organisations or legitimately constituted defence forces. This poses novel problems for defence and foreign policy and calls into question many of the assumptions that underpin traditional security thinking.

The level of violence employed is one, but by no means the only, indicator that a criminal activity has implications for security. High levels of corruption, people-smuggling and financial crimes may be just as damaging to the state and to the development and functioning of a vibrant civil society as more violent criminal activities and direct criminal challenges to national sovereignty. In an age of global commerce and communications, tax and trade fraud, money-laundering, drug-trafficking, corruption, counterfeiting and cyber-crime have the capacity to compromise the economic foundations of the state and weaken the international financial system. National economies and international markets may be distorted and dislocated by illegal transactions. Developing states, or 'economies in transition', are most at risk because individuals and elites become habituated to working outside the regulatory environment and the rule of law, which enfeebles state capacity and is injurious to human security.[89] An extended security praxis involving a more people-centred approach to security would properly locate organised crime at the hub of a new generation of transnational threats that are beyond the coping capacity of any one state and defy conventional, particularly military, solutions. Even if judged by realist criteria, it is clear that certain kinds of criminal activities have moved along the threat continuum towards the traditional concerns of national security planners.

When does crime enter the security equation? There is no clear answer to this question. Criminal organisations often metamorphose through a number of developmental stages before reaching maturity. Initially, criminal groups may be little more than loosely organised gangs, locally based and limited in their reach as well as territory. Most never move beyond this stage but some inevitably do, gradually assuming more coherent shape until they enter the national and international arena, which is usually when their activities begin to figure in political and security calculations.[90] The degree of organisational structure and operational coherence is a critical determinant of the coercive power of criminal groups. Individuals may pose serious threats to law and order and occasionally to national security, as in the case of random high-level political assassinations. In general, however, the type of criminal activity most likely to present a threat to national and international security is not random or transient but is invariably directed by groups with a recognisable structure, leadership and established modus operandi, frequently involving transnational cooperation or collaboration.

As has already been noted, not all transnational criminal organisations pose threats to security, the effects of crime are not uniformly egregious, and criminals do not operate in a discrete underworld. Criminal enterprise can be a lucrative, 'invisible' source of national income, an important source of employment and a safety net in the event of a downturn in the formal economy.[91] In Thailand, for example, prostitution supplies 300 000 people with jobs, while the extensive underground lottery is estimated to employ some 4 million people on a part-time basis.[92] The size and dynamism of the illegal economy is often an important indicator of the basic health of the legal economy. Operating parallel to the legal one, the illegal economy is 'usually symbiotic with it and for the most part institutionally embedded within it'.[93] Many TCOs engage in legitimate business transactions which are not illegal and therefore cannot be classified as criminal.[94] Others may be so ephemeral or petty in their operations that they leave little or no mark on the security fabric of the state. Only when the destabilising impact of organised crime is of sufficient import and scale to seriously endanger the two referents of security – the state and its citizens – does crime move from the law enforcement to the security domain.

Conclusion

What conclusions can be drawn from this brief survey? Perhaps the first point to note is the virtual absence of any overarching international relations theory for locating and making sense of UPMs and transnational crime. Other disciplines have a great deal to say about both subjects but, as one might expect, their interests and perspectives diverge significantly from those of international relations, although they are by no means irrelevant. The environment and security, by contrast, has attracted a surprisingly rich and vibrant literature in a short space of time as well as much disagreement over definition and scope. Environmentalists are divided on the question of whether the security-degrading effects of environmental stress are best measured by their impact on the biosphere or the state. The reservations of traditionalists, on the other hand, are more fundamental. Sceptics doubt that there is a significant causal relationship between environmental degradation and conflict, and contest the notion that environmental issues fall within the purview of international security studies.

Notwithstanding the doubts of the sceptics, and accepting their argument that much of the evidence is indeed sparse, anecdotal or inconclusive, I argue that each of the transnational issues surveyed in this chapter has a strong claim to inclusion in the taxonomy of threats to international security. Environmental decline, UPMs and transnational crime all have potentially adverse security consequences for the territorial state. Not only do they contribute to interstate tension and military conflict, but states may also be destabilised by mass population movements, and their political and economic sovereignty compromised by the activities of well-organised and well-resourced criminal groups. However, while the state may be threatened by transnational phenomena, the threat does not arise because of shifts in the balance of power and cannot be adequately explained by the realist security dilemma. The transnational challenge to state power is more diffuse and complex. With rare exceptions, the criminal threat to the state emanates from non-state actors rather than from other states; environmental scarcity reduces the capacity of the state to protect and provide for its citizens; and conflict generated by transnational forces may be played out within states as well as between them. Moreover, the transnational challenge to security extends beyond the boundaries of the state to encompass broader issues of survival and resource scarcity that affect people irrespective of national borders.

These findings may be distilled into three broad observations. First, as the term implies, transnational threats transcend the borders of the territorial state and require cooperative, international solutions. Second, transnational threats are primarily non-military in nature and constitute a broader set of security considerations relating to survival, resource allocation and the health of the planet. They are therefore unlikely to be resolved by military force or ameliorated by traditional security approaches. They can, however, cause instability that may result in violent conflict between states, as well as within states. Third, their security impact is felt most acutely in developing regions of the world which are poorly equipped, psychologically and in terms of resources, for combating them. The remaining chapters of this book attempt to correlate and substantiate these theoretical observations with 'facts on the ground' as they relate to East Asia's security.

PART I

Environmental Scarcity

CHAPTER 2

Population and Conflict

Seven environmental issues that feature prominently in the debate about the environment and security in East Asia are aggregated and analysed in Part I of this book. They are deforestation, pollution, climate change, energy, food and water scarcity and overpopulation. Rampant deforestation and worsening pollution are visible signs of the damage being inflicted on the regional ecosystem. They are also contributing to global climate change, although to what degree and to what effect is still contested. So too is the relationship between environmental degradation and resource vulnerability in East Asia, particularly of energy, food and water. Is East Asia likely to face a future energy gap, and how are environmental factors complicating the region's energy choices? Adequate supplies of water and food are crucial to human survival. Once considered abundant and free, water is becoming scarce and more expensive. Are human demands about to collide with the ability of the hydrological cycle to supply water, as the United Nation's Food and Agricultural Organisation (FAO) claims? Or will conservation and technological improvements allow governments to manage the risk without conflict? Another vital question for the region is whether or not food production can keep pace with accelerating demand as fresh water becomes scarcer and environmental degradation erodes and desiccates once productive land. Part I addresses these issues, including the likelihood of water wars in East Asia, and assesses whether energy and food crises are looming, as some modern Cassandras predict.

The common factor in all these environmental problems is human pressure on the air, land and water and the unparalleled demands that are being placed on natural resources by the sheer number of people who now inhabit the region. Unlike Western nations, anxious about the political, social and economic consequences of rapidly ageing populations,

35

developing East Asian states face the difficult and daunting prospect of having to manage substantial population growth for at least the next half-century. Overpopulation and rapid urbanisation are seldom direct causes of conflict, but in developing regions they can accelerate resource scarcity and environmental degradation, cause destabilising mass population movements and heighten anxieties about access to energy, food and water. This investigation of the links between environmental degradation and security in East Asia begins, therefore, with an examination of global population trends and the region's demographic profile.

Global Demographic Trends

Over 200 years ago, an English economist and demographer named Thomas Malthus drew attention to the link between conflict and increases in population. Malthus argued that burgeoning populations will always outrun production until checked by famine, war and ill health.[1] His gloomy prognosis has not so far been borne out because population growth from advances in health care has been offset by increased agricultural production. It is important to recognise, however, that when Malthus made his prediction in 1798 the world's population was less than 1 billion. As a result of a dramatic increase in human fertility rates and plummeting rates of mortality, at the end of the second millennium the earth was home to 6 billion people, a sixfold increase in two centuries.

No one knows for sure how long demographic growth of this order will continue; neither can anyone accurately predict the size of the world's future population. Much depends on the time-frame under consideration and the assumptions used. Most demographic forecasts are based on UN projections showing low, medium and high-growth scenarios. The differences in the projections are due to variations in assumptions about mortality and fertility rates, and to a lesser extent to migration patterns – the key variables in determining population levels and growth rates. Relatively minor changes in the variables can produce substantially different population outcomes, especially in the long term. For example, if global fertility is assumed to be 1.8 children per woman in 2025, then the world's population in 2150 would be 6.4 billion. Should global fertility average 2.2 children, the earth's population would soar to 18.3 billion.[2]

According to the United Nations' medium-variant (most likely) projections, global population is expected to reach 8 billion in 2025 and 8.9 billion by the middle of the century, before stabilising at between 10 and 11 billion people early in the twenty-second century.[3] A minority believe that greater credence should be given to the United Nations' low-variant scenario which expects world population to peak at 7.7 billion in 2040 – still a 25 per cent increase from 1999 levels.[4] Virtually no one thinks that population growth can be reduced to produce an outcome of less than 7.7 billion. Most demographers believe that the medium-variant projection of 8 billion people by 2025 will prove to be quite accurate.[5] The high-variant projection, while less likely, cannot be entirely discounted. It foresees a population of 8.6 billion by 2025 and 11.2 billion by 2050. Uncertainty over the demographic impact of AIDS, which is beginning to have a significant bearing on population growth in Africa and Asia, has further complicated the task of predicting future population levels. In its October 1998 review the United Nations revised downward from 9.4 to 8.9 billion its medium-range projections for 2050 because of declining fertility rates and rising mortality from AIDS, particularly in Africa.

These disagreements aside, several broad trends are not in doubt. First, the world now supports substantially more people than at any time in human history. It is estimated that the earth's population at the time of Julius Caesar was around 250 million and was still only 2.5 billion at the beginning of the Cold War.[6] Second, these changes have been accompanied by high rates of urbanisation. By 2015, 4.1 billion of the world's estimated population of 7.3 billion will be city-dwellers. Ninety-seven per cent of global population growth will take place in the developing world, two-thirds of it in cities.[7] Third, the rate of population increase in the twentieth century was unprecedented. More population growth occurred in the last fifty years of the twentieth century than the previous two millennia. Between 1990 and 2000, an average 80 million people were added to global population annually, more than half of them in Asia.[8]

Although the annual rate of increase has slowed to 1.4 per cent from its peak of 2 per cent in the late 1960s, the size and composition of the world's population is such that lower rates of growth will still bring about overall increases in population.[9] This is mainly due to 'population momentum', so called because relatively high percentages of people are still able to bear children as a result of past high fertility. Baby boomers will continue to procreate at least until 2010 and many of their children – over 1 billion between the ages of 15 and 24 – are in their prime childbearing years.[10] The United Nations estimates that up to two-thirds of the projected increase in population will be due to population momentum and in some developed states the ratio will be even higher.[11] Low-variant advocates are inclined to focus on falling global fertility rates without necessarily allowing for population momentum, migration from higher fertility countries or the possibility that future populations may be larger than the total fertility rates (TFR) indicate.[12] Thus the human race will continue to multiply for at least another fifty years and probably until the end of this century, despite claims to the contrary.[13] This is an important point that is often ignored or underemphasised.[14] As the United Nations points out, 'world population is certainly not going to start declining before the middle of [the twenty-first century] and then only if global fertility follows the lowest of the United Nations projections'.[15]

These demographic trends have fuelled doubts among pessimists about the earth's capacity to sustain substantially higher and denser populations without radical changes in conventional attitudes to economic growth, consumption and energy use.[16] Optimists, on the other hand, argue that the earth has sufficient ecological and physical resilience to cope with the demands being levied on it by the projected addition of several billion more people and reject the Malthusian idea that population increase inevitably leads to ecological stress, famine or conflict.[17] In their view, improved food productivity through technological innovation, better management practices, reductions in conspicuous consumption, more equitable resource distribution and the demonstrated problem-solving capacity of human ingenuity will mitigate the effects of increased human pressure on limited resources. Some, like Nicholas Eberstadt, point out that per capita output for the world has increased fourfold over the last hundred years, commodity prices have dropped, indicating that food is still fairly plentiful, and that 6 billion inhabitants is a 'triumph not a tragedy'.[18]

Population and Conflict

It would be erroneous to assume that high levels of population growth automatically lead to war or an increase in violent conflict. If so, the latter half of the twentieth century should have been a much more violent period than earlier times when both the rate of growth and population levels were significantly lower. This was clearly not the case. Even the most vicious and brutal wars of the past few decades do not compare with the global conflagrations of 1914–18 and 1939–45. Suggestions that overpopulation might lead to another pandemic and even to nuclear war seem exaggerated, and there is little evidence to support the view that Malthus was right, merely premature in his prognosis of population crash.[19] Nonetheless, violence and conflict have frequently been associated with rapid increases in population and urbanisation. John Orme has drawn attention to the link between explosive population growth and the establishment of autocratic regimes in Russia and China after the French Revolution, which was itself fuelled by the 44 per cent rise in population that took place between 1715 and 1789. The existence of a large and growing mass of unemployed and underemployed men in France first destabilised the *ancien régime* and then provided the bulk of Napoleon's formidable and highly mobile conscript army. Modern Chinese history is replete with examples of uprisings and internal wars preceded by sharp declines in the land-to-labour ratio.[20] 'Historically, the foot soldiers of rebellions against states have been landless peasants and their poor cousins recently moved to the urban slums.'[21]

In the contemporary world, rapid population growth has already drastically reduced the availability and quality of critical natural resources and living space. Global stocks of fresh water are declining as demand rises and pollution and urbanisation increase. Productive agricultural land is being eroded or given over to urban development, deforestation is proceeding apace, and many animal and marine habitats are under threat. High levels of population growth are an additional burden for developing states where fragile national institutions and the social fabric may already be strained by ethnic and religious tensions. Urban slums foster resentment, alienation and despair, and are ideal breeding grounds for the spread of radical ideologies. High levels of unemployment fuel political discontent and lead to social dislocation. Economic distortions are growing as states with rising populations find it more difficult to eliminate income inequalities and to sustain rates of economic growth sufficient to absorb excess labour and raise living standards. Population pressure and environmental degradation are responsible for large-scale movements of people, both within states and across borders. These unregulated human flows are becoming a significant potential source of conflict in many parts of the developing world, including East Asia.[22] For these reasons, large populations are now generally seen as a strategic liability rather than the hallmark of a great power.

Population Growth in East Asia

Most East Asian states are experiencing substantial increases in population and rates of urbanisation.[23] In 2000, the region contained over 2 billion people, comprising a third of the world's total population. By 2025 East Asia will be home to about 2.5 billion people, of whom 1.5 billion will live in China.[24]

East Asia already has eight of the world's fourteen largest cities, each of which has a population of over 10 million.[25] A majority of the region's people are destined to live in large urban agglomerations, which is a change of historic proportions for the previously rural, agrarian societies of East Asia. In 1950, 58 million people lived in cities with populations of over 1 million. Forty years later, that figure had swelled to 359 million – more than Europe and North America combined.[26] Moreover, the shift from rural Asia to urban Asia will accelerate in the next fifty years, aggravating urban crowding. Asia will host half the world's urban population by 2025.[27] This increase will be a primary cause of environmental degradation as cities strain to cope with the infrastructural and social demands of rapid influxes of new city-dwellers.

Table 2.1 Population growth in East Asia (millions), 1992–2025

Region/Country	1992	1999	2010	2025	2010/2025 Percentage change
Northeast Asia					
China	1182.7	1254	1394	1561	12
(Hong Kong)	6.0	6.9	7.7	7.8	.05
Japan	124.0	126.7	127.6	120.9	–5.2
South Korea	44.0	46.9	50.6	52.7	11
Taiwan	20.8	22.0	23.9	25.4	9
North Korea	23.1	21.4	23.5	25.5	9
Mongolia	2.3	2.4	2.9	3.5	20
Total	*1402.9*	*1481*	*1631*	*1798*	*10*
Southeast Asia					
Indonesia	184.0	211.8	247.5	287.2	16
Vietnam	71.1	79.5	94.2	109.9	17
Philippines	64.0	74.7	91.9	111.5	21
Thailand	58.0	61.8	67.3	73.0	9
Burma	44.5	48.1	56.6	68.1	20
Malaysia	19.0	22.7	28.4	37.0	37
Cambodia	9.1	11.9	15.5	21.2	37
Laos	4.6	5.0	6.4	8.4	31
Singapore	3.0	4.0	4.4	4.7	18
Brunei	0.3	0.3	0.4	0.5	25
Total	*457.6*	*520*	*613*	*722*	*18*
Total (East Asia)	*1860.5*	*2001*	*2244*	*2520*	*12*

Source: Population Reference Bureau, *1999 World Population Data Sheet*, www.prb.org./pubs/wpds99/wpds99_1.htm; *The Military Balance 1993–94* (Brassey's for the IISS, London, 1993); Asia 1995 (Far Eastern Economic Review Asia Yearbook, Review Publishing Co., 36th edn, Hong Kong, 1994), p. 16.

Not all regional states face the prospect of high demographic growth. Populations in Japan have stabilised, and to a lesser extent those in South Korea, Singapore and Taiwan. Both Japan and Taiwan are beginning to focus on the strategic consequences of population decline rather than overpopulation. Japan's population is expected to peak in 2007 at around 130 million and then plunge by as much as 50 per cent by century's end in the absence of measures to increase the number of births.[28] Taiwan's birth rate has slipped to a record low of 1.5 per cent which, if maintained, will see the island's population begin to decline from 2038.[29] The 'greying of East Asia', as well as gender imbalance and probable labour shortages in some states, will generate a different set of political, economic and social problems.[30] Nevertheless, overpopulation and high rates of urbanisation are the demographic forces most likely to affect

Table 2.2 Proportion of urban populations in East Asia, 1990–2025

Country	1990 (%)	2000 (%)	2025 (%)
Singapore	100	100	100
Japan	77.2	78.4	84.9
South Korea	73.8	86.2	93.7
North Korea	59.8	63.1	75.2
Brunei	57.7	59.0	72.5
Malaysia	49.8	57.5	72.7
Philippines	48.8	59.0	74.3
Indonesia	30.6	40.3	60.7
China	26.2	34.5	54.5
(Hong Kong)	94.1	95.7	97.3
Burma	24.8	28.4	47.3
Vietnam	19.9	22.3	39.1
Thailand	18.7	21.9	39.1
Laos	18.6	25.1	44.5
Cambodia	17.6	24.1	43.5
Total	*40.3*	*47.0*	*54.4*

Source: *World Urbanization Prospects: The 1994 Revision* (UN, New York 1995), Table A.2, p. 81.

East Asia's security, particularly in the region's two most populous states, China and Indonesia, which between them will account for three-quarters of the region's population by 2025. Despite two of the best-run and most generously funded population-control programs in the developing world, experts in both countries concede that their populations will soar above desirable levels before declining to more manageable proportions in another hundred years or so.[31]

China

The size of China's population and its rate of increase over the past half-century are key strategic issues for the country's government. China has long been the most populous country in the world but periodic warfare, crop failures and rudimentary health facilities meant that for most of its history mortality rates remained high and the annual rate of increase modest. The communist victory of 1949 brought an end to an extended period of civil war, greater political stability and increases in living standards which transformed China's demographic profile to one of low mortality and high birth rates. The result was a population explosion. Between 1950 and 1990, China's population grew by 571 million people and by 2020 it will probably have added half a billion more, the equivalent of another Southeast

Asia. Its projected population of 1.5 billion in 2017 will near that of the total world population in 1900.[32] As Lester Brown observes, merely to feed, house and clothe this many extra people in such a short time poses formidable problems for the Chinese Government and will further degrade the country's environment. Today there is no safety valve from overseas migration, as there was for Europe in the eighteenth and nineteenth centuries, nor is there readily accessible virgin land which can accommodate the sort of population growth China is now contemplating.[33]

These demographic realities pose problems of management, governance and social order on a scale never before experienced by any other state with the exception of India.[34] People pressure and high levels of urbanisation are significant factors in the rising level of violence and lawlessness in China.[35] The drift of people to China's megacities measures in the tens of millions and has acted as a magnet for criminal groups trading in drugs, people and contraband.[36] Illegal migration from China, aided and abetted by criminal entrepreneurs, has accelerated since the early 1990s and is a significant source of friction with other Asia-Pacific states.[37] High levels of population growth can erode the benefits of economic development and worsen income differentials. China needs to maintain a growth rate of around 7–8 per cent just to absorb existing surpluses and the 10 million new workers coming onto the labour market each year. There were an estimated 150 million surplus rural labourers, 30 million retrenched workers from the state sector and around 56 million peasants looking for work in China's cities at the end of 1997, in a labour force of around 750 million, and over 300 million in total at the end of 1999.[38] As the semi-official *Beijing Review* notes: 'unless population growth is curbed, China's increase in wealth will be offset by the ever-larger number of people who have to share it … as the contradiction between population and resources grows, environmental deterioration will follow'.[39]

While Chinese leaders have long recognised the inverse relationship between lower levels of population and higher living standards, population control has been a highly contentious domestic issue in the past and subject to sudden policy reversals which have reduced the effectiveness of family planning. In the mid-1950s, Chinese scholars warned that measures should immediately be implemented to cap population increases otherwise China would have difficulty feeding its population. But Mao Zedong took a different view. 'It is a very good thing that China has a big population', he wrote in 1949. Ten years later, on the eve of the disastrous Great Leap Forward which devastated Chinese agriculture and caused the deaths of millions of peasants, Mao asked rhetorically: 'Which is better: more people or less people? Better to have more people at present!'[40] Within two years, the famine that resulted from the failure of Mao's radical experiment in agriculture had reduced China's population by 10 million. Western scholars estimate that the total number of deaths attributable to the Great Leap Forward was probably in the order of 30 million. Reflecting on Mao's decision to abandon contraception and family planning during this period, a senior Party official later admitted that had China rigorously enforced population control the famines of 1959–62 would have been far less severe.[41]

Indonesia

Indonesia's population of 215 million will expand to 340 million by the end of the twenty-first century – more than North America's current population and half that of Europe.[42] High levels of economic and population growth and unparalleled pressure on the country's urban and rural environments are eroding the country's economic gains and undermining state capacity. Like Beijing, Jakarta remains sensitive to the security implications of large numbers of newly sacked workers joining the ranks of the terminally unemployed and socially disenfranchised urban poor. Before the Asian economic crisis took hold, it was generally accepted that Indonesia's economy needed to grow by more than 5 per cent annually to provide enough jobs to soak up new entrants into the country's 100 million-strong workforce.[43] However, Indonesia's economy contracted by over 20 per cent in 1998 and recorded negative growth in 1999, adding substantially to unemployment. A warning from the armed forces that a prolongation of the upward unemployment trend could destabilise the country was borne out by subsequent widespread disturbances and social disorder in many areas of the country.[44]

The distribution, rather than absolute size, of the population is the key issue. Java suffers from many of the population ills of coastal China and other areas of comparable density in East Asia. Over half Indonesia's total population lives on Java, the smallest of Indonesia's five major islands and one of the most densely populated areas of land in the world. A large percentage of the island's population is concentrated in a 160-kilometre corridor running between Jakarta and Bandung. In 2010, Java's urban population is likely to contain 70 million of the island's estimated 133 million people, by which time metropolitan Jakarta will be home to 22 million.[45] Java's population growth does not make conflict inevitable. Much will depend on the level of economic development as well as the degree of political and social stability. The Netherlands, for example, is one of the most densely populated states in the world and it is relatively conflict-free. For states in transition, however, chronic overcrowding and high urban densities during times of political strife are akin to highly combustible bonfires, as Indonesia has discovered since President Suharto's downfall in 1998.

In order to ease population pressures in Java, and to a lesser extent in Bali and Madura, the Suharto Government actively encouraged poor farmers to relocate to the relatively underpopulated outer islands of Kalimantan, Sulawesi and Irian Jaya through the 'Go East' transmigration and development program launched in 1990.[46] The antecedents of this program go back to the colonial period when the Dutch saw internal migration as one means of alleviating rural poverty in Java. President Sukarno followed suit after independence in 1949, but transmigration accelerated under Suharto, who saw it as a mechanism for reducing political risk as well as opening up land for development. In the thirty years between 1968 and 1998, 3.5 million mainly Javanese and Balinese migrants were offered inducements of free land in the outer islands.[47] Unfortunately, transmigration has created more problems than it has solved. Animosity between transmigrants and local villagers over land-ownership and cultural and ethnic differences regularly lead to violence and bloodshed, as Erna Witoelar, Minister of Settlements and Regional Infrastructure, acknowledged in December 2000.[48] In Western Kalimantan, settlers from the overcrowded island of Madura have been attacked repeatedly by native Dayaks and Malays. A particularly serious outbreak of violence and 'ethnic cleansing' in 1999 resulted in the deaths of several thousand Madurese. Thousands more fled, creating a serious internal refugee problem for the government.[49]

A majority of Kalimantan's Madurese settlers are 'spontaneous' migrants rather than government-assisted transmigrants. In Irian Jaya, however, most new settlers are government-assisted and in some localities they now outnumber local Melanesians.[50] Outsiders – mainly Javanese and Bugis from Sulawesi – account for 800 000 out of Irian Jaya's population of around 2 million.[51] Their presence has exacerbated the communal problems that have bedevilled Jakarta's rule since Indonesian authority was first established under UN auspices in 1963.[52] Violence flared between the island's ethnic communities in late 1995 and 1996; keen to capitalise on local grievances, the separatist Free Papua Movement (OPM) became involved in several clashes with government forces. The violence was sparked by a range of issues, including land rights, the environment, ethnic differences and hostility towards US mining firm PT Freeport Indonesia, the largest foreign company operating in Irian Jaya.[53] A significant underlying cause of the unrest, however, was the hostility between indigenous tribes and Javanese newcomers who had taken up the government's offer of free land.[54] The Transmigration Program was suspended in December 2000 because the Wahid Government recognised that its advantages were outweighed by its political, social, and financial costs.[55]

Conclusion

Neo-Malthusian predictions of 'population bombs' leading to war and civilisational decline overdramatise and distort the true nature of the links between population growth and conflict, which depend on a number of social, political and economic variables. Overpopulation is far more likely to directly affect the security of people and states in the developing world than in wealthy, well-educated and information-rich societies which are more worried about 'infertility time bombs'. Declining fertility rates, unless reversed, will cause European populations to peak and then fall precipitously after 2036, despite lengthening life-spans.[56] The same trend is also evident in a minority of developed East Asian countries, notably Japan but also in South Korea and Singapore. However, although fertility rates are falling worldwide, global trends obscure significant regional and intra-regional differences. Most East Asian states are likely to experience rapid population growth, much higher levels of urbanisation, and significant internal movements of people for the next several decades; all these will seed conflict, especially during periods of economic recession.

This is not to argue that population increase is a direct or inevitable cause of conflict. The link between population and conflict is complex, since other associated factors – energy, food and water availability, for example – are usually present. As Norman Myers observes, population growth is essentially conflict-neutral until it reaches such proportions that it overstretches the 'capacities of the natural resource base to sustain it, and the capacities of governments and other institutions to accommodate it'.[57] Nonetheless, rapid population growth, especially in urban areas, will increasingly test the institutional strength and social cohesion of East Asia's developing states and place further pressure on the region's fragile ecosystem. Overpopulation diminishes the ability of governments to provide adequate levels of food, water and other necessities of life by reducing arable land and adding to pollution and environmental stress. Even under favourable economic conditions, per capita income may improve only marginally or not at all for the poorer sections of the community when demographic increases are high. If the populations of Indonesia and China were only half their present size the governments of both countries would be far more sanguine about their ability to feed their people and to manage the domestic tensions and divisions that are never far from the surface. East Asia's economic perturbations in the late 1990s demonstrate that it is much more difficult for developing states with large labour forces to maintain political and social stability during times of rising unemployment.

Not all agree that East Asia's future will be characterised by overpopulation and labour surpluses. Sceptics maintain that even in high population growth states like China and Indonesia, labour shortfalls will begin to manifest themselves from 2010 as they approach 'labour market transition', the point at which demand begins to outstrip supply.[58] Such predictions, however, assume the continuation of pre-crisis rates of economic growth and rarely take into account the possibility that current fertility trends may be temporarily reversed for economic or political reasons. One consequence of Indonesia's economic troubles, for example, has been a plummeting rupiah, raising concerns that Indonesia could experience a mini baby boom because poorer women cannot afford the cost of imported birth control devices.[59] It may be a very long time before the transformation of labour markets in the less developed economies of East Asia provides relief from the undesirable political, social and security consequences of high unemployment and expanding populations. More importantly, if China's family planning measures based on one child per family should seriously falter, then future population growth scenarios for the region would almost certainly have to be revised upward.[60]

Thus demographic factors are likely to be a negative influence on East Asia's security environment for most of this century before populations in the less developed states begin to level off and decline. A key judgement of this book is that East Asia's expanding populations will create new resource scarcities and contribute to environmental degradation, which as the remaining chapters in Part I will show, have the potential to generate significant conflict and instability among the people and states of the region.

CHAPTER 3

Deforestation, Pollution and Climate Change

Deforestation, pollution and climate change are seldom associated with security and high politics. But like the canaries that coalminers once relied on to warn of toxic air, each is a visible reminder of the stress that human activities are placing on the earth's physical environment. Are environmental disasters like the forest fires that ravaged Indonesia in 1997 and the catastrophic floods that inundated large areas of China in 1998 naturally occurring events? Or are they the consequence of human actions and development practices that are threatening the regenerative capacity of the global ecosystem? Will temperature rises produce more extreme weather patterns this century, disrupting agriculture and precipitating destabilising shifts in the balance of power? Or is climate change of insufficient magnitude or predictability to allow informed judgements about its implications for global stability, let alone the consequences for individual regions or states? This chapter seeks answers to these questions by analysing the relationship between deforestation, pollution, climate change and security in East Asia.

Deforestation

The remnants of the great forests that once covered more than 40 per cent of the earth's land surface are receding apace as a result of land clearance for agriculture and grazing, commercial logging, urbanisation and pollution.[1] Population growth is a root cause along with the vastly increased per capita consumption of forest products such as paper and industrial round-wood. Even the use of fuel-wood and charcoal has risen – by almost two-thirds between 1968 and 1998.[2] Nearly half of the world's old-growth forests had been cleared by the end of the twentieth century. An area larger than Mexico was lost in the space of the fifteen years

47

between 1980 and 1995 and the rate of clearance shows no signs of abating. Over time, deforestation reduces the fertility of the land, causing crop failures, food shortages and population movements.[3] Aside from timber, forests contain a great diversity of products that both enrich and sustain life. Among the non-wood products traded internationally are nuts, oil and medicinals.[4] Deforestation also threatens biodiversity. Although covering only 6 per cent of the earth's land surface, the tropical forests of Southeast Asia are estimated to contain between 70 and 90 per cent of the planet's animal and plant species.[5] Forests play a crucial role in binding the ecology of the planet and protecting fragile soils from temperature and rainfall extremes and in creating their own microclimates within their canopies. Removing trees often triggers a cycle of flooding and drought that ends in substantial soil erosion and sometimes desertification.[6]

In East Asia deforestation is a major cause of soil erosion, farmland loss and poor water quality. Southeast Asia's tropical forests are the most seriously affected but the region's temperate and subtropical forests, particularly in China, are also under pressure. Almost 50 per cent of Southeast Asia's original forest cover has been destroyed.[7] The FAO puts the annual rate of loss at around 1 per cent and the World Bank estimates that forest cover in the wider East Asian region is being lost at about 1.4 per cent per annum – a substantially higher loss than any other developing region of the world.[8] Four main processes are responsible:

- 'slash-and-burn' agricultural practices;
- commercial timber extraction, both legal and illegal;
- government-sponsored transmigration schemes which accelerate the rate of deforestation in the remaining areas of virgin forest land;
- large-scale development projects, such as mining operations and dam-building, which frequently require extensive forest clearance.[9]

In some states, Thailand for example, most of the commercially valuable stands of tropical forest have already been cleared. The Philippines has seen extensive logging of its tropical forests since the Spanish stripped the island of Cebu in the seventeenth and eighteenth centuries to provide hardwood for its galleons.[10] In 1900, 70–80 per cent of the archipelago was forested compared with 20 per cent in the mid-1990s. The Philippines now imports more tropical timber than it produces.[11] In other states, notably Laos, Burma and Cambodia, loggers are indiscriminately felling large tracts of the oldest and most valuable timber with relative impunity because of weak government controls and the corruption of government officials responsible for managing and licensing timber resources.[12] The Nakai Plateau in the remote highlands area of south-central Laos has been extensively logged, mainly by a company which is

Table 3.1   Changes in forest cover in East Asia, 1990–95

Country ('000 ha)	1990	1995	Annual change %
China	133 756	133 323	−0.1
Indonesia	115 213	109 791	−1.0
Burma	29 088	27 151	−1.4
Japan	25 212	25 146	−0.1
Malaysia	17 472	15 471	−2.4
Thailand	13 277	11 630	−2.6
Laos	13 177	12 435	−1.2
Cambodia	10 649	9 830	−1.6
Vietnam	9 793	9 117	−1.4
Philippines	8 078	6 766	−3.5
South Korea	7 691	7 626	−0.2
North Korea	6 170	6 170	0
Brunei	448	434	−0.6
Singapore	4	4	0
Total	*390 028*	*374 894*	*−0.8*

Source: FAO, The State of the World's Forests, 1999, www.fao.org

a commercial venture of the Lao military and headed by one of the country's most powerful generals.[13]

In Cambodia the timber trade has been effectively criminalised because of high-level political and military corruption. In less than twenty years, Cambodia's forest cover has declined from 73 per cent to 58 per cent and commercial logging is estimated to be worth $350 million annually.[14] Since the early 1990s, senior Cambodian military officers have come to regard the country's remaining old-growth areas as personal fiefdoms and valuable supplementary sources of income. These officers either directly control logging concessions or allow timber companies to harvest trees illegally from other companies' concessions in exchange for bribes or a share of the profit. Instead of working to protect the security of Cambodia and its forest resource, they are mortgaging the country's economic future in pursuit of illicit profits and personal gain. A 1999 Asian Development Bank (ADB) Report has warned that 'uncontrolled logging, much of it illegal, threatens Cambodia's forests'; unless reversed, it 'could deforest the country in five years'.[15] According to the ADB, over 4 million cubic metres of commercial timber is harvested annually, 2.5 million cubic metres above the sustainable yield.[16] At current rates Sarawak is expected to exhaust its stocks of commercial timber before 2010.[17]

The situation is little better in Indonesia. Jakarta has permitted up to 50 per cent more logging than can be sustained in the medium term.[18]

During the Suharto era, a large proportion of the proceeds from illegal logging were siphoned off by Suharto cronies, the military, and a graft-ridden bureaucracy.[19] Unfortunately, the devastation of Indonesia's primary forests has worsened since Suharto's departure because of Indonesia's still parlous economic situation and the wood industry's crucial role as a major employer and supplier of foreign exchange. Indonesia's 120 million-hectare forests are shrinking at the rate of 1.5 million hectares a year and illegal logging already exceeds the legal cut. At current rates of logging, Kalimantan's once extensive virgin forests of commercially valuable timber will be exhausted by 2005.[20] In 1999, wood products earned Indonesia $8.5 billion and processing of timber and forest products employed 5 million people. This dramatically underlines the dilemma faced by those Southeast Asian governments that are heavily dependent on timber exports.[21] Curtailing or reducing logging in the face of entrenched interests, particularly during periods of high unemployment, risks a political and social backlash that could trigger civil strife. Failure to curb illegal logging, on the other hand, incurs the wrath of influential environmental groups and financial donors and ultimately threatens the sustainability of the whole timber industry.

China's extensive reforestation campaign follows centuries of massive forest loss, including the destruction of virtually all virgin forests.[22] Deforestation frequently has devastating human and national security consequences when it is allowed to take place in the catchment areas of major river systems. China's 6000 kilometre-long Yangtse River has always been prone to floods – about 200 have been recorded over the past twenty-three centuries. In 1998 the worst flood since 1954, when 30 000 deaths were recorded, devastated large areas of the Yangtse River basin. The 1998 flood caused the deaths of more than 4000 people and economic losses of between $15 and $22 billion, inundating valuable farmland, displacing 15 million people and placing another 75 million in direct danger.[23] In the largest peacetime deployment of the People's Liberation Army, tens of thousands of soldiers were despatched to reinforce levee banks and save the Daqing oilfields, which contribute a third of China's domestic oil production.[24] Economic losses from the Yangtse flood are calculated to have shaved up to 1 per cent off China's GDP in 1998.[25]

Those who argue that flooding of this kind is merely part of a natural cycle fail to recognise that the underlying cause of the 1998 Yangtse flood was the extensive deforestation of the river's watershed and floodplain from decades of logging and agricultural encroachment.[26] Denuded of trees, the soil is no longer able to hold the summer rains, which average 2000 millimetres annually in the upper reaches of the Yangtse's catchment area. Loose soil is washed away, raising the level of the riverbed and reducing its capacity to hold floodwaters.[27] Construction of an extensive system of dykes and levee banks has only made the problem worse. Although they reduce the frequency of flooding, man-made barriers intensify their effects once they are overwhelmed, as occurred in 1998. The Yangtse is not the only river in China at risk. A 1998 study by an international research team warned that extensive deforestation and soil erosion could lead to a disaster of similar proportions in the floodplain of the Yellow River.[28]

Pressures are growing on East Asian governments to stem illegal logging and reduce the rate of commercial timber extraction from old-growth forests. Western importers are beginning to demand certification that tropical hardwoods from Southeast Asia are being harvested legally and in a sustainable manner. However, it is doubtful whether such measures will be sufficient to bring about significant reform of Asia's timber trade. The monetary rewards and economic stakes are simply too high. In 1998, Indonesian and Malaysian exports of timber were valued at $3.9 billion and $3.5 billion respectively. Rather than conserving existing forests, both countries are intent on boosting their timber exports.[29] A new element in the equation is China, which may soon become a major importer of Southeast Asian timber and is unlikely to enforce certification. China's log shortage in 1998 equalled the combined 1997 production of commercial timber by Indonesia and Malaysia. At current rates, the primary forests of the Philippines, Cambodia and Malaysia are expected to disappear in the next decade, while those of Indonesia, which has half of Asia's remaining forests, will no longer exist by 2030.[30]

As with other forms of environmental degradation, the decline of East Asia's primary forests cannot be attributed solely to government neglect or corruption. Forests are an important part of the region's natural heritage and East Asian states argue, with some justification, that they are merely following the example set by developed countries in harvesting a valuable national resource. Malaysia, in particular, fiercely rejects Western criticism of its logging practices and maintains that its timber resources are being sensibly managed and harvested in the interests of national development. Nevertheless, current forest yields are patently unsustainable and impose high marginal costs on other critical natural resources such as water and fish, which are ecologically linked. Moreover, a great deal of the money earned from land-clearing and commercial exploitation goes into the pockets of corrupt officials and a few wealthy entrepreneurs rather than being used for the benefit of society as a whole. During the Marcos era, defence secretary Juan Ponce Enrile and armed forces chief General Fabian Ver were closely involved in illegal logging. The Philippines' experience has been the rule rather than the exception.[31] Instead of protecting, husbanding and exploiting forest resources for the benefit of the wider community, governments have all too often been the hidden hand behind illegal logging, the rampant overexploitation of timber resources, and conflicts between logging companies and indigenous people.[32] In effect, the state has become the primary cause of insecurity for those communities displaced by logging.

Pollution

Pollution is a global problem and a direct result of privileging unbridled economic growth ahead of sustainable development. When combined with other socio-economic factors such as high rates of population increase, resource scarcity, poverty and corruption, pollution may have important ramifications for regional security and foreign policy. East Asia has one of the worst pollution track records of any region in the world. Systematic abuse of the region's natural resources is causing air, water and ground pollution on such a scale that the ADB has labelled Asia 'the world's most polluted and environmentally degraded region'.[33] Asia's rivers are more polluted than in any other region of the world and by a considerable margin.[34] Air quality in virtually all the region's major cities has significantly deteriorated since the mid-1970s. According to the World Health Organisation (WHO), nine of the fifteen cities with the highest particulate (dust and soot) levels in the world and six out of the fifteen worst affected by sulphur dioxide are in East Asia. Carbon dioxide emissions per unit of GDP are three times those of Latin America, and the region will soon account for over 50 per cent of the world's incremental growth in carbon dioxide and sulphur dioxide.[35]

Government attempts to address the air-quality issue have in the main been sporadic, limited and ineffectual. The Malaysian Government's disregard for the clean-air recommendations of its own environmental experts is typical of the way in which regional governments have placed economic development ahead of environmental considerations. Much of the smog that envelops Kuala Lumpur is from local industrial and car emissions which the aborted 1994 Clean Air Action Plan was designed to reduce.[36] Hong Kong is also severely affected by air pollution. The air pollution index hit a record high in March 2000, forcing the government to belatedly announce a package of new measures aimed at improving air quality.[37] Air pollution throughout East Asia is forecast to worsen as more motor vehicles throng the region's streets, especially in China. The number of cars in East Asia is doubling every seven years. Private vehicles on the road in China increased from fewer than 150 000 in 1987 to 2 million in 1997.[38] Unless remedial action is taken, economic growth as well as the environment is likely to suffer in the long term. The economic cost of pollution is also considerable. Greenpeace calculates that the direct economic losses from pollution totalled between 3 and 5 per cent of China's

GDP during the 1990s.[39] The World Bank believes that if all the environmental imposts are added up, including health care for pollution-
induced diseases and the loss of forest and agricultural land, the true cost
of pollution and environmental degradation may be as high as 8 per cent
of GDP, which would effectively cancel out China's economic growth.[40]
This compares with the less than 0.85 per cent of GDP that China spends
on environmental protection.[41] Acid rain alone probably costs China
$1.8 billion annually.[42]

Southeast Asia's forest fires

Pollution's egregious security effect was dramatically illustrated by the
choking smog that enveloped large areas of Southeast Asia in the latter
half of 1997 and early 1998. The result of unusually severe forest fires on
the Indonesian islands of Sumatra and Kalimantan, the smog was an environmental disaster for the region with few modern parallels in terms of its
scale and political impact.[43] It affected the health of at least 20 million
Indonesians, impeded navigation through the region's busy sea-lanes and
strained relations between Jakarta and its ASEAN neighbours. The smog
also had significant political, health and economic repercussions for
Brunei, Malaysia, the Philippines and Thailand, leading the head of the
UN Environment Programme, Klaus Topfer, to declare the consequences
of the fires as catastrophic and 'a problem of global dimension'.[44]

Fire is an intrinsic part of the life cycle of Indonesia's forests, but the
1997–98 blazes were an act of man, not nature. The destruction of forests
in Kalimantan, Sumatra and, to a lesser extent, Irian Jaya and Sulawesi
began in earnest in the 1970s and accelerated in the 1990s following the
Indonesian Government's decision to significantly increase palm-oil production. Since 1985, the area of land given over to palm-oil plantations
has grown from 600 000 hectares to around 5 million hectares. Jakarta,
which earns $1 billion annually from these plantations, aims to make
Indonesia the world's largest producer by 2005.[45] Forest-burning in
Indonesia is the cheapest and quickest method of clearing land for palm-
oil plantations. Fires lit by plantation-owners on Kalimantan in 1994 created one of the worst smogs in Indonesia before 1997, forcing airports
and other facilities on Kalimantan and nearby Sulawesi to close for several weeks. Pollution in Singapore reached unprecedented levels,
Malaysia declared a public alert and both countries sought urgent talks
with Indonesia on cross-border atmospheric pollution.[46]

Two factors – a severe drought caused by the El Niño weather system
and the presence of carcinogenic particles in the smog – conspired to
increase the environmental impact of the 1997 fires. The fires spread out
of control, and prevailing winds carried a dense cloud of pollution as far

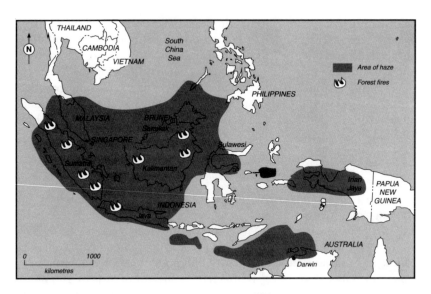

Map 3.1 Haze over Southeast Asia, September 1997
Source: Weekend Australian, 27–28 September 1997, p. 14.

as northern Australia, Thailand and the Philippines.[47] Malaysia and Singapore recorded their highest-ever levels of atmospheric pollution.[48] The smoke disrupted transport and contributed to at least two serious accidents. Factories, schools, air- and seaports, government offices and other key facilities on Kalimantan and Sumatra were closed for extended periods and Sarawak declared a state of emergency on 19 September. Economic losses from reduced manufacturing and agricultural output were compounded by a sharp decline in tourism.[49] Reduced sunlight impeded the growth of palm-oil plantations in Indonesia and Malaysia.[50] The economic costs of the fires for Indonesia, Malaysia and Singapore was initially estimated at $1.4 billion in short-term health care, lost tourist revenue and reduced industrial and agricultural production.[51] Later assessments calculated total losses at $4.4 billion.[52]

The political costs for Indonesia were equally high. Although initially blaming the fires on natural causes, principally El Niño, President Suharto was forced to issue two unprecedented apologies to neighbouring states. On 6 October, his Environment Minister Sarwono Kusumaatmadja acknowledged that 'if we don't change our ways, we won't survive as a nation. I hope this time we make doubly sure [the fires] won't happen again, otherwise we'll be out of business forever'.[53] Discontent and anger among Indonesia's normally respectful ASEAN neighbours deepened as the smog worsened. Malaysia's opposition leader, Lim Kit Siang, moved an emergency motion calling for a parliamentary debate on Indonesia's failure to put out the fires.[54] Environment Minister Law Hieng Din chided Indonesian officials for their lack of effective action.[55] Thailand's *Nation* daily newspaper blamed Jakarta for providing logging companies with subsidies to clear forests, and asked, 'who is to pay for this wanton act of destruction, if not the people of Southeast Asia?'[56] Singapore's Environment Minister, Yeo Cheow Tong, politely but pointedly reminded Indonesia that the fires could not be allowed to burn out of control.[57]

While climatic factors contributed to the severity of the 1997 and 1998 fires, they were not the primary cause. There have been major fires in non-El Niño years and conversely no fires during the course of other El Niño phenomena.[58] Speculation that the fires may have been started by small freeholders clearing their land are not supported by satellite evidence, which clearly indicates that most fires began on large landholdings under the control of business conglomerates with close connections to the Suharto family. As one Singaporean politician has pointed out, Indonesian 'government subsidies and incentives for large companies have underwritten much of the land clearing'.[59] The Suharto Government's unwillingness to enforce its own laws and regulations with regard to land clearance and forest management, combined with its inability to take strong action once the fires had started, further inflamed the situation. ASEAN's reluctance to deviate from its much-cherished principle of 'non-interference in the internal affairs of member states' reduced the capacity of Indonesia's neighbours to assist and undermined the effectiveness of a Regional Haze Action Plan.[60] Less severe fires were recorded in Kalimantan during the 1999 and 2000 dry seasons but the insipid political response belied the high environmental and economic stakes. Malaysia, Singapore and Brunei again expressed their concern to Jakarta and offered to help, but beset by a myriad of more pressing economic and political concerns, the Habibie and Wahid Governments did little to halt the slash-and-burn land-clearance practices responsible for the fires.[61]

Interstate tensions

As the Indonesian fires demonstrate, the consequences of worsening pollution may be felt beyond national jurisdictions. Japan and South Korea are increasingly concerned about the political, economic and health effects of airborne pollutants and acid rain from coal-burning power stations in China. South Korea's air quality is among the worst in the region, and the country suffers from the highest methane concentration – a key cause of global warming – in the world. However, much of the methane, along with other dangerous chemicals and particulates, originates in China.[62] Acid rain is slowly eroding the biological productivity of the sea and land, and is a long-term health and food security issue for all

Northeast Asian states.[63] China has denied responsibility for its neighbours' environmental problems and neither Seoul nor Tokyo has been prepared to make pollution a major issue.[64] This tolerance is set to be tested in the future as Chinese industrial emissions increase in line with the country's expanding economy and greater use of fossil fuels. China has an estimated 11 per cent of the world's coal reserves and coal provides 75 per cent of the country's commercial energy. With these reserves likely to last for up to 1000 years, Beijing is almost certain to exploit them fully to meet its anticipated energy shortfall.[65] As a result China is expected to become the source of nearly half the world's greenhouse gas emissions by 2010, and the world's leading source of carbon emissions by 2025.[66]

Coal-burning is not the only pollution problem with the potential to harm interstate relations in Northeast Asia. China's plans to build an extensive nuclear power industry could present Seoul and Tokyo with an environmental security dilemma. A radioactive discharge into the atmosphere could trigger a major adverse public reaction in South Korea and Japan, creating problems for their domestic nuclear industries as well as relations with China. Pollution has already intruded into the security relationship between Japan and the United States. In November 1997, US Navy officials protested to their Japanese counterparts about the fumes blowing over the military base at Atsugi near Tokyo from a large industrial waste incinerator, and urged that it be shut down. The Navy claimed that the fumes contained a toxic mix of chemicals that was damaging the health of service personnel.[67]

Pollution and the food chain

Pollution's ability to damage the food chain and diminish the capacity of developing states to provide food and water for their people has direct implications for both national and human security. In East Asia millions of hectares have been contaminated by decades of headlong economic growth, leaving large tracts of arable land infertile. The toxins dumped on this land will be difficult to clean up, and East Asia's record of combating soil pollution compares poorly with that of other developing regions. The problem is particularly acute at sea. Most of East Asia's major cities are located in coastal areas or adjacent to river systems that drain into the ocean. As cities expand, coastlines are being stripped of their protective vegetation and increasing amounts of untreated industrial and human waste are pouring into river estuaries and coastal waters. Serious marine pollution affects large areas, especially the Gulf of Thailand, Manila and Jakarta Bays, the South China Sea, the Mekong Delta and the waters off South Korea, Japan and China.[68] Even as long ago as the mid-1980s, at least a third of China's coastal waters contained significant levels of cadmium, mercury and heavy metals and the situation has worsened considerably since.[69]

One of the problems in alerting the international community to the extent of marine pollution and habitat destruction has been what Gwyn Prins calls the lack of a 'Show me!' crisis – the absence of visible signs in people's daily lives of serious environmental damage.[70] However, pollution at sea is becoming more obvious as it worsens. Discharges of nutrient-rich sewage and other forms of organic pollution are responsible for creating and exacerbating highly visible 'red tides', a generic term for micro-organisms called dinoflagellates that manifest themselves as red algae. The algae kill fish and other marine organisms, destroying natural breeding areas as well as aquaculture farms. Red tides are becoming common in Bohai and Liaodong Bays, the waters around Hong Kong and the Tumen River in North Korea.[71] One red tide in 1998 cost Hong Kong $120 million in lost fish and was described by a senior official as the island's 'worst natural disaster' in living memory.[72]

Population growth, the overuse of chemical fertilisers to improve crop yields, and the rapid increase in maritime traffic plying the region's major shipping routes have contributed to high levels of pollution in the Yellow, East and South China Seas.[73] As the search for energy has intensified, mining, oil and gas exploration has risen sharply, creating further pressures on the marine and coastal environments. Oil carried by rivers from the Beijing area and from ships and offshore drilling platforms has seriously polluted Bohai Bay. The East China Sea suffered its first major oil spill at sea in November 1971, when the tanker *Juliana* spilled 6400 tons of oil, devastating fish and other marine life.[74] In 1997, the break-up of a Russian oil tanker, the *Nakhodka*, off the Japanese coast caused significant damage to Japan's sensitive fish and aquaculture breeding grounds. The accident also became a contentious political issue as Russia refused to accept Japan's claim that Moscow should accept liability and pay compensation.[75]

Pollution is a major cause of marine habitat loss and the destruction of traditional fishing grounds in the rivers and seas of Southeast Asia. A Malaysian Department of Environment study found that of 116 major rivers surveyed in Peninsula Malaysia during 1993, only 27 per cent were pollution-free. The others were 'biologically dead' or 'dying'.[76] The Gulf of Thailand has been virtually denuded of some major fish species because of overfishing and the destruction of breeding areas caused by urban discharge into the Gulf from Bangkok and other Thai cities. Coral reefs and their rich marine life are being destroyed by blast fishing, tourist development and sedimentation.[77] The marine environment of the South China Sea is under stress from energy exploration and the increasing number of giant oil tankers transiting it from the Middle East.

Regional governments worry that a major oil spill could seriously disrupt or even close the heavily trafficked Malacca Strait.[78] A large-scale spill and subsequent closure of the Strait would have devastating economic as well as environmental consequences for the contiguous states of Malaysia, Singapore and Indonesia as well as the broader region since the Strait carries a high percentage of inter-regional trade.[79] East Asia's rising demand for oil has increased tanker traffic dramatically and heightened the risk of serious oil spills. In the mid-1990s, over 1100 fully laden oil tankers passed through the Malacca Strait annually, many with only a few metres of clearance between their keels and the channel bottom, and the number of tankers is expected to double or triple by 2010.[80] In response, Indonesia and Malaysia have significantly increased their naval cooperation and regularly pursue and fine ships caught dumping oil and waste at sea.[81]

Toxic waste

While dramatic sea chases capture the headlines, it is the cumulative effect of systemic pollution from years of unregulated and ultimately unsustainable economic development practices which represent a far more serious threat to East Asia's food and resource security. Years of using hazardous industrial wastes and pesticides is jeopardising the health and the food supply of East Asian states and accelerating the process of soil degradation caused by salinisation, overgrazing, waterlogging and erosion. Millions of hectares of land in East Asia have been polluted during the 'dirty' era of industrial development by a poisonous cocktail of pesticides, organochlorines, industrial chemicals and heavy metals. These toxins will be extremely difficult and expensive to clean up and they have rendered large tracts of arable land infertile at a time when productive farmland is shrinking because of population growth and urbanisation.[82] Unfortunately, East Asia's track record in combating soil pollution compares poorly with that of other developing regions. The extent of land degradation from all causes is above the world average and soil erosion is three to eight times higher.[83]

The generation and disposal of hazardous industrial wastes is likely to become a future source of political contention in East Asia. Three decades of rapid economic growth in conjunction with the region's laissez-faire approach to the environment has attracted many industries that are highly polluting.[84] Poorer states have long permitted or turned a blind eye to the importation of hazardous wastes from industrialised countries in the West and other parts of the region which are unable or unwilling to find suitable domestic disposal sites. However, governments are being forced to reappraise their attitudes to hazardous waste generation and disposal because of growing environmental consciousness, community opposition and recognition of the long-term health and environmental costs.

In 1998, a major row broke out between Taiwan and Cambodia over the dumping of 3000 tons of mercury-laced waste near the Cambodian port city of Sihanoukville by a Taiwanese company, Formosa Plastics. The waste had been illegally imported into Cambodia with the connivance of Cambodian Government and port officials, who were reportedly paid $3 million in bribes, and was only discovered after several people living near the dump site suddenly died while many others complained of sickness and dizziness. Under domestic political pressure to take strong action, Cambodian Prime Minister Hun Sen called in the army to cordon off and sanitise the site and demanded that the waste be returned to Taiwan. Taiwanese environmental NGOs supported the Cambodian demand and castigated Taipei for its irresponsibility. A chastened Taiwanese Foreign Minister, Jason Hu, acknowledged the damage that had been done to Taiwan's international reputation and its foreign policy interests: 'We must have the concept of being a part of the global village and respect its international laws. We cannot suffer more blows in our efforts to win international support'.[85]

Climate Change

Air pollution from industrial emissions, automobile exhausts, the burning of carbon-based fuels, change in land use and the large-scale destruction of forest cover has resulted in the build-up of 'greenhouse' gases in the earth's troposphere, or lower atmosphere. These gases – mainly carbon dioxide, methane, nitrous oxide and chlorofluorocarbons (CFCs) used as propellants in aerosols and refrigerants – have grown significantly since pre-industrial times, mainly because of human activities.[86] The Indonesian fires of 1997–98, for example, are estimated to have released 1 billion tonnes of carbon dioxide into the atmosphere, more than the total annual emissions from Western Europe's cars and power stations.[87] Analysis of ice-core samples suggests that the two key greenhouse gases of carbon dioxide and methane are at higher levels than at any time in the last 160 000 years. By 2010, concentrations of carbon dioxide are expected to be 50 per cent higher than in 1990.[88] Increased levels of greenhouse gases reduce the heat lost to space, trapping it within the lower atmosphere and causing mean global temperatures to rise over time. Already five of the hottest years on record have occurred in the 1990s.[89] Climatologists warn that over the next hundred years the concentrations of greenhouse gases accumulating in the atmosphere will eventually be of sufficient magnitude to fundamentally alter global weather patterns.

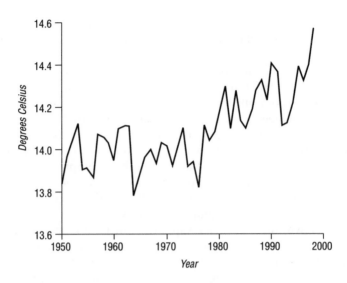

Figure 3.1 Average temperature at earth's surface, 1950–2000
Source: Vital Signs 1999, Worldwatch Institute, 1999, www.worldwatch.org

Climate and security

How might climate change affect security? There are many historical examples of climatic shifts or extremes of weather triggering conflict and even contributing to the rise and fall of civilisations and nations. Particularly intense El Niños played a crucial role in the demise of the Hittite and Akkadian empires in 2200 and 1200 BC respectively.[90] Growing aridity and frigid temperatures from a prolonged cold snap caused Huns and German tribes to surge across the Volga and Rhine into milder Gaul during the fourth century, eventually leading to the sack of Rome in 410 by Visigoths. Muslim expansion into the Mediterranean and southern Europe in the eighth century was to some extent driven by drought in the Middle East. The Viking community in Greenland died out in the fifteenth century because of a sudden cooling of temperatures across northern Europe known as the 'Little Ice Age', while weather-induced crop failures in the 1690s had adverse geopolitical consequences for Scotland and Sweden.[91]

However, these climatic changes were relatively short lived and far less significant than those now in prospect. In a world populated by 6 billion people and with natural resources already stretched, sudden deviations from global or regional weather norms could have profound consequences for international security, disrupting food production, reducing fresh-water availability for hundreds of millions of people, spreading disease, and fomenting political and social unrest. Since 50 per cent of global population is concentrated in coastal regions, sea-level rises of even modest proportions would render many cities and towns uninhabitable and could result in major population dislocations. Some countries are likely to suffer from climate change more than others. The immensely fertile American Midwest, which has played a central role in the emergence of the United States as a global superpower, could find its agricultural yields and soil fertility blighted by reductions in rainfall and extended periods of drought. Russia, on the other hand, might experience only marginal agricultural losses as previously arid areas become moister and therefore more productive.[92]

Climate change could also impose economic penalties on states forced to adopt expensive countermeasures such as building dykes or reinforcing sea walls. Wealthy countries would be able to absorb these costs better than poorer regions of the world, accentuating existing income and resource inequities and compelling the poorer 'South' to confront the richer 'North'.[93] The real problem is the unprecedented rate at which temperatures are increasing rather than the absolute size of differential warming. Spread over several centuries or a millennium, temperature rises of several degrees could be managed without major disruptions to commerce, agriculture and urban life. Compressed within the space of a single century, global warming will present far more daunting challenges of adaptation.

Pessimists like David Wirth believe that there will be no net winners from climate change, which will be responsible for major shifts in the global balance of power, 'exacerbating the risk of war'. According to Wirth, intensifying competition for land and natural resources from people dispossessed by sea-level rise could initiate new regional conflicts and aggravate old ones.[94] Shifts in rainfall patterns and temperature extremes may thus become the trigger for 'civilisational shock', instigating fundamental changes in the distribution of wealth and power.[95] Optimists, on the other hand, dismiss any direct connection between climate change and security, maintaining that climatic factors will only marginally influence tomorrow's security environment.[96] They point to significant natural fluctuations in climate patterns and short-term cyclical phenomena like El Niño and the recently hypothesised Pacific Decadal Oscillation (PDO), the causes of which are not fully understood.[97] Even if global warming does take place, they argue, many of its effects may be localised, benign or favourable.[98]

The scientific debate

Optimists have called into question the accuracy and reliability of the data used to support the case for significant climate change, especially the findings of the United Nations' expert Intergovernmental Panel on

Climate Change (IPCC). The 1995 Second Assessment Report of the IPCC concluded that:

- Mean global temperatures have risen between 0.3ºC and 0.6ºC in the past century, most of it occurring over the past 40 years. Temperatures are expected to increase another 1ºC to 3.5ºC by the end of this century.
- The early 1990s were the warmest years recorded since 1860, the first year that accurate temperature records were kept.
- In all cases the average rate of warming will probably be greater than any seen in the last 10 000 years.
- Temperatures will continue to rise beyond 2100, even if concentrations of greenhouse gases are stabilised by then.
- Sea levels have risen between 10 and 25 centimetres in the twentieth century and will rise between 15 and 95 centimetres by 2100.[99]

The IPCC made two other important findings. It identified a number of potentially serious climatic changes, including the probably heightened incidence and severity of extreme weather patterns (such as droughts, high temperatures and floods) that are expected to have a negative impact on agricultural and primary production. While acknowledging the difficulty of making accurate forecasts of local variations in weather cycles, the report concluded that the 'emerging pattern' clearly shows the weather is responding to higher concentrations of greenhouse gases.[100]

These findings are contested on three grounds by dissident climatologists and meteorologists. Although conceding that concentrations of greenhouse gases have increased and the surface of the planet is warming, they argue that temperature rises are not penetrating the free troposphere or upper atmosphere where temperatures are stable if not falling. If substantial climate change is occurring, warming should be evident right through the 10 kilometre-deep troposphere. Second, the IPCC conclusions drawn from models showing that the movement of water vapour between the surface and the upper atmosphere are not proved. The amplifying effect on global warming predicted by the IPCC may be minimal because water vapour feedback may not reach the upper atmosphere. Third, greenhouse gas-enhancing water vapour in the atmosphere could actually decrease because of the physics of cloud formation. Dissidents believe that computer climate models are not yet advanced enough to predict accurately the extremely complex dynamics of long-term climate trends.[101]

The technical and somewhat arcane nature of these arguments makes it difficult for non-specialists to come to grips with the complexities of the climate change debate, which has become highly politicised as the economic, environmental and political stakes have risen.[102] It is important to recognise, however, that expert opinion overwhelming supports the view that global warming of the order predicted by the IPCC is likely. The 1995 IPCC review represents the collective judgement of nearly 2500 of the most prominent scientists working on climate change and its conclusions were subject to extensive peer review.[103] Other independent reports by leading climatologists have endorsed the basic findings of the IPCC and the evidence for global warming has become more compelling since the 1995 report. Nineteen ninety-seven, 1998 and 1999 were the three warmest years on record and an independent panel of experts convened by the US National Academy of Science reported in January 2000 that temperatures have already risen by 0.3°C since 1979.[104] This is the highest rate of warming since the beginning of instrumental temperature measurement. There is broad scientific consensus that glaciers around the world and the polar ice caps are melting at accelerating rates and seas are continuing to warm and expand.[105]

In 2000, the IPCC conducted its first comprehensive review of climate change since 1995. Its preliminary findings reinforce and strengthen those of the 1995 report and provide further evidence that significant warming and sea-level rise are in prospect. Temperatures are now expected to increase by between 1.5°C and 6°C this century (compared with the 1°C–3.5°C predicted in 1995) because of lower emissions of sulphur dioxide which offset the warming effect of greenhouse gases. Even if atmospheric concentrations of these gases are stabilised, temperatures are forecast to continue climbing over the next several decades and sea levels will rise for hundreds more years. Robert T. Watson, the chair of the IPCC, summed up the effects in these words: 'climate change will, in many parts of the world, adversely affect socio-economic sectors, including water resources, agriculture, forestry, fisheries and human settlements, ecological systems (particularly forests and coral reefs), and human health (particularly diseases spread by insects), with developing countries being the most vulnerable'.[106]

Thus although there are still many unknowns and uncertainties about the likely severity, distribution patterns and consequences of future climate change, a great deal of the data is no longer in dispute. By the end of the 1990s, the debate had moved away from the basic science of the greenhouse hypothesis to the timing, magnitude and manageability of the expected changes.[107] Most governments around the world accept that significant global warming is not just possible but highly likely and therefore measures must be implemented to reduce its impact. This was the consensus of the 1997 Climate Summit in Kyoto Japan, which set national limits on greenhouse gas emissions in an attempt to stabilise global climate change.[108]

Climate change in East Asia

Although there is less certainty about the effect on regional weather patterns, the IPCC has identified five likely climate outcomes for East Asia:

- more intense summer monsoons, increasing the degree and frequency of destructive floods and soil erosion;
- sea-level rises which will submerge low-lying coastal plains and river deltas, placing at risk already endangered coastal ecosystems;
- changes in precipitation, which could alter river flows and affect hydroelectric power;
- decreasing fresh-water availability resulting from higher rates of evaporation and salinisation;
- greater uncertainty associated with water management and supply.[109]

Aside from the IPCC review, a number of authoritative international studies have concluded that virtually all East Asian states will experience flooding from rising sea levels, and several will be severely affected. The areas most at risk include the Yellow and Yangtse River deltas in China, Manila Bay in the Philippines, the low-lying coastal areas of Sumatra, Kalimantan and Java in Indonesia, and the Mekong, Chao Phraya and

Table 3.2 Global climate change: the scientific consensus

Issue	Statement	Consensus
Basic	Fundamental physics of the greenhouse effect	Virtually certain
Characteristics	Added greenhouse gases add heat	Virtually certain
	Greenhouse gases increasing because of human activity	Virtually certain
	Significant reduction of uncertainty will require a decade or more	Virtually certain
Projected effects by mid-21st Century	Large stratospheric cooling	Virtually certain
	Global mean surface precipitation increase	Very probable
	Reduction of sea ice	Very probable
	Arctic winter surface warming	Very probable
	Rise in global sea level	Very probable
	Local details of climate change	Uncertain
	Tropical storm increases	Uncertain
	Details of next 25 years	Uncertain

Note: Scientists are now more certain that tropical storms will increase and more confident about their ability to predict the details of local climate change.
Source: World Resources 1994–95: A Guide to the Global Environment (Oxford University Press for the UN, 1994), p. 205.

Irrawaddy deltas in Vietnam, Thailand and Burma respectively. Most of these areas are heavily populated, containing either the national capital and/or major administrative and port facilities. In most cases, the deltas and river mouths are also crucial sources of food.[110]

After many years of ignoring or playing down warnings about the potential economic and social consequences of climate change, East Asian governments are beginning to sit up and take notice as the evidence becomes more convincing. In 1995, the once sceptical Chinese Government participated in a joint study with the World Bank on greenhouse gases that analysed the effects of rising sea levels on China. The study found that without action to curb global warming, the sea is expected to rise between 70 and 100 centimetres at the northern port of Tianjin, 50 and 70 centimetres in Shanghai, and 40 and 60 centimetres in the Pearl River delta. Half of the area of the delta is less than 0.3 millimetres above sea level and the land is sinking at the rate of 0.78 millimetres annually. A 15-centimetre rise in sea levels would submerge 20–30 per cent of the delta but a 30-centimetre rise would flood nearly half. If rises of this magnitude occur, spring tides and storm surges could cause severe flooding in Tianjin, Shanghai and the Pearl River delta, all of which are major centres of industry, commerce and population.[111]

Conclusion

Deforestation, pollution and climate change are three environmental variables that are key indicators of the health of the biosphere and of the resource base on which humanity depends for its wealth and well-being. Deforestation and pollution of the water, soil and air are symptomatic of their parlous state as well as primary causes of environmental degradation, especially in East Asia, which is one of the regions most at risk. Rapid and substantial climate change in this century, which will directly affect food production and cause major population displacements, seems inevitable. The symbiotic relationship between deforestation, pollution and climate change typifies the circular, interconnected weave of today's environmental ills. Deforestation is responsible for soil erosion, acute flooding and some of the greenhouse gases that are contributing to global warming and rising sea levels. Air pollution adds to global warming and creates acid rain that eventually falls back to earth, killing trees and marine life and polluting the soil. If these were isolated developments there would be little cause for concern. They are, however, widespread and it is virtually certain that deforestation, pollution and climate change will accelerate in the decades ahead.

Forest loss, worsening pollution and the rise in greenhouse gases all have potentially serious long-term implications for security, although not necessarily in the way that traditionalists conceive. Deforestation and security are linked in two ways. Logging and land-clearance practices that alienate indigenous communities who rely on the forests for their livelihood may lead to violent confrontation and deaths.[112] But the real impact of deforestation is best measured in terms of population displacements, increases in greenhouse gases and crop damage resulting from the exposure of the soil to drought and flood-induced erosion. Floods that occur primarily as a result of human actions are a mounting cause of death and destruction, sometimes on a massive scale, as the Yangtse floods of 1998 tragically demonstrate. Worsening pollution is the unwanted legacy of East Asia's rapid economic development and is already a major environmental policy issue for the region's governments. Regional indignation over the Indonesian fires and the diplomatic difficulty between Japan and the United States over the Atsugi incinerator demonstrate that increasing sensitivity to pollution will also influence the security policy climate. Although pollution is unlikely to be a direct cause of military conflict, oil spills can cause political tensions between states, as the *Nakhodka* incident illustrates. A major spill would have adverse economic effects if it took place in a confined sea-lane such as the Malacca Strait.

The Indonesian fires highlight the political difficulties of dealing with transnational pollution issues and are a reminder of the dangers of ignoring the lessons of sustainable economic development. Further fires in Indonesia on the scale of those in 1997–98 and intensified acid rain in Northeast Asia – both of which are probable – are the two air-pollution issues most likely to have direct implications for national security and foreign policy because of their high visibility and potentially widespread impact. State capacity in Indonesia has been weakened by the combined effect of the economic crisis and political turmoil in the post-Suharto era. While in theory a liberalising Indonesia should be more sensitive to the environment, a lack of resources and Jakarta's preoccupation with political and economic survival do not augur well for the prospect of effective government action in the event of another serious outbreak of forest fires in Kalimantan or Sumatra. Should that occur, tensions with neighbouring countries could once again escalate.[113]

Pollution may be the unintended side-effect of the economic, social, environmental and demographic forces shaping East Asia's strategic environment, but it also has a security dynamic of its own. Smog from fires, acid rain, oil spills and toxic waste is an emerging source of contention between East Asian states, and its effects on human security is palpable and growing. For the millions of ordinary people whose livelihoods and health have been jeopardised, combating East Asia's worsening air, land and maritime pollution is more than just a social or environmental issue. Even if the region returns to strong economic growth, pollution will continue to degrade the food chain and place further pressure on the region's agriculture and fresh-water resources. Pollution also kills people directly. WHO estimates that of the 2.7 million pollution-related deaths that occur globally every year, half are in Asia.[114] Under economic and demographic duress, governments are more likely to pursue 'grow first, clean up later' policies that sacrifice sustainable development to political expediency. However, delaying rather than attacking the causes of pollution merely worsens the problem and shifts the burden of action to future generations, thereby increasing their insecurity.

On the evidence to date, it is difficult to see climate change alone inducing major reconfigurations of the regional or global balance of power, as some scholars have suggested. Shifts of this order presuppose substantial redistributions of the relative productive capacities of nation-states, but current climate models are still not accurate enough to describe in detail how individual states will be affected. After years of pre-varication and denial, the international community is beginning to implement a range of corrective measures that should lessen tempera-ture increases and sea-level rise in the longer term. Even so, there is now sufficient data to conclude that the rate and degree of climate change in the twenty-first century will be of a magnitude never before experienced in human history. The net security consequences are unlikely to be benign, especially for developing states which, as Peter Gleick notes, 'are least responsible for the production of greenhouse gases, least able to adapt [to] or mitigate the changes, and [have] little international or political clout'.[115] Regardless of the steps taken to cap and reduce green-house gas emissions, the rate of global warming and consequent climate change is unlikely to be reversed soon because of the build-up of green-house gases that has already taken place.

Climate change will further complicate East Asia's future security envi-ronment because weather extremes and greater fluctuations in rainfall and temperatures have the capacity to refashion the region's productive landscape and exacerbate food, water and resource scarcity in a relatively short time-span. If repetitive floods, or prolonged droughts, were to cre-ate even short-term food and water shortages during times of rising social and political tensions, regional governments might find themselves hard pressed to deal with these exigencies. Sea-level rise is of particular con-cern because of the density of coastal populations and the potential for large-scale displacements of people. It will be extremely difficult to carry out forced evacuations or relocations without conflict. The economic costs of managing the effects of climate change are likely to be substan-tial; they will include reduced economic growth and depressed incomes, which will circumscribe the ability of developing states to meet the rising aspirations of their people. Anticipating and preparing for the consequences of climate change will also compound the already formidable problems of governance. For the developing states of East Asia, global warming will prove an unwelcome additional challenge to security which will be difficult to combat without meaningful regional cooperation.

CHAPTER 4

Will There Be an Energy 'Gap'?

The next three chapters explore East Asia's resource vulnerabilities and address two key questions. Will there be sufficient energy, food and fresh water to meet spiralling demand at a time when environmental degradation is reducing arable land and fresh-water availability and when energy strategies are being complicated by environmental considerations? Under what circumstances might an emerging energy gap, and food and water shortages, lead to conflict?

Concerns about Energy

Energy and security have been linked throughout history. Competition for raw materials was an important element of interstate conflict well before the environment entered the lexicon of international security. Nations have fought for control of critical raw materials at least as far back as the Trojan War because they are finite, unevenly distributed, central to economic development and therefore have high pecuniary and strategic value.[1] Fossil fuels such as coal, oil and gas extracted from the sediments of long-dead animals and plants are the lifeblood of modern society, accounting for three-quarters of all energy used. It is doubtful, however, whether fossil fuels and their once touted replacement, nuclear power, can sustain economic growth in the twenty-first century because energy security has become increasingly intertwined with environmental issues.[2] Oil spills, acid rain, land degradation, water pollution, climate change and fear of nuclear accidents will eventually compel governments to adopt a cleaner energy system long before fossil fuels near exhaustion. Unfortunately, the transition from a 'carbon-based civilisation' to renewable sources of energy such as solar, wind and tidal power is unlikely to be smooth. It will in all probability be accompanied by significant political and strategic perturbations that will move to centre stage in the security concerns of states, especially in energy-deficient East Asia. Human security will also be threatened since access to cheap, clean energy is a prerequisite of economic and social development.

The concerns about energy security are threefold. First, it is not clear whether oil will remain affordable and available if demand maintains its upward momentum or supply is disrupted. Some time before 2010, global oil production will peak and the depletion of known reserves will pass the halfway mark. At that time the world will have used more than half its geological endowment of conventional oil and there are slim prospects of finding enough new oil to substantially alter this equation.[3] Second, environmental considerations are complicating energy choices by adding to the costs of production and usage. Coal, for example, is relatively abundant but it is also highly polluting. Governments are beginning to appreciate that the rising environmental costs of fossil fuels may circumscribe their use. Third, the reputation of nuclear power, which once promised abundant supplies of clean, cheap energy, has been tarnished by a number of well-publicised nuclear accidents over the past two decades, notably at Three Mile Island in the United States, Chernobyl in the Ukraine, and Tokaimura in Japan. Nuclear power seems unlikely to replace fossil fuel as the major future source of global energy, in part because of international disquiet about the consequences of accidental radiation fallout, nuclear weapons proliferation and the disposal of radioactive waste from nuclear power plants.[4]

Energy Security and Interstate Conflict in East Asia

The world's voracious appetite for energy is likely to fuel competition for diminishing supplies of fossil fuels and heighten national anxieties in energy-deficient states about long-term energy security. At the end of the 1990s, Asia as a whole had become the largest oil-consuming region, overtaking Western Europe in 1990 and the United States in 1997.[5] In East Asia, the perception that oil and gas may become more scarce has aggravated tensions over unresolved boundary quarrels, especially at sea. Every state in East Asia, except landlocked Laos, is involved in at least one dispute with a neighbour. Several have caused serious political tensions and military confrontation. What is new and troubling about these disputes is that they are taking place against a background of rising energy demand, diminishing energy self-sufficiency and sustained economic growth, notwithstanding the recession of the late 1990s. The drive to find and exploit new sources of energy at sea is linked to anxieties over how to secure stable and affordable long-term energy supplies.

East Asian energy concerns are rooted in the region's limited reserves of oil and the substantial increases in forecast demand for electricity and

Table 4.1 Growth in primary energy demand in East Asia, 1995–97

Country	1995[a] (%)	1996 (%)	1997[b] (%)
Malaysia	10.9	9.8	8.6
Thailand	10.7	12.4	10.9
Burma	9.7	6.1	5.9
Vietnam	9.2	14.7	12.8
South Korea	8.6	9.4	7.3
China	6.0	5.8	5.6
Singapore	5.5	6.0	5.0
Indonesia	4.1	9.0	8.7
Philippines	4.1	6.8	7.8
Taiwan	3.1	4.5	6.2
Brunei	1.7	6.2	6.5
Japan	1.6	2.1	2.5
Average	6.3	7.7	7.3

Notes: [a]1995 figures for Southeast Asian countries are an average for the period 1993–95.

[b]1997 figures are pre-economic crisis projections.

Source: Extrapolated from data in Cambridge Energy Research Associates, *Asia-Pacific Energy Watch*, Winter–Spring 1997

transport. Before the economic crisis took hold in the second half of 1997, the region's economies were doubling in size approximately every decade, and its energy use was increasing by factors of between 5 and 10.[6] The severity of the 1997–98 economic downturn, arguably the region's worst since the 1930s, caused energy demand to dip, but only temporarily. There is general agreement among energy experts that pre-crisis forecasts of long-term rises in energy demand remain valid.[7] Even at the height of the crisis in 1997, Asian oil consumption contracted by only 2 per cent and began to push up again thereafter.[8] As a result, regional demand for primary energy is expected to double every twelve years, compared with the global average of every twenty-eight years, with demand for oil expected to reach 12 million barrels per day (bpd) by 2010 – approximately the entire current daily output of oil from Saudi Arabia, the United Arab Emirates and Kuwait combined.[9]

China is likely to record the world's fastest rise in energy consumption in the first decade of this century, by which time absolute levels of consumption could equal those of all the European OECD nations combined.[10] The potential impact on world markets of China's rapidly growing demand for energy could be greater than suggested by these projections because China's per capita consumption of energy is less than 40 per cent of the world average.[11] As China's living standard improves, its per capita consumption of energy will increase.[12] In Southeast Asia, rapid urbanisation and economic growth in the second tier of 'tiger economies' has resulted in even higher relative increases in demand for electricity. Between 1993 and 1995, electricity generation in Brunei, Indonesia, Malaysia, Burma, the Philippines, Thailand and Vietnam rose by, on average, 13 per cent a year.[13] These rises slowed significantly in 1998 and 1999 but have since resumed their steep upward trend. The demand for electricity is still likely to more than double by 2010 because of continued urbanisation, industrial development and the growth of rural electrification programs.[14]

East Asia lacks the energy resources to meet its growing needs, especially oil, which is in short supply.[15] The region provides only one-tenth of the world's oil supply and has just one-twentieth (4.42 per cent) of its estimated extractable reserves.[16] Energy self-sufficiency is expected to fall from 43 per cent in 1995 to 29 per cent in 2015, by which time East Asia may have to import as much as 70 per cent of its oil.[17] This energy imbalance is most pronounced in Northeast Asia. Japan imports 88 per cent of its primary energy supplies and 90 per cent of its oil.[18] South Korea's energy dependence is higher still, North Korea has no oil at all, and Taiwan has major energy vulnerabilities.[19] China, although possessing substantial oil reserves, was forced to turn to foreign suppliers in 1993 and will probably have to import nearly 40 per cent of its estimated needs by 2010, rising to 7–8 million bpd in 2015.[20] About half of this is expected to come from Chinese-owned oilfields overseas. Imports of gas are set to double as China attempts to diversify away from coal, which currently provides over 70 per cent of its energy needs.[21] Even so, China is still expected to rely on coal for two-thirds of its energy in 2020.[22]

The situation in Southeast Asia is more complex. Cambodia, Singapore and Thailand are major energy importers. Laos, Vietnam and possibly the Philippines are likely to become modest net exporters, while Indonesia, Brunei and Malaysia are significant energy suppliers, mainly to the Asian region. But the overall picture is worsening because of accelerating domestic demand, the high cost of energy exploration and development, political uncertainties associated with some economically exploitable energy deposits, and a decline in recoverable oil reserves.[23] Malaysia may soon become an oil importer, while oil production in Indonesia, the region's largest supplier, has declined to the point where the country is expected to become a net oil importer by 2006.[24]

Will There Be an Energy 'Gap'?

Energy dependency does not necessarily translate into energy insecurity. Known global petroleum reserves are substantial. Of the 1.8 trillion barrels of conventional oil discovered – oil that flows quickly and is of good quality – some 800 billion barrels had been used at the end of 1997, leaving 1 trillion in reserve.[25] At least another 4.6 trillion barrels could be produced if prices rise.[26] The US National Intelligence Council estimates that 80 per cent of the world's oil still remains in the ground and 95 per cent of all natural gas.[27] In this sense there is no 'energy gap' nor is there likely to be one in the immediate future. However, these reassuring figures obscure some worrying long-term trends. The International Energy Agency (IEA) estimates that between 1995 and 2010, world energy demand will rise by 35–45 per cent, while demand for oil is projected to increase from 71.6 million bpd to over 115 million by 2020.[28] By 2050, global primary energy use is conservatively expected to double or triple.[29] These increases are occurring at a time when the rate of new oil discoveries is continuing to drop. The promising Caspian Basin development, for example, will at best add another three years' oil to world reserves.[30]

Although oil is not going to suddenly run out, the perception that oil may become more scarce could herald the beginning of a long-term rise in the price of oil and focus markets on the uneven distribution of remaining reserves, which are heavily concentrated in five Middle Eastern states – Iran, Iraq, Kuwait, the United Arab Emirates and Saudi Arabia. Once their share of oil production passes the critical 30 per cent threshold some time in the early part of the decade, these countries will once again be in a strong position to sharply increase the price of oil should they choose to do so.[31] This has particular significance for Asia since three-quarters of Persian Gulf oil will go to the region by 2015.[32] OPEC has already demonstrated its renewed ability to control oil prices. In the eighteen months from March 1999 to September 2000, oil prices trebled to a ten-year high of $35 per barrel.[33] Significantly, OPEC's chairman warned that even if its members wanted to, the cartel had little scope to increase production because of limited reserve capacity.[34] These developments do not bode well for East Asia because the region's energy problems are more likely to stem from short-term supply disruptions or sharp and unexpected price rises than from systemic shortfalls or physical unavailability. Although the oil crises of the 1970s did not bring about a radical shift in the balance of power because consumers introduced measures to conserve oil, diversify supplies and establish stockpiles, they did push up inflation and were largely responsible for two global recessions.[35]

Sustained oil price rises could set East Asia's recovery back and increase the region's vulnerability to recession-induced political disturbances and ethnic strife.[36] Optimists argue that the world is far better prepared for shocks of this sort, and point to the ease with which the market adjusted to the loss of Kuwaiti and Iraqi oil during the 1991 Gulf War. But petroleum stocks reached a twelve-year low in 2000 and unlike Europe or the US, East Asia has no mechanism for allocating energy in an emergency.[37]

Few states in the region have national strategic stockpiles of any significance; most states have little more than running-stocks averaging around forty days, less than half the OECD average of eighty-nine days of domestic consumption.[38] Stockpiles in China are estimated to cover only twenty days of domestic demand. China and Singapore do not even require oil firms to keep a percentage of their production in the country.

A range of potential constraints on supply could increase oil prices, including political instability or military conflict in supplier countries, sanctions, embargoes, and economic, legal, environmental and technical problems. Over 64 per cent of remaining reserves of oil are in the politically volatile Persian Gulf. The Caspian Basin development, which is attracting a great deal of interest from China, is located in one of the most strategically contested regions in the world.[39] Pipelines are particularly susceptible to disruption where they cross national jurisdictions and regions with a history of ethnic and religious antagonism. Muslim Uighur separatists in western China could, for example, sabotage China's proposed gas pipeline from Kazakhstan to Xinjiang province should their conflict with Beijing escalate.

Second, optimists argue that if markets are allowed to function efficiently, rising oil prices will force consumers to use cheaper alternatives, or encourage producers to extract oil from areas previously considered uneconomical. Markets are, however, imperfect mechanisms for allocating risk. This is especially so in the developing world where, for social, economic and regulatory reasons, rising oil prices may not prompt the expected response. Free-marketeers frequently ignore the political factors that can affect the elasticity of supply and demand. Government policies, for instance, can significantly dampen or accelerate oil demand.[40] Maximising the state's control over energy resources is an important security consideration for most East Asian governments. For example, even if the cost of alternative energy were to fall significantly, China would be unlikely for strategic reasons to reduce its use of domestic coal. Markets respond to perceptions as well as economic fundamentals. East Asia's huge latent demand for energy has the capacity to affect the oil market profoundly.[41] The issue transcends simple calculations of supply and demand. If the perception develops that shortages are possible, economic and strategic uncertainty will increase.

A related argument is that diversification of energy supplies away from oil can reduce the risk of energy shortfalls and supply disruptions. Although oil meets 51 per cent of East Asia's total energy needs, compared to a global average of just 40 per cent, there is considerable scope to develop East Asia's solar and geothermal energy, coal, nuclear power and substantial natural gas reserves.[42] Ambitious plans for three major transnational gas pipelines linking East Asian consumers with Russian and Central Asian producers as well as those within the region itself are already well advanced.[43] Diversification alone, however, will not solve East Asia's energy problems. The infrastructure costs of some of the larger gas projects are large, and there is a limit to the extent to which other forms of energy can replace oil. East Asia's future power needs may require up to $600 billion of investment annually – over 60 per cent of the world's estimated total power-sector investment – between 1998 and 2008.[44] Such large sums of money will not be easy to find, especially given the extent of capital flight that has occurred since the economic crisis. Shortages of investment funds will therefore be a further impediment to the development of serious alternatives to oil and coal.

The optimists' fourth argument is that advances in energy exploration, extraction and production technology will increase the speed with which reserves can be tapped and marketed. In addition, new environmentally friendly technology, such as that responsible for producing low-sulphur coal, can reduce the political and environmental costs of burning fossil fuels. But developing Asia cannot afford many of these new technologies – costly emission filters for coal-burning power stations, for example.[45] While technological advances may improve the region's energy imbalance, they are unlikely to redress it.

Although anxiety about future energy insecurity is centred on price instability and reliability of supply, East Asia's thirst for energy will increase competition for oil among energy-poor regional states and accentuate political and strategic differences between the major powers. In 1993, Chinese Premier Li Peng enunciated a policy of securing 'the long-term and stable supply of oil' as a primary national strategic goal.[46] Rather than buying oil on the international market, China is acquiring oilfields across the globe in a fundamental shift of energy policy. Beijing's geopolitical objective is to develop a 'strategic oil supply security system' that would make China immune to blockades, sanctions or supply disruptions. In 1997 alone, China bought up oil concessions or agreed to finance joint exploration ventures in three continents: Asia, Africa, and South America. Beijing's aggressive pursuit of self-sufficiency in energy has already ruffled feathers in Washington and Moscow. The United States has objected to China's proposal for a pipeline linking Kazakhstan with Iran because of concerns that Teheran's influence in Central Asia would be greatly enhanced. Russia opposes plans for the pipeline running through Kazakhstan to Xinjiang for fear that the former Soviet republic would come into China's sphere of influence.[47] Thus China's single-minded pursuit of energy self-sufficiency may have the unintended consequence of challenging the wider geopolitical interests of the United States and Russia as well as generating feelings of insecurity among energy-poor regional states.

Maritime Disputes in the South China Sea

Uncertainty over future energy supplies is fuelling maritime conflict in the Western Pacific. As oil exploration technology has improved, drilling has become feasible in previously inaccessible offshore sites. Oil industry analysts expect that at least forty new offshore oil and gas developments, representing $18 billion worth of investment, will come on stream in Southeast Asia between 1996 and 2006, allowing the recovery of the equivalent of more than 10 billion barrels of oil.[48]

The rise to prominence of the dispute over the Spratly Islands in the South China Sea has coincided with seismic surveys and oil exploration activities which have reinforced the view, at least in the region, that the islands sit astride large deposits of oil and natural gas.[49] China's Geology and Mineral Resources Ministry estimates that the Spratlys area holds 17.7 billion tonnes of oil and natural-gas reserves, considerably more than Kuwait's 13 billion.[50] The People's Liberation Army (PLA) has argued that these reserves must be protected from the 'predatory advances' of other states which, it complains, have taken advantage of China's tolerance and restraint.[51] The official *China Youth News* has noted that 'the South China Sea holds reserves worth US$1 trillion. Once Xinjiang has been developed, this will be the sole area for replacement of resources'. The strategic implications were made abundantly clear. The South China Sea will be 'the main fallback position for *lebensraum* for the Chinese people in the coming century ... Development southwards is perhaps a strategic orientation that [China] will have to choose'.[52]

Among the states claiming sovereignty over the Spratlys, China and Vietnam in particular are using foreign oil companies to stake out positions in deep-water zones as a precaution against future energy scarcity. The potential for conflict is already apparent. An uneasy stand-off between China and Vietnam, which followed a brief but bloody clash over the Spratlys in 1988, ended in early 1997. In March of that year, China moved the *Kan Tan III* exploration rig to a location about 65 nautical miles off the coast of central Vietnam, where it began drilling for gas. Hanoi, which claimed the area, strongly denied the Chinese Foreign Ministry's assertion that the rig was operating within its rights under international law.[53] The Vietnamese Coast Guard issued repeated warnings to Chinese vessels near the rig. When these were ignored, the official Vietnamese News Agency took the unusual step of publishing extracts of a blunt letter from the government demanding that Beijing 'stop the operation of the Kan Tan III oil rig and withdraw it from the exclusive zone and the continental shelf of Vietnam'.[54] Vietnam also threatened to widen the dispute by soliciting the support of its fellow ASEAN members and, in a bid to raise the strategic stakes, opened discussions with the United States on a possible military relationship.[55]

China's aggressive oil exploration activities in the South China Sea have heightened tensions with ASEAN generally. Indonesia's growing wariness of China's strategic intentions is directly related to concerns that Beijing's territorial claims may overlap with those of Jakarta to the north of the Natunas, a chain of 300 islands and atolls owned by Indonesia to the south of the Spratlys. The Natunas lie above an estimated 1.27 trillion cubic metres of recoverable gas – one of the world's largest offshore fields – comprising 40 per cent of all Indonesian reserves.[56] In January 1995, Indonesia's state oil company Pertamina and Exxon Corporation of the United States signed a $40 billion joint venture to exploit the fields. Production is scheduled to begin in 2003 from eighteen offshore platforms and six gas-liquefaction trains on Greater Natuna Island.[57]

Two related events illustrate the vulnerability of this massive development project to any future conflict in the South China Sea: the Chinese occupation of the Mischief Reef in the adjacent Spratlys in 1994, and Beijing's publication in 1993 of a map purporting to show the extent of China's territorial claims in the South China Sea. The Chinese boundary appeared to overlap with a portion of Indonesia's Exclusive Economic Zone (EEZ) to the north of the Natunas. In September 1996, the Indonesian armed forces staged their biggest-ever exercise in the South China Sea, involving nearly 20 000 troops, forty aircraft and fifty naval vessels. A military spokesman described the exercise as 'ensuring security for the development of the mega project in the Natunas'.[58] Given its scope and timing, and despite public statements to the contrary, the exercise was clearly meant to warn China that Indonesia would not tolerate any attempt to encroach upon the Natuna gasfield or Indonesia's contiguous EEZ.[59]

Maritime Disputes in Northeast Asia

The perceived need to protect vital resources and to maximise claims to energy-rich contested areas of sea is a major factor in two maritime disputes in Northeast Asia. One centres on a group of relatively obscure islands known as the Diaoyu (in Chinese) or Senkaku (in Japanese) located in the middle of the East China Sea and covering an area of about 7 square kilometres. Their ownership is contested by Japan, China and Taiwan. The other is over Tok-do (in Korean) or Takeshima (in Japanese), two tiny islets and a number of scattered reefs in the Sea of Japan almost midway between South Korea and Japan.

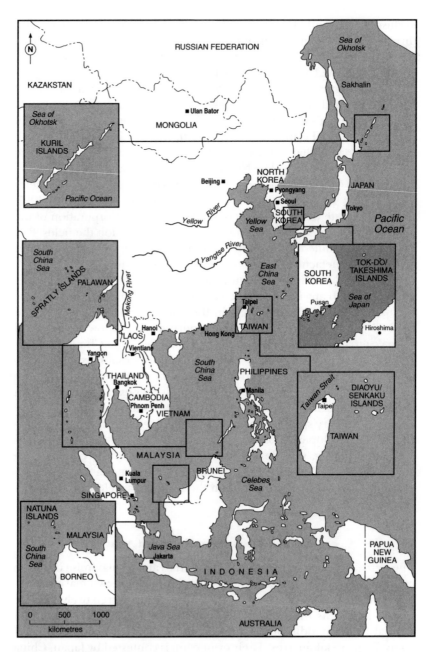

Map 4.1 Maritime disputes in East Asia
Source: Alan Dupont, 'The Environment and Security in Pacific Asia', *Adelphi Paper 319* (Oxford University Press for the International Institute for Strategic Studies, London, 1998), p. 32.

The sudden eruption of the Diaoyu/Senkaku dispute illustrates the way in which East Asia's dwindling resources and escalating energy demands are investing the region's remaining renewable stocks with new strategic and economic significance. Significantly, conflict over the island group first broke out almost immediately after a 1969 study by the UN Economic Commission for Asia and the Far East concluded that the seabed around the Diaoyu/Senkaku contained one of the richest oil and gas deposits in the world.[60] The islands are particularly important to Japan because of its energy dependence. Under international law, Tokyo has no other basis for laying claim to a share of the East China Sea continental shelf and its oil deposits.[61] In August 1970, Japan protested against Taiwan's decision to negotiate a contract with the United Kingdom's Gulf Oil to prospect for oil in an area that included the Diaoyu/Senkaku. In the following month, Japanese police tore down a flag erected by Taiwanese reporters and then in December, Beijing lodged a strong claim to ownership of the whole island group. China and Japan agreed to shelve their dispute when relations were normalised in 1972, but periodic incidents continued. China sent some fifty fishing boats to the waters around the islands in 1979 to protest against Japan's construction of a helicopter landing-pad on them.[62]

The dispute returned to prominence in 1996 following the ratification by China, Japan and South Korea of the 1982 UN Convention on the Law of the Sea (UNCLOS), and each country's subsequent declaration of EEZs of 200 nautical miles.[63] In July, right-wingers from the Japan Youth Foundation built a temporary lighthouse, erected two memorials and planted a flag on the Diaoyu/Senkakus. Two months later, Youth Foundation members returned to repair damage to the lighthouse. The Chinese Foreign Ministry issued a stern warning of 'serious damage' to bilateral relations if Tokyo did not prohibit further similar actions. Anti-Japanese demonstrations broke out in Hong Kong and Taiwan; Taipei charged Beijing with responsibility for protecting Chinese interests in the islands, while five out of six respondents in a Taiwanese newspaper poll called for military action to restore Chinese sovereignty. Tensions eventually eased when both governments realised that the situation could easily develop into a serious confrontation.[64]

Competition for energy and other marine resources is also largely responsible for the reemergence and intensification of the Tokdo/Takeshima dispute. The islands themselves, like most others which are contested in maritime East Asia, have no intrinsic value; under Article 121 of UNCLOS, they are classified as 'rocks', and therefore not entitled to a 200-nautical mile EEZ. However, ownership would allow either Seoul or Tokyo to use the islands as the basis for claiming a larger share of an area that may contain oil and gas as well as a mineral-rich sea-floor.

That these extended claims may overlap with North Korea's EEZ further complicates the issue.[65] In February 1996, well before the declaration of EEZs, a major diplomatic dispute broke out between Japan and South Korea over Seoul's plans to build a wharf on one of the islands. In response, Japan lodged an official protest, and Foreign Minister Yuki-hiko Ikeda used a nationally televised news conference to accuse South Korea of infringing Japan's sovereignty. The incident almost led to the cancellation of a scheduled summit before South Korean President Kim Young-sam and Japanese Prime Minister Ryutaro Hashimoto agreed to deal with the issue in subsequent boundary negotiations.[66]

The Nuclear Dimension

Nuclear power is destined to feature more prominently in the energy and environmental security calculations of the twenty-first century, but not in ways that strategic analysts usually envisage. The traditional secu-rity literature sees nuclear power primarily in terms of its role in the development and proliferation of nuclear weapons, or as a means by which oil-deficient states can reduce their energy dependence on politi-cally fragile or volatile areas of the world. Increasingly, however, concerns about the environmental, health and safety aspects of nuclear power are spilling over into the political and security arena. In Europe, for exam-ple, nuclear safety is a major issue in the 'enlargement' debates over the entry of Central and Eastern European countries into the European Union.[67] Domestic political sensitivity to the risks of accidental dis-charges of radioactivity from nuclear reactors has risen markedly around the world since the Three Mile Island accident in 1979 and the Cher-nobyl disaster seven years later. Although originally attractive because of its comparatively pristine environmental image, nuclear power is now widely perceived as dangerous and undesirable. As nuclear allergy spreads so will the potential for violent anti-nuclear protests. Relations between states will be strained by disputes over nuclear waste storage and the heightened risk of nuclear accidents. Public opposition to nuclear power may lead to significant reductions in planned capacity, increasing uncertainty over future energy supplies and curtailed efforts to reduce dependence on greenhouse gas-producing fossil fuels.[68]

Although less important than coal, 433 nuclear power plants neverthe-less produced around 18 per cent of the world's electricity at the end of the 1990s.[69] Unlike Europe and North America where the nuclear industry is in serious trouble for political, economic and environmental reasons, nuclear power is expanding rapidly in East Asia.[70] Energy-poor states like Japan, South Korea and Taiwan embarked on ambitious nuclear energy programs during the 1960s and 1970s. By the late 1990s they accounted for

Table 4.2 Nuclear power in Northeast Asia

No. of reactors		Energy produced (GWe)		% of energy requirements		Spent fuel (MgHM)		Country
1996	2010	1996	2010	1996	2010	1996	2010	
54	Plans to double but unlikely to be implemented	41.0	54.6	30	42	13 000	27 000[a]	Japan
12	23	8.2	22.7	36	48	3000	12 000	South Korea
3	8	4.9	7.8	30	29	1800	4000	Taiwan
3	Plans for between 16 and 18 by 2025	2.1	11.7	1.9	Insufficient data	165	3000	China
1[b]	2	—	2.0	—	Insufficient data	8000 spent fuel rods in storage	Minimal	North Korea
								Russia (Far East only)

Main problem in the Russian Far East is spent fuel from Russia's Pacific Fleet, as well as nuclear powered ice breakers and surface supply ships.

[a] This is a very conservative figure based only on reactors currently in operation or under construction. (Spent fuel figures extrapolated from David von Hippel and Peter Hayes, 'Two Scenarios of Nuclear Power and Nuclear Waste production in Northeast Asia', The Nautilus Institute for Security and Sustainable Development, Berkley, California, October 1997.)
[b] This is a 5 megawatt reactor which is currently shut down.

over 14 per cent of global installed nuclear capacity, and substantial increases in nuclear power are planned. If these plans are realised, East Asia could provide up to 48 per cent of the growth in the world's nuclear power sector between 1992 and 2010.[71] Japan, which possesses two-thirds of Asia's nuclear capacity producing 36 per cent of the nation's electricity, wants to double the fifty-three plants it operates by 2010. Nuclear power provides 41 per cent of South Korea's electricity; Seoul operates fifteen nuclear power plants and intends to build sixteen more by 2010 to meet its rising energy needs; Taiwan expects to add another four to its existing six.[72] Other states in the region have announced plans to launch new programs or expand existing ones. Between 1992 and 1997 China built three reactors, and by 2010 plans to produce eight more.[73] North Korea will acquire two 1000-megawatt South Korean light-water reactors (LWRs) under an agreement between Washington and Pyongyang in October 1994 which established the Korean Peninsula Energy Development Organisation (KEDO).[74] There are no operational power plants in Southeast Asia, but several ASEAN states have research reactors and Indonesia has seriously considered building up to twelve plants.[75]

The Nuclear Waste Problem

Northeast Asian states have already generated substantial quantities of nuclear waste, much of it highly radioactive and dangerous to human health if not shielded and handled with extreme care.[76] Even if no additional nuclear capacity were to be installed in Northeast Asia, other than those plants already under construction or which are well into the planning stage, approximately 50 000 tonnes of spent fuel would be generated between 1990 and 2020, containing 450 tonnes of plutonium. In the absence of a regional nuclear waste repository, spent fuel will either have to be recycled, which is politically contentious because it can be used to make nuclear weapons, or remain in temporary storage sites.[77] Unfortunately, much of the region's storage capacity is nearly full and most existing sites were never intended for long-term storage.[78] As a result, Northeast Asian nuclear power producers are looking to move and store their waste offshore, which is beginning to create political tensions among regional states.

Nuclear waste disposal has already emerged as a contentious issue between Taiwan and South Korea, and between Taiwan and China. Taiwan has few options for storing waste because of the lack of suitable land away from the island's densely populated urban centres, a problem it shares with Japan and South Korea. In January 1997, Taiwan announced plans to ship 60 000 tons of low-level waste to North Korea for treatment and storage under a mutually beneficial deal expected to net Pyongyang

$227 million, a substantial sum of money for the nearly destitute state.[79] The agreement prompted an unexpectedly hostile reaction from neighbouring states. South Korea denounced the scheme, claiming that it could turn the Korean Peninsula into a 'death zone'. Foreign Minister Yoo Chong-ha bluntly warned Taipei that Seoul would attempt to block the plan 'by all means'.[80] China weighed in by criticising North Korea and Taiwan for ignoring the environmental risks of the scheme and then, in a bid to extract maximum political capital from the dispute, offered to take the Taiwanese nuclear waste itself on the grounds that Taiwan was 'an indivisible part of China'.[81] Taipei was eventually forced to drop the plan, but a year later the government aired a proposal to develop a nuclear waste storage site on Wuchiu island, 14 kilometres from China's Fujian province. China's rejection of the idea was swift and unequivocal. A senior official from Fujian's Environmental Protection Bureau warned that 'Taiwan authorities will encounter strong opposition from people on both sides of the [Taiwan] straits if they persist'.[82]

The capacity of nuclear waste problems to complicate security relations between states is further illustrated by the ongoing dispute between Tokyo and Moscow over the long-standing Russian practice of dumping radioactive waste in the Sea of Japan. For more than thirty years, ocean dumping of solid and liquid radioactive waste was common in the former Soviet Union. Between 1959 and 1991, it is estimated that the amount of radioactive material dumped in the waters of the Russian Far East was equivalent to half the radioactivity released during the Chernobyl accident.[83] Political reform in Russia and the degradation of Russia's military capability in the Far East has worsened, rather than ameliorated, the problem of nuclear waste management. Moscow's preoccupation with a host of more pressing political and economic issues has left it with little interest in dealing with environmental problems in faraway Siberia.

Russian dumping of liquid waste in the Sea of Japan has continued unabated since the end of the Cold War, provoking strong opposition from Japan. In an uncharacteristically sharp 1993 diplomatic *démarche*, a senior Japanese Foreign Ministry official warned the Russian Ambassador: 'We demand that you stop this kind of dumping. We demand that you never again do this in the future'.[84] There are also serious concerns in Japan about Russia's management and processing of nuclear waste from military facilities and decommissioned nuclear submarines. At least three retired nuclear submarines from Russia's Pacific Fleet based at Vladivostok have reactor cores which are so damaged that large portions of the submarines may have to be disposed of as waste. Russia's rail transport system is too old and unreliable to move the spent fuel and other wastes out of the Far East Region to European Russia so the submarines remain at their moorings, slowly corroding with their reactors exposed to the elements.[85]

Japan has nuclear waste problems of its own making which have caused dissent at home and disputes with neighbours. Japan's plutonium cycle commits it to reprocessing the spent fuels from its commercial and research reactors, but there is insufficient domestic reprocessing capacity to handle the spent fuels that have been selected for upgrading to plutonium or mixed-oxide fuel. Japan therefore sends a proportion of its spent fuel to France and England for reprocessing. In January 1993, the first shipment of this reprocessed fuel was discreetly shipped back to Japan from France aboard the *Akatsuki Maru.* Even before the shipment left France, however, officials from Indonesia, Malaysia and Singapore expressed concern over reports that it might pass through the Malacca Strait. International and regional protests dogged the ship's journey, forcing it to take a circuitous course well south of Australia before crossing the Pacific.[86] Subsequent shipments have attracted a hostile response from international environmental groups and local Japanese citizens' groups near the fishing village of Rokkasho, where Japan has built a temporary storage facility for high-level nuclear waste. In March 1998, and again in April 1999, hundreds of protestors at Rokkasho attempted to block the unloading of the nuclear material that had been treated in France.[87] Japan has begun to arm the ships carrying the nuclear fuel because of fears that pirates may attempt to hijack the vessels and ransom its cargo.[88]

Waste disposal is central to resolution of one of the region's most intractable security problems – North Korea's suspected nuclear weapons program. For over two decades North Korea has invested considerable economic and political capital in developing an embryonic nuclear power program which is widely believed to mask the covert production of nuclear weapons.[89] North Korea operated a small, 5-megawatt nuclear research reactor at Yongbyon until 1994, described by Pyongyang as an 'experimental nuclear power station'.[90] Under the terms of the US-DPRK (North Korea) Agreed Framework negotiated in that year, Pyongyang consented to closing down this reactor, a larger one under construction, a reprocessing plant and an associated research reactor in return for two modern 1000-megawatt LWRs.[91] North Korea has about 8000 spent-fuel rods discharged from and currently stored in water pools at the site of the 5-megawatt reactor at Yongbyon. These spent-fuel rods are a source of concern because they are usable for nuclear weapons. During the early phase of negotiation for the Agreed Framework, the spent fuel was supposed to have been shipped to a third country. North Korea subsequently demanded that the two LWRs must first be constructed before the fuel rods could leave North Korea. Since then, the list of possible third-country recipients for these fuel rods has shrunk. North Korea is not willing to send them to Russia, South Korea or Japan. China appears unwilling to accept them, and transport to

France or the United Kingdom would be too costly.[92] Disposing of these rods and the spent fuel which will eventually be generated by the two LWRs is crucial to the success of the Agreed Framework and to ensuring that North Korea is not tempted to use the spent fuel for the production of nuclear weapons.

Environmental Constraints on Energy Use

Public concern over nuclear safety and potential environmental damage has stymied plans to develop nuclear power industries in the Philippines and Indonesia and is threatening the expansion plans of the Japanese, Taiwanese and, to a lesser extent, the South Korean nuclear industries. The ill-fated Bataan nuclear power plant built by President Marcos of the Philippines was an unmitigated financial disaster for the country, transgressing virtually every principle of sound economic and environmental management. Costing around $2.3 billion, it was constructed at the bottom of a dormant volcano near several earthquake fault lines only 100 kilometres from Manila and has never produced a single watt of electricity because of fears that it could trigger an environmental catastrophe should there be a volcanic eruption.[93]

The nuclear power plans developed by Indonesia in the 1990s also envisaged building plants in areas widely regarded as seismically unstable. Despite scepticism from his ministerial colleagues, the support of Baccharuddin Jusuf Habibie, at the time the influential Minister for Science and Technology, appeared to ensure that the project would go ahead. But Indonesian and foreign environmental groups mounted a vigorous campaign against nuclear power, citing fears that there could be a meltdown of the reactor core or a radioactive discharge into the atmosphere. Computer projections showed that an accidental release of radioactive materials from a planned reactor on Java's Muria Peninsula could spread over large areas of Southeast Asia and Australia.[94] In part because of escalating domestic and international pressure, as well as strong opposition from within the government itself, President Suharto decided in February 1997 to shelve the plans, designating nuclear power 'an option of last resort'.[95]

Should environmental considerations slow Northeast Asia's nuclear energy expansion plans, Taiwan, South Korea and Japan would find it difficult to reduce their high levels of energy dependence. The political climate in all three countries is far more hostile to nuclear power than it was when each began their construction programs. Taiwan's fourth nuclear power plant, conceived in 1980, has been continually delayed by protests from local residents and anti-nuclear groups. In late 2000, the newly elected President, Chen Shui-bian, announced that the government would scrap the plant altogether on environmental grounds in fulfilment of an election promise, precipitating a major political and constitutional crisis. Opponents branded the scheme as irresponsible, claiming that it would leave Taiwan vulnerable to a Chinese naval blockade since the island imports 97 per cent of its energy requirements. But 50 000 people demonstrated in support of Chen's decision to close down the plant, which he later revoked under extreme political pressure.[96] Nearby South Korea will fall far short of the sixteen extra plants it had intended to construct by 2010 and there are serious doubts about Japan's capacity to achieve its ambitious nuclear energy goals.[97] Public confidence in nuclear power has been shaken by a number of accidents in Japan, the most serious of which occurred at Tokaimura in September 1999.[98] The Tokaimura accident, the world's worst since Chernobyl, set off a chain reaction in a uranium-processing plant that took almost twenty-four hours to stabilise but not before two workers had been killed and forty-seven others exposed to higher than normal levels of radiation. Some 300 000 people within a 10 kilometre radius of the plant were confined indoors for several days as a precautionary measure against radiation poisoning.[99]

Without a substantial nuclear component, it is unclear how Japan will develop an 'energy cushion' to insure against future volatility in the supply and price of oil. Although the country's LWRs produce about 35 per cent of its electricity, most existing reactors will reach the end of their life-span between 2010 and 2020. The government's 1994 Long Term Program for Nuclear Energy planned a two-thirds expansion in capacity by 2010 – from 45 to 70 GWe. Officials of the Ministry of International Trade and Industry (MITI) accept that this figure is now unrealistic given the strength of anti-nuclear sentiment in Japan and the depressed power demand resulting from a decade of sluggish economic growth.[100] In April 2000, revised investment plans showed that only thirteen new reactors were slated to come on stream by the end of the decade, compared with the targeted figure of sixteen to twenty.[101] Public hostility has also complicated efforts to develop and operate plutonium-fuelled fast-breeder reactors. Japan's plutonium stockpile, which is forecast to reach 70 tonnes by 2010, has become a source of domestic and international contention and Japanese municipalities are becoming reluctant to store plutonium or other nuclear waste within their boundaries.[102] Even though Japan's nuclear program is fully transparent, China and the two Koreas are sensitive to the risk that plutonium might be diverted to produce nuclear weapons because of historical antipathies and Japan's technical capacity to quickly develop and deploy nuclear weapons.[103]

Despite the Japanese public's reservations about the nuclear industry's environmental and safety record, there is a recognition that Japan must continue to develop nuclear power if it is not to be held hostage to the vagaries of the international energy market. The need to reduce greenhouse gas emissions, mandated in the form of country-specific targets agreed to at the 1997 climate change conference in Kyoto, has given nuclear power a much-needed boost because of its minimal contribution to greenhouse gases and growing anxiety about global warming.[104] This newly perceived virtue has been seized on by the nuclear industry as an opportunity to reverse public opposition to nuclear power. The head of the UN International Atomic Energy Agency, Hans Blix, has argued that an expanded nuclear power industry is the best way of reducing fossil fuel emissions, and the influential Japanese business federation the Keidanren has called on the government to 'position atomic energy as the central source among the various sources of basic energy'.[105] Even so, nuclear power is unlikely to be a panacea for Japan's energy woes.

Conclusion

Much of the angst over future energy shortfalls and the scramble to increase access to fossil fuels is redolent of historical patterns of resource competition. However, current worries over energy security must be situated in an entirely different political, social, demographic and environmental landscape. East Asia's unprecedented population growth, climbing rates of energy dependence, rapid depletion of existing oil reserves and growing awareness of the environmental costs of increased energy consumption are the most prominent of a new range of transnational factors that are altering the energy security calculus in the region. In the past, access to and control over oil have tended to be seen as measures of national strength. While this view still underpins the approach of some nations to energy resources, the acquisitive impulses of earlier years are weakening. Acquiring strategic minerals by military conquest has become far less attractive, and using political manipulation or economic pressure has become more difficult. Nevertheless, competition over energy resources is contributing to conflict in East Asia and complicating the settlement of contested maritime boundaries. Island disputes in the seas of East Asia are as much about the perceived scarcity of oil and gas as they are about sovereignty and the protection of sea-lines of communication.

Attempts to deepen regional cooperation through confidence-building measures and multilateral security dialogue may help states to manage tensions over resource disputes. However, a sharp and sustained increase in the price of oil would test to the limits the region's post-Cold War security architecture and threaten a resurgence of strategic competition between the great powers for influence and control over the remaining reserves of accessible oil. East Asia's growing dependence on oil from the turbulent Middle East will make it more vulnerable to the vagaries of Middle Eastern politics than at any time in the past. Even if the more optimistic forecasts of adequate supply and stable oil prices are borne out, environmental constraints will circumscribe and complicate the energy choices of governments. Should fossil fuel usage continue its inexorable climb, as expected, rising levels of air pollution and green-house gas emissions will impoverish and degrade large areas of the region, aggravate relations between states and vitiate the health and welfare of Asians.

Although nuclear power will remain an important part of Northeast Asia's energy plans, domestic and international anti-nuclear pressure will force Japan, South Korea and Taiwan to significantly scale back their expansion plans. As a result, the use of nuclear power in Northeast Asia will continue to rank well behind carbon-based fuels as a source of electricity, while Southeast Asians are unlikely to 'go nuclear' in a major way. For these reasons, China aside, the proportion of East Asia's energy produced by nuclear power is unlikely to increase substantially. Even China may not be completely immune to the nuclear allergy that has infected much of the Western world and has now spread into East Asia. Issues of cost, both economic and environmental, as well as waste disposal and safety will constrain nuclear power's growth.

There are two important consequences for regional security. First, nuclear power's less than rosy future will increase the likelihood of energy shortfalls and reduce East Asia's capacity to manage supply disruptions or price volatility in other areas of the energy market, especially oil. Second, the storage and disposal of nuclear waste is destined to become an important security issue in its own right. Nuclear waste transcends the debate about the future of nuclear power and the proliferation of nuclear weapons. Even if all the nuclear power plants in the world were to be shut down tomorrow and every nuclear weapon dismantled, the accumulated waste of half a century would still have to be isolated, safeguarded and eventually disposed of – either in an underground repository or, less desirably, by reprocessing. Interstate tensions over the disposal of nuclear waste in Northeast Asia underline the growing capacity of a new class of energy-related environmental security issues to aggravate conflict, especially when bilateral relations are already rent by political and strategic rivalries. In an important sense, environmental issues are energy issues.[106]

CHAPTER 5

Is a Food Crisis Likely?

Concerns over East Asia's long-term food security have reemerged over the past decade as earlier impressive gains in grain production and fish catches have levelled off while demand continues to climb. Like the soil, water, and atmosphere that sustain it, food is a renewable resource. As with all resources, food is linked to security by scarcity, but the idea of food security has many different interpretations. The UN's World Food Programme (WFP) defines food security to mean that 'all people at all times have access to safe and nutritious food to maintain a healthy and active life'.[1] Indra de Soysa and Nils Petter Gledditsch focus on agriculture's importance in alleviating poverty and the subsistence crises that drive internal conflicts in developing states. From their perspective, 'the inability to meet food requirements and other basic needs drives people to adopt alternative survival strategies, one of which is to join rebellions and criminal insurgencies'.[2] The traditional security literature, on the other hand, is more concerned with the possibility that food-rich states might use food as a 'weapon' in pursuit of foreign policy goals, reflecting a wider, historical concern about dependence on foreigners for strategic resources.[3]

What Is the Concern about Food Security?

While all these themes feature in the contemporary debate about food security, the overriding concern is that population growth, environmental degradation and rising demand for a range of essential foodstuffs will lead to future food shortages that could result in widespread political and social unrest. The world is expected to consume twice as much food in the next fifty years as it has in the past 10 000 years, equivalent to a fourfold rise in the level of food production attained at the end of the twentieth century.[4] In order to meet this need, world grain production will have to increase 40 per cent by 2020.[5] Some food economists believe that this target can be comfortably met through trade and the promise of modern biotechnology, exemplified by advances in genetically modified (GM) food. However, there is good reason for caution, if not scepticism, about such best-case scenarios. The corrosive effects of environmental degradation on agriculture and the fishing industry are often underestimated and just as often ignored. The global availability of cropland fell by 25 per cent between 1975 and 1995, and there has been a steady reduction in grain yield increases since the spectacular improvements in productivity recorded during the agricultural 'green revolution' of the 1960s and 1970s.[6] Many species of fish, which are a vital source of protein, are over-exploited or in decline. East Asia's food problems are a microcosm of those of the developing world. The ability of East Asian governments to feed their people will have a major bearing on global food security because of the region's size, population and geostrategic importance.

Today's food security anxieties are redolent of those of an earlier era when there was also much apprehension about the emergence of a gap between future global food production and consumption. As populations began to soar in developing countries, and incomes rose in the wealthy, it was argued that more grain would be needed both as a food staple and to feed the growing demand for animal protein associated with more affluent diets. If these demands could not be met, there were fears that violent conflict over diminishing food supplies would result. A major 1974 UN conference on food held in Rome captured the prevailing mood of the time. Pessimists predicted that steeply rising food prices and free-falling food stocks were harbingers of a looming food crisis that would result in mass starvation in the absence of urgent remedial action.

None of this came to pass, however, largely because the green revolution dramatically improved crop yields in the developing world. Confounding the predictions of pessimists, food production actually outpaced population growth by 20 per cent in the thirty years after 1960, causing average food prices to fall by 60 per cent in the same period.[7] Both seafood and grain output registered healthy increases. As the world's fishing fleets multiplied and became more efficient, the seafood catch went from 22 million to 100 million tonnes between 1950 and 1990, while grain production virtually quintupled in the twentieth century – from 400 million tonnes in 1900 to just under 1.9 billion tonnes in 1998. Much of this increase was due to the expansion of agricultural land and technological advances in farm machinery, higher-yielding grain varieties, the use of fertilisers and the spread of irrigation. Chemical fertilisers accounted for 40 per cent of the growth in grain production, while land under irrigation has increased sixfold since 1900.[8]

By the mid-1990s, however, the green revolution had largely run its course. Agricultural and marine yield increases had begun to slow or

Table 5.1 World seafood catch and grain output, 1950–2030 (million tonnes)

	1950	1990	2030[a]
Seafood catch	22	100	100
Grain output	631	1780	2149

Note: [a] Projected.
Source: Lester Brown, *Who Will Feed China?: Wake-up Call for a Small Planet* (Earthscan Publications, London, 1995), p. 126.

stagnate, while demand continued to spiral upward. In 1994, only four years after record global grain and marine harvests, the United Nations observed:

> Global agriculture's steady gains in production over the past several decades have not fully overcome the problem of rising demand caused by soaring population growth and uneven production progress among regions. The challenge is immense: by the year 2050, global demand for food may be three times greater than today. Moreover, during the past two decades the production growth rate has declined, dropping from 3 percent annually during the 1960s, to 2.4 percent in the 1970s and finally to 2.2 percent in the 1980s.[9]

The FAO reported in 1996 that per capita food production had declined in over fifty developing countries since the mid-1970s, while food imports had increased.[10] In the same year, the Rome Food Summit reminded the international community that despite optimistic predictions in the 1970s that within a decade no child would go to bed hungry, some 840 million people still suffered from malnutrition.[11] Without more determined action, 680 million people are forecast to be without enough food in 2015 to meet their basic nutritional needs.[12] Population pressures account for some of the decline in per capita food production, while rising living standards have increased the overall demand for food, especially grain.[13] By the late 1990s, crop yield increases had begun to level off as technology was diverted to the higher priority areas of information technology, telecommunications and urban infrastructure. After rising by 38 per cent in the three and a half decades between 1950 and 1984, per capita grain production declined by 7 per cent between 1984 and 1998. Demand, on the other hand, continues to climb.[14] As a result, net cereal imports by developing countries will probably need to almost double by 2025 to around 200 million tonnes, while meat will have to increase eightfold.[15]

Environmental degradation has played a central role in slowing the growth in food productivity by reducing the global 'carrying capacity' of the land and sea – defined by Paul Ehrlich as 'the number of people that the planet can support without irreversibly reducing its capacity to support people in the future'.[16] A sixth of the world's land area and much of

Table 5.2   Net grain imports/exports, 1950–90 (million tonnes)

Country	1950	1960	1970	1980	1990
North America	23	39	56	130	110
Australia					
New Zealand	3	6	8	19	14
Latin America	1	0	4	–15	–10
Eastern Europe and Soviet Union	0	0	-2	–44	–35
Africa	0	–2	-4	–17	–25
Asia	–6	–17	–37	–63	–81
Western Europe	–22	–25	–22	–9	27

Note: Negative figures represent net imports.
Source: Lester Brown, *Who Will Feed China?: Wake-up Call for a Small Planet* (Earthscan Publications, London, 1995), p. 105.

its productive farmland has been degraded because of rampant commercial and industrial development, soil erosion and loss of soil fertility through overlogging and intensive use of pesticides.[17] It has been estimated that nearly half the 29 million tonnes gained every year from advances in technology and investments in irrigation, fertiliser and other inputs is lost because of environmental degradation.[18] Since 1981, the area given over to grain production has shrunk from 732 million hectares to 690 million hectares, while the per capita grain area has halved.[19] Protein derived from fish and other marine resources is under threat from pollution and overfishing. Less water is available for irrigation globally because of falling water tables and the insatiable demand of urban dwellers and industry for fresh water. The green revolution ultimately petered out because it transgressed many of the principles of sustainable development. There was too much reliance on irrigation, chemical fertilisers, pesticides and expensive farm equipment, which were not compatible with the environment or the needs of poorer countries.[20]

East Asia's Food Situation

Food availability in East Asia has closely paralleled global trends. From 1960 to 1990, food production exceeded population growth. Grain output doubled in China, Indonesia, the Philippines, Vietnam and South Korea in the twenty years between 1970 and 1990 and East Asian cereal production averaged 270 kilograms per person, 46 kilograms more than the world average. Asia increased its share of world cereals by 8 per cent in 1966–90 (from 33 to 41 per cent) and rice yields rose by over a third, from 2 tonnes to more than 3 tonnes per hectare.[21] However, these gains slowed significantly during the 1990s. At the end of the decade over 500 million Asians did not have enough to eat because of chronic poverty, population pressures on agricultural land, and environmental degradation.[22]

Although less important than it once was, rice is still a vital food staple providing 60 per cent of the carbohydrate and second-class protein consumed by Asians. By 2020, East Asia will need to produce 50 per cent more rice than it did in 1998, but the region's rice yields have levelled off or declined from their peaks in the 1980s.[23] Asian rice production in 1998 was 526.3 million tonnes, 16 million tonnes less than 1997, a fall which prompted a warning from the FAO that the region's food security is precariously balanced.[24] Few regional states seem likely to achieve self-sufficiency in rice. Population growth in the Philippines is expected to outpace rice production early this century. Domestic shortfalls have forced Manila to import increasing quantities of rice since the late 1980s.[25] After briefly attaining rice self-sufficiency in the mid-1980s, Indonesia has returned to its previous position as the world's largest importer of rice as well as becoming an expanding market for other food staples.[26] By 2025, China may have to import as much grain as the world produced in 1998.[27]

Fears about the impact of China's rising demand on world grain markets lie at the heart of the debate about food security in East Asia. Lester Brown, the iconoclastic president of the Washington-based Worldwatch Institute, argues that China may soon emerge as 'an importer of massive quantities of grain – quantities so large that they could trigger unprecedented rises in world food prices'. As China's consumption patterns change and the Chinese eat more livestock products and grain, subsequent price rises will overwhelm global markets, causing widespread shortages and 'an unprecedented degree of insecurity', especially in the developing world.[28] Thus food scarcity 'rather than military aggression' will become the principal threat to security.[29]

In support of these conclusions, Brown points to the fourfold expansion of China's economy since 1979. Never before in human history have the incomes of so many people expanded at such a rate. As incomes rise, China is beginning to follow the same pattern of consumption as wealthier Japan, Taiwan and South Korea, all of which diversified their diets away from a starch staple – rice – to one that included much greater consumption of meat, eggs, milk and other livestock products. However, it takes 2 kilograms of feed grain to produce 1 kilogram of poultry; pork requires 4 kilograms of feed and beef needs 7 kilograms. Brown calculates that if 1.2 billion Chinese eat more of these products, as seems likely, the country's grain imports will outstrip the world's exportable level of grain, driving up prices. 'In an integrated world economy, China's rising food prices will become the world's rising food prices. China's land scarcity will become everyone's land scarcity.'[30]

Table 5.3 Arable land area in East Asia, 1990–95

Country ('000 ha)	1990	1995	% change
China	93 287	91 977	–1.4
Indonesia	20 253	17 130	–15.4
Thailand	17 494	17 085	–2.3
Burma	9 567	9 540	–0.3
Philippines	5 480	5 520	0.7
Vietnam	5 339	5 509	3.1
Japan	4 121	3 970	–3.7
Cambodia	3 755	3 819	1.7
South Korea	1 953	1 787	–8.5
North Korea	1 700	1 700	0
Malaysia	1 700	1 820	7.1
Laos	838	875	4.4
Hong Kong	6	6	0
Brunei	3	3	0
Singapore	1	1	0
Total	*165 497*	*160 742*	*–2.9*

Source: Food and Agriculture Organisation, http://www.fao.org

Brown is not the only one to take a pessimistic view of China's capacity to feed itself. The Czech economist Vaclav Smil has documented in considerable detail China's loss of farmlands to environmental degradation. Smil calculates that 40 million hectares of farmland have been denuded since the 1950s, approximately the equivalent of all the fields in Argentina and enough to feed 350 million people.[31] With a fifth of the world's population, but only a fifteenth of its arable land, China can ill afford losses of this magnitude. Changing farming practices, such as substituting synthetic chemicals for natural fertilisers, have exacerbated the problem by moving 'China's agroecosystem further away from sustainable practices'.[32] Even Beijing concedes that 'a land crisis is approaching' as farmland loss reaches record levels.[33] In February, 1995, Jiang Chunyun, a member of the Communist Party Central Committee, conceded that 'In the long run, China's agriculture faces, on the one hand, the tremendous pressure of population growth and fast improvement in living standards and industrialization and, on the other, the severe restrictions imposed by a dwindling farmland, shortages of water resources, and a weak infrastructure'.[34]

Is a Food Crisis Likely?

Although recognising that ensuring sufficient food production is a long-term challenge, the Chinese Government has hotly disputed Brown's contention that the country is on the verge of a food crisis and points to the bumper grain harvests the country enjoyed at the end of the 1990s.[35] In 1999, Premier Zhu Rongji optimistically declared that 'China has put an end to the situation of chronic grain shortages'.[36] Chinese spokesmen have complained that Brown's arguments are merely a further example of the West's reluctance to come to terms with China's rising power.[37] Most Chinese economists, while agreeing that demand is likely to rise roughly in line with Brown's forecasts, contest his judgement that there is little scope for increases in grain production.[38] They argue that China only has to lift its annual production of grain by 1 per cent, which would see grain production rise from 500 to 640 million tonnes by 2030 when the country's population reaches its peak of about 1.6 billion.[39] In their assessment this target is 'surely attainable from either an economic or technical point of view based on the past performances of the country's agriculture and the potential of resources'.[40] The Chinese predictions are generally in line with those of the majority of international food economists.[41] The consensus of these experts is that while developing countries will increasingly become net importers of food, there will still be an increase in global food production into the twenty-first century, with cereals expected to grow at a rate of about 1.5 per cent per annum.[42] Pessimists, on the other hand, believe that the growth in cereals will not exceed 1 per cent.

Brown's focus on trends in grain production obscures the fact that China has been a net exporter of food since the mid-1980s, more than offsetting its imports of grain. The country's net food exports were valued at $2.3 billion in 1985 and had increased to $3.8 billion in 1995. By the mid-1990s, China imported only 0.4 per cent of its annual grain requirements, down from 3 per cent in the early 1980s. Grain imports are expected to rise to somewhere between 5 per cent and 10 per cent of demand but they will be offset by increases in the production of other agricultural commodities.[43] There is, therefore, considerable reason to question the worst-case predictions of a major food crisis developing in China and other developing East Asian states. Given sufficient political will by governments, and financial incentives for farmers, shortfalls in food production could be avoided. The US Department of Agriculture has argued that were China to adopt world-class agricultural technology, it could improve yields by as much as 30 per cent.[44] The Chinese Government calculates that 10 per cent of the nation's grain crop is lost because of mishandling and inefficiencies in administration and distribution; other analyses put the losses as high as 30 per cent.[45] If Beijing can halve these losses, it could reclaim 20 million tonnes annually for consumption by 2030.[46]

While Brown and his fellow pessimists may have overstated their case there are, nevertheless, grounds for concern that the balance between supply and demand is more delicately poised than many food economists are prepared to admit. At first glance, the apparently small discrepancy between low and high estimates of cereal production seems minor and hardly the basis for concerns about the world's ability to feed itself. But the difference becomes critical when compounded over several decades, producing a far less sanguine outlook than optimists envisage. Chinese estimates of future grain output exceed those of many independent studies by a sizeable margin, while its projections for grain imports are understated.[47] A major Sino-US research project on China's future food, which reviewed the major models used to calculate Chinese grain needs, concluded that China will need to import increasingly large quantities of food over the next twenty-five years.

Highlighting the uncertainties about making accurate long-term food projections, given the number of variables involved, the project nevertheless estimated that China would be forced to import between 50 million and 200 million tonnes of grain a year by 2020. Since current world grain production averages around 200 million tonnes, China's grain requirements will clearly have a major impact on the world grain market.[48] China cannot be self-sufficient in food grain as well as feed grain and livestock. With demand for beef, pork and poultry all rising, there will have to be a trade off between grain self-sufficiency and domestic meat production. Chinese subsidies costing nearly $25 billion keep the cost of domestic grain artificially high and obscure the fact that a large percentage of Chinese grain exports bring in only about a third of what they actually cost to produce. Millions of tonnes of Chinese hybrid rice are barely edible and go to waste.[49]

The FAO believes that China and East Asia's looming food shortfalls could be met by increasing domestic production and earning enough foreign exchange to import the rest. But relying on the market carries its own risks. It assumes that the export earnings of regional states will be sufficient to meet the cost of importing food. As the Asian economic crisis demonstrates, sudden economic collapse and deteriorating foreign exchange rates may preclude the import of expensive foreign food.[50] In addition, food projections are particularly sensitive to the assumptions on which they are based. For example, a 10 per cent fall in expected wheat yields or a 20 per cent increase in rates of population growth would probably result in a price rise of 30 per cent in the cost of wheat.[51] Relatively small changes in world output may thus generate large changes in volume and price fluctuations. As the gap between global supply and demand for a range of primary foods narrows, price volatility on world markets is likely to increase and will be exacerbated by the reduction in food stockpiles mandated by the implementation of the Uruguay Round agreement.[52] Without the moderating influence of substantial grain stocks, a confluence of unfavourable political, economic and climatic influences could create local scarcities. Higher prices weaken current accounts as governments strive to maintain prices at affordable levels in order to avoid sparking food riots and domestic unrest. This was precisely the situation Indonesia faced as the economic crisis took hold in early 1998, eventually forcing President Suharto's resignation.

Food economists are inclined to ignore or discount the widely different national approaches to food security. For historical and cultural reasons Asian states commonly equate minimum levels of food self-sufficiency with national security.[53] China and Japan, for example, promote measures aimed at achieving self-sufficiency in basic foods, especially rice, and rely upon strategic food stockpiles to manage price fluctuations. As one Chinese economist has argued 'it is imperative for the government to ensure a high rate of grain self-sufficiency as a necessary condition for stability'.[54] With a rural labour workforce of 400 million and mindful of the lessons of its own history, China sees grain production as crucial to maintaining the incomes of farmers and stimulating employment in the countryside.[55] Japan, although an inefficient producer of many primary foodstuffs, has resisted fully opening its agricultural markets for domestic political and security reasons. Food security is considered so important that it has been designated as one of the six major policies designed to achieve comprehensive national security.[56] East Asia's approach to food is further complicated by its symbolic and cultural importance. Rice is seen by many Asians as possessing a 'spiritual' quality that transcends its simple nutritional function.

The more optimistic forecasts of East Asia's future food production have failed to factor in the detrimental effects of environmental degradation. More than a quarter of Asian farmland is moderately or severely degraded – 'the victim of overcultivation, soil erosion, salinisation of irrigated lands and desertification'.[57] By one estimate China alone loses 12 billion kilograms of food each year from polluted farmland.[58] Half of Mongolia's cropland and a third of its pasture has been degraded.[59] Even if it were possible to put more land under cultivation, the increase would be marginal and add little to levels of food production. Biotechnology is the key to improving yields and reducing the cost of expensive fertilisers and pesticides. Genetically modified organisms (GMOs) offer the promise of higher-yielding crops that are disease-resistant and require minimal or no pesticides and chemical fertilisers. They may also be genetically enhanced to include nutritional supplements for communities that are deficient in vitamins and iron. Although the East Asian track record in using and adapting biotechnology is poor, GM crops are probably the region's best hope of reversing falling yields and attaining the large increases in food production that will be required this century. Modern transgenic technology is particularly suited to the tropics because it can help to reduce the huge crop losses (often amounting to 30 per cent) from insects and plant disease.[60]

However, it is doubtful whether biotechnology is yet capable of creating another green revolution. The main contribution of genetic research to agriculture in the foreseeable future will be to make plants more resistant to disease. Despite impressive advances, current biotechnology is beginning to approach the upper limits of the yield increases that can be obtained in cereals.[61] Although new rice strains being developed at Los Banos in the Philippines are expected to improve yields by 10–25 per cent, increases of this order are still well short of the 250 per cent gain in yields obtained in the second half of the twentieth century and they may not be enough to arrest the decline in per capita grain production that has occurred in the 1990s.[62] So far only the United States, Argentina and Canada are making extensive use of GM seeds. The backlash against globalisation that was evident at the 1999 World Trade Organisation meeting in Seattle suggests that GMOs are likely to be aggressively opposed by a coalition of environmental groups, NGOs and some European governments.[63] Opposition to GMOs has already spread to East Asia. Although China and Singapore look set to embrace the new technology wholeheartedly, consumer movements and leftist groups in Japan, Thailand and the Philippines are demanding controls on the use of GM crops, while religious factors may proscribe their use in Muslim Indonesia and Malaysia.[64]

Perhaps the greatest constraint on future food production will be the availability of water for irrigation. The expansion of land under irrigation has been a boon to agriculture and a major factor behind the impressive rates of growth in grain production recorded during the twentieth century. In the first half of the century, irrigation doubled from 48 million to 94 million hectares, and then virtually tripled again to 260 million hectares by the end of the 1990s, allowing multiple cropping, higher yields and turning previously arid areas into productive farmland. Irrigation now accounts for some 40 per cent of world food production. However, irrigated land per person has declined since 1978 and will continue falling for at least the next half-century because of population growth and natural limits to the amount of usable water.[65] Water tables are dropping across the globe and major rivers are beginning to run dry before they reach the sea as their flows are tapped for hydro-electric power and irrigation.

The reduction in the water flow of China's Yellow River is a warning of the fate that awaits other major river systems in Asia should usage exceed sustainable levels. The Yellow River provides a significant proportion of central China's irrigation requirements and food production. After flowing uninterrupted for thousands of years, the Yellow River ran dry in 1972 for the first time in recorded history and then flowed intermittently in every year between 1985 and 1997 because of massive upstream diversion of the river's water for irrigation and industry.[66] As a consequence

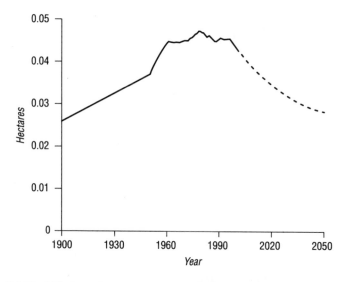

Figure 5.1 World irrigated area per person, 1900–2000, with projections to 2050
Source: Lester Brown, *State of the World 1999*, p. 124.

Shandong province, a major grain-producing area, has seen its harvests
fall, underlining the crucial relationship between water and food.[67] Water
shortages are likely to affect food production in East Asia more than any
other region of the world because of the greater dependence of Asian
states on irrigation for growing rice and cereals. China, for example, relies
on irrigation for almost 70 per cent of its grain harvest. In an era of declining water availability East Asian governments will have to choose carefully
how they allocate what was once an abundant resource. In a contest
between agriculture and industry, the other main user of water, agriculture may be the loser because water used for irrigation generally produces
a smaller economic return than water diverted to industry.[68]

Food Shortages in North Korea

Marxist and isolated North Korea is the most troubling example, in East
Asia, of a state chronically unable to feed its people. Televised images of
peasants scouring the countryside for edible roots and grass in the mid-
1990s first alerted the world to the possibility that North Korea was suffering food shortages. Reports of widespread starvation were initially
discounted partly because of suspicions that Pyongyang was playing on the
sympathies and fears of its neighbours and the international community to
extract political concessions and food aid in a bid to strengthen its hold on
power. The regime's obsessive secrecy and the lack of even rudimentary

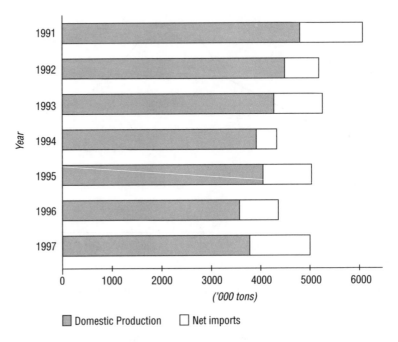

Figure 5.2 North Korean grain supplies, 1991–97
Source: South Korean National Unification Board estimates in Philip Wonhyuk Lim, 'North Korea's Food Crisis', *Korea and World Affairs* 21(4) 1997, p. 582.

data on North Korea's population, economy and agriculture also made it difficult to judge the seriousness of food shortages.

Nevertheless, by 1997, it was clear that North Korea was in the throes of a prolonged and severe famine, the worst in its modern history. The state's food shortfall had increased steadily throughout the 1990s and was compounded by adverse weather conditions in 1995–97.[69] Cereal harvests in this period were consistently 1–1.5 million tonnes short of the 5 million tonnes needed to provide a minimal level of calories.[70] The country recorded a grain shortfall of about 1 million tonnes in 1996 with the average diet down to a little over one bowl of rice a day.[71] In 1997, at the peak of the famine, North Koreans were subsisting on a daily ration of 100 grams of corn, a fifth of the daily minimum requirement.[72] According to the WFP, many city-dwellers in North Korea were receiving only 15 per cent of the daily ration given to refugees in Africa's camps.[73] Some 800 000 North Korean children were malnourished, 80 000 of them seriously.[74] This was despite the fact that international relief agencies spent more than $1 billion on food aid for North Korea between 1995 and 1998.[75] By 1999, an estimated 2–3 million people, or between 10 and 15 per cent of North Korea's entire population, had died from malnutrition and starvation.[76]

The seeds of North Korea's food problems were sown decades earlier, when the *juche* ('self-reliance') philosophy was first developed by 'Great Leader' Kim Il Sung. It is, however, doubtful whether North Korea could ever have become self-sufficient in staple foods given its generally inhospitable terrain, climate and population density. Deep-seated flaws in agricultural policy were compounded by the decline in the non-agricultural sector, which reduced the availability of key fertilisers, agricultural machinery and irrigation flows. Overshadowing this policy failure were a number of self-inflicted environmental disasters. Collectivisation was accompanied by large-scale land clearance and deforestation designed to expand the area available for cultivation. Once trees had been felled, rain washed away a large proportion of the replacement crops, causing soil erosion and serious flooding. The rate of deforestation accelerated as peasants felled trees for fuel. Then chemical fertilisers were overused and soil fertility decreased. By the mid-1980s, exhausted soils had forced North Korea into dependence on food imports, sowing the seeds of the famines of the late 1990s.[77] Without major agricultural reforms North Korea will be unable to feed its people, but improvements are unlikely while Kim Jong-il remains at the helm of the North Korean state, despite his tentative opening to the West. Fundamental economic reform would risk ushering in political change that could well prove fatal to Kim's regime.

Fish Shortages

North Korea aside, the relationship between food scarcity and security is most evident at sea. Asians are heavily dependent on the Pacific Ocean for food and it has been aptly described as the region's 'rice bowl' for the twenty-first century.[78] Fish is the main source of protein for an estimated 1 billion Asians, and fishing supports more people in East Asia than in any other region of the world. Over half the world's fish catch is taken in Asian waters, and five of the top ten fishing nations are in East Asia.[79] Unfortunately, the Pacific is showing signs of environmental degradation from coastal pollution, overfishing and unsustainable exploitation of other forms of living marine resources. Asia has already lost half its fish stocks. The depletion of fish species is a major concern in the Northwest Pacific, which provides nearly a third of the world's marine harvest.[80] Fish yields in the Yellow, South and East China Seas fell significantly in the 1990s.[81]

The decline in East Asia's reserves of fish is part of a worrying global trend. In the past fifty years the world's fish catch has risen fivefold, but because of increasing demand, per capita fish consumption has remained virtually unchanged since the late 1960s.[82] It is clear that many fish species are now at risk. In 1994, a World Bank study concluded that 'the current harvesting capacity of the world's fleet far exceeds the estimated biological sustainability of most commercial species'.[83] According

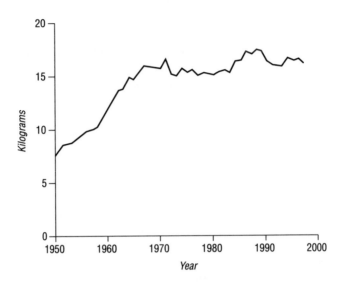

Figure 5.3 World fish catch per person, 1950–97 (kg per person)
Source: *Vital Signs 1999*, Worldwatch Institute, 1999, www.worldwatch.org

to the FAO, around two-thirds of the world's major fish species are either fully exploited or in decline.[84] Another 20–30 million tonnes of fish will probably be required to meet demand by 2010, a target that will be difficult to achieve as overfishing and poor management of fisheries threaten the ability of many species to recover and regenerate.[85] While aquaculture may meet some of the shortfall in supply, it is unlikely to become a substitute for marine fishing. Fish-farming requires far more resources than harvesting fish from the wild; it depends on an adequate supply of fresh water, which is in increasingly short supply, and it can cause significant environmental damage.[86]

State subsidies, illegal, unreported and unregulated fishing (IUU), flag-of-convenience operations and the expansion in fishing fleets are exacerbating the global and regional shortage of fish. Despite clear indications that world fisheries are in trouble, governments still provide $45 billion worth of annual subsidies to their fishing industries.[87] The practice of registering ships in countries that are not signatories to fish management regimes and treaties allows owners to fly flags of convenience and complicates efforts to control IUU.[88] A hundred and thirty-six thousand new ships have been added to the world's fishing fleets since 1989, accelerating the decline in fish numbers and causing prices to rise, a sure sign of scarcity.[89] In 1998, the bulk of the 1.2 million vessels in these fleets operated in Asian waters. China alone has an estimated 450 000 fishing boats and like many other Asian states has developed a sizeable deep-water fishing fleet.[90]

As traditional fishing grounds are exhausted, competition for remaining stocks has intensified. Countries which once welcomed foreign fishing fleets now restrict their access and quotas, while fishing nations have become much more protective of their own resources.[91] In 1981 Japan, which relies heavily on fish as a dietary staple, was allowed to catch 1.2 million tonnes in the 200-mile US EEZ; by 1988, quotas had been cut virtually to zero.[92] South Korea and Taiwan have suffered similar reductions, and their trawlers have been forced well into the South Pacific to make up the shortfall. The fishing fleets of Southeast Asia have also been compelled to move further afield, and the Chinese seem likely to join the hunt for dwindling stocks by building more ocean-going trawlers.[93] As fishing fleets grow and venture further into the Pacific, the area of ocean open to international fishing is shrinking; a large percentage of the marine resources of the Western Pacific are either claimed or contested.[94] As a result, the frequency and seriousness of incidents at sea have steadily increased as foreign trawlers have illegally encroached into other countries' EEZs and territorial waters. Gun battles have broken out between the navies of regional states intent on defending the activities of their national fishing fleets or preventing perceived territorial violations by others.

Fishing Disputes in Southeast Asia

In Southeast Asia, competition for fish and other living marine resources has historically been most intense in the Gulf of Thailand. With the third-largest fishing fleet in East Asia, Thai fishermen had begun to exhaust stocks in their traditional fishing grounds by the late 1970s and to encroach into the EEZs and territorial waters of neighbouring states.[95] In the 1980s and 1990s, seizures of Thai fishing vessels became more common throughout Southeast Asian waters, particularly in the Andaman Sea, the Gulf of Tonkin, the Luzon Strait and in the waters off Indonesia. Illegal fishing by Thai vessels became a worsening source of friction between Bangkok and its neighbours during the 1990s. In the Andaman Sea, hundreds of Thai fishing vessels regularly plunder Burma's EEZ. Burma's navy has minimal capability to protect the country's extensive coastline. The larger Thai vessels commonly carry heavy machine-guns and rocket-propelled grenade-launchers which they seldom hesitate to use if challenged. Thai fishermen also enjoy better intelligence information from radio centres that warn of approaching patrol boats.[96] In late 1998 and again in early 1999, disputes over fish threatened to escalate into serious military confrontation between Thailand and Burma following two fatal naval clashes which resulted in the deaths of several Thai and Burmese sailors. Both incidents occurred when Thai naval vessels intervened during Burmese attempts to intercept Thai fishing vessels in

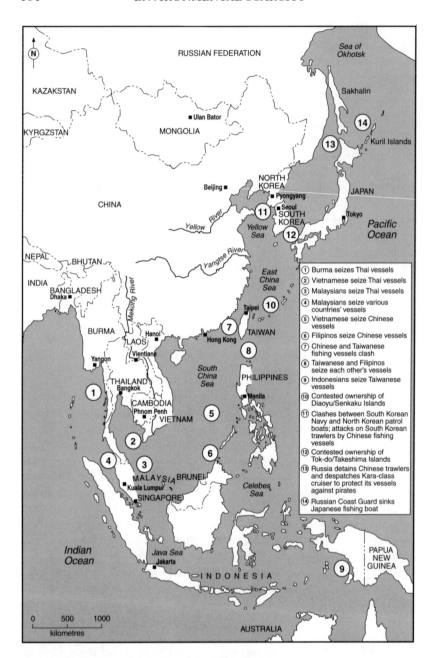

Map 5.1 Clashes over fish in East Asia, 1994–2000
Source: Alan Dupont, 'The Environment and Security in Pacific Asia', Adelphi
Paper 319 (Oxford University Press for the IISS, London, 1998), p. 52, and
updates.

contested waters of the Andaman Sea. On the second occasion, the Thai National Security Council considered deploying a squadron of F-5 fighter aircraft to the area.[97]

Since 1995, Thai fishing vessels have also clashed with the navies of Malaysia and Vietnam. On 31 May 1995, Thai and Vietnamese gunboats exchanged fire after the Thai Navy attempted to protect Thai fishing vessels from being seized by the Vietnamese Navy: a Thai fisherman and two Vietnamese sailors were killed and five of the six Thai fishing boats impounded, along with sixty-two of their crew.[98] Bangkok was forced to caution its own fishermen about illegally fishing in Malaysia's territorial waters after six trawlers were impounded by Malaysia and eighty Thai fishermen were arrested in April and May of 1999.[99] Thailand, which earns around $4 billion annually from fish exports, may be the worst offender, but it is not the only culprit. The fishing vessels of virtually all Southeast Asian states regularly intrude into neighbouring EEZs and territorial seas. Vietnam has fired on fishing boats from China, Malaysia and Taiwan, and the Philippines has seized Chinese and Taiwanese trawlers.[100] The collision between a Philippines naval patrol boat and a Chinese fishing boat which sank in July 1999 off the island of Palawan is a further illustration of the potential of these disputes to damage broader political and security ties. China condemned the Philippines' action and claimed that the fishing vessel was deliberately rammed.[101] In an earlier 1997 incident in which the Philippines arrested twenty-three Chinese nationals for illegal fishing, it warned that Manila ran the risk of ruining the 'friendly relations' between the two countries.[102]

Fish is central to the Spratlys dispute; according to one UN study, the waters around the Spratlys yield 7.5 tonnes of fish per square kilometre each year.[103] The abundance of commercially valuable tuna and shrimp has created lucrative fishing industries in virtually all the South China Sea littoral states, providing employment for millions of people as well as substantial foreign exchange earnings. Malaysia, for example, earns about $50 million a year from harvesting one species alone; the country puts the total value of tuna resources around the island of Layang-Layang in the Spratlys at around $600 million.[104] States in the region have also enacted laws and established institutions to protect their marine resources from foreign poaching. The Philippines Senate passed legislation imposing large fines on foreign poachers on 6 August 1997. In the same year Indonesia gave notice that it would ban foreign fishing vessels from its 6.5 million square kilometres of territorial waters from 2000 and inaugurated an eighteen-member National Maritime Council to 'protect the wealth and potential' of its seas against 'illegal exploitation by foreign parties'.[105] Such 'exploitation' is estimated to cost the country over $4 billion annually. In the council's inauguration ceremony, President Suharto made it clear that the protection of marine resources was closely linked with national security and defence.[106] When Abdurrahman Wahid came to power in 1999, he created a new Ministry for Marine Exploration and Fisheries and nominated combating illegal fishing as one of his government's priorities.[107]

Fishing Disputes in Northeast Asia

During the 1990s, illegal fishing, territorial/EEZ encroachments and maritime incidents in Northeast Asia have become increasingly regular. The risk of significant political and military confrontation over competition for diminishing fish and other marine resources has emerged as a genuine security issue for China, Japan, the two Koreas and Russia. In March 1999, officials at Japan's Maritime Safety Agency revealed that fishing boats, mainly from China and South Korea, had penetrated Japan's territorial waters 'several hundred times each year' and had been intercepted or chased away by Japanese patrol boats.[108] In 1996, Seoul placed its navy in the Yellow and Eastern Seas on alert after an attack by Chinese fishermen on a South Korean trawler in which eleven people were injured.[109]

North Korean patrol boats have crossed the maritime buffer zone separating North and South Korea on several occasions to protect their fishing fleet.[110] North Korean fishing vessels in search of crab during the height of the crab-fishing season crossed the buffer zone in the Yellow Sea on 15 June 1999, accompanied by torpedo boats from the North Korea Navy. Despite repeated warnings from challenging South Korean naval ships, the torpedo boats refused to turn back, precipitating the most serious armed clash between the two states since the end of the Korean War in 1953. In the ensuing fire-fight, one North Korean torpedo boat was sunk with the loss of its entire crew, while two others were damaged.[111] 'Fraternal relations' between the Chinese Communist Party and the North Korean Workers' Party failed to prevent North Korean gunboats from firing on a fleet of Chinese trawlers in 1992. In 1994, Russia despatched a Kara-class cruiser to the East China Sea to halt what the Russian Foreign Ministry called 'pirate' attacks on its vessels. Russia has also detained Chinese trawlers for illegal fishing near the island of Sakhalin.[112]

Maritime incidents involving fish resources are linked to Northeast Asia's most intractable territorial disputes. While most commentators have emphasised the geostrategic significance of the Diaoyu/Senkaku islands or the presence of oil as the underlying causes of the dispute over the islands, few seem to have recognised the importance of fish resources (Diaoyu Dao means 'fishing islands' in Chinese).[113] Taiwanese President Lee Teng-hui made it clear in August 1996 that the real importance of

these islands was fishing rights. Taiwan's national fishing association estimates that the country's ships bring in about 40 000 tonnes of fish worth
some $65 million a year from the waters around the islands.[114] Enacting
the Territorial Waters Bill in January 1999, Taiwan reaffirmed its claim to
the islands by specifically declaring them to be an integral part of the
Republic of China.[115]

In the North Pacific, the Kuril Island group is the subject of a long-
running territorial dispute between Japan and Russia. The islands have
important strategic and emotional significance for both countries
because of the way in which they were 'acquired' by Moscow at the end
of the Second World War. But fish is also central to the dispute: the Kurils
lie at the heart of one of the world's richest fishing grounds. Russia's ownership has allowed Moscow to claim an EEZ of 100 000 square kilometres
containing fish, invertebrates and water-plants with an estimated market
value of $1 billion per annum. Around 25 per cent of Russia's annual fish
catch of 6–7 million tonnes comes from the southern Kuril region.[116]
Japan's determination to reclaim the Kurils has been reinforced by the
knowledge that the region's rich marine resources would reduce the
nation's dependence on more distant foreign waters.

As the cost of deep-ocean fishing rises and other fish reserves near
exhaustion, Japanese vessels have been more willing to risk penetrating
the Russian EEZ around the Kurils. The Russian Navy has seized Japanese fishing boats on numerous occasions since the end of the Cold War.
Tensions between the two states over fishing disputes reached a peak in
1994, when Moscow allowed its border guards to open fire on foreign vessels trespassing in Russian waters. A month later, the Russian coast guard
sank a Japanese fishing boat.[117] In an attempt to reach a political accommodation, an agreement was signed in 1998 allowing Japanese vessels to
fish in the area around the South Kuril islands for the first time since the
Second World War, provided they are accompanied and supervised by
Russian border guard boats. Although the risk of military confrontation
has been reduced, the potential for conflict remains. Only a few weeks
after the agreement went into effect, several Japanese vessels intruded
into Russian waters in the South Kuril region and began fishing illegally,
using the presence of 'legal' boats to disguise their poaching. Senior
Russian border guard officials branded the poaching as a 'provocation'
and part of a deliberate strategy by Tokyo to maintain its claim to the
Kuril Islands and their bountiful marine resources.[118]

Until 1997, Japan had refrained from delineating fishing zones in the
East China Sea and Sea of Japan to avoid aggravating historical disputes
with China and South Korea over the Diaoyu/Senkaku and Tok-
do/Takeshima islands. The government took this position despite
intense pressure from the powerful domestic fishing industry, which had

complained vociferously about Chinese and South Korean illegal fishing and attacks against Japanese fishing boats.[119] Tokyo has since moved to tighten control over its own fishing grounds, while seeking to maximise access to the resources of disputed areas. In 1997, the Japanese Government declared a 200-nautical mile EEZ which incorporated the Tok-do/Takeshima group. South Korea, which has a small maritime-resource base, responded swiftly by declaring its own 200-mile EEZ. When asked to clarify the status of Tok-do by reporters, South Korea's Foreign Minister, Yoo Chong-ha, stated that the zone 'starts from the limit of South Korea's territorial waters' and that Tok-do was 'within South Korean territorial waters'.[120]

Seoul's subsequent actions underline both the capacity of these disputes to escalate, and the increasing links between maritime food resources and territorial issues in post-Cold War East Asia. Accusing Japan of violating the terms of a 1965 accord by unilaterally altering agreed fishing boundaries, Yoo Chong-ha demanded in July 1997 that Tokyo revoke its EEZ declaration until a new fishing agreement could be negotiated. The South Korean National Assembly subsequently passed a unanimous resolution protesting against Japan's 'illegal' change of the fishing boundaries.[121] Between 8 and 15 June 1997, the Japanese Maritime Safety Agency seized four South Korean fishing boats for allegedly penetrating the newly declared maritime boundary, further angering Seoul, which warned that such incidents would have grave consequences for the bilateral relationship.[122] In retaliation, South Korean trawlers continued to fish in contested waters, especially near the northern Japanese island of Hokkaido. Leaders of Hokkaido's fishing cooperatives branded the Korean actions as inflammatory and 'an act tantamount to a declaration of war'.[123]

A breakthrough in the dispute came when the Kim Dae-jung Government signed a new fisheries agreement with Japan in late 1998. The accord, which came into effect on 23 January 1999, shelved the territorial issue and established a joint fishing zone around Tok-do/Takeshima. Resistance in South Korea to the new agreement remains strong, however, and the opposition Grand National Party (GNP) succeeded in delaying its ratification for several weeks. The GNP claimed that 70 per cent of South Koreans disapproved of the agreement, believing it would damage the local fishing industry, and did not recognise Seoul's sovereignty over Tok-do/Takeshima.[124] Many influential Japanese are also dissatisfied with the outcome of the negotiations and see potential for future disputes over the linked issues of sovereignty and fish quotas. A Japanese Foreign Ministry official conceded that 'if another dispute between both countries over fishing stocks and operation regulations were to occur, it might affect the issue of Takeshima, I'm afraid'.[125]

China and South Korea have also become embroiled in disputes over fish. In contrast to the vitriol that accompanied South Korea's verbal attacks on Japan, Seoul has been restrained in its response to Chinese illegal fishing. Nevertheless, evidence of a harder line emerged during talks in 1997 aimed at renegotiating fishing agreements to accommodate both countries' newly declared EEZs. The South Korean delegation urged China to crack down on illegal fishing in South Korean waters, and President Kim Young-sam's Cabinet banned foreign fishing vessels from entering designated prohibited zones in the West Sea from 7 November 1997.[126] After protracted negotiations, China and South Korea eventually signed a fisheries agreement on 11 November 1998 which established a regime governing each country's fishing activities and marine catches in previously contested areas of the Yellow Sea.[127]

Interstate confrontation over fish and other marine living resources is emerging as a significant long-term security issue for East Asia. The declining availability of fish is a global problem but East Asia's dependence on the oceans for food suggests that disputes over fish may trigger wider conflicts between regional states unless steps are taken to manage and conserve fish stocks nationally and internationally. The number and severity of incidents at sea generated by the competition for fish has steadily increased since the end of the Cold War, notwithstanding the signing of a raft of important bilateral fishing agreements. Major wars over fish are unlikely, but as the remaining stocks of wild fish diminish, regional states will come to regard them in the same light as oil and gas – highly valuable resources that are worth contesting and defending, if necessary by military force. The competition for fish in the Pacific is also complicating and making more difficult the resolution of several festering territorial and island disputes of which the Kurils, Tok-do/Takeshima, Diaoyu/Senkaku and the Spratlys are the most prominent and intractable.

Conclusion

As these tensions over fish demonstrate, food is destined to have greater strategic weight and import in an era of environmental scarcity. While optimists maintain that the world is perfectly capable of meeting the anticipated increases in demand for essential foodstuffs, there are enough imponderables to suggest that prudent governments would not want to rely on such a felicitous outcome. Falling real food prices globally over the past few decades as a result of sharp productivity gains in industrial countries mask the fact that millions of poorer people are undernourished because they still cannot afford to purchase adequate food from existing supplies. Real food security depends on accessibility as well as availability. As Chowdhury points out, 'food security at one level does not guarantee food security at all levels'.[128]

East Asia's rising demand for food and diminishing capacity to feed itself adds an unpredictable new element to the global food equation for several reasons. The gap between production and consumption of key foodstuffs globally is narrowing dangerously and needs to be reversed. The 1996 fall in the world's grain stocks to their lowest level ever recorded and the drawing down of cereal reserves below safe levels in 1999 should be seen in this context.[129] While due mainly to short-term and probably reversible factors, grain and cereal stocks are the world's first line of defence against short-term supply disruptions. An unexpected rise in consumption or fall in production caused by climatic variables, political and social disturbances, economic mismanagement, shifts in government policies and environmental stress is more likely to precipitate food shortages when buffer stocks are low.

Food scarcity most commonly becomes a security issue as a result of sudden and unexpected fluctuations in supply and demand or, as in the case of North Korea, of political and economic failure. North Korea should be seen as a salutary if extreme example of what can happen when man-made environmental degradation, adverse weather conditions and misguided government policies combine to undermine a state's ability to feed its citizens. Nonetheless, the country's difficulties illustrate several broader points about the connections between food scarcity and security. First, even local and relatively short-term food shortages can generate social and political tensions within states which may be the precursors of more serious conflict. Second, while there is a direct link between environmental degradation and the region's declining agricultural productivity, the relationship between the environment and security is more complex: food shortages have rarely been a primary cause of major conflict between states; they can, however, contribute to state failure and death on a massive scale in developing states and aggravate interstate tensions by stimulating refugee flows and resource conflicts. Third, food shortages are generally symptomatic of flawed political and economic systems, policy failures, and lack of access because of the uneven distribution of food or income inequalities. Elites rarely suffer from hunger even in the poorest countries. A meaningful definition of food security must therefore incorporate people as well as states.

Neither a sudden fluctuation nor a failure on the North Korean scale is in prospect elsewhere in the region, nor is East Asia likely to encounter insurmountable problems in feeding itself in the immediate future. Although friction over diminishing fish supplies will increase, food shortages are most likely to threaten the security of states and people when they coincide with other threats to political and economic stability. Earlier fears that food would be used as a 'weapon' by food-rich states have faded because of the liberalisation of agricultural trade and diversified world grain markets. The real food security issue for East Asia, in the long term, is the cumulative and accelerating destruction of the region's food-producing capacity because of population pressures, urbanisation and environmental degradation. Anxieties over China's future food requirements must be seen in this light. Even though food production in China has kept ahead of population growth and further improvements in agriculture are achievable, a deteriorating physical environment in conjunction with political instability and economic failure may endanger China's food security and may have global repercussions.[130] Many developing countries in Southeast Asia are similarly vulnerable. For this reason, preserving arable land, protecting coastal and marine habitats and managing natural resources in a sustainable way may become intrinsic to the prevention of conflict.

CHAPTER 6

Water Wars

In the environmental era it has become fashionable to speculate about the likelihood of wars over the planet's fresh-water resources. Even within the traditional security literature, which has largely distanced itself from the debate about the impact of environmental degradation on international security, it is generally accepted that water scarcity is a potential cause of political and military conflict.[1] However, understanding of the relationship between fresh water scarcity, conflict and security in the academic and policy domains is often superficial and one-dimensional. It is commonly assumed, for example, that the principal strategic outcome of endemic water shortages will be to heighten the likelihood of interstate conflict in the arid Middle East. But the reality is that water scarcity is a global problem and its security consequences will not be confined to the Middle East or to relations between states. While generously endowed with water by Middle Eastern standards, East Asia is facing its own water crisis. An analysis of East Asia's water problems suggests that water scarcity is responsible for generating intra-state violence as well as tensions between states, especially when they share the resources of large river basins or underground aquifers. Dwindling supplies of fresh water are also likely to have adverse security consequences because of water's crucial role in agriculture and grain production.

Why is water in short supply?

The link between fresh water and security is the result of water's central importance to human life and economic development. We depend on continuous access to it, not only for drinking and food production, but also for industry, transport and energy.[2] Yet this most precious of natural resources is beginning to run dry. The FAO has warned that 'human demands are about to collide with the ability of the hydrological cycle to supply water'.[3] Already one-third of the world's population lives in countries with moderate to high water stress.[4] By 2025, according to the United Nations, 'as much as two-thirds of the world's population could be under [water] stress conditions' and water shortages and pollution could place global food supplies in jeopardy, possibly leading to 'a series of local and regional water crises with global implications'.[5] This is so because water and food are inseparably linked. Sandra Postel estimates that the current global water deficit is equivalent to the loss of 160 million tonnes of grain, equivalent to 80 per cent of annual grain exports. She concludes that 'as water shortages continue to mount, it is dangerous to presume, as many officials do, that there will be enough exportable grain to meet the import needs of all water-short countries at a price they can afford'.[6] Around half the world's population is without adequate sanitation or drinking water, two of the fundamental prerequisites of civilised society and human security.[7]

Three main factors are responsible for the widening gap between the demand for and supply of fresh water. First, the global supply of fresh water is limited and unevenly distributed.[8] Fresh water constitutes less than 4 per cent of the world's total water resources and most of it is locked away in glaciers and permanent snow cover; only 0.007 per cent is readily accessible for human use.[9] Many states receive little rainfall and two-thirds of the world's population live in areas that receive a quarter of the global rainfall.[10] Even in 'wet' countries, a great percentage of annual precipitation occurs during a relatively short rainy season and simply washes away.

Second, water consumption has increased exponentially because of population growth, industrial development and the expansion of irrigated farmland.[11] Global fresh-water consumption rose more than sixfold during the twentieth century at more than twice the rate of population increase.[12] As a result, per capita water supply has fallen by around 75 per cent since 1850 and the world could be using 70 per cent of accessible runoff by 2025.[13] The trend towards irrigating farmland, which provides one-third of the world's harvest from just 17 per cent of its cropland, is responsible for much of the pressure on water supply having risen from 50 million to 250 million hectares since 1900.[14] Unfortunately, only about a third of irrigation water actually reaches the plants it is intended for because of poor technology, evaporation and dispersal. Under a business-as-usual scenario, the Consultative Group on International Agricultural Research estimates that 60 per cent more water will be required for irrigation to meet the world's food supplies in 2025.[15]

Third, poor water management and conservation practices have contributed to the decline in the quality and availability of water, while over-logging and deforestation are destroying water tables and causing

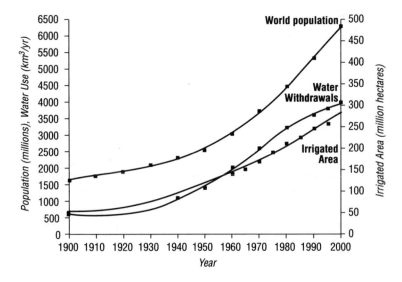

Figure 6.1 Global trends in water withdrawals, world population and irrigated area, 1900–2000
Source: Gleick, *The World's Water 1998–99*, p. 7.

siltation and salination. Wasteful and environmentally destructive farming techniques prompt soil erosion, clogging waterways, while the overuse of pesticides and chemical fertilisers pollutes water used for drinking and irrigation. The expansion of urban areas, which are often located near major river systems or in ecologically sensitive coastal areas, has further reduced fresh-water supplies.

For these reasons, water has become a scarce resource in many parts of the world: about eighty countries containing 40 per cent of the world's population suffer from serious shortages, mostly in the developing world.[16] Thus fresh water is scarcest where population and urban growth is highest. Per capita availability of good potable water is also declining in many developed states. The United Nations estimates that the number of people in water-deficient countries will increase from 550 million to 1 billion between 1999 and 2010.[17] In order to provide an adequate supply of water, as much as $800 billion in investment may be required by developing countries over the next decade. But it is difficult to see where this money will come from unless the true cost of water is reflected in its price structure and government investment priorities.

Of course there are ways of developing alternative sources of water. Water recycling is one. Another is reclaiming waste water, which may be treated and made acceptable for human consumption. Desalination plants, which remove salt from water, can go some way to reducing

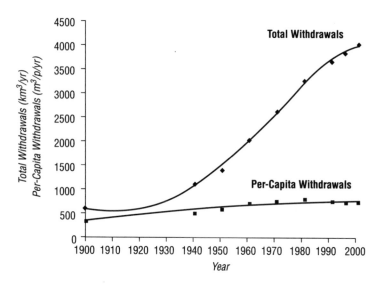

Figure 6.2 Total and per capita global water withdrawals, 1900–2000
Source: Gleick, *The World's Water 1998–99*, p. 7.

dependence on natural rainfall and groundwater, but they are not a panacea. The technology they employ is expensive because of the high energy costs associated with the purification process, and the plants themselves need large tracts of land and access to deep-water inlets. Desalination plants are therefore unlikely to make a significant contribution to the global fresh-water supply and will find favour mainly with energy-rich, water-poor states in the Middle East.[18] Other mooted solutions, such as towing giant icebergs from polar regions or redistributing water via pipelines, aqueducts, tankers and even floating nylon bags face significant political, technical and financial obstacles and are unlikely to solve the world's water problems in the foreseeable future.[19]

The key to making more water available is to reduce consumption. Significant savings have already been made in the United States and Europe by better water planning, reallocating water among users and the introduction of more efficient and cost-effective technology. Relatively simple changes can often produce surprisingly high savings. In the United States, for example, mandating the installation of high-efficiency, low-flow toilets which use 6 litres of water compared with the 23 normally used has produced a 70 per cent reduction in the water required to flush toilets. Making 1 tonne of steel now requires only 6 tonnes of water in contrast to the 60–100 tonnes used in the 1930s.[20] Fixing leaking pipes and lining aqueducts could recoup some of the 60 per cent of water lost globally because of inefficiencies in agricultural practices. Rudimentary conservation measures and charging for water would place a higher premium on the value of existing water supplies. Partly as a result of applying these new technologies and more effective water management, US withdrawals of water began to decrease in the mid-1980s despite a rising population and standard of living.[21] Nevertheless, while the application of new technology and sensible conservation practices could do much to stabilise water withdrawals, government short-sightedness, competing economic priorities and endemic political instability will almost certainly prevent recent US experience being replicated in the developing world where water shortages are most likely to occur.

Water Scarcity and Conflict

But does water scarcity necessarily lead to conflict? The historical record is ambiguous. The availability and distribution of fresh water has for centuries been a problem for the inhabitants of dry and desert regions, and has in many instances been aggravated by the often arbitrary political division of unitary river basins.[22] In the Middle East, for example, all the major rivers cross international borders and more than 50 per cent of the region's population relies on water that flows through another state.[23] The number of cases in which water is an important or contributing cause of conflict in the volatile Middle East appears to be increasing. There are currently water disputes between the nine riparian Nile states. Competition for scarce fresh water is an intrinsic part of the conflict between Israel and its Arab neighbours and a significant cause of friction between Iraq, Syria and Turkey. Their quarrel over the Euphrates River is a pertinent illustration of how water disputes may foment political and military conflict.

Several prominent political leaders have publicly stated that nations will eventually go to war over water, including the former UN Secretary-General, Boutros Boutros-Ghali, who in the late 1980s predicted that the next war in the Middle East would be 'over the waters of the Nile, not politics'.[24] Population growth in the Middle East will undoubtedly add to the pressures on the region's extremely limited fresh-water resources and increase anxiety about future water security among Arab states, since more than 85 per cent of their water originates in non-Arab lands.[25] Some analysts argue that water might eventually become more valuable than oil as a strategic resource.[26] However, emphasising the conflict potential of water shortages does not give the complete picture. Water-sharing arrangements are part of the political landscape of the Middle East, and conservation occupies an important place in the agendas of national governments. Furthermore, once cooperative water regimes are in place they usually prove resilient since the signatories calculate that they have more to lose by going to war than by mediating water disputes peacefully.[27] As already noted, technological advances, such as improved irrigation techniques and more effective water distribution systems, show that with sufficient political will, governments can considerably reduce wastage and increase the volume of usable water. Political difficulties usually arise when two or more states are forced to share scarce surface and subsurface water resources, as is the case with the Euphrates and a great percentage of the Middle East's water. Even so, for all the warnings of impending 'water wars', there is little evidence so far of actual conflict between states in the Middle East 'directly and exclusively related to the control and exploitation of water resources'.[28]

Water Scarcity in East Asia

To what extent is water scarcity likely to become a source of conflict in East Asia? Judging by the frequency and severity of flooding during the region's wet season, most of the region would seem to suffer from too much water rather than too little. East Asia is, however, beginning to encounter the quantitative and qualitative water limitations that other, drier parts of the world such as the Middle East have experienced for several decades. In Asia as a whole, per capita water availability has declined by between 40 and 65 per cent since 1950. Although the total amount of renewable water is several times annual withdrawals, rainfall and population are spread unevenly and per capita availability therefore varies considerably – from 200 000 cubic metres on the island of New Guinea to below 3000 cubic metres in China, South Korea and Thailand.[29] According to the World Bank, by 2025 most states in the region will be facing serious water shortages unless strong action is taken.[30] This steep decline is the direct result of East Asia's high population growth, the degradation of existing reserves of fresh water and the destruction of water tables through deforestation, urbanisation and environmentally insensitive agricultural practices. The depletion and pollution of groundwater is a particularly serious problem for East Asia because in most countries it supplies more than 50 per cent of fresh-water requirements.[31]

Malaysia

In March 1998, an unusual protest took place outside the house of Selangor state's chief minister. Several hundred residents from a normally peaceful and well-ordered middle-class housing estate on the southern outskirts of Kuala Lumpur gathered to protest against government inaction. The issue was not the economic recession, from which the country was still reeling, or the haze from Indonesia's forest fires, but serious

118   ENVIRONMENTAL SCARCITY

Table 6.1 Annual per capita water availability by region, 1950–2000

('000 m^3)	1950	1960	1970	1980	2000
Latin America	105	80.2	61.7	48.8	28.3
North America	37.2	30.2	25.2	21.3	17.5
Africa	20.6	16.5	12.7	9.4	5.1
Asia	9.6	7.9	6.1	5.1	3.3
Europe	5.9	5.4	4.9	4.4	4.1

Source: FAO, *The State of Food and Agriculture*, 1993, www.fao.org

water shortages afflicting most of the capital and the surrounding Klang valley. By June the Malaysian Government had been forced to impose water rationing on some 2 million people[32] – this in a country which receives 990 billion cubic metres of rainfall each year, enough to cover the entire land surface with 3 metres of water and more than 65 times the amount of water actually used by the country's 22 million people.[33]

The government attributed the shortfalls to the El Niño-induced drought, but the underlying causes were more complex and, like Indonesia's forest fires, attributable to human activities rather than the exigencies of nature. Uncontrolled deforestation from logging and tourist developments in highland catchment areas has reduced the capacity of the soil to hold water and polluted once pristine streams, forcing increasingly frequent closures of water treatment plants. Demand for water has escalated because of population growth, rising standards of living and rapid industrialisation. In the Klang Valley alone, demand is increasing by 9 per cent a year and will exceed the available supply of 3 billion litres a day by 2003 unless more reservoirs are added or wastage reduced. Loss of water pumped into the Klang Valley is high – 16 per cent because of leaking pipes and 12 per cent from theft, according to Malaysian officials.[34] The water infrastructure is old and corroding.[35] Distribution is also a problem. The water is not where it is most needed and expensive distribution systems will have to be laid. Government has been slow to address the issue despite warnings going back two decades that shortages would become endemic by the turn of the century without action to address their underlying causes.

Thailand

In Thailand, unlicensed use of ground water from Bangkok's major aquifer is depleting groundwater supplies and causing the underground water table to fall by up to 60 metres in some places, producing significant land subsidence and allowing salt water to encroach.[36] Pollution from untreated sewage and industrial waste is degrading Thailand's river systems and groundwater. The World Bank has warned the government that municipal authorities will not be able to guarantee drinking water to Bangkok's residents after 2025. Bangkok's water shortages are also taking their toll on food production. The Chao Phraya River basin is critically important because it drains virtually all northern and central areas of the country and provides most of Thailand's agricultural produce. In 1993, however, the Bangkok Metropolitan Waterworks Authority informed Chao Phraya farmers that they would not be able to plant a second rice crop because Bangkok's need for additional water meant that there was no surplus for irrigation.[37] Pressure on the Chao Phraya will continue to grow in line with Bangkok's escalating demand for water, reducing flows to the agricultural sector and the volume of rice that can be grown in the river basin.

Indonesia

After decades of environmental abuse, Indonesia is also beginning to suffer from recurrent water shortages. By 2005, Jakarta will consume 6 times as much water as it did in 1990; by 2025, an estimated 39 million people will live in the greater Jakarta area, placing additional strains on freshwater supplies.[38] Groundwater is expected to provide 27 per cent of the city's additional needs, but the water table is dropping and it is doubtful whether this target can be met. In some parts of Jakarta, seawater has penetrated groundwater up to 8 kilometres inland.[39] There are plans to draw additional supplies from rivers in West Java, but these are themselves under pressure from pollution and increased usage.[40] An associated problem is flooding caused by the destruction of the ecological system in the Jakarta area, especially the disappearance of the lakes and ponds that catch the overflow from monsoon rains.[41] In the early 1990s, a World Bank study estimated that 1 per cent of Jakarta's GDP was being spent on boiling water to make it fit for drinking.[42] In late 1995, Director-General of Water Resources Soeparmono warned that the situation was becoming dangerous.[43] Other cities in Java face comparable problems. The quality and quantity of water from the Brantas River system which supplies Surabaya, Indonesia's second-largest city, are falling rapidly because of unprecedented demand from a rising population and contamination due to urbanisation and industrial run-off.[44]

China

China does not have abundant resources of fresh water, especially in the arid north which contains 550 million people and two-thirds of its cropland. By contrast, the more humid south has four-fifths of the country's water but only one-third of the cropland, a hydrological imbalance that accentuates China's two major water problems: declining reserves and deteriorating water quality.[45] The country ranks sixth in the world in terms of its fresh-water resources, but per capita it is one of the word's most water-deficient states and its reserves of surface and underground water are being depleted at an alarming rate.[46] While China's overall population doubled between 1950 and 1990, its urban population quintupled and the area of irrigated land tripled. Since 1990, the national water deficit has grown sixfold, from 15 million tons a day to around 88 million tons.[47]

Beijing's chronic water shortages are typical. In 1999, the underground water table that supplies two-thirds of its water fell by 3.47 metres in parts of the city because of a drought and accelerating water usage for industry, irrigation and personal consumption. Over the past half-century Beijing's population has tripled and its industrial water use has increased 31 times, while the demand for irrigation has risen by a factor of 23.[48] Zhou Wenzhi, China's Vice Minister of Water Resources, admits that half the country's rivers are polluted and nearly two-thirds of its cities are facing water shortages, which costs China around 3 per cent of GDP and 20 million tonnes of grain annually.[49] The Chinese Academy of Sciences expects water usage to rise 60 per cent over the next half-century, by which time the country will be consuming an unsustainable 28 per cent of usable water reserves.[50]

The Security Implications of Water Scarcity

Unless arrested, the declining quality and per capita supply of fresh water will be detrimental to East Asia's food-producing capacity because East Asia depends on irrigated land for its food to a far greater extent than other regions. While irrigation accounts for over two-thirds of fresh water used globally, in rice-dependent states such as China, 87 per cent of water goes to agriculture mainly because rice is extremely water-intensive.[51] It takes 5000 kilograms of water to produce just 1 kilogram of rice.[52] With industrial and personal consumption accounting for a growing percentage of fresh-water use in East Asia, the net result will be less water for agriculture and an eventual fall in grain yields. Greater reliance on water-efficient crops, more effective water management and reductions in pollution can mitigate agricultural losses, but to do so on the scale needed will require a major change in the way regional states structure their economies and allocate water.[53]

Endemic water scarcity is also likely to pose considerable infrastructural and economic problems for East Asia's developing states as they struggle to meet accelerating demand and preserve existing reserves of water. Some of these challenges will undoubtedly be met by conservation measures, recourse to alternative sources of fresh water, and technological innovation. But there is a limit to the substitutability of naturally occurring water and there must be some doubt about the political commitment of regional governments to water conservation given East Asia's poor track record so far. Technology has its limits too, not least because the financial costs of desalination plants and expensive modern water reticulation systems may be beyond the means of many countries. In the longer term, if current trends continue, water-deficient states will attract significant economic growth penalties. It is estimated, for example, that water shortages cost the Chinese Government between $620 million and $1.06 billion in 1990. These costs will rise substantially in the coming decades.[54]

Population displacement caused by the construction of dams and flood-control reservoirs may prompt political instability and violence within states. In the early 1970s, the Philippines decided to exploit the hydro-electric potential of northern Luzon by building a series of dams on the Chico River. Manila planned to clear large areas of land and to relocate 140 000 people. Local tribespeople resisted the project throughout the 1970s and early 1980s. At first, resistance took the form of peaceful protest, but after the area was militarised by President Ferdinand Marcos, the conflict became violent in 1976. The communist New People's Army (NPA) portrayed itself as the protector of the rights of the local tribespeople. Although the project did not create the NPA, it made local communities sympathetic to the group's anti-government struggle, thereby prolonging its insurgency.[55] By 1980, a hundred people had been killed in fighting and the region had become ungovernable.[56] Six years later, the project was abandoned.

Of course, dams and water reservoirs have always been associated with human development and water management. They are essential for water storage and power generation and can be useful in controlling floods while keeping river channels open for marine transport during periods of low flow. It was not until the middle of the twentieth century, however, that large dams were built with the capacity to fundamentally alter the physical environment.[57] As the number of large dams in East Asia grows in concert with rising demand for energy and water they will inevitably become more contentious because of their adverse effects on the environment and human habitation despite their benefits to agriculture, power and industry.

In Malaysia, for example, there are plans to build a $526 million, 110 metre-high dam on the Selangor River to mitigate Kuala Lumpur's pressing water problems. The dam will increase the volume of water available for industry and personal use but it will also inundate 600 hectares of primary forest in an area known for its beauty and promoted by the tourist

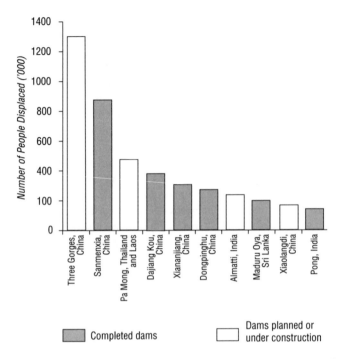

Figure 6.3 Completed and proposed dams that displace the largest number of people
Source: Gleick, *The World's Water 1998–99*, p. 79

industry as a recreation area within easy reach of Kuala Lumpur's suburbs. Opposition to the dam has grown in concert with Malaysians' rising awareness of the direct links between environmental degradation and lifestyles. The smoke haze from Indonesia's 1997 forest fires and the water shortages of 1998 have galvanised anti-dam protests and created an unusual coalition of interests opposed to the dam's construction. Businessmen, fishermen, tour operators, indigenous Temuan people and urban dwellers have joined environmental activists in arguing that the dam should not go ahead.[58] In South Korea, construction of a dam on the Tong River for water supply, flood control and power generation was cancelled by President Kim Dae-jung in June 2000 after a concerted and unprecedented campaign against its construction by environmentalists supported by a majority of the Korean public.[59]

China has the greatest number of dams in East Asia and its situation epitomises the environmental security dilemmas faced by developing states in constructing large dams. Increasing hydro-electric power, controlling floods and providing fresh water are important economic and social objectives for the Chinese Government. Supporters of large dams argue that they are environmentally friendly to the extent that they encourage diversification away from dirty fossil fuels, diminish the severity and frequency of flooding and provide fresh water for agriculture and human consumption in areas where water is in short supply. However, by the government's own admission, many of the nearly 18 000 dams built in China after 1949 were shoddily constructed and are in need of major repair. Three thousand two hundred of these dams have failed, including two in Hunan province that collapsed in 1975 leaving hundreds of thousands dead.[60] The dams have caused a significant reduction in the number of fresh-water fish because of habitat loss and interrupted water flows. Millions of people have been forced to move by rising waters as dams are filled. According to official figures, over 10 million people were displaced by water projects in China between 1960 and 1990.[61]

The massive Three Gorges scheme, which is under construction on the middle reaches of China's longest and most important river, the Yangtse, has reinforced doubts about the viability and wisdom of building dams without assessing fully their environmental and human impact.[62] The Three Gorges Dam, the largest ever built, is officially – and conservatively – estimated to cost $25 billion. But the real cost will almost certainly be much higher, perhaps as much as $72 billion.[63] It will transform the central portion of the Yangtse into a 632 square kilometre lake and generate 18 200 megawatts of electricity by 2009 – approximately the amount produced annually by eighteen nuclear-power stations or 50 million tons of coal. Apart from playing a major role in supplying China's future energy needs, the government expects the dam to control the Yangtse's periodic and disastrous floods.[64]

These are goals which would once have enjoyed considerable financial, political and popular support. The Three Gorges Dam has, however, been widely condemned on economic and environmental grounds. There is widespread scepticism in China, and internationally, about the economic viability of the project. When the Chinese Government first signed off on the project in 1992 it did so in the belief that the country would face a major energy shortfall without the hydro-electric power generated by the dam. Revised projections suggest that China's energy supply has caught up with demand and the dam's power may therefore be underused for many years.[65] The most trenchant criticism, however, has been directed at the environmental destruction caused by the dam's construction and the potential risk to human life should it be breached. The World Bank has refused finance for the project and critics warn that the lake behind the dam could become choked with sewage and industrial chemicals.[66] Many of the industrial sites which will be flooded are saturated with hazardous waste with one – the Chongqing steel mill – once described by the World Bank as among the ten most contaminated industrial sites in the world.[67] Some scientists predict that the sheer weight of the lake could trigger an earthquake, damaging the dam and threatening millions of people downstream.[68]

Environmental concerns coincide with objections against the damage that the dam will inflict on the culturally and historically significant land it will submerge. The Three Gorges project will displace more people than any dam in history – 1.3 million according to Chinese officials, but up to 1.9 million by unofficial estimates. Even more may be displaced if the government speeds up flooding of the dam's reservoir to maximise the output of electricity and reduce its interest payment on the project.[69] Beijing faces the real prospect of social unrest and violence as people are forced to move from ancestral lands. In May 1992, 179 members of the Democratic Youth Party were detained for protesting against the dam and at least 300 locals were involved in an armed clash with police near the dam site in 1993.[70] There have been periodic outbreaks of violence since, sparked by local resentment over perceptions of inadequate compensation. Government officials have also been accused of stealing money intended for compensation, which has fuelled the anger of local communities, many of whom have yet to be allocated new land for resettlement.[71]

The Interstate Dimension

Water scarcity is likely to assume wider significance when it becomes entangled with other sources of tension between states. Water security is a key strategic issue for Singapore. Because of its small size, relatively flat terrain and high population density, Singapore has never been self-sufficient in water, and relies on piped supplies from Malaysia to meet just under 50 per cent of its needs.[72] In 1997, Singapore piped around 1.5 billion litres of untreated water from Malaysia a day, of which 150 million litres were sold back in treated form. In 1961 and 1962, Singapore signed two water-sharing agreements with Kuala Lumpur. Under the 1961 agreement, which expires in 2011, Singapore's Public Utilities Board (PUB) is entitled to draw unlimited water from the Tebrau and Scudai Rivers and the Pontian and Gunong Pulai catchment areas in Malaysia's Johor state. The 1962 agreement, which expires in 2061, allows the PUB to draw up to 1.12 billion litres of water a day from the Johor River. Neither country can unilaterally abrogate these arrangements under the terms of the 'Separation Act', signed on 9 August 1965, which ended Singapore's affiliation with Malaysia.[73]

Since half of Singapore's land area is already used as water catchment, improved conservation and a pricing scheme that more accurately reflects the actual cost of water offer limited scope for increasing domestic supplies. In an effort to diversify away from its reliance on Johor, Singapore has signed an agreement with Indonesia to develop the water resources of nearby Riau province in Sumatra. Singapore hopes that Indonesia will eventually be able to supply 4.5 billion litres of water a day on a long-term basis. Mooting the possibility of future water deals with Indonesia, in January 1999 the chairman of Singapore's Economic Development Board, Philip Yeo, declared that Singapore was looking for '100 years supply at a stable price and quality ... we don't want any short-term arrangement, unlike for gas, which we can always buy anywhere'.[74] In addition to negotiating more water-sharing agreements with Indonesia, Singapore plans to build three desalination plants with the first expected to be operational by 2005.[75] These plants are expensive – about S$1 billion each – and the three plants when fully operational would produce only enough water to meet less than a third of Singapore's domestic shortfall.[76] Singapore will therefore remain dependent on Malaysian water for the foreseeable future. The water relationship between the two states is complicated by Malaysia's own impending water supply problems. Two of the country's most populous states, Negri Sembilan and Selangor – which includes Kuala Lumpur – are soon expected to exhaust their water supplies, with some Malaysian experts predicting that shortages will reach crisis point in 2010.[77]

Singapore's relations with Malaysia have historically been clouded by disagreements stemming from economic competition and political, religious and ethnic differences. These disputes have flared periodically since 1965 and on several occasions Malaysia appears to have contemplated the option of interrupting the supply of water to Singapore as a means of exerting political leverage. In his 1998 memoirs, Singapore's former Prime Minister, Lee Kuan Yew, reveals that Malaysia was prepared to use water as a means of applying economic and political pressure on Singapore after separation in 1965. According to Lee, Malaysia's then Prime Minister, Tunku Abdul Rahman, confided to Britain's High Commissioner to Malaysia on 9 August 1965: 'If Singapore's foreign policy is prejudicial to Malaysia's interests, we could always bring pressure to bear on them by threatening to turn off the water in Johor'.[78] Lee makes clear his belief that the Tunku and his Deputy Prime Minister, Abdul Razak Hussain, were confident that they could control Singapore by closing the Causeway which links the two states and cutting off Singapore's water supply.[79] Lee's typically candid memoirs elicited a curt response from Malaysian Prime Minister Mahathir Mohamad, who pointedly reminded Singaporeans that they profit from the water-sharing arrangement at Malaysia's expense since Singapore makes more money from selling the treated water back to Johor than Malaysia does from selling it to Singapore.[80]

The sharp tone of Mahathir's riposte followed an earlier and more serious row over water in 1997, again precipitated by Lee Kuan Yew.

Reflecting Singapore's concerns over perceived law and order problems in Malaysia, Lee averred that Johor state was 'notorious for shootings, muggings and car-jackings'.[81] Public and press reaction in Malaysia was overwhelmingly critical, and Ahmed Zamid Hamidi, the head of the Youth Wing of Malaysia's ruling party, the United Malays National Organisation (UMNO), urged the government to review the basis of water and air-space agreements with Singapore.[82] Johor Chief Minister Abdul Ghani suggested that Johor should consider taking over two of the three water purification plants on its soil operated by Singapore.[83]

In an unusually frank disclosure to his parliament in June 1997, Singapore's Prime Minister, Goh Chok Tong, recounted the fact that he had raised the water issue with Mahathir at the inaugural Asia–Europe Meeting in Bangkok on 2 March 1996. Goh argued that 'an agreement by Malaysia to meet Singapore's long-term water needs beyond the life of the present water agreements would remove the perception in Singapore that water may be used as a leverage [sic] against Singapore'.[84] Tensions later eased, although, when announcing price increases for water in June 1997, Singapore's Deputy Prime Minister, Lee Hsien Loong, directly linked the rises to the earlier Malaysian threats.

> You have seen how water is an item that can be used to pressure us. The bottom line is: Water is a strategic resource ... It's not like air, which you can have for free. It's not like fuel for buses or cars which you can always import any amount of ... it is something which is limited. When you run out you are up against, if not a brick wall, at least a very, very steep slope. [85]

Following a concerted attempted by Goh to smooth over differences with Mahathir in late 1997 and early 1998, Mahathir expressed his willingness to supply Singapore with water in perpetuity, provided suitable terms could be agreed. However, talks bogged down over the details of a future agreement and became hostage to the political controversy in Malaysia occasioned by the publication of Lee Kuan Yew's memoirs. In September 1998, the water talks were suspended indefinitely.[86]

The Mekong River Basin

Competition for water might also emerge as a source of conflict among the six riparian states of the Mekong River basin in mainland Southeast Asia. At 4350 kilometres in length, the Mekong forms the heart of the largest river system in Southeast Asia. Its geostrategic significance stems from the fact that it is the only major river in East Asia that flows through more than two sovereign states.[87] The Mekong is one of few river systems in the world that remains in a relatively healthy state, largely because it has not yet been fully developed. However, the river's ecosystem is under

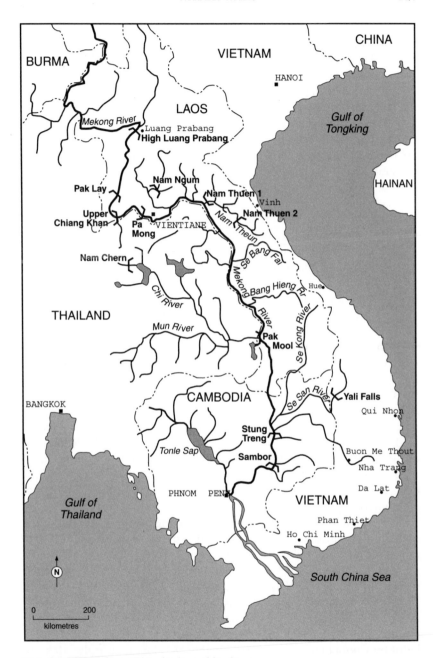

Map 6.1 The Mekong River basin and its dams
Source: Alan Dupont, 'The Environment and Security in Pacific Asia', Adelphi
Paper 31 (Oxford University Press for the International Institute for Strategic
Studies, London, 1998) p. 70.

stress from the 60 million people who directly depend on it for their livelihood and habitat.[88] The Mekong sustains the world's largest freshwater lake, the Tonle Sap, which is vital to Cambodia for fish, irrigation and transport and an important component of the entire Mekong's ecological system, acting as a natural regulator of the river's flow.[89] In 1998, the lake yielded nearly 200 000 tonnes of fish worth about $70 million.[90] The seven Cambodian provinces abutting the lake account for 40 per cent of the country's annual rice production of 2.4 million tonnes, and are home to 4 million of the nation's 9 million people.[91] Over 50 per cent of Cambodia's population live within 5 kilometres of the river and its tributaries.[92] Vietnam is arguably the most dependent of all the Mekong states on the river's resources. The rich floodplain of the Mekong Delta provides more than half of the country's rice, a substantial portion of which is exported, and around 40 per cent of its total agricultural output; some 15 million Vietnamese rely on the Mekong for fish.[93]

Thailand uses the river's waters to irrigate its arid northeastern provinces and plans to harness them for hydro-electric power. Mountainous Laos, the smallest and poorest of the states along the Mekong, sees the river as its economic salvation: 40 per cent of the rivers feeding into the Mekong originate in the mountains and highlands of Laos, and Vientiane has developed plans to build hydro-electric dams on its portion of the river to provide energy for Thailand and Vietnam. The biggest of these dams, the Nam Theun-2, is expected to generate 900 megawatts and increase Laos's GDP by about 15 per cent.[94] China is also beginning to tap the river's hydro-electric potential. The first dam across the Mekong, in China's Yunnan province, began generating electricity in 1993. China plans to build a further fourteen dams in Yunnan alone, five on the Mekong itself and nine on its tributaries. These will produce 20 000 megawatts of power, more than the capacity of the Three Gorges Dam. Altogether, some fifty-four dams are planned or are under way along the length of the Mekong and its tributaries.[95]

The idea of bringing together the states along the lower reaches of the Mekong to harness its resources for flood control, irrigation and hydropower was first mooted in the 1950s.[96] The United Nations established a Mekong Committee in 1957 but successive wars in Indochina prevented significant progress.[97] Negotiations resumed in the early 1990s and, in April 1995, Cambodia, Laos, Thailand and Vietnam signed an historic accord designed to improve the management of the river's waters under the auspices of the Mekong River Commission. Known as the 'Agreement on Cooperation for the Sustainable Development of the Mekong River Basin', the accord allows its members freedom of navigation along the river and establishes a water-sharing regime. The agreement was hailed as a breakthrough in cooperation between states which, only two decades before, were at war.

However, the agreement also contains the seeds of potential future conflict over the Mekong's resources. A key provision allows each state to divert the river's waters without seeking the approval of other members, except during the dry season.[98] This 'no-veto rule' contradicts a 1957 agreement requiring detailed studies by all parties before implementing projects that might affect the flow of the Mekong or its tributaries. Since they are not obliged to secure other states' approval for projects, signatory countries may be tempted to place their short-term interests ahead of the welfare of the river and of the wider subregion. Only eight of the fifty-four Mekong dams envisaged or in operation have been subject to environmental impact studies, and there has been no serious attempt to assess the overall effect of the dams on the Mekong's flow.[99] The minority hill tribes most likely to be affected have been largely ignored in the rush to harness the Mekong's resources. These tribal people have a history of militant opposition to central government control in China, Laos, Burma and Thailand.

China's refusal to sign the 1995 accord also raises doubts about the effectiveness of a cooperative agreement that fails to include the country with the greatest capacity to control the river's flow. China insists that whatever action it takes to exploit the Mekong's potential is purely an internal matter. The Chinese position is complicated by conflict between two politically powerful domestic interests – one favouring development of the Mekong as a transport link while the other wants hydro-power to take priority. The transport lobby opposes dams, believing that they interfere with the flow and navigability of the river. Energy-first proponents are likely to win out, which means that China's ambitious schemes for developing hydro-power will almost certainly go ahead.[100] The construction and operation of the dams will exacerbate soil loss, deforestation and land degradation in the Mekong basin, upsetting the river's ecological balance.

Forest cover in the basin has already declined significantly and as new hydro-electric dams are built, and the Mekong basin develops, the rate of deforestation will accelerate.[101] In the Tonle Sap, the ADB estimates that because of logging and other human encroachments, less than 39 per cent of the original 10 000 square kilometres of flooded forest remains. These forests form the main breeding grounds for the lake's diverse aquatic life.[102] The hydro-electric plans of China and Laos, if fully implemented, will substantially reduce the volume and impact of the river's seasonal flooding. One reservoir planned by the Chinese is of particular concern because it could hold the entire flow of the upper Mekong for up to six months.[103] A scientific study carried out on the environmental effects of damming the Mekong has found that the reduction in water volume will eventually clog its mouth. The river's salinity will also increase and its rich deposits of silt, vital for regenerating the surrounding agricultural land, will disappear. Interrupting the natural cycle of the

Mekong could be fatal for the fresh-water fishing industries of Cambodia and Vietnam.[104] It could also seriously diminish the 'carrying capacity' of the land that provides 40 per cent of Vietnam's agricultural output.[105] These are all potential bones of contention that could result in significant political tensions between downstream and upstream states unless carefully managed.

Conclusion

Perennially dry areas of the world such as the Middle East are accustomed to living without a surfeit of water. Water scarcity, however, is a fairly new experience for East Asian states and a looming resource problem which regional governments are ill equipped to deal with, psychologically and in policy terms. Much of this is due to the persistence of a no longer viable water paradigm that favours irrigation and big dam construction over conservation and sustainable development.[106] East Asia's water supply and demand are subject to much greater fluctuations than those of the Middle East because of demographic factors and wide seasonal variations in rainfall. If the wet season is late, or fails altogether, water supplies may fall abruptly and sharply. In earlier eras, when East Asia's populations were much smaller and relatively dispersed, water shortages tended to be short-term, localised and far more manageable than the man-made, systemic shortages now confronting the region. With the exception of China's arid regions, East Asia's water problems stem not from absolute shortages but relative scarcity, as per capita consumption continues to rise in line with population growth and higher usage rates, while reserves of fresh water decline.

Water shortages will affect the region's security environment in three ways. First, they will aggravate social and political tensions, adding to the internal security challenges faced by the region's developing states. Growing environmental consciousness is changing the security policy climate for large-scale water projects. Dam construction and hydro-electric schemes have entered the realm of high politics as they become lightning rods for domestic dissent and international environmental activism. Dam-related population displacement has the potential to lead to social unrest and violence, as the Philippines and China attest, although probably not on a scale that would result in major conflict or state failure. Nonetheless, environmental opposition to water-related infrastructural projects represents a new security dynamic which governments will henceforth have to factor into their planning, further complicating energy and water allocation choices.

Second, diminishing supplies of fresh water in East Asia will adversely affect key sectors of the region's economy, especially agriculture, reducing the capacity of the region's developing states to feed themselves and forcing them to import more grain. Today's water scarcity may become tomorrow's food shortages because of the crucial role played by irrigation in East Asia's food economy. Should water continue to be diverted from agriculture to meet the demands of industry and rising personal consumption, poorer states may have difficulty in meeting their grain needs in a more competitive international grain market. Without a more holistic and environmentally sensitive approach to water management and conservation, the water shortages predicted by the United Nations are almost certain to eventuate. Even if water is accorded the priority it deserves in government policies, it will take decades to repair the environmental damage that has already been done to the once pristine underground reservoirs and river systems that were millennia in the making. The deterioration in water quality will have particularly serious consequences for the health and human security of the poorer inhabitants of the region. Water-borne diseases are forecast to increase as more rivers and groundwater are contaminated by pollution and salination.

Third, water's salience as a driver of interstate conflict will increase in inverse proportion to its scarcity. This is not to argue that water wars are imminent or inevitable. As with other resource scarcity, there is no inexorable law that mandates a higher incidence of violence and conflict from the declining per capita availability of fresh water in East Asia. Interstate competition for water is virtually always played out against a complex mosaic of related political, social and economic factors. The underlying strength of the political relationship between the states that share water resources is crucial in determining whether or not water disputes will escalate into serious political or military conflict. Countries with shared values and generally cooperative relations are less likely to go to war over water than those with a history of enmity and confrontation. The extent to which water becomes a source of strategic rivalry will also be determined by the degree of scarcity that exists, the ease of access to alternative water resources, and the extent to which the waterway is shared by other states as well as their relative power to one another.[107]

It is difficult to see nations in East Asia going to war over water in the manner that some have predicted for the Middle East. Nevertheless, as economic and political interdependence grows in East Asia, the water problems of one state will become the concern of all. This is especially the case in Southeast Asia, raising the prospect that ASEAN may feel obliged to assist in adjudicating or resolving water disputes between its members. These disputes are most likely to originate in the intensifying subregional competition for the resources of the Mekong River, which could become a catalyst for the reemergence of historical grievances between the six riparian states. Maritime Southeast Asian states share no land or river borders, and so seem less likely to become involved in conflicts over water. However, as the tensions between Malaysia and Singapore demonstrate, disputes over water resources may not be confined to the ownership of underground aquifers or river systems.

This enquiry into East Asia's fresh-water vulnerabilities and the related chapters on energy and food illustrate the changing nature of resource scarcity in East Asia and the new prominence of environmental degradation for state and human security. Throughout history, the competition for resources has been a leading cause of conflict and there have been many instances of local food and water shortages resulting from war, political upheaval and economic failure. However, East Asia's current and prospective resource vulnerabilities have three characteristics that set them apart from the resource competition of earlier eras. First, they involve resources that are fundamental to survival and that were once considered so abundant that they were deemed to be inexhaustible. Second, these regionwide resource vulnerabilities are being made more acute by the destruction and degradation of the natural environment. In the case of energy, environmental factors are making it more difficult for energy-deficient states to reduce their dependence on fossil fuels. Third, although the growing scarcity of renewable resources is aggravating border disputes and creating new tensions between regional states, notably over fish and fresh water, for the most part it is the internal cohesion and stability of the region's poorer states that is most threatened by the prospect of food, water and energy shortfalls.

These scarcities have little to do with the resource competition of earlier eras and the security consequences must be measured in terms of the collective deprivation they represent for all East Asians. This analysis of the environmental causes of conflict and instability in East Asia lends empirical weight to the proposition advanced in the introduction of this book, that the security dynamics of transnational phenomena are more complex and interconnected than the Cold War drivers of conflict. Furthermore, it is clear that environmental degradation also enfeebles states economically and socially. Soil erosion, deteriorating water quality and deforestation reduce state capacity, leading to unemployment, social discontent, further neglect of the environment and destabilising internal migration. Water availability and food production are closely linked, while climate change has the capacity to adversely affect both.

PART II

Unregulated Population Movements

CHAPTER 7

Unregulated Population Movements, Ethnic Conflict and the State

Unregulated population movements have remained at historically high levels for the whole post-Cold War period. Have they become, as the United Nations claims, a 'defining characteristic of the contemporary world', and if so, what are the implications for international security?[1] In considering this question, it is important to recognise that war, persecution, religious discrimination and economic opportunity have always compelled people to migrate with, and without, the consent of their governments. History is replete with examples of communities, polities and civilisations being destroyed, supplanted or enriched by inflows of people from alien cultures and ethnic groups. Mass population movements often accompany major disturbances in the international system caused by the collapse of empires, the failure of ideologies, shifts in the balance of power and war itself.

However, the withering away of the Cold War order has been responsible for enormous changes and instabilities in the international security environment; these have triggered new waves of mass migration that are different, in many respects, from those of the past.[2] Undocumented labour migration has grown enormously in recent decades and now greatly exceeds the number of refugees fleeing political persecution. Refugees and internally displaced people are increasingly the targets of state-sponsored violence or the victims of government neglect. Many people forced to move have nowhere to go. There are no more 'new worlds' waiting to be colonised, while traditional receiving countries are becoming more reluctant to accept migrants. Whereas the direction of migration was once largely from relatively densely populated Europe to the Americas, Africa and Australasia, population movements are today typically within developing states, from the poorer South to the richer North, and increasingly

135

from the South to the South. These shifts – in the pattern of migration and the attitude of the international community towards UPMs – have been profound and are reshaping thinking about security.

Growing acceptance of the link between UPMs and international security masks sharp differences of view over whose security is being threatened – that of the refugees, displaced people and undocumented migrants concerned or that of the receiving countries who host, care and provide for them. Receiving governments tend to regard UPMs as a potential security threat because of their capacity to foment conflict with neighbours or intensify internal ethnic and social divisions. Human rights activists and NGOs, on the other hand, are more likely to see these uprooted people as the innocent victims of state policy, persecution or economic inequality for whom flight may be the ultimate survival strategy.[3] However, as this analysis of East Asia will show, these are not mutually incompatible positions. UPMs are a measure of both human and national insecurity.

The following two chapters explore the complex forces that are propelling UPMs to the forefront of international and East Asian security concerns. If contemporary UPMs are different from earlier patterns of migration, what are their underlying dynamics and why are UPMs increasing at a time when the incidence of major interstate war – a key driver of past UPMs – is declining? The answers suggest a far more complex and fluid security paradigm than that envisaged by realists, one in which states are both imperilled by, and responsible for, mass population movements that are rarely the result of power-balancing, strategic competition or ideological contention.

East Asia will continue to be one of the regions most seriously affected by UPMs as well as a primary source of illegal migrants for the developed world. There is no simple explanation for the rapid increase in UPMs that has occurred since the mid-1970s, a trend that shows every sign of continuing in the decades ahead. Several interconnected global and regional transnational forces are at work. Some are political in character and effect, others are predominantly social, economic or environmental. It is argued here that there are five major drivers of UPMs in East Asia:

- the persistence of ethnic conflict
- government policies
- the involvement of criminal groups in people-smuggling
- the rise in undocumented labour migration because of the region's sustained economic growth
- East Asia's deteriorating physical environment.

Why Do People Migrate?

The relationship between UPMs and security cannot be understood without an appreciation of the 'push-pull' forces that induce people to migrate. International population movements were generally restricted in time and place until the great European exodus to the New World began in the early 1820s. In the following hundred years, approximately 50 million people emigrated from Europe to the distant imperial colonies and emerging proto-states of Africa, Australasia and the Americas.[4] This sustained human exodus accounted for 5 per cent of the world's population of 1 billion and had enduring demographic and strategic consequences. As populations in the New World increased, the political and economic centre of gravity inexorably shifted away from Europe towards North America. The colonisation and exploitation of East Asia by the European powers eventually gave rise to indigenous independence movements and created the political and social conditions for East Asia's eventual reemergence as a locus of world power.

Why did so many people move over such vast distances to foreign shores? The New World beckoned with the promise of bounty, opportunity and above all land, while the prevailing dismal conditions in Europe, as Alfred Crosby notes, provided a considerable push. Some fled the destructive and corrosive effects of war and natural disaster, others the tyranny of dictatorship, while still more left their homes in search of profit and a better life. A population explosion and shortages of cultivable land were important catalysts; advances in transportation, especially steam power, facilitated long-distance ocean and land travel.[5] Refugees formed a significant part of the European diaspora. Often mistakenly considered a twentieth-century phenomenon, the term 'refugee' has been used since the seventeenth century to differentiate political exiles from economic migrants.[6] The early refugee-exiles were generally small in number and relatively well off compared with the peasants and urban poor who made up the vast bulk of European emigrants. The fate of radical political activists from the lower classes was usually execution or penal servitude in remote colonies.[7] Internally displaced people fleeing religious pogroms and persecution, who remained within their country of citizenship, were not regarded as refugees although the political and social causes of their flight were essentially the same.

After the First World War, the collapse of the Ottoman and Austro-Hungarian empires in conjunction with the Russian Revolution resulted in the displacement of an estimated 20 million people and the establishment of an embryonic refugee regime under the aegis of the League of Nations. While the League was able successfully to manage the initial crisis, its ad hoc approach prevented it from adequately addressing the root causes of displacement and forced migration.[8] A second major upsurge in refugee flows, numbering 20–30 million people, occurred immediately after the Second World War and led to the creation of the Office of the UN High Commissioner for Refugees. Many of these refugees were ethnic Germans driven from Russia and other parts of Eastern Europe. About 2 million are thought to have died as a consequence of exposure, starvation or outright violence.[9] It is a sobering reminder of how entrenched the problem of UPMs has since become that the UNHCR was initially given only a limited mandate and was not expected to last more than three years.[10] In the following three decades international migration flows were generally of modest size. Originating primarily in war-torn Europe, they were, to a large extent, regulated by receiving governments.[11] There were, however, periods when bouts of political and military strife stimulated substantial outflows of UPMs in specific states and subregions. Notable East Asian examples are the civil war in China during the late 1940s, the Korean War, and the long-running Indochina conflicts.

Surging Global UPMs

Notwithstanding periodic refugee 'crises', the unregulated movement of people was not an issue that commanded the attention of national security communities during the Cold War. Attitudes began to change, however, as the volume of refugees and displaced persons began to spiral upward at the end of the 1980s, dampening optimism that the end of the Cold War would herald a new era of peace and stability. An analysis of the growth in refugee numbers during the last quarter of the twentieth century is revealing. In 1975, there were around 2.4 million refugees globally, but the number of refugees and people of concern to the UNHCR grew tenfold in the following two decades, peaking in 1995 at 27.4 million. Included in this figure were 14.5 million refugees, 5.4 million internally displaced people and another 3.5 million who were not considered by the UN to have met the refugee criteria but were nevertheless considered to be in refugee-like situations.[12] Since 1995, the number of refugees has declined slightly, mainly because of the successful implementation of several ambitious repatriation programs, but they still remain at historically high levels.[13] While there are fewer asylum-seekers fleeing political persecution, the victims of forced displacement had increased to more than 50 million by the end of the decade, because of an upsurge in civil wars and internal unrest. Many of these people fall outside the care of the UNHCR.[14] To this figure can be added at least another 30 million labour migrants who are working illegally in foreign countries.[15] Altogether there are probably around 100 million refugees, internally displaced people and undocumented labour migrants worldwide.

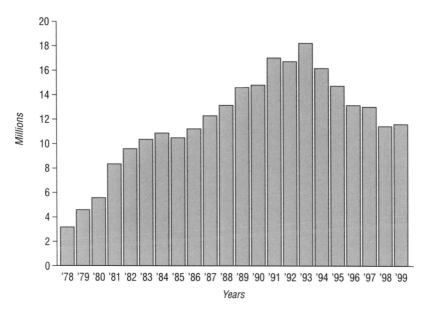

Figure 7.1 Global refugee population, 1978–99
Source: UNHCR, *The State of the World's Refugees: Fifty Years of Humanitarian Action*, 1997, www.un.org.ch/refworld/pub/state/97/ch2.htm and updated figures: www.unhcr.ch/sowr2000/toc2.htm

Three important conclusions can be drawn from these statistics. First, the volume and geographical spread of today's UPMs has few historical parallels. In the first decade after the Cold War, the number of refugees globally averaged 15 million a year, while twenty-five countries and territories were responsible for more than half a million uprooted people each, compared with only thirteen countries in 1990.[16] Even before the 1999 Kosovo crisis, sectarian conflict in the former Republic of Yugoslavia alone had created 4 million refugees and displaced people, representing the largest population movement in Europe since the end of the Second World War.[17] Second, UPMs seem to be occurring regularly and with little prior warning.[18] Third, unlike past UPMs which were episodic and driven by seminal events such as major war between states, those of the post-Cold War period have been sustained over longer periods and are being stimulated by economic opportunism and environmental decline as well as government fiat and rising levels of intra-state violence. The influence of these new drivers is evident in the falling proportion of refugees globally which, according to the UN High Commissioner for Refugees, 'now constitute little more than half of the people who are protected and assisted by the UNHCR'.[19]

Receiving countries, worried about the adverse political and social consequences of escalating levels of UPMs, have become appreciably less tolerant of migrants as public opinion has grown more hostile and fear-ful. In France, the government is determined to reduce the inflow of migrants from its former African colonies, while traditionally tolerant Germany has tightened entry requirements.[20] When the Schroder gov-ernment attempted to reform and liberalise the 1913 citizenship law it was strenuously opposed by conservative opponents who complained that the proposed reforms would divide Germany and erode national sovereignty. German angst is symptomatic of the impotence that many European nations feel when confronted with the political, social and cul-tural challenge of unregulated migrant flows. All over Europe, barriers to migrants are going up in the form of narrower, more restrictive asylum criteria, reduced migrant intakes, and increased fines and other sanc-tions for those who harbour or provide employment for undocumented migrants.[21] Some observers have predicted that once the regulatory regime governing political asylum in Europe comes into full effect, refugees may be effectively defined out of existence.[22] At least one major report has found that Europe has effectively been operating a zero immi-gration policy since the 1970s.[23]

UPMs in East Asia

Europe's growing refugee problem should not obscure the fact that 85 per cent of the world's refugees and displaced persons are located in developing states and not the affluent West.[24] At the end of the 1990s, Asia as a whole hosted more refugees and internally displaced people than any other region of the world. In East Asia there are an estimated 2–3 million refugees and internally displaced people as well as 4–5 million undocu-mented labour migrants.[25] The wave of new restrictions on migrants in Europe has yet to be emulated in East Asia, in part because many regional states already have strict citizenship requirements and narrowly defined refugee criteria. However, East Asian governments have become far more sensitive to the political and security ramifications of UPMs than they were during the Cold War. Illegal migration features regularly in 'second-track' security forums like CSCAP and the security 'roundtables' held annually in Kuala Lumpur.[26] The subject is also discussed in multilateral 'first-track' forums such as the ASEAN Regional Forum (ARF) and appears with increasing frequency on the security and foreign policy agendas of regional states.

The state with the greatest capacity to affect the future volume and direction of UPMs is China, because of its location, size and population. China has land and sea borders with over half the countries of East Asia and a serious unemployment problem. Large numbers of people have relocated from rural to urban areas, forming a vast itinerant pool of potentially disaffected citizens numbering more than 100 million people.[27] China is also a significant source of illegal migrants for East Asia and North America. Increasing numbers of Chinese will be prepared to risk the hazards and costs of clandestine emigration if the government cannot offer them a reasonable prospect of employment, or an adequate social security system to replace the 'iron rice bowl' once provided by the state. An admittedly worst-case scenario, but nevertheless one which virtually all China's neighbours fear, is that major internal political instability or civil strife could stimulate a refugee crisis that would dwarf all previous UPMs, creating a serious security problem for the whole region.

However, affluence rather than instability is a more likely catalyst. Emigration climbs when countries emerge from poverty. It is no coincidence that the rise in people-smuggling from China has paralleled its economic resurgence. Jack Goldstone estimates that even under favourable scenarios of political stability and economic growth, illegal Chinese migration to the United States will probably increase by a factor of 10, rising to between 200 000 and 300 000 by 2005.[28] Extrapolating from these estimates, there is a high probability that more and more illegal Chinese migrants will seek employment opportunities closer to home in East Asia. If these predictions are borne out, migration-induced tensions between China and the rest of the region could reawaken latent historical animosities and fuel anxieties about China's potential to promote its political and strategic influence through its expanding diaspora. The new wave of Chinese migrants are, on the whole, more assertively nationalist than their predecessors, having grown up in a China that is now an established global power. Consequently, they are more likely to identify with China than with their adopted countries, which over time could inflame extant anti-Chinese feeling in receiving states.

Upwardly mobile Chinese workers are already seeking their fortune in Japanese cities and towns, giving rise to fears that areas like Kabuchiko, Tokyo's largest entertainment district, are being taken over by Chinese business and criminal interests and are becoming a magnet for illegal workers from China.[29] Officials in Moscow harbour the fear that sparsely populated Siberia may be infiltrated and eventually overwhelmed by illegal immigrants from China's adjacent provinces.[30] Russians have not forgotten how China almost succeeded in annexing Manchuria by encouraging Han Chinese to settle there during Tsarist times before the Russian army forcibly expelled or killed the newcomers and sealed the border.[31] In many Southeast Asian states, tensions between Chinese émigré communities and indigenous groups are never far from the surface and commonly erupt into intercommunal violence and confrontation during periods of political instability and economic recession.

Uncontrolled migration from China, both actual and hypothetical, is by no means the only concern of East Asia's receiving states. Virtually every country in East Asia has experienced significant population movements over the past few decades and many governments see UPMs as an emerging security issue for the wider region.[32] South Korean officials, who once made much of the threat posed by a hostile, nuclear-capable North Korea, are these days more inclined to worry about an inflow of refugees from across the border in the event of the collapse of the North Korean state. Some 200 000 North Koreans thought to be living illegally overseas, mainly in China and Russia, could constitute the vanguard of a major refugee problem for Moscow and Beijing if living conditions in North Korea were to deteriorate further.[33]

In ethnically diverse Southeast Asia, the emergence of UPMs as a serious security issue can be traced back to the well-documented and long-running saga of the Vietnamese 'boat people', an exodus which began in 1975 after the fall of South Vietnam and continued unabated for twenty years. The United Nations estimates that 840 000 people departed Vietnam by boat during this period, although the real figure is almost certainly higher as many perished at sea or were captured and killed by pirates.[34] Around 200 000 made their way to Hong Kong; the remainder ended up in temporary refugee camps throughout East Asia before eventually being resettled in the West or repatriated to Vietnam.[35] Vietnam's neighbours were forced to bear a large proportion of the political and economic costs associated with the continuing refugee outflow. By the end of the 1980s, tolerance and understanding of the boat people's plight had given way to compassion fatigue and the perception that many of the boat people were economic migrants rather than genuine refugees fleeing from political persecution.

Hong Kong was the first to break ranks in 1988 when it declared that each newly arrived Vietnamese would henceforth be individually screened for refugee status rather than being automatically classified as a political refugee. A year later, first-asylum countries in East Asia reached agreement with the UNHCR and Western resettlement states on a Comprehensive Plan of Action which endorsed the Hong Kong approach of individual refugee assessment, and mandated resettlement in third countries or repatriation by June 1996.[36] In January 1996, the Chinese government renewed its warning to the United Kingdom that it must accept responsibility for the entire repatriation and resettlement costs of the 21 000 Vietnamese boat people remaining in Hong Kong before the mid-1997 handover of the colony to Beijing. This warning came almost at the same time that a meeting of ASEAN delegates in Bangkok made it clear to Vietnam that it must accept the repatriation of some 40 000 Vietnamese who were still in camps around the region. Vietnam's ASEAN colleagues argued that such people were not bona fide refugees and therefore not entitled to resettlement in another country. Malaysia and the Philippines took steps to forcibly repatriate the remaining Vietnamese from holding camps in their respective countries, and other East Asian states soon followed suit.[37] The remaining elements of an estimated 1.5 million Vietnamese refugees were finally resettled or repatriated in 1998.[38]

Compared with the extensive media and scholarly coverage of the Vietnamese boat people issue, other UPMs in Southeast Asia have received scant attention despite the political and social tensions they are generating.[39] Thailand, for example, gave sanctuary to 360 000 Lao asylum-seekers between 1975 and 1997 in addition to providing a temporary home for 160 000 Vietnamese and large numbers of Cambodians.[40] Thailand has also been a reluctant host to refugees and illegal migrants from Burma. Senior Thai officials calculate the number of illegal migrants at between 500 000 and 700 000, but some NGOs believe that the real number may be as high as 1.75 million. Another 500 000 to 1 million internally displaced people are camped along Burma's eastern border with Thailand, forming a human reservoir of potential refugees and illegal workers.[41] Substantial numbers of refugees fleeing domestic instability in Cambodia have maintained an almost permanent presence at border refugee camps inside Thailand since the mid-1970s.[42] Worsening civil strife in Indonesia has forced many ethnic Chinese to flee and caused large-scale population displacements in Kalimantan, the Moluccas and East Timor.

Ethnic Conflict and Migration

As Indonesia attests, ethno-nationalism remains a primary source of political and social tension in East Asia and has long been responsible for refugee flows and forced migration, particularly among the multi-ethnic states of Southeast Asia. Since recorded history began, East Asia has been shaped by the migration of successive waves of ethnically distinct traders, seafarers, warriors and their communities, moving south and east from the hinterland and extremities of China and Mongolia into Japan, Korea, and Southeast Asia. They, in turn, were followed by seaborne traders, scholars and priests from Arabia and Persia, and then by the colonising European powers who stimulated the first intra-regional labour flows. The enduring legacies of these historical movements of people include the development of an influential and ethnically separate Chinese diaspora numbering over 50 million people;[43] the establishment of patterns of conquest (of existing communities by new arrivals) and assimilation (of the new arrivals by established communities); and a recognition by East Asia's political and military elites that migration straddles the divide between high and low politics.[44]

Of course, East Asia is not the only region rent by ethnic strife. Ethnic differences in multi-ethnic states, which constitute the vast majority of the world's nearly 200 nations, continue to exert a powerful, discordant influence on the international system and are a root cause of the intra-state violence that has supplanted classical interstate warfare as the dominant form of contemporaneous conflict. Of the twenty-three major conflicts recorded in 1994, eighteen were due primarily to communal rivalries and ethnic challenges to states. These, and other ethno-nationalist clashes, accounted for three-quarters of the world's refugees and displaced persons.[45] Although the level and frequency of ethnic and religious warfare globally has subsided after peaking in the mid-1990s, in East Asia ethno-religious rebellions have spread and intensified in the wake of the economic crisis and a resurgence of political Islam.[46]

The four states considered to have the most significant subnational ethnic conflicts are China (Tibet, Inner Mongolia and Xinjiang); Indonesia (Aceh, Kalimantan, the Moluccas and Irian Jaya); the Philippines (Mindanao); and Burma (several ethnic minority groups, especially the Karen, Shan, Kachin and Wa).[47] By their very nature, however, ethnic conflicts are seldom confined within the borders of a single state. Vietnam's border dispute with Cambodia, for example, has been complicated by ethnic tensions and the trans-border movement of minorities, particularly from Vietnam to Cambodia. In 1993, before the UN-sponsored elections in Cambodia, up to 50 000 mainly illegal Vietnamese migrants crossed into Cambodia in order to take advantage of a construction boom in Phnom Penh and economic opportunities elsewhere in Cambodia.[48] The Khmer Rouge seized on their presence to reignite traditional anti-Vietnamese sentiment among Cambodians, claiming that the Vietnamese were once again seeking to impose their hegemony on the country. The presence of a substantial Vietnamese community in Cambodia remains a sensitive political and security issue for both Phnom Penh and Hanoi.[49]

When people flee across national borders as refugees their choice of refuge is determined as much by ethnic bonds as geographical proximity or ease of access. Kathleen Newland has drawn attention to the reality that ethnicity is not only a cause of flight but also largely determines where people go and how they are welcomed by receiving countries.[50] States that share common borders frequently become unwilling hosts to refugees because their ethnic make-up is the same as those of persecuted or defeated ethnic minorities seeking asylum. In 1991, 280 000 Muslim Rohingya refugees uprooted by the Burmese Army sought asylum in Bangladesh, mainly because of ethnic and family ties.[51] Ethnicity may also be a reason for refusing sanctuary. The reluctance of Southeast Asian countries to permanently resettle Chinese and Vietnamese boat people was partly motivated by fear of upsetting their own delicate ethnic balances.

Ethnic minorities, forced to become refugees in neighbouring states because of political persecution, commonly prosecute wars and political violence against their former governments, fuelling tensions between their home and host states. Ethnic and religious violence in China's remote but strategically important western province of Xinjiang has compelled many indigenous ethnic Uighurs, the oldest Turkic people in the world, to flee into neighbouring Kazakhstan, Kyrgyzstan and Tajikistan.[52] The root of the problem is the Uighur belief that China is deliberately encouraging Han migration to the resource-rich province in order to disempower and isolate the Muslim Uighurs, who are already a minority in Xinjiang. Agreements opposing separatism signed in 1996 between China and these states have done little to deter Uighur dissidents from carrying out cross-border sabotage, bombings and other acts of violence into Xinjiang Province.[53] The conflict is likely to intensify after warnings by the exiled leader of the Eastern Turkestan Freedom Organisation, Erkin Alptekin, that Uighurs intend to step up their campaign against Chinese rule. In June 2000, Alptekin spoke for many Uighurs when he complained that population transfer, birth control and the systematic Sinoisation of the Uighur language were driving his people 'into a corner'.[54]

Multi-ethnic Indonesia is a pertinent illustration of how ethnic rivalries, in concert with religious differences and misplaced government policies, can inflame intercommunal tensions, leading to violent conflict and internal displacement, sometimes on a large scale. In March 1999, President Habibie's foreign policy adviser, Dewi Fortuna Anwar, addressed a gathering in Canberra of senior military officers and defence officials from Indonesia and Australia. She warned that unless religious and ethnic conflicts in Indonesia were controlled, they could cause the failure of the Indonesian state and result in refugee flows on a scale not seen since the end of the Vietnam War. Such flows, Anwar maintained, would not only threaten Indonesia's security but also 'the stability of the Asia and Pacific region as a whole'.[55] The reasons for her concern are not hard to find. Beset by economic problems and political turmoil, ethnic conflict has flared across the Indonesian archipelago, especially in Kalimantan and the once tranquil island of Ambon, best known as the centre of Indonesia's centuries-old spice trade.

In southwest Kalimantan, ethnic clashes between indigenous Dayaks and immigrants from the island of Madura date back to the 1950s. They became more frequent during the 1990s as the Dayaks came under increasing economic pressure from a steady influx of commercially astute and culturally assertive Madurese migrants, whom the Dayaks feared would eventually dispossess them of their land and traditional way of life.[56] A serious outbreak of hostilities in late 1996 and early 1997 resulted in the slaughter of over 600 Madurese and forced many thousands out of their homes and villages.[57] Malaysia temporarily closed the border crossing points into Sarawak and reinforced police border units.[58] Worse was to follow. A second bout of ethnic cleansing in January 1999 forced virtually the whole Madurese community to flee for their lives amid previously unseen levels of violence and bloodshed. Hundreds more were killed and at least 29 000 settlers were evacuated by the Indonesian armed forces. Plans to resettle the Madurese on two islands near the provincial capital of Pontianak foundered when they were branded as 'an insult to the dignity of the whole Madurese community' by local legislators.[59]

Intercommunal tensions fuelled by ethnic and religious differences partly account for the equally bloody clashes between Muslims and Christians on the island of Ambon that began in the same month as the Dayak led anti-Madurese pogrom. Like Kalimantan, however, migration was a cause as well as a consequence of the conflict. For centuries Muslim Bugis, Buton and Makassarese – colloquially known as 'BBM' – from South Sulawesi have ranged across the Indonesian archipelago. During the 1950s many of them settled in Ambon, reinforcing the ethnic, religious and geographic divide between the Muslim north and Christian south of the island. Antipathy towards the BBM migrants from native Christians grew in direct proportion to their commercial and political success. Antipathy turned to alarm when a Muslim governor was appointed in 1992 and Muslims began to make inroads into the bureaucracy, traditionally dominated by Christians.

A seemingly trivial street brawl between a Christian bus driver and Muslim passenger was the match that ignited long-suppressed emotions. During a three-month period beginning on 19 January 1999, as many as 1000 people were killed and the island's economy and infrastructure devastated. More than 50 000 BBM, Javanese and Sumatran settlers fled Ambon in one of the largest forced displacements of people in Southeast Asia since the Vietnam War. This human tragedy was made more poignant by the fact that returning BBMs found themselves unwelcome in their South Sulawesi home towns because of demographic pressures and recession-induced economic hardship.[60] Widespread fighting and civil disorder spread throughout the Moluccas and into neighbouring Sulawesi in the following months. By June 2000, at least 3000 people had been killed and another 110 000 internally displaced people were either sheltering in Ambon or had sought refuge elsewhere in the archipelago, forcing President Wahid to announce a state of emergency.[61]

Ethnic differences also played a role in the East Timor conflict and the mass population movements that preceded East Timor's independence. Throughout the twenty-four years of Indonesia's occupation, the predominantly Catholic indigenous East Timorese resented Javanese and Bugis domination of the island's economy and political institutions.

Many East Timorese regarded Muslim immigration from other parts of the archipelago as a deliberate attempt by Jakarta to change the island's ethnic and religious balance. Rising Christian hostility towards the Muslim community precipitated anti-Muslim riots in 1995, forcing many Javanese and Bugis from East Timor.[62] In the backlash that followed, several prominent Indonesian Muslim organisations urged the Suharto Government to take a firmer hand against Timorese 'dissidents' and threatened retribution against Christian communities.[63] Following President Habibie's decision, in January 1999, to allow the East Timorese to choose between independence or integration with Indonesia, a second wave of 26 000 Javanese and Bugis fled the island.

The Role of the State

While states worry about population movements that are outside their control, governments themselves often determine their scale, direction and composition. Sometimes this is a function of government weakness rather than a conscious policy decision. UPMs are commonly associated with politically weak or disrupted states, but even relatively strong central governments may be incapable of controlling outlying regions where borders are contested, porous or too long to police effectively.[64] However, refugees and displaced communities are also manipulated and exploited by states to further foreign policy or strategic interests.[65] During the Balkans conflict whole communities were displaced or expelled as a deliberate act of state policy. In 1995, Tadeusz Mazowiecki, the UNHCR's special rapporteur in Bosnia, observed that 'the population transfers were not the consequence' of the war in Bosnia, but its purpose'.[66] Yugoslav President Slobodan Milosevic emptied Kosovo of ethnic Albanians in a calculated act of ethnic cleansing designed to entrench Serb dominance over the province. Over 1 million Kosovo Albanians were forced to flee, mainly into neighbouring Macedonia and Albania, in one of the largest refugee flows seen in modern European history.[67] On several occasions, Yugoslav Army units used the displaced Kosovo Albanians as human shields to deter NATO air strikes.[68]

Several months later, in scenes chillingly reminiscent of Kosovo, thousands of East Timorese were uprooted when pro-Indonesian militia attacked their villages and threatened further violence if they did not vote for integration in the UN-sponsored August 1999 ballot.[69] Following the overwhelming rejection of autonomy with Indonesia by nearly 80 per cent of East Timorese voters, virtually all of East Timor's 830 000 people were displaced as the result of the militia campaign of intimidation and violence. A quarter of a million East Timorese were forced at gunpoint into military trucks and taken across the border into West Timor in an apparent attempt, by the Indonesian military, to discredit the ballot and to eliminate the support base of the East Timorese resistance. Many others simply disappeared or were killed by marauding bands of militia.[70]

Beijing's policy of settling ethnic Han people in Tibet and Hanoi's decision to allow Vietnamese farmers to cross the border and establish themselves in eastern and southeastern Cambodia after its 1978 invasion are two instances where East Asian governments have encouraged migration primarily for political and security reasons. In both cases, the underlying objective was to secure sensitive border regions and circumscribe the influence and activities of troublesome indigenous communities. There are strong indications that Hanoi manipulated the flow of boat people to extract aid and concessions from the West during the 1980s. The Vietnamese Government initially did little to prevent vessels illegally departing the country when most were filled with ethnic Chinese from southern Vietnam. During the 'high tide' of this exodus in the late 1970s and early 1980s, up to 50 000 mainly Sino-Vietnamese refugees were arriving on East Asian shores and across land borders every month, fuelling suspicion among ASEAN receiving states that Vietnam was intent on using the refugees to subvert and destabilise non-communist Southeast Asia.[71] After concerted international pressure, Hanoi began actively to discourage illegal emigration, and outflows quickly dwindled to about 6000 a month.[72] Vietnam's willingness to stem the flight of people from its shores was clearly a quid pro quo for Western agreement to support Vietnam's integration into the world economy, which was, and remains, one of Hanoi's principal economic and foreign policy objectives.[73]

Elsewhere in Southeast Asia, the presence of large numbers of Burmese refugees along Thailand's western border has been a major source of contention between Rangoon and Bangkok for many decades. Thai and Burmese officials have met on numerous occasions to discuss the cross-border flow of refugees, but efforts to resolve the problem have been hampered by mutual suspicion and Rangoon's belief that the Thai military has aided some of the insurgents fighting the Burmese Government.[74] In January and February 1997, Rangoon sanctioned a series of provocative cross-border raids by the Burmese Army and its surrogate Democratic Karen Buddhist Army on several large refugee camps inside the Thai border populated by ethnic Karens. The Karen refugees were loyal to the Karen National Union, the only major ethnic army in Burma that had refused to accept Rangoon's ceasefire offer. Thousands of refugees were compelled to flee and hundreds of buildings destroyed.

The timing and ferocity of the attacks seemed inopportune coming on the eve of Burma's admission into ASEAN. But the State Peace and Development Council (SPDC) shrewdly calculated that Thailand's reaction would be muted by its desire not to encourage further Karen migration. By instigating violence against the camps, the Burmese clearly hoped to force the Karen National Union into negotiations, destroy their support base in the refugee camps and pressure the Thais into repatriating the refugees back to Burma. Although the Thai Army rushed heavy reinforcements to the Mae Sot area immediately after the incursions, including armoured personnel carriers and helicopter gunships, the Chavalit Government resiled from taking strong political or military action against the encroaching Burmese forces for fear of inflaming the situation. Some Thai Army units forced Karen refugees back across the border into Burma, drawing criticism from Thailand's liberal press and the United States, as well as expressions of concern from the UNHCR. About 100 000 Karen and Karenni continue to eke out a living in Thai refugee camps along the border with Burma.[75]

Thailand has not been averse to manipulating refugee communities for its own political and strategic ends. For almost two decades, Thailand tolerated Khmer Rouge units operating from refugee camps inside Thailand because Thai governments of all political persuasions regarded the Khmer Rouge as a useful buffer against the traditional enemy, Vietnam. Soon after invading Cambodia in Christmas 1978, the Vietnamese Army succeeded in cantoning the bulk of the Khmer Rouge forces in jungle redoubts along the Thai border, forcing thousands of fleeing civilians into Thailand. Vietnam's occupation of Cambodia created alarm and consternation in Thailand, reawakening deep-seated fears that Vietnam was intent on dominating Indochina.[76] Following the time-honoured tradition of 'my enemy's enemy is my friend', the Thai military high command elected to arm and supply Khmer Rouge soldiers and allow them to use the refugee camps on the Thai side of the border as a sanctuary from pursuing Vietnamese forces. The Thai Army also provided assistance to other Cambodian factions among the refugees and attempted to create a *cordon sanitaire* along their eastern border. Frustrated that they were not able to eliminate the Khmer Rouge camps inside Thailand, the Vietnamese army deliberately targeted the refugee camps, shelling them regularly during the 1980s and occasionally straying across the border in 'hot pursuit' operations which precipitated several serious border clashes with the Thai Army.[77]

In the interests of enhancing its political, strategic and trade links with Beijing, Rangoon has allowed Chinese businessmen and migrant workers into northern Burma since a peace settlement was concluded with the Chinese-sponsored Burmese Communist Party and the Wa ethnic minority in the early 1990s.[78] This was a major change in policy for the fiercely independent Burmese and would have been inconceivable during former President Ne Win's long tenure in office. Chinese businessmen and migrant workers, mainly from Yunnan province, have moved into northern Burma, taking advantage of burgeoning Sino-Burmese ties to purchase shops, restaurants, hotels and karaoke bars. In the late 1990s, a second wave of Chinese agricultural workers and labourers whose lands had been inundated by flooding in southern China began to appear, some of whom held Burmese identity cards obtained from corrupt officials. One million Chinese are estimated to have entered Burma between 1996 and 1999, many of them illegally.[79] Fearing a backlash from local communities and worried about the strategic implications of excessive dependence on China, Burma's SPDC has tightened up on cross-border trade and Chinese migration.[80] A wholesale repatriation of Chinese migrants is unlikely, however, while China remains Burma's most important ally and trading partner.

In order to exert political pressure on other states, political leaders have even threatened to encourage illegal migration. Former US President Jimmy Carter was put on notice by his Chinese counterpart, Deng Xiaoping, that the United States might not welcome the consequences of a more liberal Chinese attitude towards human rights. When Carter complained to Deng about restrictions on the movement of Chinese citizens during an official visit to Beijing in the late 1970s, Deng responded by asking Carter how many million Chinese migrants the United States would like to take.[81] Malaysia's combative Prime Minister, Mahathir Mohamad, argued at the height of the Asian economic crisis that developing nations should swamp Europe and the United States with illegal migrants if they insisted on recolonising the South using globalisation as a pretext. In an attack on the Group of Seven (G7) industrialised nations, the World Bank, the International Monetary Fund (IMF) and the European Union, Mahathir asserted that 'people mobility' was the ultimate weapon of the developing South. 'Masses of Asians and Africans should inundate Europe and America', he said, if undeveloped nations were not 'allowed to prosper in a borderless world'.[82]

It is not uncommon for governments to forcibly uproot their people for economic reasons, to relieve population pressures, or as a means of social control. In 1997, Laos initiated a plan to relocate 300 000 families, representing nearly a third of the country's total population. The government in Vientiane justified this massive displacement by arguing that it would reduce or eliminate unproductive agricultural practices and allow the construction of dams and infrastructure deemed critical to economic development. However, the scheme has contributed little to the security or welfare of the affected families, who have suffered widespread impoverishment, emotional trauma and high mortality rates.[83]

In some instances, entire classes of people whose existence is considered to be inimical to the interests of the ruling elite have been relocated, expelled or eliminated. Vietnam tacitly encouraged the departure of several hundred thousand long-standing ethnic Chinese residents back to

China before and after military hostilities with Beijing in 1979, of whom 285 000 are still in southern China.[84] Pol Pot's Khmer Rouge expelled the 300 000 Vietnamese residents of Cambodia in 1975, and systematically eliminated other minority groups like the Chams before turning their machetes, hoes and guns on their own population.[85] Some 450 000 people were forced to flee Cambodia into Vietnam and Thailand during the Khmer Rouge's four-year reign of terror from 1975 to 1979.[86] They were the fortunate ones. Almost the entire Cambodian population of 8 million people became part of a massive slave labour force, who lived and died at the whim of Khmer Rouge cadres. Two million did not survive.[87] The Khmer Rouge is not the only Marxist regime in East Asia to use population relocation as an instrument of policy. In 1999, the regime of Kim Jong-il began a five-year program intended to relocate up to 2 million people from Pyongyang and other cities to the countryside.[88] The aim of the program was to increase agricultural production in the famine-stricken nation and lessen the potential for civil unrest in the politically sensitive cities. If fully implemented, it would be the largest forcible relocation of people in East Asia since the Khmer Rouge depopulated the cities and towns of Cambodia.

Conclusion

Ethno-nationalist conflicts, far from proving evanescent as Marxist theorists once argued, have increased in intensity and frequency in many parts of East Asia and will remain a leading cause of UPMs, notwithstanding claims to the contrary.[89] Indonesia's post-Suharto travails account for some of the rise in ethnic violence, but it must be remembered that ethno-nationalism is endemic throughout the region and will remain a potent cause of instability in Southeast Asia and in China's fractious outlying provinces of Xinjiang and Tibet. Ethnic differences are a primary cause of refugee diasporas that have spawned festering insurgencies along China's borders with Tajikistan and Kyrgyzstan and Burma's border with Thailand.

Governments themselves have become part of the problem in the sense that they may be the direct or indirect cause of migration and refugee movements. Not only do governments pursue policies designed to compel, encourage or prevent migration, but they are usually the final arbiters of whether people will be allowed to leave or enter.[90] Moreover, as has been shown, their decisions are often based on security rather than humanitarian considerations, as evidenced by the large numbers of Khmer refugees camped inside Thailand's eastern borders during the 1980s who became innocent pawns in a high-stakes strategic game between Vietnam and Thailand. There is a also a growing trend for governments to implement policies deliberately aimed at displacing or dispersing sections of their own population, often ethnic minorities, who are considered troublesome, dangerous or undesirable. Finally, the sharp rise in the number of internally displaced people suggests that the frequency and severity of intrastate conflict in East Asia is increasing since internal displacements are usually the result of domestic turmoil and civil war.

CHAPTER 8

People-smuggling, Undocumented Labour Migration and Environmental Refugees

In the decade after 1988, around 19 million people moved within or between the countries of the Commonwealth of Independent States (CIS), representing nearly one in every thirty of the region's inhabitants.[1] At the time, this surge in migration seemed to be consistent with the thesis that UPMs are largely determined by the incidence and severity of war and ethnic upheavals since these extraordinary population movements coincided with the disintegration of the old Soviet empire as its constituent states were reshaped by irredentism, ethno-nationalist struggles and civil wars. Since the mid-1990s, however, a measure of stability has returned to Russia and its former satellites, while globally there has been a marked reduction in the frequency and severity of military conflict. Why, then, have UPMs remained at historically high levels?

One explanation is that modern war is producing proportionately more refugees than previous eras of conflict because civilian populations are being deliberately targeted or are suffering 'collateral damage' such as occurred, for example, during the Kosovo crisis.[2] Even allowing for this possibility, the sustained rise in UPMs cannot be attributed solely to the vagaries of modern warfare. Other forces are clearly at work that have little to do with violent conflict or regime change. Demographic pressures in developing states are contributing to internal migration as well as pushing people overseas in search of employment and economic opportunity. The information revolution and advances in telecommunications have made the inhabitants of the poor South acutely aware that other countries enjoy higher incomes and substantially better living standards. Transnational criminal organisations offer a ready and affordable means of escape from the drudgery and hardship of life at home. This new breed of economic migrants, as Gerald Dirks reminds us, does not see migration merely as a desirable option but as one of the few available

153

courses of action to escape the consequences of overpopulation and diminishing employment opportunities.[3] Environmental degradation reduces incomes and may make human habitation so inhospitable that people sometimes have little choice other than to migrate. This chapter examines the economic and environmental drivers of UPMs, the influential role played by criminal organisations, and the challenges these present for East Asian governments.

People-smuggling

The smuggling of human beings by transnational criminal organisations has become a defining characteristic of illegal migration and a major political and security issue for the world community.[4] This reality was dramatically and tragically underscored by the deaths of fifty-eight Chinese illegal migrants who suffocated in the back of a truck at the Channel port of Dover while being smuggled to the United Kingdom in June 2000.[5] The European Union has witnessed a massive increase in people-smuggling from other parts of Europe, the Balkans, Russia and China since the mid-1990s and governments are struggling to cope with the problem. The rise in people-smuggling has been paralleled by an increase in the sophistication and organisation of the smugglers to such an extent that, according to the head of Britain's immigration service, they have acquired 'infrastructures, communications and surveillance capabilities far in excess of anything that the law-enforcement agencies' can muster.[6] The International Organisation for Migration estimates that mainly Russian, Albanian, Yugoslav and ethnic Chinese gangs moved some 500 000 people into the European Union in 1999, a 500 per cent increase in less than six years.[7] Globally, about 4 million people are being smuggled or trafficked across international borders every year, earning TCOs $7–12 billion annually and rivalling the profitability of the drug trade.[8]

Asian TCOs engaged in people-smuggling range from small-time local 'entrepreneurs' geared to making a quick dollar, to sophisticated international crime syndicates such as the Japanese yakuza and Chinese triads. The triads and other ethnic Chinese criminal groups, colloquially known as 'snake-heads', are responsible for much of the illicit global and regional trade in people. Thriving in the comparatively free-wheeling political and economic milieu of post-Deng China, Chinese criminal gangs regard people-smuggling as core business and a lucrative complement to other forms of criminal enterprise. They have established elaborate global networks to facilitate the movement of illegal migrants which are also used for smuggling drugs and other illicit contraband. Typically, ethnic Chinese are moved by sea or air to the United States from clearing houses in Cambodia and Thailand via South and Central America. Even faraway Greenland and the tiny Pacific island of Vanuatu have been used as transit stops for Chinese illegals en route to the United States.[9]

China has been a major source of migration on at least two other occasions. After the fall of the Ming dynasty in 1644, a large number of migrants from China's southern coastal provinces opposed to the Manchus spread out across Southeast Asia, followed by a second and much later wave of migrants in the mid-nineteenth century who also settled mostly in Southeast Asia.[10] Others journeyed to more distant Australia and the United States, lured by the promise of gold and bounty. These earlier migrations were driven by war and conflict in China, but the contemporary exodus has quite different dynamics and characteristics. Fundamental economic and social change has created a massive floating population in China of over 100 million people seeking employment opportunities or a better lifestyle.[11] Until the 1980s, controlling this large transient population was essentially an internal problem for China because of restrictions on overseas travel and the low incomes of most prospective migrants. The loosening of travel restrictions has coincided with a steep rise in average incomes and improved access to the global information network, stimulating a desire and demand for emigration in China that has been exploited by organised crime.[12]

A second important difference is that the current migrants are from all over China and not just the southern coastal provinces, although Fujian still provides a high percentage of all Chinese illegal migrants. The main destinations are Southeast Asia, Europe, North America, Australia and Canada, but since the mid-1990s entrepreneurial criminals have opened new markets for their human cargoes in Japan, the Russian Far East, South Africa and Latin America. The paucity of reliable data and the clandestine nature of the enterprise make it difficult to obtain a clear picture of Chinese people-smuggling, but TCOs were probably earning around $3.5 billion annually in the mid-1990s from smuggling Chinese migrants to East Asia and the West.[13]

The dramatic grounding in 1993 of a Chinese ship carrying illegal immigrants to the United States brought home to a global audience both the scale of people-smuggling from China and the audacity and resources of the smugglers. The *Golden Venture* ran aground on a sandbar within sight of the Statue of Liberty, spilling its unfortunate passengers into the waters off the New York borough of Queens. Most were quickly apprehended by US officials under the full glare of television cameras. Of the 261 people on board, ten drowned, 245 were arrested and six escaped. It later emerged that the operation had been organised by Kwok Ling-kay, the then head of the notorious Fuk Ching Triad, the largest of the Fujianese gangs.[14] The incident reverberated in Washington where a newly elected President Clinton directed the National Security Council to take charge of the investigation and to develop and coordinate a response to the traffickers. People-smuggling had clearly become a matter of national security in the eyes of the Clinton administration, a perception that was shared by many other governments in the West and increasingly in East Asia. Not long after the *Golden Venture* incident, Indonesia's Immigration Director and the chief of Thailand's National Security Council both declared illegal Chinese immigration a threat to their respective country's national security.[15]

TCOs have capitalised on burgeoning intra-regional trade and travel to target Southeast Asian states as end destinations for illegal migrants from China as well as using them as staging posts for onward destination to the West. Cambodia and Thailand are central to the trade, with a steady stream of Chinese illegal migrants entering by land, air and water, including along the Mekong River, assisted by a variety of trafficking and smuggling organisations. In 1997, Cambodian police estimated that there were about 10 000 Chinese illegal migrants living in Cambodia awaiting trans-shipment to other countries.[16] Thailand is also a gateway, sending up to 100 000 illegal Chinese migrants annually on to third countries.[17] Many of the criminal groups are not only highly organised but have consistently shown a capacity to corrupt public officials and penetrate the agencies responsible for security and immigration.

Police investigations into Sino-Thai people-smuggling rackets provide revealing insights into how organised criminal groups manage and control the flow of illegals from China to Thailand and other destination countries. Potential Chinese migrants who are willing to pay the substantial fees involved first contact brokers, who may be Thai or Chinese.[18] The brokers typically use a down payment from the intending migrants to obtain airline tickets and arrange travel documentation such as visas and passports. These are usually forged, but legitimate travel documentation is sometimes obtained from corrupt officials. In other cases, illegals enter Thailand as tourists and then melt into the local community while immigration officers, co-opted by the traffickers, feed false departure data into the computer records. Customs, immigration and airline staff in the pay of the brokers ensure that the documentation of the illegal migrants is not thoroughly checked and generally facilitate their movement through the barriers designed to protect against illegal entry. Residences and hotels in Bangkok and outlying districts are used by the brokers as temporary holding areas, where the illegal migrants can be safely kept until it is time for them to depart to their destination country.[19]

Sometimes the route is by land, but increasingly it is by ship and air or a combination of all three. In southern China, a favourite point of egress is via the Golden Triangle region into Thailand at the border crossing point of Mae Sai. On this route the main facilitator is the Eastern Shan

State Army, a notorious narco-insurgent group which has diversified from drugs into people-smuggling.[20] Others travel by land and ship to Hong Kong and Singapore before flying to the United States, Japan and Canada. The most prominent people-smugglers are the Fuk Ching gang in the United States and several Taiwanese criminal groups with strong ancestral and family ties in neighbouring Fujian province – the source of 90 per cent of the Chinese illegals smuggled into the United States.[21] The Hong Kong triads have a competitive advantage in moving people by air because of Hong Kong's strategic position as an Asian hub for international carriers, but the Taiwanese dominate the seaborne trade.[22] It is relatively easy for Taiwanese fishing trawlers to pick up illegal migrants at sea just outside Chinese territorial waters and transport them to other destinations in East Asia. The Taiwanese gangs have become so proficient that they are believed to be responsible for much of the illegal smuggling of Chinese immigrants worldwide.[23]

The cost of passage varies depending on the level of service provided, the mode of transport, the distance to be travelled and the barriers that have to be overcome. A billet on a small fishing vessel from Fujian province to Australia might be obtained for as little as $600–$700. At the upper end of the scale, an air ticket to the United States or Australia complete with documentation and coaching on what to tell suspicious customs officials costs $20 000 to $30 000, but can go as high as $47 000.[24] The fifty-eight Chinese who died in the back of a truck at Dover paid about $22 000 for their passage.[25] Criminal gangs may provide loans to cover costs, which the migrants have to repay, usually at exorbitant rates. The lives of the illegal immigrants who use the services of criminal gangs are often placed at risk, either as the result of hazardous crossings or more commonly because they are unable to repay loans to the criminals who finance their passage. It is not uncommon for Chinese smuggled into destination countries to be effectively held prisoner in 'safe house' dormitories while they work off their debts to the gangs – the men in menial employment and the women possibly forced into prostitution. Failure to repay debts can result in death or disfigurement. Extortion and blackmail are commonly used to persuade families in China to pay off the debts of their sons and daughters in the West.[26]

Northeast Asian states are also becoming targets for criminally assisted migration.[27] Authorities in Japan, South Korea and Taiwan are concerned by the rising number of Chinese migrants entering illegally by air and sea. The Japanese Government despatched a mission to Beijing in March 1997, hoping to persuade China to stem the flow of illegal migrants and crack down on the smuggling organisations.[28] Although their Chinese interlocutors agreed to cooperate, the flow of illegal migrants into Japan has shown no sign of falling.[29] Chinese gangs appear

increasingly willing to form cross-cultural liaisons with non-Chinese criminal groups. They have enlisted, for example, the services of 'moonlight-
ing' Korean fishermen who are happy to supplement their regular
income by smuggling people on a fee-for-service basis. Chinese are not
the only human cargo carried by regional people-smugglers. Ethnic
Koreans from China have been intercepted attempting to land clandes-
tinely in South Korea on fishing vessels, while groups from Bangladesh
and the Middle East have been caught trying to enter Australia via Mer-
auke in Irian Jaya and other exit ports in Indonesia.[30]

There is a thriving illegal trade in Indonesians wanting to work in
Malaysia, Singapore and Saudi Arabia. The small Indonesian island of
Bintan is used by local criminal gangs as a staging post for smuggling
Indonesians from all over the archipelago to Malaysia and Singapore. At
any one time up to 3000 would-be migrants are camped in squalid conditions on the island, watched over by gang members while they wait their
chance to cross the Strait of Malacca. Singapore is only forty-five minutes
away but 80 per cent of migrants are destined for Malaysia. A one-way
crossing to either destination costs less than $200.[31] Although the smug-
glers have fewer resources at their disposal than the larger Chinese gangs
based in other parts of the region, their organisational and entrepreneurial skills are nonetheless impressive. In late 1997, the Indonesian
Government arrested 700 agents and brokers involved in counterfeiting
travel documents and identity cards for illegal workers. They were operating an organised network that Indonesia's Minister for Manpower,
Abdul Latief, described as stretching 'from the villages in Indonesia to
Saudi Arabia'. According to Latief, most of the estimated 150 000 illegal
Indonesian workers in Saudi Arabia hold forged passports.[32]

Criminals are also cashing in on the growing international trade in
women – what some observers have called the 'feminization of migration'.[33] In the 1990s, 50 per cent of the 35 million people who crossed borders in search of better employment opportunities were women,
compared with 15 per cent in the 1970s and 25 per cent in the 1980s.
Human rights NGOs estimate that 1–2 million of these women are trafficked every year by TCOs to supply the global sex industry.[34] In East Asia,
nearly two-thirds of all Indonesians and Filipinos employed overseas are
female; they are in demand primarily as domestic labourers and as entertainers.[35] For many years, women from Thailand and the Philippines have
worked illegally in Japan, Hong Kong and Singapore as waitresses,
singers, entertainers and prostitutes.[36] Up to 60 000 young women, mainly
from Burma, were smuggled into Thailand to service the sex trade
between 1991 and 1997.[37]

As immigrant women from Burma, China, Laos and other low-cost
states in East Asia move into Thailand, Thai sex workers are being forced

further afield in search of higher incomes.[38] Asian women make up a small but rising percentage of the 500 000 female sex workers imported into Western Europe.[39] Rising numbers of women are also being sought as wives for female-deficient communities throughout the region as a result of a growing gender imbalance. Males outnumber females by a significant proportion in China, Hong Kong, Taiwan, Burma, Brunei, the Philippines, South Korea and Malaysia because of improvements in medical technology such as ultrasound scanners, the preference in many Asian societies for boys rather than girls, and China's one-child policy.[40] Since the early 1990s, ethnic Chinese women from the poorer provinces of northern Vietnam have been smuggled into southern China by criminal organisations as brides for Chinese men unable to find wives among their own communities.[41] These women, like their counterparts in other parts of the region, are extremely vulnerable because of their status as illegals. Yet it is they rather than the criminals who traffic in them who are often considered by governments as the lawbreakers and as threats to national security.[42]

Undocumented Labour Migration

The illegal trade in women is merely one aspect of a broader social phenomenon which is adversely affecting the region's political and security environment. Undocumented labour migrants form a growing proportion of UPMs in East Asia, exceeding the number of refugees and internally displaced people.[43] At least 4–5 million foreign workers in East Asia are undocumented, a trend which is likely to strengthen as intra-regional economic and income disparities widen.[44]

Labour migration has been a feature of regional population movements since the Western colonial powers began to import workers, administrators, teachers and indentured slaves from other parts of their far-flung empires at the end of the seventeenth century.[45] Labour migration within East Asia, mainly from China, continued unabated for nearly three centuries until disrupted by the decolonisation process and the rising fear of communism in the early years of the Cold War.[46] The ending of restrictions on Asian migration to the United States, Canada and Australia in the 1960s and the infrastructure boom in the Middle East generated by rising oil prices stimulated a second wave of labour migration which, by one estimate, totalled nearly 12 million workers in the twenty years to 1989. South Korean engineers and construction workers were the first East Asians attracted to the oil-rich but labour-poor Middle East. Others soon followed, especially Filipino women, who generally found employment as maids and domestic workers.[47]

Globalisation, sustained economic growth and declining fertility rates in the more mature regional economies are largely responsible for a third wave of labour migration which the Asian economic crisis dampened but did not extinguish.[48] Initially characterised by emigration from developing Southeast Asia to industrialised Northeast Asia, these labour flows have become more complex and multidirectional since the early 1990s. Two other factors have facilitated intra-regional migration. A large and vigorous international migration industry has sprung up in the region, much of it clandestine or operating on the fringes of the legal regulatory system. Mushrooming diaspora communities of foreign workers in labour-scarce countries have strengthened important social networks and fostered the development of influential pro-migration constituencies.[49] Probably less than half of all labour migrants in East Asia are employed under legal contracts and bilateral labour agreements between receiving and sending states; the remainder are undocumented, although not necessarily unsanctioned by governments. During the region's long economic boom, receiving states were inclined to turn a blind eye to undocumented foreign workers because they were considered to be a cheap and convenient temporary solution to domestic labour shortages.

Sending countries derive significant economic benefits from their nationals working overseas, who remit money, acquire valuable skills and develop useful personal and business networks.[50] Remittances are a major source of foreign exchange and may be crucial to the economic health and development of poorer states, in many cases exceeding official development assistance.[51] It is estimated, for example, that overseas remittances were worth $4.93 billion to the Philippine economy in 1995, nearly enough to cover the nation's $6 billion trade gap.[52] Thailand earned around $2.6 billion from its 210 000 workers overseas in 1999, and Indonesia hoped to receive $12.5 billion in remittances in 2000 before economic recession forced a downward revision of this figure.[53] China, a relative newcomer as a labour-exporting country, earned over $1 billion in 1994 from money received by 150 000 legal migrant workers in 158 countries, while remittances made up over half Vietnam's hard-currency earnings in the late 1980s.[54] These figures do not include the substantial sums of money and goods sent home privately which do not show up in the official statistics.

Before the economic crisis, labour migration in Southeast Asia was mainly from the less developed, labour-surplus states of Indonesia, Burma and the Philippines to more affluent Singapore, Malaysia, Brunei and Thailand. Thailand and Malaysia are labour importers as well as exporters, while Cambodia and Laos are probably net importers of labour.[55] These labour migration trends are likely to resume and strengthen as Southeast Asia's economic recovery gathers steam. In Northeast Asia Japan, Taiwan and Hong Kong remain popular destinations for Southeast Asians. China is a growing source of labour migrants for Taiwan, Japan and South Korea, and there is a sizeable Korean community in Japan from both sides of the divided peninsula. Many countries in East Asia are experiencing substantial internal movements of people – from rural communities to the larger cities and urban agglomerations, and from depressed regions to more economically vibrant areas. In Vietnam before the economic crisis took hold, 20 000 temporary workers a day were being attracted to Ho Chi Minh City from the countryside.[56] China's large transient labour force will continue to grow for at least another two decades before the country approaches labour market transition.[57]

Accurate national statistics on intra-regional and external labour migration are difficult to come by for many countries in East Asia. There are no time-series or internationally comparable statistics on the flows of skilled and unskilled labour in the region, either legal or undocumented.[58] Just as the term 'refugee' is subject to different interpretations and is frequently used to include people who do not meet refugee criteria, it is not always clear how statistics for labour migration have been compiled or interpreted. Accurately assessing numbers of undocumented labour migrants is hindered by administrative and financial obstacles to the collection of data and by the unwillingness of most East Asian states to publish statistics on labour migrants. Their reluctance stems from domestic political sensitivities and a desire not to offend sending states, which may be neighbours and important trading partners.[59]

Malaysia was the largest importer of foreign labour in East Asia before the recession took hold and has one of the highest concentrations of illegal workers. In 1997, Malaysia supported 2.2 million foreign labourers out of a total workforce of 10 million of whom only 900 000 were documented.[60] As many as half a million Indonesians and Filipinos work illegally in the Malaysian state of Sabah on the island of Borneo.[61] The Philippines is the leading regional exporter of labour and the second largest globally after Mexico.[62] Of the 4.2 million expatriate Filipino workers in 1994, almost half (1.8 million) were undocumented.[63] Thailand is home to between 750 000 and 1 million undocumented workers, mainly from Burma but increasingly from China, while approximately a million Thais are employed overseas, many of them illegally.[64] Once impoverished Cambodia has an estimated 1 million Vietnamese illegally working in construction, infrastructure development and the sex trade.[65]

China aside, Northeast Asian states are overwhelmingly importers of labour. Taiwan and Japan host substantial numbers of foreign workers from less developed regional states attracted by higher living standards and the reluctance of many Japanese and Taiwanese to do menial or dirty work. Japan's workforce includes nearly half a million foreigners, the majority of whom are undocumented.[66] In the mid-1990s, there were at

Table 8.1 Undocumented labour migration in East Asia, 1999

Receiving country	Estimated No. of undocumented foreign workers	Sending country
Malaysia	1.3 million	Indonesia, Bangladesh, India, Philippines
Thailand	750 000–1 million	Burma and China
Japan	333 000	Thailand, China, South Asia and Middle East Countries
Taiwan	100 000	China, Malaysia, Philippines, Indonesia and Thailand
South Korea	85 000	China and Philippines
Singapore	10 000	Malaysia, Philippines and Thailand
Cambodia	1 million	Vietnam
Burma	500 000–1 million	China
Total: 4.1–4.8 million		

Sources: ASEAN Economic Bulletin 12(3) 1995; *Asia-Pacific Magazine* 13,
13 December 1998; Philipp Martin, 'Migration on the Move', *Asia-Pacific Issues*
29, December 1996; various East Asian newspapers; and interviews with
officials from regional labour ministries.

least 100 000 illegal labour migrants in Taiwan and their numbers have
been swelled by a steady influx of people smuggled from China by Taiwanese and Chinese criminal gangs.[67] South Korea is emblematic of the
transformation of East Asia's labour markets. Until the mid-1980s, the
country was a major exporter of labour, mainly to the Middle East, but
since its economy went into overdrive it has become a magnet for undocumented labour migrants and has experienced one of the most rapid
migration transitions of any state in East Asia.[68]

The steady growth of intra-regional labour migration has been a
mixed blessing and presents East Asian states with some difficult choices.
There is a growing realisation that uncontrolled labour migration can
upset the precarious social and ethnic balance of multicultural states and
be a source of political tensions between sending and receiving states.
The dilemma for East Asia is that intra-regional labour migration is inextricably linked with economic development, bringing tangible benefits
for both receiving and sending states. The growth prospects of the more
developed regional economies like Japan, Taiwan, South Korea, Singapore and Malaysia are already dependent, to varying degrees, on the
availability of cheap foreign labour because of structural imbalances in
their own labour sectors and declining birth rates. Their reliance on foreign labour is set to increase as their economies mature and diversify.
Indeed, labour shortages may eventually become the main impediment
to sustained economic growth in several East Asian states.[69]

Thailand and Malaysia epitomise this new security dilemma. Bilateral relations have been strained by the steady influx of undocumented labour migrants into Malaysia from third countries using Thailand as a convenient staging area.[70] Both countries stepped up joint military patrols along key border crossing points in 1996 to stem the flow of illegal workers from Thailand, and Malaysian army units subsequently extended their patrols to include isolated beaches and coastal areas used as disembarkation points for illegals arriving by boat.[71] Deportations have increased significantly and Malaysia's armed forces have been given additional powers allowing them to detain illegal immigrants at the border and to conduct regular sweeps of areas known to harbour foreign workers. Much to Thailand's chagrin, however, Malaysia is building a fence along their common land border to stop the infiltration of illegal workers and smugglers in a none too subtle demonstration that it has little faith in the efficacy of Thailand's border control measures.[72] Thai officials maintain that they are doing all they can to stem the flow and have been critical of Malaysian attempts to push illegal workers, mainly Bangladeshis, back across the border into Thailand. The Deputy Secretary of Thailand's National Security Council, General Kachadpai Burutpat, warned in February 1997 that the Malaysian policy was creating unnecessary tension between the two countries.[73]

On the other hand, the Malaysian government estimates that it needs to import around 2.5 million foreign workers if it is to fulfil the ambitious economic goals laid out in its Vision 2020 plan.[74] The labour-rich Indonesian island of Sumatra was once considered a desirable source of workers because of strong historical ties and close ethnic, linguistic and religious affinities. In the late 1980s, Malaysia began to allow a steady flow of 'temporary' workers across the Malacca Strait from Sumatra. At first, local Malays welcomed the Indonesian migrant workers because it was felt that they would bring significant economic benefits and 'strengthen the position of the Malays in the country's delicate communal balance'.[75] As the number of legal and undocumented Indonesian migrants has grown, however, so has resentment against them among the communities in Malaysia that are most affected. The Indonesian migrants are increasingly seen as responsible for Malaysia's rising crime rate and squatter problems, of adding to the demands on an already strained social infrastructure, and of creating a potential fifth column should there ever be another 'Confrontation' with Indonesia.[76]

Tensions in the bilateral relationship increased markedly when Malaysia took steps to forcibly repatriate Indonesian illegal workers in 1997, a move quietly supported by Singapore, which shared Malaysia's anxieties about the potential security threat posed by the unregulated inflow of Indonesian workers.[77] The Singapore Government-controlled *Straits Times* declared: 'Malaysia was right to make a move on the problem because it was beginning to have security implications ... Malaysia's action, if anything, was overdue'.[78] Over 10 000 Indonesians were interned in heavily guarded camps and rioting broke out when they realised they were to be deported.[79] Eight were killed in one incident as well as a Malaysian policeman. The muted response from Jakarta belied private expressions of anger and bitterness by Indonesian officials at the peremptory treatment of the deportees.[80] In the first direct involvement of the Indonesian Armed Forces, naval vessels were despatched to pick up 1500 undocumented Indonesian migrants from the port of Pasir Gudang in Malaysia's Johor state in January 1997.[81] Malaysian apprehension about the social, security and health threat to the country from undocumented labour migrants, especially from Indonesia, escalated as the economic crisis worsened.[82] Foreign Minister Abdullah Ahmad Badawi publicly voiced these concerns in March 1998: 'It can cause instability in Malaysia. It will affect us socially and perhaps ... even politically. We must make sure there are jobs available for Malaysians. Charity must begin at home'.[83]

Such strains are likely to be magnified when guest workers or illegal migrants are culturally dissimilar or of a different race or ethnic background. The Flor Contemplacion issue, which soured relations between the Philippines and Singapore in 1995, underlines the capacity of disputes involving migrant workers to erode trust and goodwill even between friendly states. Contemplacion was a Filipino maid who was hanged in Singapore in March 1995 after being found guilty of murdering another maid and her 4-year-old Singaporean ward. At the time the case became a *cause célèbre*, three-quarters of the 90 000 maids employed in Singapore were from the Philippines. Bilateral relations were at an all-time high, so much so that the *Straits Times* had run a cartoon in February depicting the relationship as a couple in love. Barely two months later, thousands of Filipinos took to the streets, burning the Singaporean flag and an effigy of Singapore's President Ong Teng Cheong in response to Contemplacion's imprisonment and subsequent execution. The Ramos Government came under heavy public pressure to ban the employment of Filipinos overseas and at one stage the President feared for his own political survival as the Philippines teetered on the brink of severing relations with Singapore. Two Philippine ambassadors, the Labour Minister and the respected Foreign Minister, Roberto Romulo, were forced to resign, while Singaporean investment in the Philippines dropped from a record $65 million in 1994 to $3.7 million in late 1995.[84]

Environmental Refugees

East Asia's deteriorating environment is a relatively new contributor to the sustained rise in regional UPMs, demonstrating the circular causality between the health of the environment, population movements, and conflict. Environmental change in the form of naturally occurring droughts, floods and pestilence has been a significant factor in forcing people to migrate since the beginning of recorded history. So has war-related environmental destruction. However, demographic pressures, modern development practices and the rapid pace of social and economic change are giving rise to concerns that a new class of displaced people, 'environmental refugees', is being created in poorer states.[85] Some scholars contend that environmental refugees now constitute the fastest growing proportion of refugees globally. Norman Myers, for example, forecasts that the number of these refugees will double by the year 2010 and continue increasing thereafter, while Jacobson has predicted that by 2050, refugees from environmental causes could exceed all others by a factor of six.[86]

These figures must be treated with caution as the links between environmental degradation and UPMs are not well established, conceptually or empirically. There are unresolved problems of definition and the extent to which there is a direct causal relationship between environmental change and UPMs is not entirely clear. Since most of the people forced to move because of environmental factors remain within the boundaries of their home state, strictly speaking they are not refugees. Many definitions do not distinguish between people displaced by naturally occurring climatic events and those displaced by human activities. El-Hinawi, for example, defines environmental refugees as 'those people who have been forced to leave their traditional habitat, temporarily or permanently, because of a marked environmental disruption that jeopardized their existence and/or seriously affected the quality of their life'.[87] The conceptual waters are further muddied by disputes over whether population displacements are due to cumulative or 'catastrophic' environmental change.[88]

Nevertheless, it is becoming more and more apparent that human-induced environmental degradation is stimulating UPMs by reducing incomes, especially in rural regions, or by rendering the environment so unhealthy and unpleasant that people feel compelled to move.[89] Once again, it is the poorest and least developed regions of the world that are most at risk. It is no accident that Africa has the greatest number of refugees per capita, many of whom can be broadly classified as environmental refugees since their economic impoverishment is rooted in the erosion of their physical environment and means of livelihood.[90] Human-initiated deforestation leading to catastrophic floods and desertification are responsible for a significant proportion of population displacements in Africa. Conflict sometimes ensues as communities forced to move out of despoiled areas clash with their neighbours in their search for diminishing sources of food, potable water and arable land.

Although East Asia has been less affected than Africa, continuing population growth, high rates of urbanisation, pollution and climate change are likely to increase the overall numbers of environmental refugees. The UN Environment Programme has investigated the likely environmental impact of global warming on Thailand, Malaysia and Indonesia. It found that significant coastal areas in all three countries would be permanently flooded by rising sea levels, notably Bangkok and much of the equally densely populated coastline of northern Java, causing major population dislocations.[91] A study by the World Bank and the Chinese Government on climate change and its implications for sea-level rise along the Chinese coast concluded that up to forty-eight cities could be submerged by 2050, including Shanghai. The study estimated that should sea-level rises of the magnitude forecast occur, as many as 76 million people in Chinese coastal cities could be displaced – more than the entire populations of medium-sized states such as France, the United Kingdom or Thailand.[92]

North Korea is the most egregious East Asian example of a state where government neglect of the rudiments of sound environmental management and sustainable development has forced people to move in large numbers. In 1995, North Korea suffered the worst floods in living memory; they caused widespread damage, left over 500 000 homeless and affected up to a quarter of North Korea's population of 23 million. The flood damage was so severe that the fiercely independent North Korean regime took the unprecedented step of asking the United Nations for emergency aid. Although the floods were natural events, the consequences were magnified by rampant deforestation and North Korea's dysfunctional agricultural system. The combined effects of the country's natural and man-made environmental disasters caused a sharp rise in the number of North Koreans seeking refuge and food in the Yanbian region of China's Jilin province, where ethnic Koreans comprise about 40 per cent of the 2.1 million local population.[93] The floods devastated crops, prolonging and worsening the country's famine. As the number of refugees escalated, Beijing offered emergency food aid and established refugee holding camps. Fearing that some North Koreans would attempt the hazardous land and sea crossing across the Demilitarised Zone, South Korean officials also set up refugee camps and a system for dealing with large inflows of North Koreans.[94]

Up to 400 000 North Korean environmental or 'food refugees' crossed over into China in 1998, most of whom returned after begging or scrounging food, although significant numbers have remained in Jilin.[95] China had no choice but to tighten security on what was once its most relaxed and lightly policed frontier. At the height of the influx of North Korean refugees in late 1998, Chinese border guards temporarily closed the 1300 kilometre-long border and repatriated any North Korean refugees caught.[96] By mid-1999, the famine had so debilitated ordinary

North Koreans that the normally zealous North Korean border guards were doing little to stop people crossing into China, often demanding only a share of the food they brought back as the price of passage. China also relaxed its attempt to repatriate North Korean illegals in the knowledge that most would return to North Korea to feed their families.[97] Humanitarian considerations were clearly overshadowed in the minds of all North Korea's neighbours by the prospect that the Marxist state might collapse with little warning if the refugee flows continued. China, in particular, feared that officially recognising them as refugees would open the floodgates to an even greater flow of destitute North Koreans.[98]

Conclusion

A number of important conclusions can be drawn from this analysis. The unregulated movement of people is a global phenomenon that has long historical antecedents. Its emergence as a significant security issue in the modern era must be seen against the backdrop of rising populations in the poor South, growing income disparities between and within states, and the liberating effects of the revolution in communications and information technology. The huge increase in the number of refugees, displaced persons and illegal migrants recorded since 1975 has shifted international attention from the plight of these itinerants to the consequences of their flight. Receiving states worry about the harmful effects of UPMs, especially during periods of political and economic turbulence. Cross-border movements of refugees and illegal migrants can impose heavy economic and financial burdens on developing countries, seriously destabilise border regions and, in extreme cases, help to precipitate the downfall of governments – as East Germans discovered in 1989.[99] People forced to move by war and conflict, or government fiat, almost always suffer abuses of fundamental rights and denial of basic freedoms. Illegal migrants, drawn by the promise of a better life, may find themselves hostage to the whims of unscrupulous people-smugglers or confined for lengthy periods within the walls of holding camps pending deportation or relocation. The security of people and the security of states are intimately linked – when governments fail, neglect or exploit their people, population displacements often result.[100]

The unregulated movement of people is a seminal transnational security issue that will demand greater attention from policy-makers in the early twenty-first century. Refugees will account for a significant proportion of future regional UPMs, but the forced displacement of people who remain within the borders of their home countries is likely to be more conspicuous in future patterns of migration. Indeed, there is no essential difference in their plight since they are all victims of conflict or persecution.[101] The causes of contemporary UPMs are multidimensional, increasingly complex, and interlinked in ways that do not avail themselves of easy solutions. Repression, ethno-nationalism and the exploitation of minorities by governments in pursuit of foreign policy and national security goals will continue to reap a grim human harvest of refugees and displaced people, but they will be exacerbated by a number of new factors. Chief among them are the growth of criminally assisted people-smuggling, undocumented labour migration, and the widespread and accelerating destruction of the environment. Although governments play a central role in determining population movements, non-state actors can be equally influential. Combating criminally assisted illegal migration is a major security challenge for East Asia. People-smuggling threatens the integrity and inviolability of national borders and erodes the authority of governments; trafficking in women promotes the spread of AIDS and drug addiction, undermines state capacity, and jeopardises the health, welfare and security of those being trafficked.

Undocumented labour migration has important implications for state security as well as economic and social policy. There are risks associated with hosting large illegal migrant communities, not least of which is their potential for exposing and accentuating existing ethnic divides. Migration-driven political tensions between Malaysia and its Thai and Indonesian neighbours underline how undocumented labour flows can aggravate relations between states. Dealing with the repatriation of unwanted workers to their home states poses its own set of national security problems as well as raising concerns about the welfare and safety of those being repatriated. Ecological stress will be a contributing cause of UPMs in East Asia, because of demographic pressures and the parlous state of the region's natural environment. The direction of these environmental refugee flows will be overwhelmingly from rural to urban areas within developing states, increasing unemployment among an underclass of already socially alienated and politically marginalised urban poor.

To summarise, the unregulated movement of people is representative of the new class of transnational issues that are reshaping East Asia's security environment. The sustained surge in UPMs is destabilising states internally, aggravating trans-border conflicts, creating political tensions between sending and receiving states, and jeopardising the human security of its many victims. Its principal drivers, however, are far removed from those responsible for the strategic competition of the Cold War years and they are largely beyond the purview of the realist school of thought. These drivers are social, economic and environmental as well as political and strategic, and the UPMs they stimulate cannot be stemmed or effectively deterred by military force. States are commonly the chief instigators of population movements, especially within their own borders, but powerful non-state actors are becoming extremely influential in determining their flow and direction.

Another defining aspect of UPMs in East Asia is the interconnectedness and non-linear relationship between its causal variables, which is characteristic of transnational security issues more generally. A large proportion of illegal migrants are driven by population, environmental and economic forces – but new migrants, regardless of whether or not they cross borders, impinge on the living space of others, threaten their security and add to environmental stress in a self-sustaining cycle of migration and instability. Finally, and contrary to the assertions of traditionalists, it is misleading to classify UPMs as merely the unintended consequences of military conflict – they are now a root cause of instability and insecurity in East Asia. More than half of the region's UPMs are undocumented labour workers who leave their home countries voluntarily in search of economic opportunity, not because of war or conflict.

PART III

Transnational Crime and AIDS

CHAPTER 9

Transnational Crime

Part III of this book deals with two separate but related transnational issues. The first two chapters chart the rise of transnational criminal organisations globally and in East Asia, and show how activities like drug-trafficking have moved along the threat continuum towards the traditional concerns of national security planners. They also scrutinise the structure and operations of the most prominent organised criminal groups in East Asia, identify the reasons for their emergence and assess the nature and gravity of the threat these non-state entities pose to the region. Drug-trafficking is by no means the only illicit activity conducted and controlled by organised crime, but it is certainly one of the most destructive and insidious and for this reason it warrants detailed analysis. Chapter 11 focuses on an infectious disease, AIDS, which has reached epidemic proportions in parts of Africa and threatens to do the same in East Asia. It illuminates the close connection between organised crime, drug-trafficking and HIV transmission and argues that AIDS will have severe consequences for regional stability unless its spread is arrested.

The internationalisation of crime and the criminalisation of war have become key strategic issues for East Asia, reinforcing the need for a more holistic approach to security and underlining the complexity of the transnational challenge to regional security. As the historian Martin van Creveld argues, there is a clear link between war and crime: soldiers may become criminals, criminals become soldiers, war become criminalised, and shadow states exploit the resulting ambiguities.[1] Capitalising on the opportunities provided by economies in transition and a thriving global market for their unlawful products and services, a new breed of Asian criminal entrepreneur has acquired a level of financial and political influence which exceeds that of many states. Borders are no longer serious impediments to criminal transactions and transnational criminal organisations are taking advantage of the jurisdictional limitations on national police forces and weak international cooperation on law enforcement to maximise their illicit profits. Sovereignty-bound East Asian governments, on the other hand, have been hamstrung by their attachment to the paramount regional 'non-interference' norm and their slowness to recognise that the expansion in major crime can only be combated by international cooperation.[2]

Unless contained, the spread and institutionalisation of transnational crime will not only be a major obstacle to the development of vibrant civil societies in East Asia's democratising states but also erode the performance legitimacy of the region's authoritarian regimes. TCOs are supplanting the functions of government, while criminal violence threatens the stability of regional states and the survival and well-being of millions. In countries like Burma, North Korea and Russia, crime and politics are virtually indistinguishable, either because the state has been co-opted by the criminals or because the people who run the state are themselves criminals. The economic and societal impact of transnational crime is no less severe. The 'laundering' of vast sums of money by TCOs weakens national economies, while people-smuggling and drug-trafficking may be as injurious to life and social harmony as war itself.

The Rise of Global Crime

Although crime, like war, has been associated with the dark side of human nature for millennia, its intrusion into the international security domain is a late twentieth-century phenomenon.[3] In 1992, three years after the breaching of the Berlin Wall symbolised the end of the Soviet political and military challenge to the West, the former head of the CIA, James Woolsey, declared:

> These examples demonstrate that the threat from organized crime transcends traditional law enforcement concerns. They affect critical national security interests. While organized crime is not a new phenomenon, today some governments find their authority besieged at home and their foreign policy interests imperiled abroad. Drug trafficking, links between drug traffickers and terrorists, smuggling of illegal aliens, massive financial and bank fraud, arms smuggling, potential involvement in the theft and sale of nuclear material, political intimidation and corruption all constitute a poisonous brew – a mixture potentially as deadly as some of what we faced during the cold war.[4]

Woolsey was not alone in expressing this view. John Kerry, an influential US senator, argued that the rise of powerful, well-organised and well-funded international criminal groups was a new threat to global order and stability. 'This is something that none of us has ever experienced before. It is not ideological. It has nothing to do with right or left, but it is money-oriented, greed based criminal enterprise that has decided to take on the lawful institutions and civilized society.'[5] A senior US official labelled international crime as a 'major threat to world stability and US national security', while the head of the German criminal intelligence agency, the BKA, asserted that organised crime had become the 'chief enemy of international security'.[6] These sentiments were echoed by leaders of the G7 industrialised nations at their 1995 summit in Halifax, Canada, who declared in a post-summit statement that transnational criminal organisations were a growing threat to their security.[7] Three years later at the Birmingham summit in the United Kingdom, the G8 nations asserted that organised crime was not only a threat 'to our own citizens and their communities ... but also a global threat which can undermine the economic basis of societies'.[8]

Not all were convinced by these declarations and assertions. Academic dissenters argued that Western defence and security communities were exaggerating the threat of transnational organised crime in their search for a post-Cold War *raison d'être*.[9] Internal government sceptics, on the other hand, while prepared to accept that transnational crime had become a serious international problem, saw the issue as primarily one of law enforcement rather than international security. Nonetheless, by the end of the 1990s, transnational crime had firmly entrenched itself on the agendas of the United Nations, the European Union and the Clinton White House.[10] The transformation in US thinking was underlined by President Clinton's May 1998 announcement of a comprehensive 'International Crime Control Strategy' which set out a five-point program to combat transnational crime.[11] In his covering letter to the strategy, Clinton wrote: 'international crime today is more than a law enforcement problem. It is a formidable threat to America's security and it demands a concerted response'.[12]

Why is Crime a Security Issue?

There are a number of explanations for crime's emergence as a significant international security issue. Renewed nationalist, ethnic and tribal conflict has stimulated the clandestine arms trade and created new markets for illicit drugs and contraband. The disintegration of the Soviet Union ushered in a period of weak central government in Russia and eastern Europe, which assisted the global spread of organised crime. As one expert on the Russian mafiya observed, during the communist era 'the government kind of ran the criminals', whereas afterwards 'the criminals are kind of running the government'.[13] In addition, the steady erosion of the moral and political authority of secular states in the developing world over the past quarter of a century has led to an upsurge in lawlessness in extensive areas of Central Asia and Africa.

The same global forces that are transforming international society and the world economy are also changing the way criminals are organised and do business. Urbanisation and the growth of megacities increase both the intensity and the density of economic activity, allowing criminal enterprise to flourish. Global cities are congenial environments for today's criminal organisations and excellent incubators for those of the future.[14] Economic activity across the world has been 'stretched' and deepened as the spatial and temporal constraints on the flow of labour, capital and information weaken.[15] Improvements in communications technology and transportation, in conjunction with the development of a global market for drugs, have cemented the power of existing criminal syndicates and provided enhanced opportunities for newcomers, as has the introduction of electronic banking, which improves the speed and security of illicit money transfers. The extension of economic activity into cyberspace via the Internet and the emergence of a truly global trading and financial system has given TCOs the tools and access to penetrate the cyber-economy and extend networks of influence and patronage. Networking across national borders enables TCOs to develop a high degree of operational mobility and to establish alliances and associations with other criminal groups.[16] Law enforcement agencies, on the other hand, have been hampered by jurisdictional impediments, political inertia and bickering over turf.

Over the past three decades, the Sicilian mafia, Chinese triads, Japanese yakuza and the North American La Cosa Nostra have been joined by a new breed of extremely powerful and ruthless TCOs. They include the Colombian and Mexican drug cartels, Lebanese and Nigerian gangs, the narco-warlords of Burma, and the Russian mafiya.[17] Like their legitimate counterparts in business, today's TCOs are far more willing than in the past to form tactical alliances and strategic partnerships in order to increase their commercial leverage and access to global markets. The desire to maximise profits overrides ethnic affinities and national loyalties. The Cali cartel has agreements with Italian crime syndicates to distribute cocaine in Italy and has recruited former Czech intelligence officers, Polish businessmen and Russian criminals to ship cocaine to Europe. The once fiercely parochial Sicilian mafia has established an effective money-laundering operation by enlisting the services of their Russian counterparts.[18] Nigerians have become bag-carriers, couriers and enforcers for a variety of TCOs, while Korean and Vietnamese gangs perform similar functions for the yakuza and triads respectively. Chinese people-smugglers have even employed Canadian Mohawk Indians to ferry illegals across the St Lawrence River into the United States.[19]

Highly sophisticated and well-established TCOs are not the only criminal groups cashing in on the lucrative trade in illegal goods and services. Smaller family ventures and 'freelancers' form part of the criminal challenge to international security. Typically, this new class of criminals may own legitimate businesses such as travel agencies or export/import companies. Their illegal activities and associations tend to be episodic and fleeting, making them almost invisible to law enforcement agencies. When they operate within closely knit ethnic and family units the already difficult task of exposure and arrest becomes even more problematic. Both the larger organised gangs and the smaller kinship networks are characterised 'by a high degree of role differentiation'. The bosses manage and are appropriately remunerated; a host of lesser lights execute the many specialist tasks that may be necessary to complete the operation or transaction.[20]

The Russian mafiya exhibits virtually all the characteristics of successful modern TCOs and is best characterised as 'a series of loose and flexible networks of semi-independent criminal entrepreneurs' who collectively have attained substantial political influence and financial power in post-Soviet Russia.[21] The mafiya is aggressive, internationalist and deeply rooted in Russian society. Although generally lacking the discipline and organisational structure of La Cosa Nostra, the yakuza and the triads, they are no less formidable or resourceful. In the mid-1990s, Russian law enforcement officials estimated that nationally, 8000 criminal gangs employed about 100 000 gang members and, indirectly, another 3 million Russians working in illegal enterprises.[22] By one calculation, 35 per cent of the nation's GDP was derived from criminal transactions, while between 15 and 35 per cent of all Russian banks and up to 80 per cent of all joint ventures with the West were run by the mafiya.[23] The mafiya now probably control around 40 per cent of the Russian economy.[24]

Russian TCOs routinely carry out high-profile contract killings, launder billions of dollars in revenue and control a significant proportion of the illicit global arms and drug trade. So brazen and widespread have their activities become that serious questions are being asked about the viability of the Russian state and its commitment to the rule of law. A 1997 survey found that more than 50 per cent of Russians believe that the mafiya, not the Kremlin, run Russia. Boris Yeltsin, the putative leader of Russia for most of the 1990s, conceded that organised crime 'is destroying the economy, interfering in politics, undermining public confidence, threatening individual citizens and the entire nation'.[25] Russians appear to live not by law but by understandings that have been characterised as a cross between 'a bandit's code and [a] feudal code'.[26] Russian organised crime has diversified its activities outside Russia and Europe and, like many other TCOs, subcontracts work to a range of freelance specialists in everything from communications encryption to money-laundering. In the Russian Far East, the aptly named Russian Far Eastern Association of Thieves acts as a de facto trade association for a variety of local TCOs, including an increasing number of ethnic Chinese gangs who are proliferating in the growing Chinese émigré community.[27]

The borderless world in which TCOs operate offers numerous opportunities for the acquisition of illicit wealth. At the end of the twentieth century, the financial and human resources at the disposal of the major TCOs surpassed that of many states. It is this development, perhaps more than any other, which accounts for their new-found ability to threaten international security. In the public mind, La Cosa Nostra is the stereotypical crime family – rich, powerful and omnipresent. But in many ways La Cosa Nostra is yesterday's TCO. The US Federal Bureau of Investigation (FBI) estimates that at the height of its influence in the 1970s and 1980s, the organisation consisted of approximately twenty-five families and 2000 active members. Although La Cosa Nostra maintains overseas networks, most of its profits derive from its American operations. By contrast, the Colombian cocaine industry is a truly global enterprise employing around 100 000 people. In their heyday, during the early and mid-1990s, the major Colombian cartels outperformed most Fortune 500 companies and probably made more in a week than the American mafia did in a year.[28]

Other TCOs command comparable wealth and influence. Drug money accounts for 25 per cent of Pakistan's gross national product.[29] Based on its narcotics revenue alone, the Italian mafia is estimated to be richer than 150 sovereign states, while the Chinese triads and Japanese yakuza make profits that would be the envy of most large multinationals.[30] According to the director of the US Drug Enforcement Agency, the Mexican drug-trafficker Amado Carillo Fuentes earned $10 billion a year before his death in 1997 and paid $800 million in annual bribes to corrupt officials for protection.[31] At the global level the revenues generated by TCOs are enormous, even by the standards of developed states and major multinational corporations. Bill Gates, the head of Microsoft Corporation and reputedly the richest man in the world, accumulated a personal fortune of $100 billion before a US government anti-trust case in 1999 left him $40 billion poorer.[32] By comparison, organised crime turns over US$1.5 trillion a year, and the IMF estimates that half a trillion dollars, or 2–5 per cent of global GDP, is illegally laundered through banks and financial institutions, illustrating the formidable financial power and global reach that modern TCOs have acquired.[33]

East Asia's Crime Problem

The factors responsible for the spread of crime internationally are also making their presence felt in East Asia. Globalisation, decades of strong

Table 9.1 Major transnational criminal organisations

	Major Activities	Size	International Connections
Cocaine Cartels	Headquartered mainly in Colombia and Mexico, the cocaine cartels manage the entire cycle of cocaine from production to distribution around the world.	The cartels employ individuals in a rigid pyramid structure, with heads of families in control of geographic areas gathered together as loose business coalitions. Their objective is to maximize profit.	Cosa Nostra La Cosa Nostra Triads Yakuza
Triads	The activities of the Triads are extremely diversified. They cover drugs, money lending, gambling, racketeering, service sector investment, money laundering and running of clandestine immigration systems.	The Triads employ upwards of 170,000 persons in a fairly traditional pyramid structure headed by a Boss, Underboss, and Recruiting boss. The majority of the organization is made up of 'soldiers'. Known Triads are: 'Sun Yee On' Hong Kong, '14K' Hong Kong, 'Wo Federation' Hong Kong, 'United Bamboo' Taiwan Province of China, 'Four-Seas Band' Taiwan, and 'Great Circle' China.	The Triads are pervasive and are known to be active throughout Asia, Europe and the USA, although their main activities center around Hong Kong, Burma, Taiwan Province of China, The Philippines and the USA.

Table 9.1 Major transnational criminal organisations (*continued*)

	Major Activities	Size	International Connections
Yakuza	The Yakuza are involved in all types of crime in Japan including racketeering, business fraud, drugs, prostitution and pornography. Within the Asian drugs scene they are very active in trafficking methamphetamine.	There are approximately 60,000 full time Yakuza and 25,000 associates. The organizational structure is extremely complex and involves thousands of small gangs, and many families.	Yakuza are known to have links to organized crime in the USA, Columbia, Germany, China and the CIS.
Cosa Nostra	Perhaps the best known organized crime group, Cosa Nostra has become mainly involved in international drug trafficking, serving as a clearing house for international agreements and drug routes. It also services the financial and laundering needs of many smaller crime groups. Other activities include extortion, loan sharking and skimming public works contracts.	A vertical organization of roughly 5,000 members in regional and provisional commissions.	Based in the Italian island of Sicily, Cosa Nostra has established networks of affiliates in every continent. It has ties with all of the major drug trafficking organizations including the cartels, La Cosa Nostra, and Mafia groups headquartered in the former Soviet Union.

La Cosa Nostra (New York)	La Cosa Nostra is involved in drug trafficking, illegal gambling, arms trafficking, prostitution, extortion, skimming public and private works contracts, usury, business activities, including construction and food retailing, and influencing unions, mainly in the USA.	The organization comprises 3,000 individual 'soldiers' in 25 families, five of which are based in New York and which hold the greatest prestige and influence.	The primary connections of La Cosa Nostra are the cocaine cartels and the Cosa Nostra, and Mafias headquartered in the former Soviet Union.
Mafia groups (headquartered in the former Eastern Block)	Trafficking in drugs, raw materials, nuclear materials and weapons. Also involved in money laundering, white slavery, extortion, currency smuggling and counterfeiting.	Three million members in 5,700 gangs of which at least 200 have highly sophisticated structures with dealings in 29 countries.	Groups in the USA, the cocaine cartels and the Cosa Nostra.

Source: UN Crime and Criminal Justice Division, *Crime*, No. 26/27, November 1995, Annex III and *World Drug Report 1997*, p. 132.

economic growth, market liberalisation, booming intra-regional trade, the rise of the biggest middle class in history and the development of regional growth triangles have facilitated illicit business as well as legitimate enterprise.[34] East Asia's rapid modernisation has made governments in the region acutely vulnerable to criminal penetration and allowed TCOs unparalleled access to the indispensable tools of their trade – sophisticated information systems, high-speed data transfer links, electronic banking and world-class transport and communication hubs. Asian use of the Internet is increasing by more than 50 per cent a year and there has been a comparable rise in criminal exploitation of the Web, which takes two principal forms. One is computer hacking for financial gain and the other is the use of the Internet for more traditional criminal purposes such as drug-trafficking and money-laundering. In Thailand, for example, amphetamine dealers have been using the Internet to sell their product directly to a regionwide market and to launder the proceeds.[35]

Furthermore, as the political scientist Robert Leiken notes, developing states are transitional, not traditional, and transition involves institutional and cultural contention which breeds corruption.[36] Developing states are more vulnerable to corruption because their political and bureaucratic elites are poorly paid and the moral code that underpins traditional society often breaks down during the modernisation process. In East Asia, as the economic crisis conclusively demonstrated, insufficient priority has been accorded to the rule of law, prudential management and financial accountability. All these developments in conjunction with ineffective law enforcement and the widespread availability of small arms have weighted the scales firmly in favour of the criminals.

Asian organised crime first appeared on the international law enforcement agenda in 1978 when a conference on the subject was convened in the United States attended by fifty investigators. Less than twenty years later, a similar conference attracted over 1000 participants from more than twenty countries. In his keynote address, FBI director Louis Freeh declared Asian organised crime to be no longer an emerging issue but 'an established crime problem that threatens the security of many countries'.[37] The first regional attempt to address the security implications of transnational crime was the 1996 meeting of the ASEAN Regional Forum, the region's premier security forum.[38] The chairman's report noted: 'The Ministers also agreed to consider at the next ARF meeting, the question of drug trafficking and related transnational issues, such as economic crimes, including money laundering, which could constitute threats to the security of the region'.[39]

Taking its cue from the ARF, the 6th Meeting of the CSCAP Steering Committee established a study group on transnational crime which later became a full working group co-chaired by Australia, the Philippines and Thailand. The first meeting of this working group considered a list of nineteen criminal activities thought to have implications for regional security which was later refined into eight 'crime types' deemed worthy of further attention.[40] They were arms-trafficking, drug production, international corporate/white-collar crime, smuggling of nuclear materials, counterfeiting, illegal migration, money-laundering and technology crimes. A longer list of forty-four separate transnational criminal activities also appears in a 1998 paper written by the Australian co-chair.[41]

Regional interest in the subject of transnational crime mirrors the sharp rise in Asian crime that crosses over into the security domain. Taiwan's crime rate has climbed steadily since the 1949 martial law decree was lifted in 1987, while across the Taiwan Straits the Chinese Government has publicly voiced its anxiety about the rising level of crime nationally.[42] According to the president of the Supreme People's Court, Ren Jianxin, about half of the 482 927 criminal cases recorded in 1994 were for crimes which 'posed a grave threat to national security or public safety', such as murder, rape, armed robbery, drug-trafficking and kidnapping.[43]

Until the mid-1990s, it was common for Indonesian officials and law enforcement officers to discount organised crime as a major national problem, arguing that Indonesia was relatively unaffected by the activities of large overseas crime syndicates. The contract assassination of a prominent local businessman and a sudden influx of the drug 'ecstasy' into the country via a sophisticated international network controlled by non-Indonesian TCOs caused a major reassessment and led President Suharto to urge the police to pay greater attention to the problem of organised crime.[44] In the neighbouring Philippines, one of the major disincentives to foreign investment is the country's spiralling level of crime. During his tenure as president, Fidel Ramos was forced to crack down on criminal gangs in response to a rash of kidnappings of foreign businessmen and armed robberies which Ramos admitted threatened political stability.[45] But the Philippines faces a far greater security challenge from the resurgent Abu Sayyaf group, which purports to be fighting a war of liberation in the south of the country but which frequently resorts to the kind of anarchic criminal violence more often associated with Africa, Latin America and Central Asia.[46]

The criminalisation of war and internal conflicts is a trend that is evident elsewhere in East Asia. The remnants of the pro-Jakarta militias, once united in their determination to keep East Timor a part of Indonesia, have degenerated into semi-autonomous gangs, pursuing their own narrow interests and using criminal violence against the UN peacekeeping forces and vulnerable East Timorese border communities. In Burma, many of the former ethnic insurgents who formerly opposed the central government are now free to pursue a range of criminal pursuits provided they do not directly challenge the authority of the military regime in Rangoon. One of these groups, the United Wa State Army (UWSA), dominates the Asian heroin and amphetamine trade and has established a large settlement in the Mong Yawn valley just across the border from Thailand which has all the hallmarks of an emerging criminal state.[47]

The UWSA provides the military muscle and protection for the drug caravans that ply their trade in the tri-border region of Burma, Thailand and Laos. Its 15 000 to 20 000 troops are well armed and equipped with mortars, heavy machine-guns and Russian made SA-7 surface-to-air missiles, which makes the UWSA a formidable military force by any standard and arguably the most potent narco-insurgency in East Asia. Thailand regards the activities of the UWSA and its drug-running operations as a serious threat to Thailand's national security. If the fragile ceasefire with Rangoon should fail, the SPDC may find it virtually impossible to reassert its notional control over the UWSA or the fiefdom that the UWSA is carving out in the Shan hills.[48]

While weak governments are commonly exploited for criminal purposes, some states are directly complicit in the spread of transnational crime. Persistent though fragmented reports of North Korean involvement in criminal transactions date back to the mid-1970s. The closed nature of North Korean society at first made it difficult to determine whether these were the actions of individuals or the results of a conscious policy decision by the regime.[49] Since the mid-1990s, however, there has been a marked escalation in the intensity and scope of drug-trafficking by North Korean diplomats and officials, as well as smuggling and counterfeiting by these officials. Given the tight control that the ruling Korean Workers Party exercises over all levels of North Korean society, it is extremely unlikely that this increase in criminal activity could have taken place without the explicit endorsement of the Party leadership, including Kim Jong-il himself.

Information gleaned from US, South Korean and Japanese intelligence agencies and police investigative reports leaves little doubt that Pyongyang is deliberately using the instruments of state power for criminal purposes. In 1994, the Korean Workers Party established a special office to coordinate attempts to obtain foreign currency which also seems to be in charge of all 'crime for profit activity'. Bureau No. 39, which is directly answerable to Kim Jong-il, uses North Korean diplomatic missions, government offices overseas and trading enterprises as fronts for a range of criminal enterprises. Much of the money obtained is channelled through the Kaesong Bank and diplomatic pouches are routinely used for illicit purposes.[50] Pyongyang has also begun to use the services of the yakuza and other TCOs to gain access to their narcotics distribution networks and markets.[51] The money obtained is used to prop up North Korea's ailing economy, buy elite loyalty, support diplomatic missions and finance intelligence operations.[52]

Asian Organised Crime: the Triads

North Korea aside, the reality is that transnational organised crime in East Asia is dominated by non-state actors, principally Chinese triads, the Japanese yakuza and Chinese and Vietnamese ethnic gangs who operate independently from the triads and yakuza as well as in association with them. Asian crime is often associated in the public mind with the activities of the triads, whose origins go back to the mid-eighteenth century. The word 'triad' is actually of English coinage and is derived from the society's emblem, which is a triangle bounded by the Chinese characters for heaven, earth and humankind.[53] Shrouded in mythology, the triads were originally thought to have been established by priests from a Shaolin monastery intent on overthrowing the Qing Manchu dynasty and restoring the vanquished, indigenous Mings.[54] Recent historical research suggests, however, that the antecedent of the triads was the Heaven and Earth Society (Tiandihui in Chinese). This patriotic society was founded in Fujian province by a Chinese monk in 1761 as a mutual protection and self-help organisation for the lower classes. It was based on a pseudo-familial network of acquaintances, and in some cases kinship.[55] Like today's triads, Tiandihui members were bonded by ritual and ceremonies designed to inculcate a sense of brotherhood, organisational loyalty and devotion to the aims of the society.

As the Tianhdihui extended its reach throughout Southeastern China and internationally, its patriotic impulses were debased and corrupted by involvement in criminal enterprise, especially the opium trade. Triad political influence reached its zenith under the Kuomintang in the 1930s and 1940s.[56] By some estimates as many as 100 000 people, or 3 per cent of Shanghai's population, were associated in some way with organised crime during this period.[57] So pervasive was the influence of the triads that Wang Jinrong, a notorious crime boss and head of the Qing Gang, was appointed as the Inspector-General of Police in the French concession in Shanghai.[58] The Qing Gang fled China for Taiwan in 1949, shortly before the communist victory on the mainland, and founded several other secret societies that later evolved into the Bamboo Gang, Pine League and Taindao League in Taiwan and the Triade, Sap Sie Kee (14K) and Suihuang in Hong Kong and Macau.[59] By the time of Hong Kong's return to China in 1997, there were some 150 000 triad members on the island out of a total population of 6 million; 30 000 formed a hard core of active members who had undergone initiation rights, while another 120 000 could be activated if needed. The preeminent Hong Kong group is the Sun Yee On, with around 40 000 members, followed by the Wo Shing Wo and Sap Sie Kee, with about 25 000 and 20 000 members respectively.[60]

The magnitude, diversity and geographical scope of their operations and their propensity for violence have given the triads a deserved reputation as the most serious Asian criminal threat to law and order and regional security. Triads engage in a wide range of criminal activities such as drug-trafficking, smuggling, money-laundering, bribery and extortion. They are an integral part of the global heroin trade and have extensive links with other ethnic Chinese and Asian gangs, as well as some of the largest and most notorious non-Asian TCOs. Their influence extends beyond their traditional bases in Hong Kong, Macau and Taiwan into mainland China, Japan and most of Southeast Asia as well as Australia, the United States, Canada and Europe. After a four-decade absence, the triads have reemerged in China following the economic reforms initiated by Deng Xiaoping in 1979 and have established political connections that extend all the way to the Politburo, the inner sanctum of the Chinese Communist Party.[61] During the 1930s and 1940s, senior Chinese communist leaders maintained close relationships with triad groups such as the Red Spear Society and the Elder Brother Society, although their activities were proscribed during Mao's rule.[62] Deng himself was quite sympathetic to the triads, remarking in 1984 that 'not all Chinese secret societies are bad, many societies are patriotic'.[63]

The degree to which Hong Kong-based triad groups have taken root in China over the past decade was thrown into sharp relief in 1993 by the public comments of Tao Siju, China's Minister for Public Security. In words reminiscent of Deng's earlier pronouncement, Tao declared:

> Triads are not all bad, some are good people and are patriotic ... Regarding such organisations as triads in Hong Kong, as long as these people are patriotic and as long as they are concerned about the stability and prosperity of Hong Kong, we should unite because I tend to believe the more people we unite the better.[64]

In a revealing example of how the communist leadership tolerates and even uses secret societies, Tao disclosed that his ministry had mobilised 800 triad members 'to guard a Chinese leader against potential danger when he was travelling abroad'.[65] Triad inroads into China are particularly evident in traditional strongholds like Shanghai and Shenzen. Hong Kong Special Branch officers believe that the Shanghai Gentlemens Club is run by the Sun Yee On triad in conjunction with senior members of the Shanghai police force. Other triads, once aligned with Taiwan, have been lured away from their former Kuomintang patrons with the promise of lucrative business opportunities in the Shenzen special zone adjacent to Hong Kong.[66]

The recrudescence of triad influence in China could not have taken place without the complicity of Chinese officials, which does not augur well for China's ability and willingness to limit triad activities in Hong Kong. Contrary to the expectations of many Western observers, the handover of the former British territory did not spur a mass exodus of triad members from Hong Kong.[67] As one senior Hong Kong police officer remarked at the time, 'who are these criminals supposed to be fleeing from?' Why emigrate when there are 'many more lucrative money-making opportunities in the territory and across the border in booming southern China'?[68] In the years since China assumed control of Hong Kong, few triad members are known to have relocated overseas and it is unlikely that they will do so. Aside from the top leadership, most have criminal records, are poorly educated and would be disinclined to move from a familiar environment to an almost certainly hostile foreign country unless they were forced to do so by the Chinese Government. Beijing has shown no inclination to rein in the Hong Kong-based triads. On the contrary, there are indications that the triads are moving to consolidate their position by developing access to the new power-brokers in Hong Kong and by penetrating key government institutions.[69]

There are striking parallels between Hong Kong and Macau. Most of Macau's gangs originated in Hong Kong and like their triad brothers they have maintained close links with the mainland, mirroring the symbiotic relationship between criminal groups and political rulers throughout China's long history.[70] Organised crime was so entrenched in Macau under the Portugese administration that before the assumption of Chinese control in 1999, over 28 per cent ($2.1 billion) of the island's gross national product came from gambling and the 4600-strong police force was outnumbered by some 12 000 active triad members.[71] For many years the triads and police lived in an uneasy coexistence, but the relative calm was shattered in 1997 as rival triad groups fought over gambling rights and positioned themselves in preparation for Macau's return to China. For nearly three years, bloody internecine gang warfare involving assassinations, bombings, kidnappings and violent shoot-outs were a regular occurrence and seriously threatened Macao's political and economic stability. Tourism dropped dramatically, as did gambling revenues.

By the end of 1999, organised crime had degenerated into disorganised crime, eventually forcing the Chinese Government's hand. Banker Edmund Ho, China's chief executive designate for Macau, promised to 'first address corruption, crime ... and exhaust all possible legal means to smash criminal gangs'.[72] One thousand elite soldiers from the PLA were deployed to Macau to ensure security and on 24 November 1999, Chinese courts sentenced three prominent triad members to death and gaoled the leader of the 14K for fifteen years.[73] Yet the triads have remained and prospered because the object of Beijing's crackdown was not to eliminate them but to ensure that they operated within acceptable parameters. In exchange for eschewing the anarchical gang warfare that nearly destroyed Macau's gambling-dependent economy in the late 1990s, the triads have been allowed to continue their lucrative criminal activities.

Triads are also very much part of Taiwan's underworld. The largest and most infamous triad clan is the United Bamboo Gang, which was estimated to have 40 000 active members at its zenith in the early 1980s before internal attrition and police operations reduced membership to 10 000. Other major Taiwanese gangs are the Four Seas, Sung Lian and the Heavenly Way Alliance. Their memberships range from several hundred to around 2000 in the case of the Four Seas.[74] The Taiwanese gangs have overseas cells in many Western and Asian countries and have been implicated in criminal activities in China's Fujian province since the 1980s.[75] Many Taiwanese legislators are known to have triad and gang connections – between 5 and 10 per cent by the government's own estimates, although the real figure is almost certainly a great deal higher. Some 20 per cent of provincial legislators and 33 per cent of elected officials at county level have triad affiliations. One senior politician, Luo Fu-tsu, has even admitted to being the 'spiritual leader' of the Heavenly Way Alliance.[76]

Despite a much-publicised 1997 crackdown on crime and the passage of an Organised Crime Prevention Statute, no national legislators, even those with well-known triad connections, have been incriminated – not surprisingly, perhaps, since former president Lee Teng-hui sought triad assistance when he wrested control of the party away from the old Kuomintang guard in 1987.[77] Since then triad influence in all sectors of Taiwanese life has steadily increased, including in the defence forces. In April 1998, the former director of the Defence Ministry's Military Affairs Bureau, Lieutenant General Liu Hsueh-ta, was arrested for leaking classified material to local defence contractors with triad connections. Liu was the highest-ranking officer ever arrested for corruption.[78] Triad members and their corrupt associates in bureaucratic and political circles are believed to have siphoned off US$26 billion from government public works projects between 1991 and 1996.[79]

Nonetheless, triad involvement in organised crime can be overstated.[80] The great majority of triad members are not active criminals – perhaps only 10 per cent according to estimates by the Hong Kong police.[81] Those triad members who do engage in hard-core crime are not as organised, as omnipresent or as deeply embedded within tightly knit, reclusive ethnic communities as is commonly supposed.[82] There is no central controlling body or the equivalent of La Cosa Nostra's 'boss of bosses', and ethnic and kinship ties are frequently subordinated to a stronger imperative – the desire to make money. It is not unusual for gangs belonging to the same society to compete and fight with each other, or for triads to seek tactical alliances with other societies.[83] Officials working at the national level, as well as politicians and the Western press, tend to regard all triads as well organised, highly structured and heavily engaged in crime. Those working on the ground with direct operational experience see greater variation in triad criminal involvement and more instability in their organisation.[84] The latter view is probably closer to reality. As Chu Yiu-kong argues, triads are 'neither a highly centralised nor a totally disorganised organisation but ... are loose cartels which organise in such a way that non-triad groups are excluded from gaining access to their organisational power'.[85]

Ethnic Gangs

Much organised crime in East Asia is carried out by ethnic Chinese groups that are not secret societies and have only the most cursory affiliation with the triads. Chinese gangs have sprung up in many parts of Southeast Asia, Australia, Europe, the United States and wherever there are significant ethnic Chinese enclaves. Rather than forming a homogeneous Chinese criminal diaspora, these groups operate as autonomous entities, often in competition with longer established triads. The smaller street gangs are rudimentary in their organisation, and typically consist of young men in their teens or twenties who engage in petty rather than major crime.[86] However, some of the larger Chinese gangs such as the Big Circle Gang, which is particularly active in Europe, are expanding rapidly and their operations are beginning to rival those of the triads.

Other non-ethnic Chinese gangs and organisations are gaining in influence, notably the Vietnamese, Thai and minority tribespeople of northern Burma.[87] Vietnamese and Sino-Vietnamese gangs have developed a reputation for violence and are considered more versatile than their Chinese counterparts. Based in Vietnam and emerging out of newly established émigré communities in the West, many young Vietnamese men initially found employment with triads as enforcers, but in the 1990s some branched out to form their own gangs. Prominent Vietnamese gangs such as BTK (Born to Kill) and 5T are heavily engaged in criminal activities ranging from extortion and home invasions to more serious crimes such as narcotics-trafficking and money-laundering. Other gangs active in East Asia with international connections include Nigerians, Koreans, Pakistanis, Russians, Australians, Europeans and Americans from both continents.[88]

The Japanese Yakuza

Organised crime groups in Japan are generally referred to as *yakuza*, although strictly speaking the Japanese term *boryokudan* is more accurate because it includes all forms of organised crime in Japan, not only those that conform to the particular traditions and beliefs of the yakuza. The name *yakuza* is derived from the sum of the numbers by which one loses the traditional card game *hanafunda: ya* equals eight, *ku* nine and *za* three.[89] The yakuza trace their origins back to the Ronin, samurai who carved out a living in seventeenth-century Japan providing protection against marauding bands of outlaws and bandits in exchange for money. But the true antecedent of the yakuza was the prototype criminal organisation Bakuto, which emerged in the eighteenth century during the Tokugawa era.[90] Over the years the various yakuza clans insinuated themselves into the innermost reaches of Japanese society and developed a dense, highly structured web of criminal linkages within their individual families and subcultures. Yakuza members swear loyalty and fealty to a hierarchically organised leadership structure, and are distinguished by a culture which emphasises ritual, servitude and group identity based on quasi-familial Confucian lines.[91] All power is concentrated in the leader of the clan (*oyabun*) and a member's status within the organisation is mainly determined by income.[92]

There are an estimated 53 000 full yakuza members and 24 000 associate members divided into 2300 groups and subgroups.[93] The largest family is the Yamaguchi-gumi, which dominates the densely populated Kyoto–Osaka industrial belt in the south of Japan's main island, Honshu. Other major groups are the Inagawa-kai, the Sumiyoshi-kai, Toa Yuai Jigyo Kumiai and Sumiyoshi-rengo.[94] Not all yakuza activities are criminal in nature and in many respects yakuza values mirror those of mainstream Japanese society. Nevertheless, their essential purpose is illicit profit, and violence and intimidation are routine tools of trade. What sets the yakuza apart from most other organised criminal groups in East Asia is the degree to which they have acquired political influence in their home state and commensurate financial muscle.

Yakuza criminal operations are extensive in scope, ranging from petty crime to major fraud, arms-smuggling, extortion and drug-trafficking. Since the early 1950s, the yakuza have cornered the domestic drug market for stimulants, especially crystal amphetamines known colloquially as 'ice'.[95] Taking advantage of the speculative fever of the late 1980s, when real estate prices and the local stock market recorded surreal increases, the yakuza gravitated from their dealings in drugs and prostitution at the fringes of the economy into the heart of the Japanese financial system. Initially they began buying into real estate and development projects. They then moved into finance lending and preyed on smaller lenders such as the *jusen* (housing loan corporations) and credit unions. As prices collapsed, banks and financial institutions were left holding US$350 billion in bad loans, at least $35 billion of which was owed by the yakuza.[96] The problem for the banks and the government was that these debts were effectively uncollectible because the yakuza refused to pay.

The few banks brave enough to attempt collection wound up with dead or badly frightened executives.[97] In the mid-1990s, the yakuza dominated the real estate market and made more loans to individual Japanese than the legitimate banking system. They also controlled a substantial part of the Japanese stock market and ran in the order of 20 000 legally constituted businesses.[98]

Yakuza political influence stems from their close links to the Liberal-Democratic Party (LDP) which has dominated Japanese politics since the Second World War. There are allegations that the yakuza has effectively become an underground government and that its coercive power over the LDP is comparable to that wielded by the mafia over the Christian Democrats in Italy.[99] While this may overstate yakuza influence, the close relationship between organised crime, big business and political parties has been an enduring feature of Japan's postwar political and economic landscape. During the 1960s, the LDP employed the yakuza to put down radical students and labour militants, while individual LDP politicians have used the yakuza to further their political ambitions. Yakuza families have channelled money into the LDP over a long time in return for political favour and patronage.

Although their activities are overwhelmingly concentrated in Japan, the yakuza have established one of the largest criminal confederations in the world, extending well beyond their Japanese base into the United States, Australia, South Korea and Southeast Asia.[100] Hawaii has become a major money-laundering centre for the yakuza since the upsurge in Japanese tourism to the island. The yakuza have strong connections with Korean criminals, financing South Korean-based laboratories which supply most of the world market for ice and using Koreans as couriers and enforcers.[101] Cooperation with the triads and ethnic Chinese gangs is more limited and tenuous. The yakuza are wary of Chinese criminals and have a healthy respect for their competitive instincts and entrepreneurial talents. Chinese gangs and triads began to move into Japan's entertainment industry in the late 1990s, taking over many bars and brothels and forcing out the local criminals. Acknowledging the business acumen and ruthlessness of the Chinese, one yakuza summed up the difference between the groups in this way: 'For Japanese yakuza, the most important thing is staying alive, and making money is second. But for the Chinese gangsters, the first thing is money. The second thing is money. And the third thing is money'.[102]

Conclusion

The globalising forces of the information age are transforming the way in which criminals organise and operate. Not all criminal associations are threats to security and the business conducted by criminals is not always illegal. But in their search for illicit profits, transnational criminal groups are challenging the political authority of governments, undermining the economic foundations of states and threatening the welfare and liberty of millions of people around the world. Crime is firmly entrenched on the international security agenda of the twenty-first century, but the scale and diversity of criminal transactions poses formidable challenges for law enforcement, foreign policy and defence. While governments remain sovereignty-bound, criminals are increasingly sovereignty-free, operating with relative impunity across borders made permeable by the transnational flow of people, money and information.

Developing states are most at risk because of their relatively fragile institutions and the scarcity of resources, both human and capital, needed for effective crime prevention. In East Asia, a number of insurgent movements have sacrificed their political aims and revolutionary elan on the altar of Mammon and transnational criminal groups have amassed enormous wealth and significant military power. Endemic corruption underpins and sustains major crime and habituates people to working outside the regulatory environment and the rule of law. Government officials are routinely co-opted and corrupted by TCOs, while governments themselves may directly engage in criminal activities, as North Korea attests.

Coordinating effective regional responses is difficult because the nature and pattern of criminality is constantly evolving and the level and type of crime varies between countries and subregions. White-collar crime predominates in developed Japan, Taiwan, South Korea and Singapore, whereas violent challenges to national governments are more characteristic of East Asia's developing states. Pornography, protection rackets and home invasions clearly have implications for individual liberty and personal safety, but seldom do they impinge on the sovereign interests of the state in the manner of war or major political and economic instability. On the other hand, trafficking in drugs, arms and contraband, piracy, money-laundering, counterfeiting and cyber-crime all have important implications for regional security because these activities subvert the political authority of governments and imperil the economic and social foundations of the state.

Many criminal organisations are venture-specific, coming together in loose, transient arrangements for a particular operation and then quickly disbanding after the illicit transaction has been completed. Chinese heroin groups increasingly work in this way, while the Colombian and Mexican drug cartels are structured and organised along more permanent and hierarchical lines.[103] The scope and focus of the illegal activities conducted by transnational criminal organisations also varies considerably and shapes their organisational dynamics. The Cali cartel concentrates on narcotics whereas the Russian mafiya, in the tradition of its Sicilian counterpart, is far less discriminating and oversees a wide repertoire of criminal transactions. Similarly, the Japanese yakuza and other Asian criminal organisations operate across a wide range of illegal activities.[104] Modern triads cannot be characterised by one organisational type. Some are well organised with extensive international connections; others are far less structured. In virtually all cases they are highly adaptive. Triad authority is also more diffuse and their associations more ephemeral than in the past.[105]

The triads and yakuza are the two dominant transnational criminal organisations in East Asia but other ethnic gangs are beginning to make their presence felt, especially the Vietnamese. Each has distinct cultures but they share a propensity for violence; both are adept at penetrating state institutions and operate with little regard for sovereign borders or, by definition, the rule of law. By virtue of their natural aggression, adaptability and impressive financial resources, triads are the greatest organised criminal threat to the region. Although less agile and structurally more rigid than their triad counterparts, the yakuza are embedded to a far greater degree in mainstream Japanese society than are the triads in their home environments. But their reach is not as extensive as those of the triads nor are they as formidable beyond Japan. The regional picture is completed by a bevy of smaller entrepreneurial criminals, some of whom play important roles in facilitating major crime.

The influence and capabilities of the triads, yakuza and other emerging criminal groups should not be exaggerated. Triads are more loosely affiliated and less disciplined than popular fiction would suggest and the vast majority of their members are not involved in serious crime. Outside Japan, the yakuza are heavily reliant on the relatively small Japanese diaspora in East Asia and are not as effective internationally as the triads or some of the non-triad Chinese and Vietnamese gangs with whom they compete. There is no centralised, overarching authority or pan-Asian criminal imperium, and the scale and intensity of organised crime fluctuates according to the opportunities for illicit profit, the degree of government complicity, and the efficacy of national and regional programs for combating and preventing crime. Nevertheless, economic integration and the increasingly porous nature of East Asia's borders are providing TCOs with unparalleled opportunities to acquire illicit wealth. Wealth in turn provides the incentive and means to contest the authority and prerogatives of state power and diminishes the ability of governments to protect their citizens from the predations of organised crime.

CHAPTER 10

Drug-trafficking – An Emerging Threat

The drug trade is arguably the most serious of the multitude of criminal endeavours that diminish the security of states and their citizens. It is also emblematic of the growing capacity of non-state actors to challenge the centuries-old monopoly over the instruments of coercive power enjoyed by nation-states. Traffickers of illicit narcotics bring untold suffering to millions, distort international economic and trading patterns, infiltrate and suborn political, business, judicial and military elites and transform power relationships to the detriment of good government and the rule of law.[1] Increasingly, drug-traffickers are allying themselves with separatist and terrorist groups, serving as 'cash cows' in return for protection and access to paramilitary resources.[2] In some cases, the drug-traffickers and insurgents are one and the same; in others, the state is complicit or sponsors drug-trafficking to the detriment of its own people and those of other states. Like many emerging transnational challenges to security, the illicit trade in narcotics is not new, but the global reach of today's drug-traffickers and their accumulation of enormous wealth sets them apart from their predecessors. As Giorgio Giacomelli, executive director of the UN International Drug Control Program, has written: 'All over the world, individuals and societies face an illicit drug problem whose scale was unimaginable a generation ago ... as drug abuse affects more and more countries, the power of international drug trafficking organisations threatens to corrupt and destabilize the institutions of government'.[3]

Aside from a handful of studies focusing on the narco-politics of the Golden Triangle, there has been surprisingly little analysis of the wider dimensions of the contemporary drug trade in East Asia and its impact on the security of the region.[4] Yet East Asia would appear to have many of the underlying conditions that transnational criminal groups have exploited in other regions of the world to reap rich financial and political rewards.

194

Narcotics-trafficking has grown enormously in sophistication and volume in conjunction with the spread of Asian organised crime. While the production and consumption of narcotic substances has a long history in East Asia, there are several disturbing new developments which have forced narcotics-trafficking onto the regional security agenda for the first time.[5] Once mainly a producer of heroin, East Asia has become a major heroin consumer and an emerging market for a new class of designer drugs like 'ice' and 'ecstasy'.[6] Drug dependency is on the rise, including in states with no recent history of drug addiction such as China and Vietnam, while drug money is distorting regional economies and exacerbating corruption and political instability. Narcotics-trafficking is now big business in the region and one of the few enterprises to flourish during East Asia's economic crisis as impoverished and unemployed workers turned to drug-dealing to supplement their meagre incomes.

The Global Narcotics Trade

The extent to which the illicit drug trade has begun to reshape East Asia's security environment cannot be grasped without an understanding of its global dynamics and characteristics. The international drug trade is centred on four main types of drugs. The most widely abused and heavily trafficked by volume is cannabis, which is derived from the plant of the same name and is consumed by at least 140 million people worldwide. However, cannabis is far less potent than cocaine, heroin, or amphetamine-type stimulants (ATS), which, if taken on a regular basis, are habit forming and can have serious social and health consequences.[7]

Between 3.3 per cent and 4.1 per cent of the world's 6 billion people are regular users of illicit drugs; of these an estimated 21 million are cocaine and heroin addicts while another 30 million suffer from ATS abuse.[8] In the mid-1990s the annual profit from narcotics-trafficking was around $400 billion, or 8 per cent of international trade – equal to the combined GDPs of Indonesia, Malaysia and Thailand.[9] The OECD believes that illicit drugs cost its member states over $120 billion annually for medical treatment, policing and in lost production.[10] In the United States alone, 1.7 million people regularly use cocaine and the government estimates that every dollar invested in the drug trade reaps $12 240 for traffickers.[11] Although these figures must be treated with some caution, given the difficulty of calculating precisely the value of an industry that is inherently non-transparent, they lend credence to claims that a culture of drug-taking has entrenched itself globally, enriching and empowering today's drug lords to a degree that has few precedents.[12]

Latin America is the region most closely associated in the public mind with the illicit drug trade, and for good reason. Cocaine is Latin America's

second largest export after petroleum, accounting for 3–4 per cent of the
GDPs of Peru and Bolivia and employing half a million Andeans.[13] Virtually all the cocaine produced for export comes from Peru, Bolivia and
Colombia and is largely destined for the North American market.[14] Before
its demise in the mid-1990s, approximately 70 per cent of the global trade
in cocaine was controlled by the Medellin cartel.[15] Drug syndicates and
narco-insurgents have at various times directly challenged the political as
well as the economic sovereignty of Colombia, and to a lesser extent Bolivia
and Peru. Since the 1980s, the government of Colombia has been in a virtual state of war with drug-traffickers that has resulted in the deaths of over
1200 judges and 5000 police officers.[16] In the late 1990s, Colombia's drug
lords joined with the country's largest rebel group, the Revolutionary
Armed Forces of Colombia (FARC), in a powerful alliance that benefited
both, to the detriment of the Colombian state, illustrating how internal
conflicts are being criminalised by narcotics-trafficking.[17]

While Colombia and other Latin American states dominate the
cocaine trade, Asia is the leading producer of heroin – an analgesic, narcotic and potentially addictive drug refined from the cultivation of the
immature fruit of the opium poppy, *Papaver somniferum*. Ninety per cent
of opium is grown in the Golden Triangle (Burma, Thailand and Laos)
and Golden Crescent (Afghanistan, Iran and Pakistan) for a global market. In 1996, at the high point of its production, the Golden Triangle produced 65 per cent of all illicit opium and sustained a heroin industry
worth US\$160 billion annually, four times the value of the international
arms trade in that year.[18] Burma produces the lion's share of the Golden
Triangle heroin, but its cultivation of illicit opium fell significantly at the
end of the decade, largely because of the effects of drought.[19] Nevertheless, the country remains the world's second largest heroin producer
after Afghanistan, accounting for 80 per cent of total Southeast Asian
production.[20] Despite the fall in the area given over to opium poppy cultivation, more efficient cropping and extraction techniques have substantially increased heroin yields so that there has been no noticeable fall
in overall heroin production.[21]

The reason for heroin's profitability and hence its attraction to organised crime is that the mark-up is extremely high both in absolute terms
and relative to most other commodities. A single kilogram of heroin typically doubles in price by the time the narcotic reaches its first transshipment point in the Thai city of Chiang Mai; it triples again in Bangkok and
eventually sells for between two and six times the Bangkok price in New
York.[22] Profits can be even higher still, depending on demand, availability, purity and exchange rate fluctuations. A 700-gram brick of heroin
costs a wholesaler in Australia around US\$53 000. When adulterated with
other chemicals and sold in small 20-milligram bags, each bag retails for

Table 10.1 Potential illicit opium production, East Asia, 1991–99 (metric tonnes)

Country	1999	1998	1997	1996	1995	1994	1993	1992	1991
Burma	1090	1750	2365	2560	2340	2030	2575	2280	2350
China					19	25			
Laos	140	140	210	200	180	85	180	230	265
Thailand	6	16	25	30	25	17	42	24	35
Vietnam	11	20	45	25					
Total E Asia	1247	1926	2645	2815	2564	2157	2797	2534	2650

Source: International Narcotics Control Strategy Report 1999, Released by the Bureau for International Narcotics and Law Enforcement Affairs, US Department of State, Washington, D.C., March 2000, www.state.gov/www/global/narcotics_law/1999_narc_report/seasi99.html

about $25, which means that 1 kilogram of heroin on the streets of Sydney is worth between $650 000 and $750 000.[23]

While heroin production stabilised during the second half of the 1990s, the use and abuse of ATS has soared, particularly in North America, Europe and East Asia. Despite their modern image, the first amphetamines – the progenitors of designer drugs like ecstasy – actually first appeared over a century ago. In the 1930s they were regarded as having beneficial therapeutic qualities and were enthusiastically promoted; they are still widely prescribed for a range of medical conditions. Ecstasy was synthesised and patented in 1914, but was never marketed until rediscovered in the 1970s by American psychiatrists who valued its capacity to facilitate interpersonal communication and empathy. Ecstasy is the quintessential modern drug. Its popularity is due in part to its much sought after side-effects which include feelings of serenity, well-being, enhanced performance and a mild euphoric 'rush'.

Ecstasy and other synthetic stimulants have been cleverly marketed to a new generation of younger drug-takers as relatively benign, fashionable narcotics – an image that belies their addictive properties. These drugs have no counterpart in nature and can be reproduced in virtually unlimited quantities from existing chemicals, unlike heroin, cocaine and other plant-based drugs. They can also be altered structurally to increase their potency.[24] In the absence of reliable data, it is difficult to know how much ATS is produced globally but a crude picture can be obtained by analysing seizure rates. Global seizures of ATS increased slowly from 281 kilograms in 1976 to 1.3 tonnes in 1990, but thereafter they exploded, far exceeding that of any other drug type. With 30 million regular users, for the first time, in 1996, the abuse of ATS surpassed that of heroin and cocaine combined, and consumption of ATS has soared since, presenting a new drug challenge for already hard-pressed security and law enforcement officials.[25]

East Asia's Drug Problem

The Shan hills of northeastern Burma form the apex of the Golden Triangle, producing around 90 per cent of all heroin exported from the region – enough to satisfy the US market for heroin many times over.[26] One reason for Burma's domination of the heroin trade in the 1990s was the break-up of the Burmese Communist Party (BCP) into its constituent tribal elements following the surrender of the predominantly Burmese leadership in 1989.[27] In the previous three decades the BCP had conducted a violent armed struggle against the central government from its base in the Shan state. Eschewing involvement in the drug trade during its ideologically pure formative years, the BCP turned to narcotics-trafficking in the 1970s to finance its war against the Ne Win government

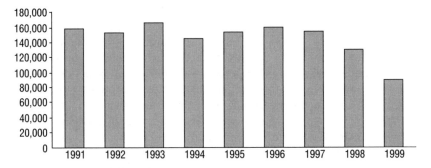

Figure 10.1 Opium cultivation in Burma, 1991–99 (in hectares)
Note: Serious drought was responsible for low crop yields in 1999.
Source: International Narcotics Control Strategy Report, 1999, Bureau for
International Narcotics and Law Enforcement Affairs, US Department of State,
Washington, D.C., March 2000, www.state.gov/www/global/narcotics_law/1999_
narc_report/seasi99.html

and subsequently became a major heroin player. Far from heralding a decline in Golden Triangle heroin production, the demise of the BCP had the opposite effect, resulting in a substantial increase as splinter groups competed for market share and became full-time traffickers.[28] Fearful that the remnants of the BCP might form alliances with disaffected urban youth alienated by the army's crushing of the 1988 pro-democracy movement, Rangoon negotiated a series of understandings with them. In exchange for promises not to attack government troops or move into government-controlled areas, the Burmese military government gave the former insurgents virtual freedom to engage in 'private' business activities, a euphemism for narcotics-trafficking.

A second reason for the rise in Burmese heroin production is that influential members of the SPDC have been co-opted by the drug lords who control the heroin trade in much the same way as the Colombian and Bolivian governments have been penetrated by the cocaine cartels.[29] The SPDC has denied allegations of complicity in narcotics-trafficking, pointing to the 3000 casualties the army has suffered since 1988 in the war against drug insurgents.[30] There is little doubt, however, that the regime has permitted and even encouraged known drug-traffickers like Khun Sa and the family of former drug lord Luo Xinghan to establish themselves as leading business figures. As much as 60 per cent of all private investment in Burma is drug-related.[31] Many of the ceasefire agreements negotiated with tribal minorities allow them to continue their narcotics cultivation and trafficking activities, and elements of the Burmese Army are almost certainly involved in the heroin and amphetamine trades.[32] There is evidence that the government has financed much of its arms build-up over the past decade from taxes levied on heroin refineries.[33] Far from benefiting Burma, however, drug money has seriously distorted the national economy and Rangoon's development priorities. Rather than being directed towards much-needed infrastructure, industry and social services, most money derived from narcotics-trafficking is channelled into non-essential real estate or marginally productive enterprises such as hotels, karaoke bars and restaurants.

Although it could be argued that Burma is an isolated, albeit egregious, case of a drug-tainted state largely quarantined from the economic life and the security concerns of the wider East Asian region, the evidence suggests otherwise. Burma has become the hub of a global heroin industry, and other East Asian states are being drawn into a regionwide market and distribution network for illegal narcotics dominated by Asian criminal organisations and Burma's drug barons. China is emblematic of East Asia's emerging drug security problem. In 1949, there were estimated to be 20 million drug addicts in China before the opium trade was ruthlessly stamped out by the communists[34] – to such an extent that in the mid-1960s China proudly proclaimed itself to be a 'country without narcotics'.[35] However, drug-trafficking and opium addiction has reemerged as a serious issue since the watershed 1979 modernisation campaign transformed the political and social climate in China. Initially, the drug problem was confined to the provinces adjacent to the Golden Triangle and Xinjiang Province in the far west of the country – the natural point of entry for Central Asian drugs. As China's modernisation gathered steam, high-grade heroin began to make its appearance throughout the country, especially in the larger cities like Beijing and Shanghai as well as Fujian province, which is adjacent to Taiwan.[36]

By the mid-1990s, the drug problem had become serious enough to attract the attention of senior Party officials in Beijing. A nationwide anti-drug campaign was launched in April 1997, and in May of that year, Ruan Zhengyi, the deputy director of China's Public Security Bureau, acknowledged that 'the problem of drugs has returned to China with a vengeance'.[37] Three years later, a special white paper on narcotics control published by the State Council noted that the number of drug addicts in China 'has kept rising, drug related cases have constantly increased, the drug scourge is becoming more serious with each passing day, and the situation is grim for the anti-drug struggle'.[38] China's seizure of heroin in 1999 exceeded that of all other Asian countries combined, lending weight to the State Council's assessment. The once drug-free state is now the principal route for heroin smuggled out of Burma.[39]

In the Philippines the escalating level of drug dependence and the power of local drug lords has become a major social, political and security issue. A study by the Philippine National Police Narcotics Group paints a grim picture of the corrosive effects of drugs on the social and political fabric of the nation. The Philippines has 1.7 million drug-users, and the annual turnover of the illegal drug trade in the Philippines was estimated to be US$9.5 billion (251 billion pesos) in 1997, which represented more than half that year's national budget. Over 80 per cent of this money is derived from the crystalline stimulant methamphetamine hydrochloride, known locally as 'shabu' and abroad as 'ice', which was once manufactured from stimulants brought in from China and Taiwan. However, the discovery and destruction of local manufacturing or recrystallisation laboratories is clear evidence that domestic involvement in ATS production is on the rise.[40]

The Philippines also produces a substantial quantity of cannabis and other banned drugs locally, valued at US$1.8 billion (46.5 billion pesos) in 1997, and it has become a major transshipment point for heroin destined for Europe and the west coast of the United States.[41] It does not, as yet, have a significant domestic heroin problem. President Ramos declared drug addiction 'a threat to national security' in 1997 and a senior Philippine senator, Ernesto Herrera, has warned that without resolute action the Philippines could be transformed into a narco-state. According to Herrera, 'drug money is corrupting and co-opting elements in immigration, customs, the police and the military. It has even penetrated the ranks of court officers and some well-placed public officials'.[42] Alleged connections between drug-dealers and members of the Filipino elite has become a contentious domestic political issue and spilled over into the 1998 presidential campaign. The soon to be elected Vice-President, Gloria Macapagal-Arroyo, was forced to defend herself against politically inspired claims by her opponents that she had ties to local drug lords.[43]

In virtually every country in the region, corrupt government officials and members of the security forces have been recruited by organised crime. In some cases corruption has reached right into the heart of the state organisations responsible for countering drug-trafficking. Cambodia's Interior Minister, General Khieu Sopheak, has admitted that corrupt elements in the national police and armed forces are involved in the narcotics trade.[44] A last-minute confession by a convicted Lao drug courier in July 1996 led to the arrest and conviction of a number of senior Vietnamese police officers who were found guilty of complicity in the largest and most serious case of drug-smuggling discovered in Vietnam to that date.[45] Two cases in 1999 implicated senior customs and public security officials in heroin-trafficking from Laos.[46] In Indonesia a police captain admitted to being part of a local drug syndicate after having been found with hundreds of ecstasy tablets in his possession, while some two dozen Manila policemen were placed under surveillance in 1997 because of their close association with known drug-dealers.[47]

Why Has Drug-trafficking Entrenched Itself in the Region?

The rise in illicit narcotics production and trafficking in East Asia stems from a complex amalgam of domestic and international causes. North Korea's moribund economy and dysfunctional state apparatus has forced its diplomats to supplement their embassy finances by engaging in a range of government-sponsored criminal activities. In Burma, the diversification of heroin producers into amphetamine production can be seen as a logical extension of existing narcotics-trafficking by ethnic Chinese drug lords responding to changing demand, while the political instability and endemic corruption that has pervaded Cambodia since Vietnam's withdrawal in the early 1990s has created an ideal operating environment for organised crime in that country.

More generally, the spread of illicit drugs has been facilitated by East Asia's long period of sustained economic growth and the establishment of world-class regional communication and transportation networks. New road, river and air routes have benefited the drug-traffickers, allowing them to move their illicit contraband to international markets with relative ease; at the same time these routes preserve the anonymity of the transactions and the identity of the middlemen who play a vital role in laundering drug profits and linking the producers with their distributors and final markets. Regional growth triangles, what Robert Scalapino calls 'natural economic territories', have helped to accelerate cross-border trade and reduce the border restrictions and choke-points which once circumscribed the free flow of drugs between East Asian states.[48] The area encompassing the Golden Triangle has been subsumed within a wider economic development quadrangle that links Burma, Thailand and Laos with southern China, creating new market opportunities and distribution routes for the opium warlords of Burma and their triad associates operating out of hubs such as Hong Kong and Bangkok. These two cities have effectively become the corporate headquarters and key distribution centres for the traffickers who control East Asia's drug trade.[49]

The regional economic crisis provided a further boost to the drug trade and the activities of organised crime. As unemployment escalated, impoverished and unemployed workers saw narcotics-trafficking as an economic lifeline. Thousands were involved as couriers, spotters, facilitators and dealers, usually at the base of the industry pyramid. Many also became users, including government workers.[50] For heroin-producers and wholesalers, profits soared because the narcotic was paid for in Thai baht and then sold overseas in US dollars or other hard currencies.[51] The Thai baht almost halved in value against the US dollar at the height of the economic crisis, representing a considerable windfall profit for the narco-bosses at the top of the pyramid. Conversely, the declining budgets of East Asian governments reduced the amount of money available for drug interdiction, opium poppy replacement crops, and cooperative regional responses.[52]

The sophistication and reach of today's Asian drug-traffickers has few historical parallels. Once based on family or local identity, with limited international connections, the trafficking of narcotics in East Asia is now more commonly distinguished by strategic alliances and integrated networks which enable organised criminal groups to span East Asia into the global market. James Mills has characterised these networks as a kind of criminal imperium, 'an underground empire as ruthlessly acquisitive and exploitative as any nineteenth-century imperial kingdom'. According to Mills, this imperium maintains its own armies, diplomats, intelligence services, banks, merchant fleets and airlines, and seeks 'to extend its dominance by any means, from clandestine subversion to open warfare'.[53] However, Mills overstates his case. The illicit drug trade and the relationship between drug-traffickers and their criminal associates is better understood in more prosaic terms. As Phil Williams argues, TCOs are more alliances of convenience based on strictly economic considerations rather than elements of a global criminal conspiracy.[54]

The alliances may be tactical or strategic in nature, or between small as well as large transnational criminal organisations. This is especially the case in East Asia where drug-traffickers tend to be more loosely configured and less hierarchically organised than, for example, the Colombian cartels or the Sicilian Cosa Nostra.[55] The popular Western image of an inscrutable oriental crime mandarin orchestrating the activities of a monolithic crime cartel is at variance with the reality of drug-trafficking in East Asia. This illicit trade encompasses an extremely diverse range of organisations, from highly organised transnational criminal groups to traditional tribal producers, small-scale family business operations and ephemeral, entrepreneurial 'marriages' of convenience between individuals and groups. In a typical operation, opium grown by the ethno-insurgent groups of Burma will be processed and refined into heroin in their well-equipped and staffed laboratories along the Chinese and Thai borders. The heroin is then passed onto Chinese and Thai ethnic criminal networks for transshipment by heroin brokers in Bangkok, Hong Kong, Ho Chi Minh City, Manila and Taipei.[56]

Increasingly, growers are diversifying into processing and distribution, extending the geographical spread of their operations by taking advantage of new heroin distribution routes which have opened up in southern China, Laos, Cambodia and Vietnam.[57] Most of the heroin produced in the Golden Triangle was once moved almost exclusively overland through Thailand to Bangkok, by sea from Thailand to Hong Kong, or from Burma across the southern Chinese provinces of Yunnan and Guangxi, to Guangdong, Hong Kong and Macau.[58] But there are now multiple land, sea and air routes throughout the region. Burmese heroin is frequently moved from the Shan hills of Burma, through Mandalay and then to Rangoon, Moulmein or other seaports for shipment to Singapore and Malaysia.[59] Some travels westward across the Bangladeshi border to developing markets in India and Bangladesh. Drug-running into Taiwan is also highly organised. Heroin is often hidden inside fishing trawlers which ply between the Fujian coast and the port of Hehliu near Taipei. At other times drugs are carried in container ships sailing between Bangkok to the port of Kaohsiung and Taipei.[60]

Cambodia has become a significant producer as well as a major alternative to Thailand as a heroin transshipment state.[61] Drug-traffickers have taken advantage of Cambodia's unstable political environment and weak law enforcement capabilities to move heroin by sea from the southwestern port of Koh Kong and by air from Phnom Penh's Pochentong airport.[62] Even Buddhist monks have been caught up in the trade as couriers.[63] In 1999, Cambodia's National Authority for Combating Drugs reported that illegal drug laboratories had begun to appear in the northwestern and southwestern parts of the country and that the number of Cambodian addicts was on the increase.[64] Laos, which has traditionally been a major producer of opium – the third largest after Burma and Afghanistan – is rapidly becoming a major distribution route with a significant proportion of the drugs making their way across the border to the Vietnamese coastal city of Da Nang for shipment to the United States and Australia.[65] Nearly a hundred cases involving drug-trafficking across the Laos–Vietnam border were detected between 1993 and 1999.[66]

Ho Chi Minh city has become an important new centre for heroin distribution, some of which is finding its way down the Malay peninsular into Malaysia, Singapore and Indonesia. While Singapore's tough anti-drug laws have circumscribed drug use in the city-state, traffickers are exploiting Singapore's well-developed financial and shipping infrastructure for the transit of narcotics and the laundering of drug profits.[67] From Singapore and Malaysia, drugs are moved by boat or air to Brunei, the Philippines, Indonesia and eventually Australia and New Zealand.[68] Australia has become a major market for Burmese heroin. A heroin seizure in October 1998, one of the largest on record, netted 400 kilograms of heroin that had made its way from Burma overland to China's Yunnan province and then by boat to the Australian east coast.[69] TCOs based in Bangkok use Nigerian couriers to carry heroin into Jakarta's Soekarno Hatta airport via commercial flights for onward distribution to Australia, the United States and Europe.[70]

East Asia as a Major Drug Market

Long the primary producer of heroin, Asia now has two-thirds of the world's heroin-users and the region as a whole has gravitated from being a producer of drugs for consumers in the West to the world's largest market for illegal drugs.[71] Until the late 1980s, virtually all the heroin from the Golden Triangle went to the United States or other non-Asian markets, but today much of it is destined for East Asia. In a worrying new trend, with potentially serious long-term security and health consequences for the region, the number of addicts has begun to rise steeply.

Thailand is estimated to have 500 000 heroin addicts, which is more per capita than the United States, while Burma has between 400 000 and 500 000.[72] Narco-traffickers respect neither borders nor political, cultural or religious divides. Relatively developed Muslim Malaysia has around 160 000 addicts while still impoverished Communist Vietnam has at least 200 000.[73] Vietnamese police officials estimate that up to 15 tonnes of heroin are entering Vietnam every year, an increasing percentage of which is finding its way onto the domestic market. This figure seems to be supported by the number of Vietnamese students being arrested for possessing heroin and the rise in the number of registered drug addicts to 97 000 at the end of 1999.[74] There is also evidence of a substantial increase in opium cultivation in the mountainous northwestern provinces of Lai Chau, Son La and Nghe An, while in China heroin addiction is escalating rapidly and already exceeds that of any other East Asian state.[75] Between 1991 and 1999, the number of registered drug addicts in China rose from 148 000 to 681 000, over two-thirds of whom are addicted to heroin.[76] These figures are extremely conservative and almost certainly understate the real level of drug dependency.

There has been an even more dramatic rise in the production and consumption of amphetamine-type stimulants, which seem likely to replace heroin as the future drugs of choice in the region. Stimulants have been present in East Asia for many years but were once largely confined to Japan and South Korea, which have significant methamphetamine problems.[77] However, the new designer drugs have a much wider appeal and have penetrated most regional states. The rise in ATS production may prove to be a seminal transformation of the narcotics trade.[78] The Thai Office of the Narcotics Control Board believes that ATS generates more profits for traffickers than all the heroin consumed locally in Southeast Asia and exported from the region.[79] Thailand is the nation most seriously affected by the wave of stimulants flooding into East Asia. Known locally as *ya ba* ('madness medicine'), ATS have only been readily available in the country since the early 1990s, but by 1998 Thailand had more *ya ba* users than heroin addicts.[80] Retailing at around 67 US cents a tablet, they are much cheaper than heroin, which makes them affordable for low-income earners.[81] According to Thailand's Narcotics Control Board, more than 100 million amphetamine tablets were smuggled into the country from laboratories in Burma and Cambodia in 1997, but by 2000 the number had increased dramatically to 600 million, and an estimated 1 million Thais were regular amphetamine abusers.[82] So serious has the problem become that in September 2000 Admiral Dennis Blair, head of the US Pacific Command, pledged to supply the Thai military with counter-narcotics training and equipment, including possibly Blackhawk helicopters.[83]

There are two main reasons for the sudden upsurge in ATS production and consumption in East Asia. Modernisation and rapid economic growth has stimulated the demand for ATS because of their performance-enhancing characteristics, which temporarily increase well-being and productivity. It is no coincidence that the first serious users of ATS in Thailand were long-distance truck and bus drivers.[84] In the early 1990s, students and factory workers began to emulate the ATS habits of these drivers, spreading the drug culture more widely into areas of the community not previously affected. Following a trend first noticed in Europe and North America, designer drugs like ecstasy have become an accepted part of the East Asian disco and party scene, which has contributed to their rapid spread among young urban users.[85] ATS were initially imported into the region from Europe, but as demand for the new class of drugs grew, heroin-producers in the Golden Triangle began to switch some of their production to ATS. The first ATS laboratories were only established in the early 1990s but they have since proliferated rapidly, particularly along Burma's border with China. Hundreds of chemists have been recruited from Europe to staff these new laboratories and others have sprung up in Vietnam and the Philippines.[86]

A second reason for the spread of ATS is that they are attractive to producers as well as consumers, although for different reasons. Even though the profit margins are less than for comparable amounts of heroin, because ATS are sold locally and in volume they produce a quick return on investment and the manufacturing process is more flexible.[87] The laboratories used for manufacturing ATS are smaller, more mobile and therefore more difficult to detect than those required for refining heroin. While a major part of the heroin market is geographically distant from the Golden Triangle, necessitating the maintenance of a lengthy and expensive distribution network, the ATS markets are increasingly in East Asia. ATS are well entrenched in Taiwan, Japan and South Korea, but China has seen the most dramatic increase, with seizures doubling in 1999 from the previous year.[88] Cambodia and Indonesia are emerging as significant new markets for ecstasy. In Indonesia, for example, schoolchildren initially employed as go-betweens and couriers often become addicted themselves, following the Thai trend in which young traffickers, turned addicts, form an extremely efficient network of drug-dependent distributors.[89] There are indications that amphetamines were widely used by Indonesian soldiers in East Timor and by members of the Jakarta

Military Command, and its use has become prevalent among young professionals, teenagers and prostitutes.[90]

Drugs, Security and the State

Aside from its often tragic and devastating consequences for individual users and addicts, East Asia's heroin problem and the escalating ATS trade have the potential to destabilise those countries most affected and inflame relations among regional states. Narcotics-trafficking is blurring the boundaries between politics, crime and terrorism in many parts of East Asia. China's hesitant overtures towards the fundamentalist Taliban regime have been motivated by fear that a hostile Afghanistan, which is now the largest producer of opium in the world, could further encourage the spread of drugs and radical Islamic politics into China's Xinjiang province, fuelling ethnic separatism among the Uighurs.[91] Heroin from Pakistan and Afghanistan is already finding its way into Xinjiang and arms and explosives used by the separatists have been traced to Afghanistan. Uighurs have long enjoyed close ties with the various Afghan groups and some have trained and fought with the Mujahideen since 1986. Many are receiving training in Taliban religious schools, or *madrassas*. The nightmare scenario for China's leaders is that the Uighurs may use drug money and their Taliban connections to finance and strengthen their already serious challenge to Beijing's rule in Xinjiang.[92]

Thailand's increasingly fraught relations with Burma are rooted in Bangkok's frustration over the SPDC's inability or unwillingness to control the cross-border flow of drugs into Thailand's northern provinces. Key members of the Thai political and military establishment believe that Burma is deliberately flooding Thailand with heroin and amphetamines, which they regard as more lethal to Thailand than 'bullets and bayonets'.[93] Thailand's National Security Council has declared the narcotics trade the number one threat to national security and ordered the closure of several border crossing points in 1999 in a pointed warning to Burma that Thai patience with cross-border drug-trafficking is wearing thin.[94] In July of that year a 1000-strong Thai force, supported by armoured cars and helicopter gunships, attempted to seal off a 50-kilometre stretch of its western border. Several fire-fights ensued with the United Wa State Army, the most powerful of the narco-insurgent groups operating from bases in Burma's Shan State. Thai troops were instructed to shoot first and ask questions later if the Wa ventured across the border, and elite ranger units were given the green light to aggressively locate and destroy drug laboratories inside Burma.[95] In April 2000, the Thai Deputy Foreign Minister, Sukhumbhand Paribatra, admitted that Thailand was supporting regular clandestine cross-border operations against Wa-controlled areas in Burma.[96]

The involvement of the SPDC in narcotics-trafficking has sharpened divisions in ASEAN over Burma's membership and the organisation's attachment to the norm of non-interference in the internal affairs of member states which is one of its core principles. Senior Thai officials commonly express regret at having sponsored Burma's 1997 admission into ASEAN and Thai criticisms of Burma's tolerance of drug-trafficking have become sharper and less veiled.[97] In unusually blunt words, Samai Charoenchang, Thailand's chairman of the House Committee on Parliamentary Affairs, accused Burma of direct involvement in amphetamine-trafficking in August 1999, and declared: 'Once the ASEAN countries learn about these facts, they will definitely not be willing to befriend a country which allows its ethnic minorities to produce goods, drugs, that genocidally kill mankind'.[98] Implicit in Samai's warning was the threat to resume military assistance for ethnic tribes traditionally opposed to the Wa, like the Karen and Shan.[99] The Royal Thai Army Commander in Chief, General Surayuth Chulanond, has gone further, making clear that he is determined to 'win the war against drugs even if it meant fighting a border war against drug armies or the army of Myanmar [Burma]'.[100]

If Burma is a state under the influence of narcotics-traffickers, North Korea seems on the verge of becoming a fully fledged narco-criminal state. Driven by its desperate need for hard currency, the regime of Kim Jong-il has distinguished itself in East Asia by being the only government directly engaged in drug-trafficking. North Korea is a rarity in the typology of narco-states in using the apparatus of the state for trafficking in illicit drugs. Narco-states are usually so defined because legitimate government institutions have been thoroughly penetrated and compromised by non-state criminal actors. There are, however, no known criminal organisations operating in North Korea because the North Korean Worker's Party rules with an iron fist. In effect, the state itself has been criminalised by Kim Jong-il.

Reports of North Korean drug-trafficking date back to the 1970s but were at first difficult to substantiate. Since the mid-1990s, however, evidence that the regime of Kim Jong-il is directly involved in the drug trade has become overwhelming. In January 1995 two North Koreans, one of them in possession of a North Korean diplomatic passport, were arrested by Chinese police while attempting to sell 6 kilograms of opium in Shanghai.[101] A North Korean consular official was taken into custody for a similar offence in Shenyang.[102] These were not isolated incidents. North Korean Government-sponsored drug-smuggling has been reported in at least thirteen countries.[103] Two diplomats from the North Korean Embassy in Mexico were arrested at Moscow's international airport in February 1998 for smuggling 35 kilograms of cocaine into Russia.[104] North Koreans have also been involved in some curious criminal alliances.[105] In June 1994, the Russian police announced its largest drug seizure to that time: $2.5 million worth of factory-produced heroin from capitalist Taiwan which was smuggled by North Koreans into Russia's Far Eastern Maritime District.[106]

North Korea is estimated to produce about 50 tonnes of raw opium a year and to have begun manufacturing methamphetamines in 1996 after floods severely reduced that year's opium crop. Pyongyang probably earned in the vicinity of $100 million from heroin and methamphetamine exports in 1997 and appears to be stepping up production of ATS, much of which is finding its way into Japan.[107] North Korea has also been linked with the appearance, in Japan and elsewhere in the region, of the synthetic drug philopon, an ATS similar to 'speed'. In May 1999, a shipment of 100 kilograms of philopon produced in North Korea and destined for Japan was confiscated at a South Korean port. According to Japanese and South Korean investigators, the shipment was the first known case of cooperation between North Korea and the yakuza to supply the Japanese philopon market, estimated to be worth $40 billion annually, but it was not the first time that drugs bound for Japan from North Korea have been intercepted.[108] In April 1997, Japanese police apprehended a North Korean ship that was found to be hiding drugs produced in China. Eighteen months later, Japanese maritime police officers confiscated 300 kilograms of drugs from local smugglers who had offloaded the drugs from a North Korean vessel disguised as a fishing boat anchored off Japan's east coast.[109] Japanese police have also seized large quantities of rohypnol, a controlled though not illicit substance more commonly referred to as the 'date rape' drug, which was being smuggled into the country by a North Korean diplomat posted to Syria.[110]

Conclusion

Combating the illicit production and distribution of narcotics has long been regarded as a matter for law enforcement agencies. This is demonstrably no longer the case. The internationalisation of crime and the ability of narcotics-traffickers to undermine the political and economic sovereignty of states has already made the drug trade a significant security issue for many states and a primary strategic concern for the most seriously affected. Heroin and designer drugs are destroying the lives and livelihoods of countless individuals who are the principal victims of what is now a huge illicit industry that will be extremely difficult to contain, let alone eradicate.

Aside from China's historical experiences with opium addiction in the nineteenth century and again in the first half of the twentieth century, drug-trafficking has seldom figured in the security calculations of East Asian states. Even in Burma, the drug trade is commonly portrayed as the incidental by-product of a more fundamental threat posed by insurgent groups fighting for independence, limited autonomy or political change. In the 1970s and 1980s, when Asian criminal organisations used heroin from the Golden Triangle to establish markets in North America and Europe, they attracted little policy attention from regional producer states and even less in the way of effective countermeasures, despite the ire and concern of Western states. However, as they contemplate the security implications of their recently acquired status as consumer states, the indifference of East Asian governments towards narcotics-trafficking has been shaken. No longer can it be argued that drugs are someone else's problem or the consequence of societal failure in the West. East Asia is especially vulnerable because most of its nations are poorly equipped to fight the drug problem. As a new, predominantly Asian, narco-aristocracy entrenches itself throughout the region the drug problem of one state will become the problem of all.[111]

It is important, however, not to overestimate the threat or to misconstrue the nature of the forces that are driving the illicit drug trade in East Asia. With the possible exception of Burma, the situation in East Asia cannot yet be compared with the most severely affected states in Latin America. The deleterious effects are unevenly spread and not all have implications for security. Nevertheless, drug-trafficking in East Asia represents a growing threat to the political stability, social harmony and economic development of the region. The security effects are felt most acutely at the national and subnational level, but the burgeoning trade in illicit drugs also has the capacity to complicate relations between states. East Asia's developing drug culture reflects international trends as well as regional proclivities. The intensive cultivation and widespread availability of traditional plant-based narcotics like heroin, as well as synthetic ATS, is very much a global phenomenon, as is the associated rise in the power, wealth and reach of organised criminal groups.

Although the scale and corrosive nature of the contemporary drug trade is greater than anything previously experienced in the region, there is no dominant criminal syndicate or oriental 'boss of bosses' controlling and manipulating the trade. If there were, the task of combating illicit drugs would be considerably easier than it has proved to be. Rather, regional governments are faced with a multiplicity of criminal groups and constantly shifting alliances. Typically these are tactical rather than strategic in nature, forming and dissipating in response to changing market conditions in much the same way as legitimate business enterprises adapt to new commercial realities. In East Asia, the locus of the trade has become more diffuse, spreading from the sanctuary of the Golden Triangle into southern China and Southeast Asia. ATS are challenging heroin as the main drugs of choice for a new generation of Asian addicts, although heroin still exerts a powerful influence. As in other afflicted areas of the world, large-scale drug-trafficking is circumscribing the capacity of states to govern, corrupting the political process, distorting economic and development priorities and imposing enormous social and health costs on the region and its people.

In the most seriously affected country, Burma, drug-traffickers operate with relative impunity in areas that are effectively outside the control of the government and employ significant military force to protect and maintain their business interests. Burma's sovereignty is arguably as much under threat from the anti-state imperatives of criminals trafficking in heroin and ATS as it is from ethnic separatists or insurgents. More to the point, these groups are often indistinguishable from one another for all practical purposes. In other parts of the region, particularly southern China, Laos, Vietnam and Thailand, drug-traffickers pose a less severe but still significant threat to the state. Their activities and operations frequently violate the sanctity of the region's borders and weaken the authority of national governments, especially when carried out with the connivance of officials responsible for security and customs. As the region's first example of a proto-criminal state, eccentric North Korea is a further reminder that far from being coterminous, national security and human security may be fundamentally opposed. Finally, the transnational criminal challenge to East Asia's security undermines one of the fundamental premises of the realist school of thought: that interstate violence defines the security problematique. North Korea aside, the organisations that control serious crime in East Asia are non-state entities that are sovereignty-free. Although TCOs can pose a military threat to the authority of the state, the soft power of money and drugs are usually the preferred means for achieving criminal ends rather than the barrel of a gun.

CHAPTER 11

The AIDS 'Pandemic'

AIDS, or the Acquired Immune Deficiency Syndrome, is perhaps the best known of a new class of highly infectious diseases that will rival war as a major cause of death and impoverishment in the twenty-first century. Since it was first isolated in 1983, the proliferation of the Human Immuno-deficiency Virus (HIV) which causes AIDS has been sudden, traumatic and devastating in its consequences, especially for the developing world.[1] AIDS epitomises the transnational challenge to international security. It is a global, non-military phenomenon that strikes indiscriminately at its human victims, weakening the socio-economic foundations of states in transition and corroding government institutions. Although AIDS would exist without crime, narcotics-trafficking and the sex trade have been central to its spread. The nexus between organised crime and AIDS is characteristic of the close interrelationship and circular causality of many contemporary transnational security issues. As rates of heroin addiction increase, unprotected sex between injecting drug-users (IDUs) and their partners, who may include sex workers, facilitates HIV trans-mission.[2] AIDS-ravaged countries become ever more vulnerable to the predations of organised crime and the cycle intensifies as it is repeated. AIDS is one of the few diseases to justify the term 'pandemic' since it is killing more people than any other infectious disease.[3] By the end of 1999, 18.8 million people had died from the effects of the HIV virus and 34.3 million were infected.[4] Virtually all those who are HIV-positive will eventually die from AIDS unless there is an immediate and revolutionary medical breakthrough, a remote prospect at best. The disease is set to claim more lives in the first decade of this century than all the wars fought in the twentieth century, making it a key issue for foreign policy and international security as well as public health.[5]

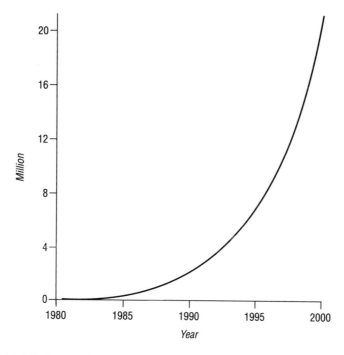

Figure 11.1 Estimates of cumulative AIDS deaths worldwide, 1980–99
Source: UNAIDS, *Surveillance Documents and Reports*, and *AIDS Epidemic Update*
(June 2000), all on www.unaids.org/hivaidsinfo/index.html; *Vital Signs 1999,*
Worldwatch Institute, www.worldwatch.org.

Although the devastation wrought by AIDS is most evident in sub-
Saharan Africa, the global epicentre of the disease has now shifted
emphatically to Asia. About 8 million Asians had AIDS or were HIV-positive in 1999, and Asia as a whole will soon overtake sub-Saharan Africa as
the region with the most number of HIV infections.[6] Another 4 million
Asians died from tuberculosis in 1998.[7] Because of its lengthy incubation
period, the full impact of AIDS is yet to be felt, but the extent and speed
of its penetration is alarming health authorities and NGOs working in
the field of health care. The head of the UN program on HIV/AIDS has
warned that Asia is at the beginning of an 'epidemic wave'.[8] Health
experts are worried that they are losing the fight to stem the advance of
the disease as most countries in the region are already affected, some
quite seriously. Unless there is a sudden and dramatic reversal of this
trend – and there is little to suggest that a generalised turnaround in HIV
infection rates is likely – AIDS is destined to become a major security
issue for the region.

What is AIDS?

There are two different strains of the HIV virus. HIV-1 is the most common and is primarily responsible for the AIDS pandemic. HIV-2 also causes AIDS and was once mainly confined to West Africa but it has expanded to other regions of the world.[9] Once erroneously labelled the 'gay disease', 75 per cent of all HIV infections are actually from heterosexual contact, very often involving injecting drug use.[10] HIV attacks the body's immune system, thereby making carriers susceptible to a range of infections, one or more of which will ultimately prove fatal. Infected individuals normally take eight to ten years before they display obvious symptoms and several more years to develop full-blown AIDS.[11] For this reason statistics showing the number of confirmed AIDS cases substantially understate the true level of HIV infection. Six million people were infected in 1998 compared with 8.9 million for the whole of the 1980s, indicating the disease's accelerating rate of transmission.[12] HIV is also largely responsible for the reemergence of tuberculosis, the second biggest infectious killer after AIDS.[13]

The initial wave of HIV was concentrated in Africa before spreading to homosexual men and IDUs in Western states during the late 1970s. Because of higher standards of health care and education and the availability of expensive new drug therapies, the spread of AIDS has been largely contained in the West but it has wreaked enormous damage in sub-Saharan Africa, which accounts for seven out of ten HIV infections globally and nine out of ten AIDS deaths. In Botswana and Zimbabwe, two of the nations hardest hit, the average life expectancy has dropped to pre-1950 levels, wiping out decades of social and economic progress.[14] One in three adults in Botswana is infected, the highest level of HIV infection in the world.[15] South Africa and several neighbouring states are in the midst of an explosive epidemic in which infection rates have reached 20 per cent or over of the entire adult population, compared with less than 1 per cent for most industrialised countries. Without a low-cost cure, Botswana, Namibia and South Africa may lose over a fifth of their populations by 2010.[16] In another six sub-Saharan states life expectancy will drop to 40 years or less in the same time-frame.[17]

AIDS and International Security

In the first post-Cold War decade, AIDS rated only a passing mention in the taxonomy of threats to international security despite abundant evidence that the disease was set to devastate sub-Saharan Africa and was spreading rapidly across the globe. The slowness to recognise the threat from AIDS can be attributed to a complex mix of genuine ignorance, denial, social taboos and a widespread conviction in the West that AIDS

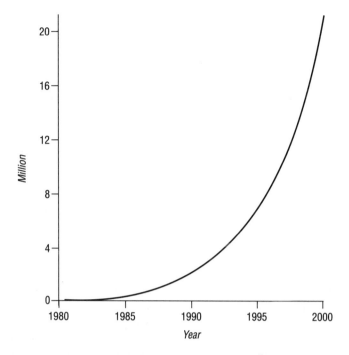

Figure 11.2 Estimates of cumulative HIV infections worldwide, 1980–99
Source: UNAIDS, *Surveillance Documents and Reports,* and *AIDS Epidemic Update
(June 2000),* all on www.unaids.org/hivaidsinfo/index.html; *Vital Signs 1999,*
Worldwatch Institute, www.worldwatch.org.

was largely under control in the developed world and would therefore
have only a marginal effect on Western security interests.[18] However, as
the immensity of the disease's impact has become more apparent, intelligence agencies and national security communities around the world
are beginning to sit up and take notice. An attitudinal turning point was
the decision by the Clinton Administration in early 2000 to declare AIDS
a threat to US national security, citing the disease's capacity to destroy
governments and foment ethnic conflict.[19] This followed an assessment
by the National Intelligence Council that the infiltration of AIDS and
other infectious diseases into the ruling elites of developing states could
intensify internal power struggles over scarce resources as well as having
a severe social and economic impact in developing countries.[20]

    What makes HIV such an insidious and dangerous virus is that its long
incubation period allows it to spread much more effectively than other life-
threatening viruses. Ebola, for example, is a haemorraghic fever which kills
its victims brutally but quickly, so that there is less opportunity for it to
become an epidemic. To use Chris Beyrer's military analogy, Ebola and

other comparable diseases go off like cluster bombs, whereas HIV is more like a landmine, lying undetected for long periods before being triggered and exploding.[21] Of course, there have been epidemics and pandemics throughout history. Some, such as the Black Death that ravaged Europe in the fourteenth century and the influenza epidemic that swept the globe at the end of the First World War, were more lethal than AIDS in the sense that they killed a higher percentage of the world's population in a shorter space of time. The Black Death of 1347–50, a virulent composite of three diseases – bubonic plague, septicaemic plague and pneumonic or pulmonary plague – is estimated to have reduced Europe's population by as much as a third, or 30 million people. The influenza epidemic of 1918–19 probably killed about 40 million people worldwide.[22]

However, the number of deaths globally from AIDS is approaching 20 million and by 2010 is likely to surpass the number of people killed by the 1918–19 influenza pandemic and the Black Death. This grim statistic aside, the HIV virus has a number of unique characteristics that makes it difficult to combat and magnifies its social impact.[23] As Whiteside and FitzSimons note, 'HIV differs from previous killer diseases in that it has a long incubation period; is predominantly sexually transmitted; its symptoms are diverse; it is fatal; and it hits two specific groups – the young sexually active population and infants infected before or during birth'.[24] AIDS infects and debilitates the body politic as well as the bodies of its victims, destabilising states in the developing world and reversing their hard-won economic gains. The virus's long gestation period and the lingering death that those afflicted generally suffer also makes AIDS a high-cost disease in terms of its demands on public health systems and the depletion of an infected country's human capital. In 1994, the total direct and indirect cost of HIV/AIDS globally was around $500 billion, or roughly 2 per cent of the world's GDP, and it has since climbed significantly.[25]

AIDS intensifies poverty, causes demographic imbalances, places great strains on social services and tax systems and affects the middle class as well as the poor, reducing the number of teachers and skilled workers. These are problems for industrialised states as well as the developing world, but there is an important difference. In Western Europe, North America, and mature economies like Australia and Japan, AIDS is a serious social and health concern but it is seldom a national security problem. Developing countries, on the other hand, have fewer resources at their disposal to devote to AIDS prevention. Once HIV infection rates approach or exceed 5 per cent of the adult population, the generally accepted benchmark figure denoting an epidemic, then combating AIDS becomes fundamental to national survival.[26] Moreover, AIDS-related insecurity is not confined to the domestic arena. AIDS-affected nations may become a source of concern to neighbours if they are seen to be a potential source of HIV transmission or the disease is considered to be symptomatic of a rise in criminal activity and drug-trafficking.

Another reason for treating AIDS as a security issue as well as a public health crisis is that transnational criminal organisations are important vectors in the spread of HIV/AIDS. AIDS flourishes where drug-trafficking, people-smuggling and the sex trade are rampant. All three criminal activities have played an important role in the proliferation of the disease, especially in Asia. AIDS enters the human body through unprotected sexual contact, blood transfusions and increasingly through needle-sharing by IDUs. It is no coincidence that the first groups to experience the rapid phase of HIV spread in Thailand, Burma, Malaysia, Vietnam and China's Yunnan province were IDUs.[27]

As drug addiction increases, so does the level of HIV infection. There is a marked correlation between the location of drug-smuggling routes and the spatial distribution of AIDS. Recent outbreaks of AIDS have closely followed the opening up of new distribution networks and markets for heroin. As Lierly observes, 'the narcotics pipeline is a leaky one that has addiction and AIDS as a by-product'.[28] Trafficking in young women for the entertainment industry has compounded the problem. A significant proportion of undocumented labour migrants are young, single women destined for the sex trade who eventually return infected with HIV to their home regions, where the virus soon finds new hosts. Almost regardless of national circumstances, once epidemics mature, transmission from sex worker clients and IDUs to their partners becomes the most common route of female infection.[29]

Military forces can be important vectors in the spread of AIDS within their own countries and internationally, as members of multinational peacekeeping and peace-making forces.[30] Peacetime infection rates among military populations are on average 2–5 times higher than among civilians, and during conflicts the risk of infection soars dramatically, sometimes by as much as 100 times the civilian average.[31] Combat-readiness rates may be eroded and peacekeeping operations complicated if there is a high prevalence of AIDS among the civilian populace or the peacekeeping troops themselves.[32] HIV and AIDS may pose a strategic threat to the worst-affected defence forces because of the loss of skilled manpower, military leadership and morale.[33] Fifty per cent of all new AIDS infections occur among 15–25-year-olds, the age group that is the seedbed for military recruitment.[34]

The cost of testing for HIV and caring for military personnel, who usually have a lifelong entitlement to military-funded health care, will consume an increasing proportion of defence budgets. AIDS is a particular problem for the armed forces of developing states since they are heavily dependent on young male conscripts for the bulk of their personnel. In

Africa, the incidence of AIDS among military personnel is on average three times higher than the civilian population. In some armies, infection rates have already reached epidemic proportions, hollowing out units and drastically reducing their operational effectiveness. Fifty per cent of the Congo's army is estimated to be infected with HIV, while in Uganda two-thirds of officers and enlisted soldiers are HIV-positive and in some units 100 per cent of the personnel have AIDS.[35] Airforce units in other African countries have been forced to reduce flying time because many air crew are too sick to fly.[36] The most severe impact is often on the officer corps and senior non-commissioned officers, whose skills are less easily replaced than those of short-term conscripts.

AIDS in East Asia

In East Asia, the epidemiology of the disease and estimated prevalence rates show considerable diversity. North Korea has virtually no HIV because of Pyongyang's tight control over its borders and people, but AIDS has been reported throughout China and exists to varying degrees in every other East Asian state, especially Thailand, Burma and Cambodia, which have the highest levels of infection.[37] While Japan, Taiwan, South Korea and the Philippines show few signs of hosting 'explosive epidemics' and Singapore and Brunei seem relatively unaffected, WHO has cited a high level of underreporting and under-diagnosis of HIV in the region.[38] For this reason, caution is necessary in drawing definitive conclusions about the level of HIV infection in those countries where the level of AIDS appears low.[39]

Thailand

The first known case of AIDS in the region was reported in Thailand in 1984. Within a decade, some 600 000 Thais had become infected, with the number rising to 1 million in 2000, representing the fastest rate of HIV transmission ever documented.[40] So entrenched has AIDS become in Thailand that the nation's capital, Bangkok, has earned itself the dubious reputation of being the AIDS capital of Southeast Asia. The rapid and early spread of the disease stems from the country's position as a major transit country for heroin from the Golden Triangle; widespread ignorance of the link between unprotected sex, drug use and AIDS in the 1970s when the disease was first seeded; and the relaxed attitude of Thais towards casual sex. It was once common practice for young Thai men to visit prostitutes regularly and to eschew the use of condoms. The rate of infection has been particularly high among Thai army units based in areas of northern Thailand adjacent to the Golden Triangle. In 1993, the prevalence rate among new recruits nationally reached 3.5 per cent, a sevenfold increase in five years.[41]

Table 11.1   Epidemiology of HIV/AIDS pandemic in East Asia, 1999

Country	No. of HIV/AIDS Infections
China	500 000
N. Korea	<100
S. Korea	3 800
Japan	10 000
Mongolia	<100
Brunei	<100
Cambodia	220 000
Indonesia	52 000
Laos	1 400
Malaysia	49 000
Burma	530 000
Philippines	28 000
Singapore	4 000
Thailand	755 000
Vietnam	100 000
Total E. Asia	2 253 200

Source: UNAIDS, Global AIDS Epidemic – Update, June 2000
www.unaids.org/epidemic_update/index.html.

Faced with the grim evidence of a widespread and worsening epidemic, Thailand initiated a nationwide education campaign in 1991 that encouraged 'safe sex' through the use of condoms. Within five years, condom use rose from 50 per cent to 90 per cent and HIV infection rates began to drop dramatically.[42] Indicative of the success of the safe sex campaign was the 80 per cent fall in the incidence of HIV among military recruits in northern Thailand between 1991 and 1995, and a further decline between 1995 and 1999.[43] AIDS remains a heavy social and economic burden for the country, but the resolute measures taken by Thai governments have succeeded in averting a national catastrophe, demonstrating the importance of high-level political support and well-funded public education programs.[44] Unfortunately, Thailand is a beacon of light on an otherwise gloomy horizon. Several other regional states are manifesting the same pattern and rate of infection recorded by Thailand in the late 1980s and early 1990s. There is little evidence, however, of a willingness to follow Thailand's example in AIDS prevention, in part because condom promotion is as politically sensitive as the subject of AIDS itself.

Cambodia

Cambodia is succumbing more quickly than any other Southeast Asian state and now, at 4 per cent of its adult population, has a higher infection rate than either Thailand or Burma, although it did not report its first positive case of HIV infection until 1991.[45] The situation has deteriorated to such an extent that a senior WHO official has predicted that Cambodia faces an HIV/AIDS epidemic potentially as devastating as anything suffered under the murderous Pol Pot regime.[46] One hundred and forty-four thousand Cambodians were HIV-positive in 1998 and the UN Development Programme forecasts that 500 000 people – close to one in twenty of the population – will be infected by 2006.[47] Peter Piot, executive director of UNAIDS, believes that Cambodia will have to spend about $2.8 billion annually on AIDS treatment by 2007, an enormous financial burden for a country whose total GDP in 1998 was only $3.6 billion.[48] Like Thailand, the main form of transmission is through heterosexual intercourse. Less than 15 per cent of men use condoms regularly and nearly half of all sex workers surveyed in Phnom Penh were HIV-positive in 1997.[49]

HIV has made particularly serious inroads into the military and law enforcement agencies. The US Agency for International Development found that 80 per cent of police and military surveyed in 1997 had visited a prostitute in the previous twelve months, with few having used condoms.[50] Given this incidence of commercial sex and Cambodia's spiralling drug problem, estimates that as many as 12–17 per cent of the security forces are HIV-positive do not seem unreasonable.[51] This is an extremely high level of infection by world standards and does not augur well for the future vitality and readiness of Cambodia's armed forces. Even higher rates of infection have been recorded among military units in Koh Kong province bordering Thailand.[52] With the demise of the Khmer Rouge, AIDS has moved to the top of the security agenda in Cambodia. Underlining the magnitude of the threat, the Defence Ministry's senior health official, General Veng Bun Lay, declared in 1999, that 'HIV-AIDS is now the military's only enemy. It could devastate our plans for reform and reduce our capability. We are very worried'.[53] There are well-founded fears that AIDS will soon kill more Cambodians than malaria, mines, or the once feared Khmer Rouge.[54]

Burma

Although AIDS is patently out of control in Burma, the SPDC has steadfastly refused to accept that the country is in the middle of an AIDS epidemic which has the potential to surpass both Cambodia and Thailand in terms of death and social dislocation.[55] In fact the SPDC has indirectly assisted the spread of HIV by tolerating drug-trafficking and discouraging NGOs from establishing AIDS prevention and education programs in Burma.[56] Although the first cases of HIV were not recorded until 1988, within a decade 86 000 people had died from AIDS and another 440 000 were HIV-positive.[57] At the end of 2000, there were probably between 1 and

1.2 million cumulative infections.[58] Experienced observers like Chris Beyrer believe that Burma is the country in East Asia most likely to repli-cate the experience of sub-Saharan Africa.[59] Of particular concern is the extremely high rate of transmission among commercial sex workers and IDUs. Eighty per cent of Burmese women working in the sex trade in Burma and neighbouring Thailand are expected to become infected with HIV.[60] AIDS is rampant in Burma's numerous prisons, where homosexual-ity is common, heroin is widely available and needle-sharing the norm. Infection rates among the Tatmadaw, the Burmese armed forces, are also on the rise and may have exceeded 8 per cent of all soldiers by 2000, although the lack of reliable data makes it difficult to be sure.[61]

China

Although the known rate of HIV infection in China is still low by the stan-dards of Thailand, Cambodia and Burma, it has begun to gather pace. Unlike Western countries and some Southeast Asian states where AIDS is mainly an urban phenomenon, AIDS in China has generally spread from rural border areas to the cities.[62] A major outbreak of AIDS in China could dwarf anything yet seen in East Asia, or even globally, because of the coun-try's large population and escalating drug use. According to official Chi-nese figures there were only 4500 cases of HIV infection in mid-1996 but, unofficially, government experts concede that the real number was closer to 100 000 since only about 5 per cent of all HIV cases are reported.[63] UN and WHO figures show a figure of 400 000 infections in 1997, rising to 1 million in 2000–2001.[64] China has taken some measures to confront its AIDS epidemic. In 1996, Beijing launched an AIDS awareness campaign to combat public ignorance and sanctioned an AIDS prevention program for high-risk groups such as long-distance truck-drivers, migrant workers and prostitutes.[65] The effectiveness of the program has been attenuated, how-ever, by a lack of resources and public stigmatisation of HIV sufferers.[66]

In China, transmission through heterosexual activity is rising in line with a relaxation of social mores and the reemergence of a thriving sex industry. Prostitution, like drugs, was thought to have been eradicated during the Mao era, but China's Public Security Department estimates that there are now between 3 and 4 million prostitutes plying their trade throughout the country.[67] HIV has also been spread by Chinese women returning home after having worked in the Thai sex trade and by IDUs. At the end of 1999, 72.4 per cent of all reported cases of AIDS in China were injecting drug-users and more than 50 per cent of IDUs were HIV-positive in the worst affected province of Yunnan.[68] The northwestern region of Xinjiang is set to overtake Yunnan as the province with the most number of carriers due to an upsurge in heroin-trafficking, but populous

Henan province may not be far behind. Some 500 000 to 700 000 people were thought to be infected in Henan at the end of 2000 because of unhygienic blood transfusion practices and donation irregularities associated with a thriving trade in blood products.[69]

Vietnam and Laos

HIV 'take-off' occurred later in Vietnam than other Southeast Asian states. By 1993, however, it was clear that the disease had entrenched itself among sex workers and IDUs and was spreading into the general populace. Drug-trafficking and tourism have facilitated the spread of HIV/AIDS in Vietnam.[70] Needles are used extensively without sterilisation and the rate of heroin addiction continues to climb. At the end of 1997, 88 000 Vietnamese were conservatively estimated to be HIV-positive or suffering from AIDS and more than 300 000 were expected to be infected by 2001.[71] Inward-looking and rural Laos was effectively quarantined from the drug and AIDS epidemic in neighbouring states during the 1980s and first half of the 1990s. However, the opening up of the Lao economy and the 1994 construction of a major bridge over the Mekong into Thailand will make the country more susceptible to drug and HIV penetration.

Malaysia and Indonesia

Religious and cultural differences have had little effect on the rate of HIV/AIDS transmission in the region. Islam has not proved a barrier to the spread of HIV in Malaysia or Indonesia, where the AIDS epidemic has exhibited a similar pattern of development to that of non-Islamic Southeast Asia. While acknowledging the efforts of her father's government in responding to AIDS, Marina Mahathir has highlighted the resistance to AIDS education among conservative Muslims in Malaysia and Indonesia, who associate the disease with 'immoral and depraved behaviour'.[72] This was certainly a factor in the Suharto government's initial reluctance to accept that AIDS had become a serious problem for Indonesia.[73] Only when the evidence to the contrary became overwhelming did Jakarta reassess its position, but some Indonesian health officials still persist in understating the real level of infection.[74]

In 1994, the newly appointed Indonesian National AIDS Commission concluded that AIDS 'has left the linear growth phase of the epidemic and is now in the early exponential growth phase'. Projecting three growth scenarios, the commission estimated that HIV infections would range from a low of 600 000 to a high of 2 million by 2005, depending on the effectiveness of a national AIDS prevention strategy and transmission variables.[75] An ASEAN task force on AIDS reported in closed session that the AIDS epidemic in Indonesia could soon rival that of Thailand. Almost all the factors required are present, including 'high-risk sexual behaviour, poverty, high prevalence of sexually transmitted diseases, a demand for tourist industry [sic], increasing population mobility and many seaports frequently visited by sailors from high-prevalence countries'.[76] UNAIDS and WHO studies show that Malaysia had an even higher number of HIV/AIDS cases than Indonesia at the end of 1997 and that the disease is no longer restricted to commercial sex workers and IDUs.[77]

Why Has AIDS Reached Epidemic Proportions in East Asia?

As this survey of the epidemiology of HIV/AIDS makes clear, there is no single explanation for the proliferation of the disease in East Asia. Multiple factors are at work, the most salient of which are East Asia's opening up to the world; increasing trans-border flows of itinerant fishermen, truck-drivers, nomadic tribal groups and foreign tourists; intra-regional labour migration; drug-trafficking; and the growth of transnational crime.

Official ignorance, denial and an unwillingness to discuss sexual matters openly have assisted HIV's spread in East Asia.[78] Typical of the widespread reluctance to confront reality is the assertion by the head of Burma's social welfare department that 'there can be no prostitution in our country because it is illegal'.[79] One Indonesian health minister in the late 1980s refused to countenance the likelihood of AIDS developing into a serious problem for Indonesia because, in his view, Indonesia had no homosexuals.[80] The economic crisis has also slowed attempts to improve AIDS awareness and prevention. Struggling with shrinking budgets and preoccupied with more pressing priorities, programs for AIDS prevention and treatment have been emasculated at the very time they have been most needed. Rising prices have led to the removal of expensive imported drugs like AZT from government health insurance schemes. The downturn in business has forced many female sex workers to return home, accelerating infection rates in rural areas.[81] At the same time more people have entered the drug trade as distributors and users, sowing the seeds of a second wave of HIV infection.[82]

One of the main reasons for the rapid spread of HIV in East Asia has been the stimulus provided by organised criminal groups, through their control of the burgeoning drug trade and commercial sex industry and their prominent role in facilitating undocumented labour migration. The strong connection between intravenous drug use and the sex trade in Thailand, Burma, China, Malaysia, Vietnam and, to a lesser extent, Singapore is well documented.[83] Drug use, particularly in areas adjacent to the Golden Triangle, established an initial 'reservoir of infection' for the AIDS epidemic, largely accounting for the severity of the problem in Thailand and Burma.[84] As the illicit heroin industry grew in sophistication during the 1970s and 1980s, the narcotics-traffickers who control the Golden Triangle began to encourage addicts in Burma and northern Thailand to switch from traditional opium-smoking to taking heroin intravenously.

Since needles were not in abundant supply, needle-sharing was common among heroin addicts, who then infected their families and local prostitutes.[85] In some cases needles were almost as expensive to obtain as heroin. By 1995, 80 per cent of the HIV/AIDS population in Thailand and 66 per cent in Burma were IDUs, extremely high proportions by world standards.[86] The same pattern has been repeated elsewhere in the region. Clusters of HIV infection can be found in China all along the ancient southern silk road linking Burma with central Asia and Europe, which in recent times has become a major heroin route from the Golden Triangle. Subtype C of HIV-1, which is endemic in Burma, is the most common strain of HIV among drug-users in Yunnan province, accounting for about four-fifths of all China's AIDS sufferers.[87]

Infected Thai prostitutes among the 40 000–50 000 working illegally in Japan under the aegis of the yakuza helped spread HIV to Japan and were sent back to Thai brothels often unaware that they had contracted the virus. When the supply of young Thai women began to dry up, partly because of more effective education programs implemented by the Thai government, criminal groups turned their attention to other sources of young women, mainly from Burma, Vietnam and China, where the cycle has been repeated. The HIV virus continues to be propagated via the largely unsuspecting clientele of East Asia's many brothels, karaoke bars, nightclubs and massage parlours. The extension of the sex trade into the broader entertainment area – a strategic objective of those criminal groups involved in prostitution – has also caught within its net a considerable number of Filipino women working as singers, dancers and waitresses.[88]

Not all prostitution is controlled by organised crime. Grassroots prostitution is often the preserve of small-time independent operators who recruit their 'ladies of the night' from poor villages and migrant populations. But once profits start to climb, organised crime moves in. Prostitution has become a lucrative add-on to the drug trade, amounting to hundreds of millions of dollars annually for the triads, yakuza and mainland Chinese gangs involved in the business. The extensive distribution and operational networks used for the movement of illicit narcotics are easily adapted to smuggling prostitutes, many of whom are unwitting carriers of HIV/AIDS. Taiwan's Bamboo Gang, for example, is responsible for an extensive chain of bars and nightclubs on China's Hainan Island which operate with the blessing of local public security officials.

Hong Kong triads run prostitution rings under the cover of nightclubs and karaoke bars in Hong Kong, Macau and increasingly mainland China. International cooperation is a feature of the sex trade, as it is for illicit narcotics. The triads and yakuza cooperate in the movement of prostitutes to Japan, and the Russian mafiya has developed a profitable assisted trade in Russian and Eastern European women to Macau and other East Asian cities.[89]

Conclusion

After years of prevarication and denial, governments in East Asia and the West have begun to accept that AIDS is not merely another infectious disease that can be treated as a biomedical problem and allowed to play out in distant and 'overpopulated' Africa. AIDS has become a major global cause of human and state insecurity, flourishing in and reinforcing conditions that can lead to war, social violence, humanitarian emergencies and economic collapse. If HIV continues to proliferate in East Asia, as seems likely, the virus will undermine civil society, slow the democratisation process and intensify poverty, resource scarcity and conflict, directly affecting the national security interests of afflicted states, the region's collective security interests and the lives of millions of people. What is especially worrying about the AIDS pandemic is that even though Asia has already overtaken Africa as the epicentre of the disease, its full impact will not be felt for perhaps another decade because of HIV's lengthy incubation period. Around 4 million East Asians were HIV-positive at the end of 2000 and as many as 20 million may be infected by 2010.[90] Unlike Europe or the United States, HIV is permeating the whole of society in the countries in which it is endemic, striking down people during their most productive years when they have most to contribute and would normally require little health care.[91] Average life expectancy has plummeted in the African states ravaged by AIDS and the same will occur in East Asia unless the progress of the disease can be arrested and reversed.

Unfortunately, a cure for AIDS remains elusive, partly because of HIV's mutation rate, which makes it difficult to develop an effective vaccine. Expensive new therapies are gradually becoming available in the West that can contain the rate of infection by preventing HIV from replicating itself in the body. They are not, however, a panacea. For most AIDS victims in developing states the cost of these therapies and treatments is prohibitive, notwithstanding the well-publicised decision by five major pharmaceutical companies to slash the cost of AIDS drugs for poorer nations.[92] Even if drugs like AZT become affordable, most developing states lack the supporting medical and social infrastructure to make drug treatment work, casting doubt on the transferability and efficacy of Western anti-AIDS strategies for the worst-affected countries in East Asia.[93] Thailand has demonstrated that it is possible to curtail infection rates by using simple and cheap prophylactics, but financial, social and cultural barriers are likely to inhibit their use in other regional states.

In addition to the strains it will impose on public health systems, forcing governments to redirect precious resources towards palliative care for those infected, AIDS will circumscribe social and economic development more generally in East Asia. Managing and mitigating its impact is, therefore, a core development issue.[94] The vice-president of the Asian Development Bank has aptly characterised AIDS as 'the enemy of the Asian promise', threatening much of the hard-won economic gains of the past four decades.[95] Judging by the number of HIV infections recorded in the region, the economic impact of dealing with AIDS will be substantial. AIDS has already cost East Asian economies billions of dollars in revenue, market share and health care.[96] The investment firm McGraw-Hill has calculated that Asian economies would forfeit in the order of US$38–52 billion in lost production and spiralling health expenditure between 1995 and 2000, while others estimate that Southeast Asia could sacrifice between 1.7 per cent and 2.3 per cent of GDP, although this figure is contested.[97] What is not in dispute is that the disease will devastate the social fabric of many communities at the local and family level, reduce economic vitality, exacerbate regional labour shortages, push up wages and encourage migration.[98] One other side-effect will be a distortion in the demographic profile of affected states, from the normal, healthy pyramid structure to a chimney shape, as reduced numbers of young adults are left to support relatively large numbers of children and older people.[99]

AIDS-related economic and social stress will also be a serious political and strategic problem for developing East Asia, destabilising countries, reducing the coping capacity of governments and hollowing out conscript armies. AIDS-weakened states could in turn become a source of regional instability and create anxieties that they may facilitate the spread of HIV into neighbouring countries. Not all states will be equally affected. The available evidence suggests that AIDS could emerge as a first-order security issue for China, Vietnam, Cambodia, Thailand and Burma, while Japan, Taiwan, Singapore, Brunei and the two Koreas should remain relatively unaffected. The jury is still out on the archipelagic states of Malaysia, Indonesia and the Philippines, although it is conceivable that all three could experience epidemics on a scale comparable to that of mainland Southeast Asia. Much will depend on government action at the national and regional level. As Thailand has demonstrated, effective public education is the key to combating the disease, but no other regional state has yet been able to emulate Thailand's record in reducing HIV infection. Despite its success in restricting the disease, Thailand may still lose 1–2 million of its people prematurely because of AIDS. China is already in the early stages of an AIDS epidemic. Without a determined effort to reverse this trend and to attack the causes of AIDS, China's National Centre for AIDS Prevention and Control has forecast that HIV/AIDS infection in China could reach 10 million by 2010. If this forecast proves accurate, AIDS-related deaths in China would equal all the fatalities from armed conflict in East Asia between 1945 and 1999.[100]

Conclusion

To recapitulate this book's central themes, I have argued that a new class of transnational threats is emerging which will be increasingly influential in determining East Asia's strategic future. Unfortunately, the drivers of these threats are not well understood by scholars and policy-makers working in the field of international relations, who are for the most part heavily influenced by realist assumptions about security. The problem is that realism's self-professed conceptual parsimony and its preoccupation with military conflict between states does not equip it for dealing with forces that are essentially non-military in nature and unrelated to the competitive behaviour of states. Environmental degradation, UPMs and transnational crime are representative. Far from being peripheral or irrelevant to the security concerns of states, as realists maintain, their capacity to destabilise states internally as well as to aggravate relations between them is real, and rising. However, the security-degrading effects of these transnational phenomena extend beyond the boundaries of the territorial state to encompass individuals who may live outside its protective embrace or who feel threatened by the coercive power of their own governments.

Although the balance of power still explains much about the causes of geopolitical rivalry and military conflict in the current milieu, realism's limited worldview suggests that a new template is required, cut to fit and discern the more complex strategic patterns of the twenty-first century. Extended security provides an alternative conceptual framework for thinking about security which recognises that transnational forces are compelling a shift in the security paradigm, upward and outward to include the biosphere and non-state actors.[1] Consequently, future security policy will need to be more nuanced, less reliant on military force as the primary instrument for achieving security, and more cognisant of non-military, transnational threats.

The Implications for Theory

Since the transnational security agenda has a number of important implications for international relations theory in general, and the realist security orthodoxy in particular, these themes warrant further elaboration. The argument advanced here and in the introduction is that notwithstanding its various permutations and hypotheses, realism is unable to capture the evolving security dynamics of the post-Cold War world. Many of these are in fact conflicting, rendering the theory less determinate and coherent than its disciples avow.[2] Any theory that purports to represent the complexity of a world in transition must be sensitive to the inevitable shifts in the relationship and salience of the variables that cause and accentuate conflict. Moreover, its underlying assumptions and core beliefs must be continually subject to rigorous inquiry and not sanctified as unassailable doctrine. It is unreasonable to expect concepts rooted in the experiences of yesterday's Europe to retain their theoretical preeminence in a world that is in the throes of one of the most far-reaching transformations in history. This is not to argue that the realist baby should be thrown out with the conceptual bathwater. Twentieth-century realism provided unique insights into the structure and dynamics of the Cold War order and still contains much that is apposite today. Increasingly, however, realism is incapable of capturing the determining changes in the international and East Asian security environments and of grasping the requirements of an extended security praxis.

Even though the territorially constructed state remains the principal actor in the international system and the standard vehicle for political expression, it ought not to be enshrined as the only legitimate security referent. As advocates of human security argue, more weight should be given to protecting the individual from hunger, thirst, disease and repression since the security of the state has no real meaning if divorced from its human constituents. Human security and national security are threatened in equal measure by transnational phenomena. The forced displacement of people by governments is injurious to the security of those individuals compelled to move. Conversely, the large-scale, unregulated movement of people across borders threatens the sovereignty and internal cohesion of affected states, especially when illegal migrants and refugees are of different ethnic or religious backgrounds.

Contrary to the assertions of realists, the security of the state is not synonymous with the security of its citizens. To the extent that authoritarian regimes lack political legitimacy they cannot be said to represent fully the interests of their citizens. In multi-ethnic states, minority groups frequently regard the state as the principal threat to their survival rather than the protector of basic freedoms and rights; citizenship, for these

people, is a fundamental source of their insecurity. Failed states, by definition, have abrogated their responsibility for anyone's security. A balanced and inclusive definition of security should therefore incorporate
both people and states. However, the dichotomy between human and
national security should not be exaggerated since the two referents of
security are seldom mutually exclusive. It is only necessary to differentiate between the two when the state, through tyranny or neglect, forfeits
its right to act as the political embodiment of its citizens.

Realism's equation of security with the maintenance of political independence and the territorial integrity of the state ignores the reality that
in an interconnected world the notion of sovereignty is far more elastic
than it once was. It is true that sovereignty has never been absolute or
unquestioned, but in today's world borders are regularly breached by
transnational forces that are exogenous to realism's constructs and largely
beyond its comprehension. Realists assume a monopoly over the instruments of political, economic and military power which states now rarely
enjoy. The American realist Kenneth Waltz once wrote: 'as men live in a
world of states, so states exist in a world of states'.[3] In the world of the
twenty-first century, however, states will be forced to cede a large measure
of control over the totems of sovereignty, namely borders, capital, people
and territory.

National power will increasingly be shared with non-state actors that
have at their disposal resources and influence that may equal, or even
exceed, those of many states. As Simmon observes, they are 'changing
societal norms, challenging national governments and ... muscling their
way into areas of high politics'.[4] Unfortunately, not all non-state actors are
benign or eschew the use of force. Some organised criminal groups have
demonstrated a penchant for high levels of violence and a capacity for
military action rivalling that of national defence forces.[5] However, while
transnational challenges to security are becoming more salient and
numerous, they are relatively immune to traditional enforcement strategies, do not conform to national borders and are usually beyond the jurisdiction of individual states.[6] They may also result from domestic
institutional weakness or policy failure rather than the calculated actions
of a rival state.

War has traditionally been considered the main threat to international security because of the large number of deaths it causes and the
threat it poses to the functioning and survival of the state. If judged by
these criteria, it is clear that some of the non-military, transnational
threats explored in this book are potentially as detrimental to human life
and the economic and political stability of nation-states as military
threats. AIDS, for example, is already responsible for the entirely preventible deaths of large numbers of East Asians. Unless arrested, it will

cripple whole communities and even countries. Deforestation in the upper reaches of the Yangtse River was a major factor in the catastrophic floods that inundated huge areas of China's main grain-producing region in 1998 and swept away thousands of its inhabitants. The paradigm shift that is already apparent – away from the military, state-centric view of security that predominated during the Cold War towards an extended notion of security – is being given added impetus by the rise of powerful transnational influences. Military threats, while still to be guarded against, no longer dominate the security agenda.

Far from representing a dilution or over-stretching of security, the concept has been enriched by attempts to widen its focus and make it more relevant to the contemporary world. Realist notions of security are unable to provide a satisfactory analytical framework for assessing and understanding the impact that environmentally generated conflict, UPMs and transnational crime are having on the security of states and their people. This is particularly so in East Asia, which is more vulnerable to their destabilising effects than more developed regions of the world. In the words of Fidel Ramos, the former President of the Philippines, 'other powers are arising in Asia that have nothing to do with states'.[7] Yet the ability to control the more egregious of these transnational powers and forces is beyond the capacity of any one state, placing a premium on effective international cooperation.

Incorporating the core transnational agenda into an extended security praxis does not have to result in conceptual muddle, nor does it require a radical redefinition of security. Richard Betts' metaphor suggests a way in which traditional military concerns and the non-military transnational agenda can be conceptually reconciled. Imagine security as a composite of three concentric circles, each of which encourages a particular kind of focus and analytical approach. Residing within the inner circle or core is military science, which is mainly concerned with the technology, organisation and tactics employed in fighting wars and winning battles. In the middle circle is strategic studies dealing with 'how political ends and military means interact under social, economic and other constraints'. The outer circle encompasses the broader field of security studies, which Betts defines as everything bearing on the security of a polity. Environmental security, UPMs and transnational crime can be accommodated within this outer circle without diminishing in any way the integrity, coherence or relevance of the other two circles.[8]

How Serious is the Threat?

These broad theoretical observations aside, what specific conclusions can be drawn about the seriousness of environmental degradation, UPMs and transnational crime for East Asia's security? Some environmentalists have been guilty of alarmist talk of the effects of ecological degradation, conjuring up images of environmental breakdown leading to violent conflict and, eventually, social and political anarchy in the developing world. Those who see a close connection between environmental degradation and military conflict exaggerate their case: there are few examples of environmental problems being the primary cause of major sub-national conflicts or interstate wars. It must be remembered, however, that war is usually the result of multiple forces and there is little agreement on the identity and primacy of its causal variables, notwithstanding the considerable intellectual energy and scholarly endeavour devoted to the subject.[9] While ecological pressure may not be the ostensible or direct cause of military conflict, it is having a discernible impact on East Asia's security – far more than traditional security analyses have generally allowed. Military conflict is not the only yardstick for measuring the security-degrading effects of a deteriorating physical environment. Ecological factors will be increasingly important in shaping the economic and political environment in East Asia and, by extension, its security environment. East Asia suffers from many tensions that have environmental sources, especially within states. Understanding security in East Asia therefore requires an understanding of environmental issues and their interaction with the other variables that cause conflict and instability.

Neo-Malthusian claims that uncontrolled population growth will eventually overwhelm the planet's coping capacity, resulting in famine and war, must also be treated with caution. There is no evidence of a direct link between population growth and conflict. Much depends on the ability of the resource base to sustain expanding populations and the political and economic circumstances against which this expansion takes place. Nevertheless, violence and conflict have historically been associated with rapid increases in population and urbanisation, and are more likely to occur in an era of environmental scarcity. The effects of rising populations will continue to be felt in East Asia for the rest of this century, aggravating political and social tensions within states and accelerating the decline in the region's stocks of natural resources. Urbanisation, particularly the expansion of the region's megacities, is spawning a host of environmental ills, reducing the availability of primary renewables like fresh water and arable land and therefore the ability of developing states to provide for their people. Rapid population growth reduces the benefits of economic development, creating large pools of unemployed and politically disenfranchised urban poor. The ability of China and Indonesia to effectively manage their projected population increases will be critical to the stability and prosperity of the whole region. Demographic pressures on the environment are set to reduce the carrying capacity of the land in

East Asia's two most populous states, and will be most severely felt in and near major cities. Other regional states will have to deal with their own population problems as well as considering the consequences of population growth in China and Indonesia.

Deforestation, pollution and climate change are symptomatic of the declining health of the global and regional environments and illustrate the circular connections between contemporary environmental problems and conflict. Although they are unlikely to cause major military conflict between states, their implications for security cannot be evaluated only in these terms. Forest loss reduces the productivity of the land and intensifies the effects of naturally occurring floods and droughts, with potentially disastrous consequences for human life and habitation. Deforestation can lead to significant internal unrest when indigenous communities resist commercial logging and exploitation of their forest homes. Unless reversed, East Asia's worsening pollution will have serious consequences for public health and economic development and will contribute to food and water problems. Pollution assumes greater political prominence when major oil spills and forest fires increase tensions between states and call into question the priorities and competence of governments. As in the case of the Indonesian fires, pollution can help to reshape the political agenda, and hence the overall security-policy climate, in significant ways. Major forest fires, acid rain and oil pollution at sea are three pollution-related issues most likely to have direct implications for foreign policy and regional security.

Pollution and deforestation are responsible for the rise in greenhouse gases that are at the heart of concerns about global climate change. Rapid climate change now seems inevitable in this century. Some states could be profoundly affected, others less so, and not all climate change will be deleterious. On balance, however, the net security effects are unlikely to be benign. The economic cost alone of managing climate change in East Asia will be substantial, particularly if sea-level rise forces large numbers of urban dwellers to relocate and if fertile coastal strips, crucial to cropping and grazing, are rendered unusable by salt water intrusion. Fluctuations in rainfall patterns and greater temperature extremes could disrupt agriculture and worsen food, water and resource scarcity. More extreme weather patterns are also likely to result in greater death and destruction from natural disasters, adding to the burden on poorer states.

Environmental degradation is heightening regional anxieties about future supplies of energy, food and water at a time when the security margins for all three are becoming disconcertingly thin. While there is no absolute shortage of oil, concerns about energy security are rooted in East Asia's limited reserves of oil and rising demand for electricity and transport. Environmental issues will complicate energy choices as the transition from highly polluting fossil fuels to cleaner sources of energy gathers speed. In the short term this may exacerbate oil shortages resulting from sudden price rises, distribution problems or disruptions to supply, adding to strategic uncertainty. The perception that oil may become scarce, or more expensive, is accentuating friction over unresolved maritime disputes, while the region's dependence on oil from the volatile Middle East is increasing. Nuclear power, once touted as an environmentally clean alternative to fossil fuels, has a serious public image problem and is unlikely to become a substitute for oil or greenhouse gas-producing coal. Nuclear waste disposal is destined to become a significant regional security concern, underlining the capacity of a new class of energy-related environmental issues to foment political and military conflict in East Asia.

Like the putative US–Soviet 'missile gap' of the 1960s, fears of an approaching food deficit in East Asia may prove unfounded. Modern-day Cassandras are inclined to underestimate the resilience of the global food economy and the capacity of modern technology to increase grain and cereal production. Should serious shortfalls develop, East Asia could trade its way out of a short-term crisis as other regions have done in the past. But this is not a reason for complacency. The gap between production and consumption of grain and cereals has narrowed dangerously in the past decade, while East Asia's and China's rising demand for grain has added an unpredictable new element to the global food equation. Food economists who are sanguine about the capacity of food supply to stay comfortably ahead of demand through innovation, biotechnology and loss reduction do not seem to have grasped just how much arable land is being desiccated and laid waste by environmental degradation and urban development. Localised food shortages can destabilise states, particularly when they occur against a background of political and economic turbulence. As the North Korean famines of the 1990s demonstrate, food insecurity is more often a function of government ineptitude, insouciance or policy failure than the result of actual scarcity, although for the millions of North Koreans who have died from starvation this distinction is entirely academic. More broadly, food seems destined to have greater strategic weight and import in an era of environmental scarcity.

Once considered abundant and free, fresh water is becoming scarce and more expensive. It is an open question as to whether or not conservation and technological improvements will allow governments to manage future water shortages without conflict. The auguries are not favourable and suggest that water scarcity will become a major security issue for East Asia even though wars are unlikely to be fought purely over water. The extent of the problem will vary significantly within and between states. China, Indonesia, Singapore and Thailand suffer endemic water shortages and other states may soon be affected. Long-term trends in use and supply point towards an accelerating deterioration in the region's reserves of fresh water. There is little prospect of reversing the trend without substantial and meaningful regional cooperation. Water disputes in Southeast Asia have the capacity to widen tensions between Malaysia and Singapore, and eventually to reawaken traditional animosities between the riparian states of the Mekong River. Aside from its importance for industry, the declining availability of fresh water will heighten regional insecurity because of irrigation's critical role in hydro-electricity generation and rice-growing. Indeed, water's central importance to food production may well prove to be the most fundamental security linkage of all.

UPMs are inextricably linked to other transnational security issues as well as more traditional causes of conflict in a complex web of interdependence which is altering the strategic calculus of many states. In an era characterised by rapid economic, social, technological and environmental change, the unregulated movement of people will be a growing source of domestic instability and interstate tension throughout the developed and developing world. Security is threatened because UPMs challenge the authority of governments in receiving states, accentuate the permeability of borders, widen internal political and social divides and levy heavy financial imposts on poorer countries. They can also be a source of military conflict between states. It should not be forgotten, however, that people forced to flee as a result of war or persecution are also victims, as are those exploited by criminal gangs capitalising on the expanding trade in undocumented foreign workers. How to reconcile the needs of these itinerants with the obligation and right of governments to protect their territory, institutions and citizens poses moral and practical dilemmas not easily resolved.

No state in East Asia has been able to immunise itself from the explosion in UPMs that has taken place in recent decades, a trend that shows no sign of being reversed any time soon. While migration has been an enduring feature of the region's political and social development, enriching East Asian societies as well as destroying them, today's UPMs are far more numerous, of a qualitatively different order and the product of multiple and diverse drivers. Ethno-nationalist conflicts, identity struggles and repression are the main catalysts of refugee flows and internally displaced persons in the region. However, demographic, environmental and economic forces are playing an increasingly influential role and are largely responsible for the rise in undocumented labour migrants who are being moved and exploited by mainly Asian people-smugglers. The future level of undocumented labour migration from China is the wild card in the migration pack. China's middle class is leaving in record numbers, seeking economic opportunity in more affluent parts of the globe. As incomes increase, emigration will become more affordable and living overseas a viable and much sought after option. Should Beijing prove unable or reluctant to stem the exodus, migration-induced tensions could increase further in East Asia as well as in Europe and North America.

The new prominence of people-smuggling in regional defence and foreign policy underscores how certain criminal activities have crossed over from law enforcement into the international security domain, blurring the distinction between them. War is being criminalised, criminals are becoming soldiers, and criminal violence is undermining regional stability and jeopardising the lives and security of countless individuals. The criminal challenge to East Asia's security stems from the ability of a new breed of transnational criminal organisations to exploit advances in knowledge, communications technology and financial services to acquire wealth, power and political influence on a scale that is without parallel in human history. In the process they are co-opting and corrupting the institutions of government, de-legitimising the state, subverting the rule of law, abetting the spread of AIDS and threatening the lives and livelihoods of people everywhere. Police and security forces struggling to combat rising crime are hamstrung by jurisdictional limits on their powers and embryonic regional cooperation. Criminals, on the other hand, are effectively sovereignty-free and have demonstrated an impressive ability to form transnational partnerships that span borders as well as ethnic and linguistic boundaries.

Not all criminal activities are threats to security, not all serious crime is organised, and there is no criminal imperium or Asian boss of bosses of the kind often portrayed in popular fiction. But sophisticated, highly organised criminal associations like the triads and yakuza feature prominently in East Asia's criminal landscape and their influence extends well beyond the region. At one end of the organisational spectrum are states like Burma and North Korea that are either complicit, or actively engaged in, criminal acts. At the other end are relatively small but extremely agile entrepreneurs involved in a multitude of illicit transactions that vary in their gravity, scope and consequences for regional security. Drug-trafficking is arguably the most serious because of the enormous sums of money concerned, the corruption it engenders and its association with insurgent movements, the sex trade and the spread of AIDS. As Karen Tellis argues, when drug power penetrates government institutions it 'devalues and disempowers those engaged in legitimate activity and discourages people from pursuing commercial and political ends within a system of law'.[10] East Asia is one of the principal producers of heroin and ATS but in recent years it has also become a major consumer of illicit drugs. Although the illicit production of drugs is geographically concentrated in the Golden Triangle region of mainland Southeast Asia, narcotics-trafficking is now an Asia-wide problem that shows every sign of worsening in the years ahead. In every sense, the production and consumption of illicit drugs is a first-order security issue for the region that warrants considerably more intergovernmental attention, resources and cooperation.

HIV/AIDS is representative of a new genre of infectious diseases which have become so detrimental to human life in many parts of the developing world that their security fall-out is commensurate with that of armed conflict and major war. Within the next decade the total number of AIDS-related deaths is projected to exceed those of human history's two other great pandemics, the Black Death and the influenza epidemic of 1918–19. However, the number of deaths caused by AIDS is not the only reason for its increasing salience for international and regional security. The disease is killing and blighting the prospects of whole generations in many developing countries, placing an intolerable burden on public health systems and exacting a heavy economic as well as human toll. Drug-trafficking, people-smuggling and the sex trade are crucial vectors in the rapid spread of AIDS in East Asia, highlighting the symbiosis between the disease and organised crime. The political, social, health and economic effects of HIV/AIDS will be felt across the region as the epicentre of the pandemic shifts from Africa to Asia in this decade. Thailand has shown that HIV infection rates can be stabilised and reduced, but widespread official ignorance, complacency and sexual taboos have reduced the effectiveness of regional responses to the pandemic. Unless these attitudes are reversed, AIDS threatens to kill millions more East Asians, reversing much of the hard-won economic progress of recent decades and destabilising the worst affected states.

More broadly, the maritime disputes in the South and East China Seas illustrate how the interweaving of traditional and transnational security concerns is driving conflict in the region. As traditional fishing grounds are depleted, the competition for the remaining stocks of fish and other living marine resources is intensifying throughout the Pacific Ocean, while maritime disputes and illegal fishing are on the rise. Declining reserves of fish and escalating demand for energy is increasing political and military tensions between states fighting to maintain their share of a shrinking resources cake. Without the pressure of climbing populations, high levels of energy dependency and the exhaustion of fish and other marine living resources, the maritime sovereignty issues in the Western Pacific would almost certainly not have attracted the same degree of prominence, nor proved as difficult to resolve. Even the residual conflicts of the Cold War are being reshaped by transnational forces which are blurring the conceptual and policy boundaries between high and low politics. South Korea has become uncomfortably aware that the barrels of the massed guns of the North Korean Peoples Army may pose less of a threat to its security than a famine-ridden, collapsing North Korean state.

For much of the twentieth century, securing control over oil and other non-renewable energy resources was a central strategic objective of the great powers and a leading cause of war. Although the contest for oil and strategic minerals will continue to feed interstate rivalry, the cumulative impact of a deteriorating natural resource base, overpopulation and climate change on state capacity and human security could prove a greater long-term danger for East Asia. As Norman Myers observes, 'when one problem combines with another problem, the outcome may not be a double problem, but a super-problem'.[11] It is the erosion of the planet's primary renewable resources which differentiates modern resource scarcity from that of the past. Not only are some key renewables becoming increasingly scarce but there are few, if any, real substitutes for them. What, for example, can replace fresh water? Technology can provide answers to some of the environmental ills that beset East Asia, but for struggling states and impoverished communities they may not be practical, affordable or politically palatable.

In a world where the limits of sustainable development have already been reached, environmental scarcity will circumscribe the power of all states. Resource availability will become, in the words of Robert Mandel, 'a determining constraint, or a "ceiling", on national power', rather than a 'determining opportunity, or "floor", on national power'.[12] States will be compelled to devote more capital and energy to preserving their natural resources from misuse, neglect and overexploitation. Developing states are particularly vulnerable to a range of atmospheric, terrestrial, and aquatic environmental pressures.[13] A degraded natural resource base will diminish the security of people, as well as states, pushing more people into penury, devaluing their lives and sometimes threatening their very survival. Environmental degradation resulting from human action cannot be compared with the random damage inflicted by naturally occurring earthquakes, tidal waves, storms and drought. The reality is that most contemporary environmental problems are caused by human actions. Unintended or not, the consequences of failing to preserve the physical environment will have direct consequences for the political and economic health of nation-states and the well-being of humankind.

One question that arises is whether it is possible or, indeed, desirable to rank in importance the transnational threats discussed in this book. There are some obvious pitfalls in doing so. For a start, different countries have different problems. Developed Japan, South Korea and Singapore are less vulnerable to the resource scarcities which bedevil their poorer neighbours and are more concerned about population decline

than overpopulation. It could also be argued that far from assisting scholars and policy-makers to understand better their dynamics and characteristics, attempting to prioritise transnational issues risks obscuring
their interconnectedness and works against the development of comprehensive solutions.

Nevertheless, within the taxonomy of threats to the region, fresh water
scarcity and AIDS stand out as potential first-order security issues. So
might climate change in the not too distant future, depending on the
extent of sea-level rise, the effect on regional agriculture production and
the frequency and degree of destructive cyclones, floods and drought.
Fresh water scarcity and AIDS, however, are here-and-now issues. As we
have seen, the availability of adequate supplies of fresh water is essential
to human survival and to virtually every aspect of economic development. Unlike most other resources, however, there are no real substitutes
for water; it is already in short supply throughout the region and critical
shortages are beginning to develop in a number of the most populous
states. Unless there is an immediate and major effort to reverse these
trends, water shortages could seriously jeopardise East Asia's stability in
the decades ahead, retarding agricultural and industrial growth, compelling internal migration and increasing water disputes between states.
AIDS is the other transnational issue with the potential to threaten the
security of the whole region because of the scale of the pandemic, the
accelerating rate of HIV transmission, its association with the region's rising level of drug addiction, and the numerous deaths it will cause. Few
other threats are likely to rival AIDS or fresh water scarcity in magnitude
or gravity during the next few decades.

Lessons for policy-makers

There are a number of important lessons for policy-makers. First, the
agencies responsible for formulating and implementing national security
policy are often poorly equipped, intellectually and organisationally, for
dealing with transnational issues which tend to fall across bureaucratic
jurisdictions rather than neatly fitting into them. Many are complex –
most are beyond the authority and competence of defence and foreign
ministries and require whole-of-government responses. Security is becoming the concern of a far greater range of actors, placing a higher premium
on effective coordination and cooperation. Environmental planning,
health, immigration, agriculture, energy, customs and police agencies
are legitimate bureaucratic stakeholders in the fight against transnational
threats. But they are frequently excluded from the national security
decision-making process or have insufficient policy clout to make a significant contribution. Typically, no single department has ownership of a

transnational security problem because governments are still structured along the same functional lines that they were fifty years ago. A more comprehensive and inclusive approach to security planning at the national level is essential for dealing with the transnational security agenda.

Second, East Asian states have rarely addressed transnational threats as a region. No multilateral organisation has been prepared to take on the role of formulating an overarching strategy for dealing with regional transnational security issues, and there is still insufficient appreciation of the multidimensional nature of the linkages between these issues and security. Even at the national level, few states in East Asia have effectively integrated the environment, illegal migration or transnational crime into national security planning. Regional governments need to cooperate more closely in finding solutions to problems that concern them all. Rather than establish new bodies to assist national governments in this task, better use could be made of existing organisations. Developing effective regional responses should be a priority task for East Asia's premier multilateral security organisation – the ASEAN Regional Forum. So far, the ARF has not done enough in this area. Although transnational issues feature rhetorically in the comprehensive approach to security adopted by the ARF, they have not yet found their way into the organisation's confidence-building processes. Nor have they yet been taken up substantively in regional preventive diplomacy, which is an important but under-utilised tool in the ARF's diplomatic armoury.

Transnational security issues should be at the heart of the ARF's experiment in confidence-building and preventive diplomacy. They are generally less politically sensitive than 'hard' security issues like nuclear and chemical weapons proliferation, which are usually contentious and frequently carry with them the grievances and accumulated strategic baggage of the Cold War era. Moreover, unlike many of the most serious political and military disputes confronting the region, which are either bilateral or peculiar to one particular subregion, the most pressing transnational security problems are seldom amenable to unilateral or bilateral resolution. For this reason they are well suited to the cooperative security framework of the ARF. There is still a window of opportunity to prevent phenomena like environmental degradation, UPMs, transnational crime and other transnational issues from entrenching themselves as primary sources of regional conflict. A commitment by the ARF to place transnational issues at the heart of its future confidence-building and preventive diplomacy agenda would be a far-sighted initiative and one likely to find favour with most regional states.[14] It would also strengthen the ARF's hand and renew faith in the contribution that multilateral diplomacy can make to conflict prevention in East Asia.

On the evidence presented in this book, the following subjects have persuasive claims for inclusion in a transnational basket of CBMs and preventive diplomacy measures for East Asia. Collectively, they constitute a new security agenda for the region:

- conflict over fresh water
- declining regional fish stocks and maritime resource competition
- drug-trafficking
- AIDS
- unregulated population movements
- pollution, with particular emphasis on acid rain, deforestation and forest fires.

How might measures to combat them be organised and operationalised? A useful model is the Maritime Information Exchange Directory (MIED) which was agreed on at a July 1992 Western Pacific Naval Symposium Workshop in Sydney. The idea behind the MIED is that participating navies would share information on a range of maritime activities, many of them related to transnational security issues such as UPMs, maritime pollution/environmental concerns, fisheries infringements and suspicious activity such as narcotics-trafficking. Based on the MIED model it ought to be possible, for example, to set up a regional surveillance centre to track and provide information on UPMs to participating governments. The centre's purpose would be to act as an early warning system of potentially destabilising mass migrations, to provide data on regional trends in UPMs and to assist in the identification and apprehension of criminal groups engaged in people-smuggling. Information relevant to specific movements, including numbers, intended destinations and current locations (especially useful for tracking boat people) could also be part of the centre's mandate.

A third lesson for policy-makers is that transnational phenomena will inevitably force changes in national intelligence priorities, strategic studies and defence planning. Intelligence collection and assessment is already beginning to reflect the demand by governments for a more integrated analysis of security trends, as well as for specific reporting on transnational developments. Indeed, no analysis of East Asia's security environment in the twenty-first century would be complete without a thorough audit of the region's stocks of natural resource and an evaluation of the destabilising consequences of UPMs and transnational criminal activities. The desire for a more comprehensive approach to strategic analysis that would include non-military influences was responsible for the 1996 directive by US Vice President Al Gore, that US intelligence agencies begin to assess the effect of environmental, social and economic factors on national and global security.[15]

As the salience of transnational influences grows, those responsible for predicting strategic trends will need to draw on a far broader range of disciplines for advice than has previously been the case. It may well be, as

Simon Dalby believes, 'that some ecological literacy will become an indispensable part of the intelligence community's tool kit'.[16] Certainly, it
would be futile to judge the security implications of AIDS without access
to informed medical opinion, just as it would be folly to attempt a strategic analysis of climate change without consulting climatologists. There are
also important implications for curriculum development and the way in
which strategic studies and international relations are taught at universi-
ties. More emphasis on interdisciplinary research and the cross-fertilisa-
tion of ideas is essential for developing better theory, as well as policy.

An extended security praxis strengthens the hand of those who argue
that modern military forces must be configured and employed for conflict prevention and constabulary tasks as well as conventional war-fighting and hybrid forms of warfare.[17] This is not an argument for attenuating
the core war-fighting tasks of the military but rather for a sensible and
modest reordering of defence priorities to include some capacity for combating non-military threats and conducting military operations other
than war. Asian defence forces are not well equipped doctrinally, organisationally or in resource terms to deal with the new transnational challenges they face, and they may have to make significant adjustments to
their modus operandi and force structures. It is already becoming common practice for military units in many regions of the world to take on
more responsibility for monitoring the health of the physical environment, and to use their organisational and technological strengths to assist
other agencies in repairing environmental damage. Equipment such as
radar and other surveillance systems may have to be reconfigured and
more agile platforms purchased so that they can monitor the small,
extremely fast-moving boats used for transporting drugs and other illegal
contraband across maritime borders.[18] At a more fundamental level, conflict itself is being transformed by transnational forces and non-state
actors. If Robert Kaplan's somewhat apocalyptic vision of a pre-modern
formlessness invading the battlefields of the underdeveloped world is
only half right then future conflict, as well as conflict prevention, will pose
demands of a very different order on defence forces and policy-makers.[19]

It is tempting for governments in the West to dismiss transnational
phenomena as predominantly afflictions of the world's poorer states. In
a sense they are right. Struggling communities and impoverished nations
are clearly more vulnerable to the effects of environmental degradation;
they are the source of most of the world's refugees and illegal migrants;
and they are particularly susceptible to the ravages of AIDS and exploitation by unscrupulous criminal organisations. But this is not a reason for
Western complacency. Policy elites sitting in their comfortable offices in
Europe, North America, Japan and Australia would do well to reflect on
the fact that 4.8 billion of the world's 6 billion people currently reside in

the developing world. By 2025, another 2 billion people will be living in countries where the basic necessities of life will almost certainly be in short supply. In an interconnected world, where time and space have been compressed by the forces of globalisation, the problems of the developing world are everyone's problems.

Of course, it is important not to inflate the transnational challenge to East Asia's security or overstate the spillover effects. With resolute action, many of the worst-case scenarios envisaged by pessimists may not come to pass. Indeed, it is to be fervently hoped that they do not. But in assessing political and strategic risk in East Asia, security planners ought to ask themselves what would be the consequences of a failure to reverse the decline in energy, food and water sufficiency, or the rise in HIV transmission, drug addiction and people-smuggling? The answer is that a continuation of these trends will have overwhelmingly negative outcomes for regional peace and stability. Ultimately, that is the reason why environmental degradation, UPMs and transnational crime must be accepted as core security issues for East Asia.

Notes

Introduction

1 East Asia is defined here as that part of Asia bounded by Burma, the Russian Far East, the Philippines and the Indonesian archipelago (including East Timor).

2 See, for example, Robert Jervis, 'The Future of World Politics: Will It Resemble The Past? *International Security* 16(3) 1991–92, p. 64.

3 One of the first to coin the term 'new agenda' was Fred Halliday in 'International Relations: Is There a New Agenda?', *Millennium: Journal of International Studies* 20(1) 1991, pp. 57–60. So-called 'gray-area' phenomena, defined as 'threats to the stability of nation-states by non-state actors and non-government processes and organizations', are also located within the new security taxonomy: James F. Holden-Rhodes and Peter Lupsha, 'Horsemen of the Apocalypse: Gray Area Phenomena and the New World Disorder', in Graham H. Turbiville Jr (ed.), *Global Dimensions of High Intensity Crime and Low Intensity Conflict* (Office of International Justice, University of Illinois, Chicago in cooperation with Mr Graham Turbiville Jr, Director, Foreign Military Studies Office, United States Army, Fort Leavenworth, Kansas, 1995), p. 10. Holden-Rhodes and Lupsha list as examples of gray-area phenomena ethno-religious-nationalistic conflicts, weapons proliferation, conflicts over scarce resources, the spread of AIDS and other infectious diseases, the globalisation of organised crime, drug-trafficking, economic warfare and conflicts over technology and emigration and famine. Although incorporating an expansive list of threats, much of the literature on gray-area phenomena is confined to organised crime and low-intensity conflict – the so-called 'gray war'. The notion of grey-area phenomena is also articulated in Max G. Manwaring (ed.), *Gray Area Phenomena: Confronting the New World Disorder* (Westview Press, Boulder, Colo., 1993) and Peter Chalk, 'Grey-Area Phenomena in Southeast Asia: Piracy, Drug Trafficking and Political Terrorism', Canberra Papers on Strategy and Defence No. 123 (Strategic and Defence Studies Centre, Australian National University, Canberra, 1997).

4 Paradigm is used here to mean a basic theory or philosophy about the meaning and practice of security. There is a vast body of literature on realism. The standard realist text is Hans Morgenthau, *Politics Among Nations: The Struggle*

for Power and Peace (Alfred Knopf, New York, 5th edn, 1973), while that of neo-realism or structural realism is Kenneth N. Waltz, *Theory of International Politics* (Addison-Wesley, Reading, Mass., 1979). Other important realist works include Waltz's *Man, the State and War: A Theoretical Analysis* (Columbia University Press, New York, 1959); Robert Gilpin, *War and Change in World Politics* (Cambridge University Press, 1981); John Mearsheimer, 'Back to the Future: Instability in Europe After the Cold War', *International Security* 15(1) 1990, pp. 5–55. For a useful restatement of the realist case see the collection of essays edited by Benjamin Frankel in the special issue entitled 'Realism, Restatements and Renewal', *Security Studies*, 5(3) 1996.

5 See Morgenthau, *Politics Among Nations* pp. 167–72, 178.

6 Richard Rosencrance, *The Rise of the Trading State: Commerce and Conquest in the Modern World* (Basic Books, New York, 1986), p. 8.

7 Arnold Wolfers, 'National Security as an Ambiguous Symbol', *Political Science Quarterly*, 67(4) 1952, p. 483. See also William Wohlforth, 'Realism and the End of the Cold War', *International Security* 19(3) 1994–95, pp. 91–129.

8 Barry Buzan, *People, States and Fear: The National Security Problem in International Relations* (Wheatsheaf Books, Sussex, 1983), p. 8.

9 'Balance of power' can have two distinct meanings. One denotes the general distribution of power among states. The other is best understood as the prevention of any one state from establishing hegemony by means of countervailing alliances. On the balance of power see Richard Betts, 'Wealth, Power and Instability', *International Security* 18(3) 1993–94, p. 35; Hedley Bull, *The Anarchical Society: A Study of Order in World Politics* (Macmillan, Melbourne, 1977), p. 24. There is insufficient space here to provide a comprehensive analysis of the different variants of realism. In brief, neorealism differs from classical realism in two important respects. Neorealists postulate that states form a structure with an identifiable set of behavioural regularities that provide a guide to the operation of the international system as a whole as well as to the behaviour of individual states. A second major departure in neorealist thinking is the belief that 'the ultimate concern of states is not for power but for security'. As Kenneth Waltz notes, this 'is an important revision of realist theory': Kenneth Waltz, 'Realist Thought and Neorealist Theory', *Journal of International Affairs* Summer 1990, p. 36. Realists also differ on the question of whether states seek to maximise their relative power vis-à-vis other states. Defensive realists contend that states are primarily concerned with maintaining the existing distribution or balance of power; that security is usually readily obtainable without recourse to war or conflict; and that defensive strategies will generally suffice to maintain national security even in a competitive world because the international system 'provides incentives only for moderate, cautious and restrained behaviour on the part of states': Benjamin Frankel, 'Restating the Realist Case: An Introduction', *Security Studies* 5(3) 1996, p. xvi. On defensive realism see Joseph Grieco, 'Anarchy and the Limits of Cooperation: A Realist Critique of the Newest Liberal Institutionalism', *International Organization* 42(3) 1988, pp. 498–500; Jack L. Snyder, *Myths of Empire: Domestic Politics and International Ambition* (Cornell University Press, New York, 1991), pp. 10–13; Fareed Zakaria, 'Realism and Domestic Politics: A Review Essay', *International Security* 17(1) 1992, pp. 190–6. Offensive realists demur. In their view security is scarce. Therefore states are more inclined to maximise their power through aggressive strategies because of uncertainty and fear about the intentions of others and because the anarchical nature of

the international system dictates such behaviour. The search for security compels states to engage constantly in a struggle for survival which encourages influence-maximising behaviour. While absolute security is unattainable, a state 'with more power is more secure than a state with less power': Frankel, 'Restating the Realist Case', p. xviii. The clearest statements of offensive realism are Mearsheimer, 'Back to the Future', pp. 5–56 and 'The False Promise of International Institutions', *International Security* 19(3) 1994–95, pp. 5–49. See also Sean M.Lynn-Jones, 'Realism and America's Rise: A Review Essay, *International Security* 23(2) 1998, pp. 157–8.

10 Inis L. Claude Jr., *Swords Into Plowshares: The Problems and Progress of International Organization* (Random House, New York, 1971), p. 14.

11 This is the classical security dilemma first articulated by the American realist John Herz in *Political Realism and Political Idealism: A Study in Theories and Realities* (University of Chicago Press, 1951), pp. 2–15.

12 Arnold Wolfers, *Discord and Collaboration*, (Johns Hopkins University Press, Baltimore, 1962), p. 150.

13 Paul Kennedy, for example, who has written extensively on the connection between wealth and power, considers that 'all of the major shifts in the world's *military-power* balances have followed alterations in the *productive* balances': Paul Kennedy, *The Rise And Fall of the Great Powers* (Fontana Press, London, 1988), p. 567. There is a considerable body of literature on the relationship between economics and security. Among the most informative are Klaus Knorr and Frank Trager (eds), *Economic Issues and National Security* (University of Kansas Press, 1977), especially the chapters by Robert Gilpin and Clark A. Murdock; Rosencrance, *The Rise of the Trading*; Fred Bergsten, 'The Primacy of Economics', *Foreign Policy* 87, Summer 1992, pp. 3–24; Robert Gilpin, 'The Economic Dimension of International Security', in Henry Bienen (ed.), *Power, Economics and Security: The United States and Japan in Focus* (Westview, Boulder, Colo., 1992); Edward Mansfield, *Power, Trade and War* (Princeton University Press, 1994); Stuart Harris, 'The Economic Aspects of Security in the Asia/Pacific Region', *Journal of Strategic Studies* 18(3) 1995, pp. 32–51.

14 David Held and Anthony McGrew, 'Globalization and the liberal democratic state', in Yoshikazu Sakamoto (ed.), *Global transformation: Challenges to the state system* (United Nations University Press, Tokyo, 1994), p. 60.

15 Jessica T. Matthews, 'Power Shift', *Foreign Affairs* 76(1) 1997, p. 50.

16 Liberalism, like its antithesis realism, has an equally long pedigree in international relations. For a cogent analysis of modern liberal thought, as conceptualised in neoliberalism, see Robert O. Keohane, 'Institutional Theory and the Realist Challenge After the Cold War' in David A. Baldwin (ed.), *Neorealism and Neoliberalism: The Contemporary Debate* (Columbia University Press, New York, 1993). The seminal statement of interdependence theory is Robert O. Keohane and Joseph S. Nye Jr., *Power and Interdependence* (Scott, Foresman & Co., Glenview, Ill., 1989). Other important liberal institutionalist works are Robert Axelrod and Robert O. Keohane, 'Achieving Cooperation under Anarchy: Strategies and Institutions', *World Politics* 38(1) 1985, pp. 226–54 and Kenneth A. Oye, 'Explaining Cooperation Under Anarchy: Hypotheses and Strategies', *World Politics* 38(1) 1985, pp. 1–24. In the 1940s and early 1950s, the dominant mode of liberal thought was encapsulated in functionalist integration theory, which evolved into neofunctionalist integration theory in the 1960s and interdependence theory in the 1970s. See

Joseph Grieco, 'Anarchy and the Limits of Cooperation: A Realist Critique of the Newest Liberal Institutionalism', *International Organization* 42(3) 1988, p. 486.

17   Robert O. Keohane and Joseph S. Nye Jr., 'Globalization: What's New? What's Not? (And So What?)', *Foreign Policy* 118, Spring 2000, p. 114. On globalisation see Thomas Friedman, *The Lexus and the Olive Tree* (Farrar, Straus & Giroux, New York, 1999) and David Held, Anthony McGrew, David Goldblatt and Jonathan Perraton, *Global Transformations: Politics, Economics and Culture* (Stanford University Press, 1999) for a comprehensive survey of the academic literature.

18   Keohane and Nye, *Power and Interdependence*, pp. 24–5.

19   Cited in ibid., p. 3. A succinct exposition of the reasons for the balance of power's Eurocentric nature and its declining relevance can be found in 'Not quite a new world order, more a three-way split', *Economist* 20 December 1997, pp. 41–3. See also Robert Cooper, *The Post-Modern State and the World Order* (Demos, London, 1996). Cooper contends that the balance-of-power system effectively came to an end with the collapse of the Soviet Union in 1989.

20   See, for example, Daniel Deudney, 'The Case Against Linking Environmental Degradation and National Security', *Millennium: Journal of International Studies* 19(1) 1990, p. 461.

21   For an analysis of this conflict see Beno Wasserman, 'The Cod War', *Contemporary Review* 225(1302) 1974, pp. 7–13.

22   On this point see Joseph A. Camilleri, 'Security: Old Dilemmas and New Challenges in the Post-Cold War Environment', *Geojournal* 34(2) 1994, p. 136.

23   Michael E. Brown (ed.), *The International Dimensions of Internal Conflict* (MIT Press, Cambridge, Mass., 1996), p. 1. Many ethnic minority groups are effectively stateless, few states are ethnically homogeneous (where one group comprises over 95 percent of the state's population), and borders seldom correspond to natural ethnic, linguistic or cultural boundaries. Of 161 states surveyed in one study only forty-one were found to be ethnically homogeneous. Few ethnic groups have their own state: Gunnar P. Nielsson, 'States and "Nation Groups": A Global Taxonomy', in Edward A. Tiryakian and Ronald Rogowski (eds), *New Nationalisms of the Developed West* (Allen & Unwin, Boston, 1985), Table 2.1, pp. 30–1, 33.

24   Not only have interstate wars become relatively rare but internal conflicts have on the whole been much bloodier, featuring great 'collateral damage' to civilian populations caught up in the fighting or its immediate aftermath. Nearly 90 per cent of war-related casualties during the 1990s were civilian: Indra de Soysa and Nils Petter Gleditsch, *To Cultivate Peace: Agriculture in a World of Conflict*, PRIO Report 1/99 (International Peace Research Institute, Oslo, 1999), pp. 7, 13–15.

25   Robert Gilpin, 'Economic Interdependence and National Security in Historical Perspective', in Knorr and Trager, *Economic Issues and National Security*, p. 26.

26   Schroder argues persuasively that 'bandwagoning' – joining the stronger side even though this meant insecurity vis-à-vis the protecting power – was actually more common in Europe than balancing, especially for smaller powers: Paul Schroder, 'Historical Reality vs Neo-realist Theory', *International Security* 19(1) 1994, pp. 117, 147–8.

27 Dating back to at least the third century BC, although Chinese suzerainty was not widely established in Southeast Asia until the arrival of the Sui and Tang dynasties in the seventh century. For an overview of the relationship between China and other East Asian proto-states, see Keith W. Taylor, 'The Early Kingdoms', in Nicholas Tarling (ed.), *The Cambridge History of Southeast Asia: From Early Times to c. 1800*, vol. 1 (Cambridge University Press, 1992), pp. 137–81.

28 Nicola Baker and Leonard C. Sebastian, 'The Problem of Parachuting: Strategic Studies and Security in the Asia/Pacific Region', in Desmond Ball (ed.), *The Transformation of Security in the Asia/Pacific Region* (Frank Cass, London, 1996), p. 16.

29 ibid., p. 20.

30 For a discussion of ASEAN's approach to security see Amitav Acharya, 'A New Regional Order in South-East Asia: ASEAN in the Post-Cold War Era', Adelphi Paper no. 279 (Brassey's for the IISS, London, August 1993).

31 Muthiah Alagappa (ed.), *Asian Security Practice: Material and Ideational Influences* (Stanford University Press, 1998), p. 674.

32 On constructivism (located within this conceptual family or associated with it are several overlapping strands of thought variously described as critical theory, postmodernism, post-structuralism and reflectivism) see the various articles written by Alexander Wendt, notably 'Anarchy Is What States Make of It: The Social Construction of Power Politics', *International Organisation* 46(2) 1992, pp. 391–425 and *Social Theory of International Politics* (Cambridge University Press, 1999); and Andrew Linklater, 'The Question of the Next Stage in International Relations Theory: A Critical-Theoretical Point of View', *Millennium: Journal of International Studies* 21(1) 1992, pp. 77–98. According to constructivists, realists are guilty of creating a mindset that actively works against the interests of peace and security by conditioning elites to regard conflict and competition as natural and preordained. Constructivists favour the formation of security communities, the marrying of state interests with those of international society, and the creation of norms that encourage peaceful change and transform the way states think about themselves and other units in the system: John G. Ruggie, 'International Structure and International Transformation: Space, Time and Method', in Ernst-Otto Czempiel and James N. Rosenau (eds), *Global Changes and Theoretical Challenges: Approaches to World Politics for the 1990s* (Lexington Books, Lexington, Mass., 1989), p. 30. Wendt is associated with a 'thinner', less radical version of constructivism which acknowledges the existence of material forces like power and interest but argues that anarchy has no determining logic and asserts that theorising about international politics should begin with 'the distribution of ideas and especially culture': Wendt, *Social Theory of International Politics*, p. 371. On the importance of culture in determining strategic preferences and perceptions of security, see Alastair Ian Johnston, 'Thinking about Strategic Culture', *International Security* 19(4) 1995, pp. 34, 55; Winifred L. Amaturo, 'Literature and International Relations: The Question of Culture in the Production of International Power', *Millennium: Journal of International Studies* 24(1) 1995, p. 2.

33 Alagappa, *Asian Security Practice*, p. 649. China, for example, retains a strong consciousness of its civilisational identity and a subliminal memory of the patron–client relationship that once defined its responses to other East Asian polities. Thailand and Vietnam have historically battled for influence in chronically weak Cambodia, and contemporary attitudes will continue to be

shaped by their long- standing strategic rivalry and strong sense of cultural and ethnic separateness.

34 This is the definition of security that will be used throughout this book unless otherwise specified.

35 Gwyn Prins and Robbie Stamp, *Top Guns and Toxic Whales: The Environment and Global Security* (Earthscan, London, 1991), p. 20. Prins is not the only scholar to take this view. See also Michael Renner, 'Environmental Dimensions of Disarmament and Conversion', in Kevin J. Cassidy and Gregory A. Bischak (eds), *Real Security: Converting the Defense Economy and Building Peace* (State University of New York Press, Albany, 1993); Richard Falk, *This Endangered Planet: Prospects and Proposals for Human Survival* (Random House, New York, 1971); and the numerous writings of Norman Myers, in particular *Ultimate Security: The Environmental Basis of Political Security* (Norton, New York, 1993).

36 Alexander Carius and Andreas Kraemer, '"Complexificacao" of environmental security', paper prepared for the Seminar on Global Security Beyond 2000: Global Population Growth, Environmental Degradation, Migration, and Transnational Crime, University of Pittsburgh, 2–3 November 1995, p. 13.

37 The United Nations is best placed to make such a determination, although in practice consensus is unlikely to be easy or even achievable.

38 The genesis of the idea of human security was a 1994 report of the UNDP, which asserts, *inter alia,* that 'the concept of security has for too long been interpreted narrowly ... It has been more related to nation states than people. Forgotten were the legitimate concerns of ordinary people who sought security in their daily lives': UNDP, *Human Development Report 1994* (Oxford University Press, 1994), p. 22. See also Gareth Evans, in 'Cooperative Security and Intra State Conflict', *Foreign Policy* 96, Fall 1994, pp. 6–11; Mel Gurtov, *Global Politics in the Human Interest* (Lynne Reinner, Boulder, Colo., 1991), p. 4; Camilleri, 'Security', p. 131; Keith Krause and Michael C. Williams, 'From Strategy to Security: Foundations of Critical Security Studies', in Keith Krause and Michael C. Williams (eds), *Critical Security Studies: Concepts and Cases* (University of Minnesota Press, 1997), p. 44.

39 UNDP, *Human Development Report 1999: Globalization with a Human Face,* www.undp.org/hdro/Backmatter2.pdf. The notion of human security has attracted powerful support from UN agencies, NGOs and an emerging coalition of like-minded states. Some, like Canada and Norway, have traditionally been strong advocates of human rights. It is no coincidence that these two Western states are the principal organisers of the 'Lysoen Process' which has been instrumental in promoting and attempting to operationalise human security. In East Asia, both Japan and Thailand have identified human security as a desirable national development and foreign policy goal. 'Human security and human development are two sides of the one coin', according to former Thai Foreign Minister, Surin Pitsuwan: H. E. Surin Pitsuwan, 'Statement by H. E. Dr. Surin Pitsuwan, Foreign Minister of the Kingdom of Thailand', at the Ministerial Meeting on Human Security Issues of the 'Lysoen Process' Group of Governments, Bergen, 19 May 1999, p. 1. The late Japanese Prime Minister, Keizo Obuchi declared that human security would be one of the essential principles of Japan's foreign policy: Ramesh Thakur and Steve Lee, 'Defining New Goals for Diplomacy of the 21st Century', *International Herald Tribune* 19 January 2000, p. 8.

40 Canadian Foreign Minister, Lloyd Axworthy, quoted in Astri Suhrke, 'Human Security and the Interests of States', *Security Dialogue* 30(3) 1999, p. 269.

41 Ramesh Thakur, 'From National to Human Security', in Stuart Harris and Andrew Mack (eds), *Asia-Pacific Security: The Economics-Politics Nexus* (Allen & Unwin, Sydney, 1997), pp. 53–4.

42 On the centrality of the individual in Western liberal philosophy see Emma Rothschild, 'What is Security?', *Daedalus* 124(3) 1995, pp. 53–98.

43 See Barry Buzan, 'Human Security: What it Means, and what it Entails', paper presented at the 14th Asia-Pacific Roundtable, 3–7 June 2000, particularly pp. 3–7; Ole Waever, 'Securitization and Desecuritization', in Ronnie Lipschutz (ed.), *On Security* (Columbia University Press, New York, 1995).

44 'Second track', as distinct from the official 'first track' security process, refers to the formal security dialogue between academics, business people, NGO representatives and officials acting in a non-official capacity that has become institutionalised over the past decade.

45 'Concepts of Comprehensive and Cooperative Security', *CSCAP Newsletter* 6, June 1997, p. 2. For an analysis of CSCAP and its record, see Desmond Ball, 'The Council for Security Cooperation in the Asia Pacific: Its Record and Its Prospects', Canberra Papers on Strategy and Defence no. 139 (Strategic and Defence Studies Centre, Australian National University, Canberra, October 2000).

46 'Concepts of Comprehensive and Cooperative Security', p. 2.

47 *North–South: A programme for survival*, Report of the Brandt Commission (Pan, London, 1980).

48 Richard Ullman, 'Redefining Security', *International Security* 8(1) 1983, p. 133.

49 UNHCR, *The State of the Word's Refugees 1997–98: A Humanitarian Agenda*, www.unhcr.ch/refworld/pub/state/97/ch1.htm.

50 Vice-President Al Gore, *Opening Statement in the Security Council Meeting on AIDS in Africa*, 10 January 2000, www.un.int/usa/00_003.htm; 'US vows $228m for AIDS war', *Australian* 12 January 2000, p. 8.

51 NSC 68, *United States Objectives and Programs for National Security*, 14 April 1950 was written for President Truman by a special State and Defense Department Study Group headed by Paul Nitze. The full text of the once top-secret document can be found in Thomas H. Etzold and John Lewis Gaddis (eds), *Containment: Documents on American Policy and Strategy, 1945–1950* (Columbia University Press, New York), pp. 385–442.

52 *A National Security Strategy for A New Century*, October 1998, www.whitehouse.gov./WH/EOP/NSC/html/nschome.html. Transnational security issues featured prominently in all the major iterations of US national security policy during the Clinton presidency.

53 ibid. See also the introduction of the 1999 National Security Strategy, released on 5 January 2000, usinfo.state.gov/regional/ea/easec/natsec2k.htm.

54 Lorien Holland, 'Running Dry', *Far Eastern Economic Review* 3 February 2000, p. 19.

55 See, for example, Thomas Homer-Dixon, 'On the Threshold: Environmental Changes as Causes of Acute Conflict', *International Security* 16(2) 1991, p. 83; Mark Levy, 'Is the Environment a National Security Issue?', *International Security* 20(2) 1995, pp. 56–7.

56 The existing scholarly material on transnational security tends to deal with the subject from a broad theoretical or a country perspective. A notable

exception is the article by R. T. Maddock: 'Environmental Security in East Asia', *Contemporary Southeast Asia* 17(1) 1995, pp. 20–37.

57 The Woodrow Wilson Center, for example, lists thirty-seven transnational problems ranging from acid rain to nuclear waste, genetic engineering and infectious diseases. See Franklyn Griffiths, 'Environment in the US Security Debate: The Case of the Missing Arctic Waters', *Environmental Change and Security Project* (Woodrow Wilson Center) 3, Spring 1997, p. 17.

58 In any empirical study there is a fine line between providing enough factual information to support the arguments being advanced and data overload. Where possible, the data and facts contained within these pages have been incorporated into graphs, tables and maps that convey a sense of the dominant trends and discernible regionwide patterns. Although there are clearly many parallels with other regions of the world, the temptation to expand the book's geographical scope beyond East Asia has been resisted in the interests of manageability and coherence.

1 Transnational Issues and Security

1 The term 'environmentalists' is used here not in its general sense but rather to denote those who share the view that there is a discrete and important environmental dimension to security which has been neglected in the traditional security literature.

2 Harold and Margaret Sprout, *Toward A Politics of the Planet Earth* (Van Nostrand Reinhold, London, 1971), pp. 23–4. On the concept of 'environmental security', see Richard Ullman, 'Redefining Security', *International Security* 8(1) 1993, p. 133; Maddock, 'Environmental Security in East Asia', p. 20; Jennifer Tuchman-Mathews, 'Redefining Security', *Foreign Affairs* 8(1) 1993, p. 162; Levy, 'Is the Environment a National Security Issue?', pp. 37–41; Stephen Libiszewski, 'What is an Environmental Conflict?', Occasional Paper No. 1, Environment and Conflicts Project, Swiss Peace Foundation, Bern, 1992, p. 3.

3 Paul Ehrlich wrote a number of influential books. Perhaps the best known is *The Population Bomb* (Ballantine Books, New York, 1968). Rachel Carson is generally accepted as one of the founding 'mothers' of the environmental movement as a result of her widely read book *Silent Spring* (Houghton Mifflin, Boston, 1962).

4 Disciples of 'securing the environment' are generally suspicious of the motives of security specialists in entering the debate on the environment. These interventions have been characterised as a dangerous reinforcement and legitimation of 'a militaristic mindset' and a barrier to the development of an effective response to environmental decline. On this point see Lorraine Elliott, *The Global Politics of the Environment* (New York University Press, New York, 1998), p. 219.

5 In ancient Greece, Gaia was the Goddess of the Earth.

6 According to Lovelock, a cybernetic or feedback system seeks an 'optimal physical and chemical environment for life on this planet': Norman Myers (ed.), *The Gaia Atlas of Planet Management* (Pan Books, London, 1985), p. 100. See also James E. Lovelock, *Gaia: A New Look at Life on Earth* (Oxford University Press, 1979). Others, notably Harold and Margaret Sprout, have also argued for an understanding of the 'interrelated whole' which is the global ecosystem: *Toward A Politics of the Planet Earth*, pp. 14–17.

 7 Robert D. Kaplan, 'The Coming Anarchy', *Atlantic Monthly* February 1994, p. 58.
 8 Michael Renner, cited in Simon Dalby, 'Security, Intelligence, the National Interest and the Global Environment', *Intelligence and National Security* 10(4) 1995, p. 187.
 9 See Barry Buzan, *People, States and Fear: An Agenda For International Security Studies in the Post-Cold War Era* (Harvester Wheatsheaf, London, 1991), especially p. 131; Tuchman-Mathews, 'Redefining Security', pp. 162–77.
10 Desmond Ball, Nancy Viviani and Ross Garnaut, 'Economics and Security: Towards Greater Cooperation in the Asia/Pacific Region', paper prepared for the Conference on the Asia-Pacific Region: Links Between Economics and Security Relations, Institute on Global Conflict and Cooperation, University of California, San Diego, 13–15 December 1993, p. 28.
11 Shaukat Hassan, 'Environmental Issues and Security in South Asia', Adelphi Paper no. 262 (Brassey's, for the International Institute of Strategic Studies, London, 1991), p. 24; Dalby, 'Security, Intelligence, the National Interest and the Global Environment', p. 183. There is also concern that some elements of the broad ecological movement may become progressively more militant in pursuit of their political agendas, and move outside the boundaries of national and international law. This may pose threats to states in the form of ecologically inspired terrorism or low-level conflict: George Joffe, 'The Impact on Security of Demographic and Economic Change', G. A. S. C. Wilson (ed.), *British Security 2010*, proceedings of a conference held at Church House, Westminster, November 1995, p. 38.
12 Ullman, 'Redefining Security', pp. 138–45. See also the studies by Arthur Westing (ed.), *Global resources and International Conflict* (Oxford University Press, 1986); Ronnie Lipschutz, *When Nations Clash: Raw Materials, Ideology and Foreign Policy* (Ballinger, Cambridge, Mass., 1989).
13 See, for example, the various writings of Thomas Homer-Dixon, especially 'On the Threshold: Environmental Changes as Causes of Acute Conflict, *International Security*, Fall 1991, 16(2), pp. 76–116 and Gwyn Prins and Robbie Stamp, *Top Guns and Toxic Whales: The Environment and Global Security* (Earthscan Publications, London, 1991).
14 Such conflict could be generated by competition over 'environmental goods' or by environmental changes which generate or contribute to the 'chain of events that produce it': Richard A. Matthew, 'Rethinking Environmental Security', in Nils Petter Gleditsch et al. (eds), *Conflict and the Environment* (published in cooperation with NATO Scientific Affairs Division, Kluwer Academic Publishers, Dordrecht, The Netherlands, 1997), p. 73. There are two other interpretations of environmental security in the security literature. One explores environmental warfare – the explicit targeting of an adversary's resources or physical environment aimed at degrading or destroying his capacity to prosecute war. See, for example, Arthur Westing (ed.), 'Environmental Warfare: an overview', in *Environmental Warfare: A Technical, Legal and Policy Appraisal* (Taylor & Francis, London, 1984). The most commonly cited examples of modern environmental warfare are the second Indochina War, and the 1991 Gulf War. During the Indochina conflict, the United States sprayed large areas of Vietnamese rainforest with defoliants like Agent Orange in an attempt to deny cover to the North Vietnamese and their Viet Cong allies. The Iraquis deliberately destroyed or disabled a large percentage of the petroleum rigs in Kuwait for punitive and economic reasons, in the process causing substantial damage

to Kuwait's environment and the maritime ecology of the Gulf. A second distinct area of research is concerned with the use of national defence forces and military assets to monitor environmental change and to assist in protecting or rejuvenating the environment. See, for example, Robert K. Ackerman, 'Defence Machinery Gears Up to Fight Environmental Threat', *Signal* December 1990. For a comprehensive discussion of the many aspects of environmental security see Gleditsch et al., *Conflict and the Environment*, especially pp. 15–91.

15 Deudney, 'The Case Against Linking Environmental Degradation and National Security', pp. 461–4.

16 ibid., p. 465; Levy, 'Is the Environment a National Security Issue?', p. 40.

17 Lothar Brock, 'The Environment and Security: Conceptual and Theoretical Issues', in Gleditsch et al., *Conflict and the Environment*, p. 20.

18 For example, glass in fibre-optic cabling is replacing copper as a communication conduit and composite materials are lessening the amount of steel used in automobiles and aircraft.

19 Deudney, 'The Case Against Linking Environmental Degradation and National Security', pp. 470–1. See also Ronnie Lipschutz and John P. Holdren, 'Crossing Borders: Resource Flows, the Global Environment, and International Security', *Bulletin of Peace Proposals* 2(2) 1990, pp. 121–33.

20 Homer-Dixon, 'On the Threshold', pp. 56–7.

21 Kazuo Takahashi, *Sustainable Development: Environment and Security*, paper presented at Concurrent Workshop VI, Ninth Asia-Pacific Roundtable, Kuala Lumpur, 5–8 June 1995.

22 W. Harriet Critchley and Terry Terriff, 'Environment and Security', in Richard Schultz, Roy Godson and Ted Greenwood (eds), *Security Studies for the 1990s* (Brassey's, New York, 1993), p. 337; Dalby, 'Security, Intelligence, the National Interest and the Global Environment', p. 178.

23 Dalby, 'Security, Intelligence, the National Interest and the Global Environment', p. 184.

24 Homer-Dixon, for example, suggests that the causal links and connections between environmental degradation and security are not tight or deterministic and that the violence stemming from environmental degradation and resource scarcity is usually an indirect consequence of economic and institutional dislocation caused by resource stress: Homer-Dixon, 'On the Threshold', p. 78; 'Correspondence', *International Security* 20(3) 1995–96, p. 191.

25 Robert Mandel quoted in Schultz et al., *Security Studies for the 1990s*, p. 347.

26 John McCormick, *The Global Environmental Movement* (Belhaven Press, London, 1989), p. vii. McCormick provides an excellent survey and analysis of the roots and development of the broader environmental movement.

27 Alfred W. Crosby, *Ecological Imperialism: The Biological Expansion of Europe, 900–1900* (Cambridge University Press, 1986), p. 53. See also Crosby's account of the ecological destruction of the vast pampa grasslands of Argentina by mainly Spanish settlers in the nineteenth century: ibid., pp. 160–1.

28 Dalby, 'Security, Intelligence, the National Interest and the Global Environment', p. 177; Carius and Kraemer, '"Complexificacao" of environmental security', p. 7.

29 On this point see Alagappa, *Asian Security Practice*, pp. 647–9.

30 There are a variety of often confusing terms used in the migration lexicon, among which are 'asylum flow, mass expulsion, ethnic cleansing, disaster-induced displacement, development-induced displacement, forced migration,

internal displacement, population transfer, population exchange, involuntary repatriation and imposed return': UNHCR, *The State of the Word's Refugees 1997–98: A Humanitarian Agenda*, www.unhcr.ch/refworld/pub/state/97/ch3.htm

31 Barbara Harell-Bond, 'Refugees and Displaced Persons in South Asia: The Challenge to Academia', *Regional Centre for Strategic Studies Newletter* 4(2) 1998, p. 5.

32 Some examples are Charles P. Kindleberger, *Europe's Postwar Growth: The Role of Labor Supply* (Harvard University Press, Cambridge, Mass., 1967); Wolf R. Bohning, *Studies in International Labour Migration* (Macmillan, London, 1984); Sidney Klein (ed.), *The Economics of Mass Migration in the Twentieth Century* (Paragon House, New York, 1987).

33 For a cogent summary of the various theories of migration see *World Population Monitoring 1997: International Migration and Development* (Department of Economic and Social Affairs, Population Division, UN, New York, 1998), pp. 141–7.

34 Jack A. Goldstone, 'A Tsunami on the Horizon? The Potential for International Migration from the People's Republic of China', in Paul J. Smith (ed.), *Human Smuggling: Chinese Migrant Trafficking and the Challenge to America's Immigration Tradition* (Center for Strategic and International Studies, Washington, D.C., 1997), pp. 48–9.

35 Fred Halliday was one of the first to predict that migration would become a major security concern in the post-Cold War world: 'International Relations: Is There a New Agenda?', pp. 59–60. Some early studies which analyse migration from a political or security perspective are Michael S. Teitelbaum, 'Immigration, refugees, and foreign policy', *International Organization* 38(3) 1984, pp. 429–50; Leon Gordenker, *Refugees in International Politics* (Croom Helm, London, 1987); Kimberly A. Hamilton and Kate Holder, 'International Migration and Foreign Policy', *Washington Quarterly* 14(2) 1991, pp. 195–211. Other significant works are Myron Weiner, 'Security, Stability and International Migration', *International Security* 17(3) 1992–93, pp. 91–126; Gil Loescher, 'Refugee Movements and International Security', Adelphi Paper no. 268 (Brassey's for the IISS, London, 1992).

36 Also referred to as 'high' and 'low' policies: Edward Morse, 'The Transformation of Foreign Policies – Modernization, Interdependence and Externalization', *World Politics* 22, 1969–70, pp. 371–2. See also Gerald E. Dirks, 'International Migration in the Nineties', *International Journal* 48, Spring 1993, p. 191.

37 Hania Zlotnik, 'International Migration 1965–96: An Overview', *Population and Development Review* 24(3) 1998, p. 429; Leon Bouvier, Dudley L. Poston Jr, and Nanbin Benjamin Zhai, 'Population Growth Impacts of Zero Net International Migration', *International Migration Review* 31(2) 1997, p. 295.

38 Waever, 'Securitization and Desecuritization', p. 65.

39 Maddock, 'Environmental Security', p. 177.

40 Demetrios G. Papademetriou and Philip L. Martin, 'Labor Migration and Development: Research and Policy Issues', in Demetrios G. Papademetriou and Philip L. Martin (eds.), *The Unsettled Relationship: Labor Migration and Economic Development* (Greenwood Press, New York, 1991), pp. 8–9.

41 See Sadako Ogata's foreword in *The State of the Word's Refugees 1997–98: A Humanitarian Agenda* (Oxford University Press, New York, 1997), p. iii.

42 Teitelbaum, *Immigration, Refugees, and Foreign Policy*, pp. 429–30.

43 See Aristide R. Zolberg, 'International migrations in political perspective', in Mary M. Kritz, Charles B. Keely and Silvano M. Tomasi (eds), *Global Trends in Migration: Theory and Research on International Population Movements* (Centre for Migration Studies, New York, 1981), pp. 3–27.

44 Teitelbaum, *Immigration, Refugees, and Foreign Policy*, p. 429.

45 Peter Nyers, 'Emergency or Emerging Identities? Refugees and Transformations in World Order', *Millennium: Journal of International Studies* 28(1) 1999, p. 11.

46 According to the 1951 UN Convention Relating to the Status of Refugees and its 1967 Protocol, a refugee is 'any person who, owing to a well-founded fear of being persecuted for reasons of race, religion, nationality, membership of a particular social group or political opinion, is outside the country of his nationality and is unable, or owing to such fear is unwilling, to avail himself of the protection of that country'. The definition now used by the UNHCR has been broadened significantly to include: 'persons recognized as refugees under the 1951 United Nations Convention relating to the Status of Refugees or its 1967 Protocol, the 1969 Organization of African Unity (OAU) Convention Governing the Specific Aspects of Refugee Problems in Africa, persons recognized as refugees in accordance with the UNHCR Statute, persons granted humanitarian status and those granted temporary protection': *Refugees and Others of Concern to UNHCR: 1998 Statistical Overview*, www.unhcr.ch/statist/98oview/intro.htm.

47 The millions of people displaced by the war returning to their homelands in 1945 and 1946 constituted the first wave.

48 Harell-Bond, 'Refugees and Displaced Persons in South Asia', pp. 3–4.

49 Adrienne Millbank, 'Global population movements, temporary movements in the Asia-Pacific region and Australia's immigration program', Research Paper no. 13, 1994, Parliamentary Research Service (Department of the Parliamentary Library, Canberra, 1994), p. 7.

50 Jacqueline Desbarats, 'Institutional and Policy Interactions among Countries and Refugee Flows', in Mary M. Kritz, Lin Lean Lim and Hania Zlotnik (eds), *International Migration Systems: A Global Approach* (Clarendon Press, Oxford, 1992), p. 282.

51 Since 1993, the UNHCR has included in its statistics figures for internally displaced persons, as well as others 'of concern', but it is not always clear how the figures for these latter two categories are arrived at or how comprehensive they are. The UNCHR concedes that part of the problem is the lack of agreement on how to define internally displaced people. For the purposes of this analysis, the UNHCR definition has been accepted. The term will be used to denote 'those persons who, as a result of persecution, armed conflict or violence, have been forced to abandon their homes and leave their usual place of residence, and who remain within the borders of their own country': UNHCR, *The State of the Word's Refugees 1997–98: A Humanitarian Agenda*, www.unhcr.ch/refworld/pub/state/97/ch3.htm.

52 Of the states that constitute East Asia, only China, Japan, South Korea, Cambodia and the Philippines have signed the 1951 Convention and/or its 1967 Protocol. Figures extrapolated from *World Refugee Survey 1995* (US Committee for Refugees, Washington, D.C., 1995), p. 47. Hong Kong and Taiwan are not included in this list, the former because it is now part of China and the latter because it is not a member of the United Nations.

53 Buzan, *People, States and Fear*, p. 94.

54 Eighty-six per cent of the foreigners residing legally in Japan are of Korean descent: Hania Zlotnik, 'International Migration 1965–96', 24(3) 1998, p. 453.
55 Weiner, 'Security, Stability and International Migration', pp. 96–7.
56 Paul Smith, 'Immigration Alters Military Role', *Defense News* 12–18 May 1997, pp. 27–8; Margot Cohen, 'Deport and Deter', *Far Eastern Economic Review* 23 April 1998, p.16; 'Navy nabs another 85 illegal migrants', *Canberra Times* 8 November 1999, p. 3.
57 Margaret E. Beare, 'Illegal Migration: Personal Tragedies, Social Problems, or National Security Threats?', *Transnational Crime* 3(4) 1997, p. 15.
58 Also referred to as transnational organised crime – the two terms tend to be used interchangeably. I have excluded terrorism from my discussion of transnational crime since criminal motivation is primarily economic while those of most terrorist groups is political.
59 These are only some of the subjects listed for study by the CSCAP Working Group on Transnational Organised Crime. See the report by John McFarlane of the Australian Federal Police in the *AUS-CSCAP Newsletter* 6, April 1998, pp. 6–7.
60 Jay S. Albanese, 'Models of Organized Crime', in R. J. Kelly, K. L. Chin and R. Schatzberg (eds), *Handbook of Organized Crime in the United States* (Greenwood Press, Westport, 1994), p. 78.
61 James D. White, 'The Map of the City: Putting an Asian Face on Crime', *Technological Forecasting and Social Change* 52, 1996, p. 201.
62 The United Nations defines an organised criminal group as 'a structured group [of three or more persons] existing for a period of time and having the aim of committing a serious [transnational] crime [through concerted action by using intimidation, violence, corruption or other means] in order to obtain, directly or indirectly, a financial or other material benefit'. Article 2 of the revised draft *United Nations Convention against Transnational Organized Crime* (UN General Assembly [AC.254/4/Rev.5], 16 November 1999) is quoted in John Morrison, *The Trafficking and Smuggling of Refugees: The End Game in European Asylum Policy?*, pre-publication edn, July 2000, originally commissioned by the UNHCR Policy Research Unit, Centre for Documentation and Research, www. unhcr.ch/evaluate/reports/traffick.pdf. For an alternative definition see Phil Williams and Ernesto U. Savona, 'The United Nations and Transnational Organized Crime', *Transnational Organized Crime* Special Issue, 1(3) 1995, p. 3.
63 R. T. Naylor, 'From Cold War to Crime War: The Search for a new "National Security" Threat', *Transnational Organized Crime* 1(4) 1995, p. 32.
64 Denny F. Pace and Jimmie C. Styles, *Organized Crime: Concepts and Control* (Prentice-Hall, Englewood Cliffs, N.J., 1975) cited in Sheldon X. Zhang and Mark S. Gaylord, 'Bound for the Golden Mountain: The social organization of Chinese alien smuggling', *Crime, Law and Social Change* 25, 1996, p. 3.
65 Albanese, 'Models of Organized Crime', p. 87.
66 Naylor, 'From Cold War to Crime War', p. 46.
67 This theme is explored in Dwight C. Smith, 'Paragons, Pariahs, and Pirates: A Spectrum-Based Theory of Enterprise', *Crime and Delinquency* 26, July 1980.
68 S. Mastrofski and G. Potter, 'Controlling Organized Crime: A Critique of Law Enforcement Policy', *Criminal Justice Policy Review* 2(3) 1987, pp. 269–76.
69 Several other iterations and permutations of these theories can be found in Doug Greaves and Susan Pinto, 'Redefining Organised Crime: Commentary

on a Recent Paper by Phil Dickie and Paul Wilson', *Current Issues in Criminal Justice* 5(2) 1993, pp. 223–4. See also 'The Use of Models in the Analysis of Organised Crime', Occasional Paper no. 9/96, Office of Strategic Crime Assessments, Canberra, 1996.

70 Shelley, 'Transnational Organized Crime', p. 464.
71 Godson and Olson, 'International Organized Crime', p. 20.
72 The preceding two paragraphs and the accompanying graphs draw on John Ciccarelli, 'Crime as a Security Threat in the 21st Century', *Journal of the Australian Naval Institute* November–December 1996, pp. 43–4.
73 Louise I. Shelley, 'Transnational crime: An Imminent Threat to the Nation State?', *Journal of International Affairs* 48(2) 1995.
74 Linnea P. Raine and Frank J. Cilluffo, *Global Organized Crime: The New Empire of Evil* (Center for Strategic and International Studies, Washington, D.C., 1994).
75 See Naylor, 'From Cold War to Crime War', pp. 48–50.
76 Clair Sterling, *Crime Without Frontiers: The Worldwide Expansion of Organised Crime and the Pax Mafiosi* (Little, Brown & Co., London, 1994), pp. 1–5.
77 Phil Williams, 'Transnational Criminal Organizations: Strategic Alliances', *Washington Quarterly* 18(10) 1995, p. 58.
78 D. Black, *Triad Takeover: A Terrifying Account of the Spread of Triad Crime in the West* (Sidgwick & Jackson, London, 1991), cited in Chu Yiu-kong, 'International Triad Movements: The Threat of Chinese Organised Crime', *International Triad Movements*, Research Institute for the Study of Conflict and Terrorism, July–August 1996, p. 1.
79 Williams, 'Transnational Criminal Organizations', p. 58.
80 Phil Williams, 'The Geopolitics of Transnational Organized Crime', paper presented at the seminar on Global Security Beyond 2000, sponsored by the University of Pittsburgh, 2–3 November 1995, p. 13.
81 Roy Godson and William J. Olson, 'International Organized Crime', *Society* January–February 1995, p. 21. See also Shelley, 'Transnational Organized Crime', p. 469.
82 Rensselaer W. Lee, 'Global Reach: The Threat of International Drug Trafficking', *Current History* May 1995, p. 210. See also Michael J. Dziedzic, 'The transnational drug trade and regional security', *Survival* November–December 1989, p. 534.
83 Phil Williams, 'The Geopolitics of Transnational Organized Crime', p. 13 and 'Transnational Crime: A New Security Threat', *Strategic Survey 1994–1995*, (IISS, London, 1995), p. 25.
84 James Rosenau, *Turbulence in World Politics: A Theory of Change and Continuity* (Princeton University Press, 1991), p. 36.
85 Kaplan, *The Coming Anarchy*, p. 49.
86 Alan Dupont, 'New Dimensions of Security', in Denny Roy (ed.), *The New Security Agenda in the Asia-Pacific Region* (Macmillan, London, 1997), p. 41. Some pessimists see criminal groups acquiring the means to militarily threaten nation-states for the purposes of extortion. Others envisage highly organised criminals acquiring the capability to manufacture their own nuclear weapons or seize control of military satellites and communications systems in order to redirect military weapons: Richter H. Moore Jr, 'Wiseguys', *The Futurist*, September–October 1994, pp. 35–7.
87 'Drug-smuggling sub found high in mountains', *Reuters* 9 September 2000.
88 Stefan Leader and David Wiencek, 'Drug Money: The fuel for global terrorism', *Jane's Intelligence Review* February 2000, p. 49.

89 Samuel D. Porteous, 'The Threat from Transnational Crime: An Intelligence Perspective', *Commentary* 70, Winter 1996, p. 4.
90 Naylor, 'From Cold War to Crime War', p. 46.
91 Phil Williams and C. Florez, 'Transnational criminal organizations and drug trafficking', *Bulletin on Narcotics* 46(2) 1994, pp. 23–4.
92 Chang Noi, 'There's Money Everywhere for Thai Police', Bangkok, The Nation in English, *Foreign Broadcast Information Service-TDD-97-006-L*, 25 February 1997.
93 Naylor, 'From Cold War to Crime War', p. 43.
94 The Chinese triads, for example, use their networks for licit and illicit purposes. So does the Sicilian Cuntrera-Caruana clan which, during the 1990s, established a wine bar, travel agency and antique business in the United Kingdom as fronts for the importation of cannabis from Kashmir and heroin from Thailand: 'International Crime' in *Strategic Assessment 1997: Flashpoints and Force Structure*, p. 202.

2 Population and Conflict

1 Neville Brown, 'Climate, Ecology and International Security', *Survival* 31 (6) 1989, p. 121.
2 *United Nations Population Fund News Feature*, 'Era of Rapid Population Growth Is Not Over' (Information and External Relations Division, New York, 2 September 1998); *The State of World Population 1998* (UN Population Fund, New York, 1998), p. 21. Two point one children per child-bearing woman represents 'replacement fertility', the minimum level necessary to offset deaths.
3 Unless otherwise indicated, the population statistics used in this analysis are taken from: *World Population Prospects: The 1996 Revision* (Population Division, Department for Economic and Social Information and Policy Analysis, UN, New York, 1996), Annexes 1, 2 and 3; *Population Newsletter* 62, Department for Economic and Social Information and Policy Analysis, UN Secretariat, December 1996, pp. 1–3; *World Population Projections to 2050* (Population Division, Department of Economic and Social Affairs, UN Secretariat, New York, 1998), Executive Summary, pp. 1–2.
4 See, for example, Nicholas Eberstadt, 'Research: Too Few People', *Prospect* 25, December 1997, p. 51.
5 Robert Engelman, 'Human Population Prospects: Implications for Environmental Security', *Environmental Change and Security Project Report*, pp. 48–9, 51; *World Resources 1994–95: A Guide to the Global Environment* (Oxford University Press for the UN, 1994), p. 27; private discussions with Australian demographers.
6 Rahul Singh, 'Food for thought: Too many people can hamper development', *Far Eastern Economic Review* 22 September 1994, p. 21.
7 *Asia 1997 Yearbook* (Hong Kong, Far Eastern Economic Review, 1996), p. 69; Singh 'Food for thought', p. 26.
8 *Concise Report on the World Population Situation in 1993: With Special Emphasis on Refugees* (UN, New York, 1994), p. 12; *Population Newsletter*, no. 62 (Department for Economic and Social Information and Policy Analysis, UN Secretariat, December 1996), p. 1; author's calculations from UN data in *World Population Projections to 2050*.
9 *United Nations Population Fund News Feature*, 'Era of Rapid Population Growth Is Not Over'.

10 *United Nations Population Fund Press Summary*, 'The New Generations' (Information and External Relations Division, New York, 2 September 1998), p. 1. The continuing increase in world population is also partly due to the fact that people are living much longer than they were a century ago. On this point see Nicholas Eberstadt, 'Six Billion Reasons to Cheer', *Asian Wall Street Journal* 13 October 1999, p. 6.

11 *The State of World Population 1998*, p. 21.

12 Because the TFR does not measure women's actual experience and may not adequately account for women choosing to have children later in life: ibid. p. 20.

13 Population growth may be as great in the next fifty years as it has in the past fifty: *United Nations Population Fund News Feature*, 'Era of Rapid Population Growth Is Not Over'.

14 To illustrate, while demographic growth rates were higher in the period 1950–55 than they were in 1985–90, the respective annual increases in global population were 47 million and 88 million: *Concise Report on the World Population Situation in 1993*, p. 14.

15 *The State of World Population 1998*, p. 20.

16 Tim Dyson of the London School of Economics contends, for example, that the population 'explosion' is 'probably the single most important thing happening in the world': '100m births a year for the next 50 years', *Straits Times* 13 October 1999, p. 16.

17 Rahul Singh, 'Growing Pains: Cairo conference debates world's demographic future', *Far Eastern Economic Review* 22 September 1994, p. 20; Engelman, 'Human Population Prospects', p. 53.

18 Eberstadt, 'Six Billion Reasons to Cheer', p. 6.

19 Brown, 'Climate, Ecology and International Security', p. 131.

20 For example, the collapse of the Ming dynasty, the Taiping rebellion and the revolutions of 1911 and 1949: John Orme, 'The Utility of Force in a World of Scarcity', *International Security* 22(3) 1997–98, p. 158.

21 Indra de Soysa and Nils Petter Gleditsch, *To Cultivate Peace: Agriculture in a World of Conflict*, PRIO Report 1/99 (International Peace Research Institute, Oslo, 1999), p. 35.

22 For elaboration see Alan Dupont, 'Unregulated Population Flows in East Asia: A New Security Dilemma?', *Pacifica Review* 9(1) 1997, pp. 1–22.

23 For East Asia as a whole, TFRs declined from 2.8 to 2.3 in the period 1975–90. However, there were significant regional variations. Southeast Asia's TFRs fell in the same period from 4.8 to 3.7, set against a world decline of 3.8 to 3.4. Data extracted from *World Population Prospects: The 1992 Revision* (UN, New York, 1993), Table A.12.

24 *Concise Report on the World Population Situation in 1993: With Special Emphasis on Refugees*, pp. 12–13.

25 ibid., p. 34.

26 William McGurn, 'City Limits', *Far Eastern Economic Review* 6 February, 1997, pp. 34–7; World Bank discussion paper prepared by Clive Bardon and Ramesh Ramankutty, cited in Florence Chong, 'Asia's economies may cost the Earth', *Australian* 30 March 1994, p. 39.

27 ADB figures cited in Johanna Son, 'Megacosts keep megacities unhealthy', *Jakarta Post* 23 April 1997, p. 5.

28 One 1998 Japanese government publication, only half in jest, fretted that unless Japanese women have more babies 'Japan's population will be …

about 500 people in the year 3000 and about one person by the year 3500':
Eriko Amaha, 'Baby Blues', *Far Eastern Economic Review* 16 July 1998, p. 13.

29 'Island mulls measures to halt drop in workforce', *Hong Kong Standard* 6
    March 1999, p. 7.

30 For a good analysis of these issues see Nicholas Eberstadt, 'Asia Tomorrow,
    Gray and Male', *National Interest* 53, Fall 1998, pp. 56–65.

31 China's ideal population is considered by Beijing to be about 700 million: J.
    Song and J. Y. Yu, 'The Stability of Population and Population Control Poli-
    cies', in Hermann Schebenell (ed.), *Population Policies in Asian Countries*
    (Drager Foundation and Center of Asian Studies, University of Hong Kong,
    1984), p. 517.

32 Lester Brown, *Who Will Feed China?: Wake-up Call for a Small Planet* (Earthscan
    Publications, London, 1995), pp. 35–6.

33 ibid., pp. 40–1.

34 On current projections India will overtake China as the world's most popu-
    lous state before 2050.

35 Chinese Public Security officials have expressed concern at the growing level
    of unrest and violence, particularly in areas of high unemployment: Susan V.
    Lawrence, 'Mercury Rising', *Far Eastern Economic Review* 27 April 2000, p. 26.
    See also Greg Austin, 'The Strategic Implications of China's Public Order
    Crisis', *Survival* 27(2) 1995, pp. 7–23.

36 For an interesting overview of the rise of global cities, and their role as incu-
    bators of both organised and random crime, see Williams, 'The Geopolitics of
    Transnational Organized Crime', p. 8.

37 Japan's concern about the dramatic rise in the number of Chinese illegal
    migrants was underscored by its decision to send a delegation of lawmakers
    to China in March 1997 for discussions with Chinese security and foreign
    ministry officials: Yoshiko Matsushita, 'Japan fights immigrant wave', *Asia
    Times* 25 April 1997, p. 2.

38 Pamela Yatsko and Matt Forney, 'Demand Crunch', *Far Eastern Economic
    Review* 15 January, 1998, pp. 44, 46; Ma Jisen, 'The Politics of China's Popu-
    lation Growth', *Asian Perspective* 21(1) 1998, p. 50; Lynne O'Donnell, 'A City
    on the scrapheap', *Australian* 14 February 2000, p. 7.

39 Cited in Alan Burnett, *The Western Pacific: Challenge of Sustainable Growth* (Lon-
    don: Allen & Unwin, 1993), p. 77.

40 Ma Jisen, 'The Politics of China's Population Growth', pp. 39, 42.

41 The official was Shao Lizi, a former member of the Political Council, the
    forerunner to China's Politburo: ibid., p. 44. China's current leaders have
    repeatedly emphasised the importance of population control. In noting the
    World Day of Six Billion People in October 1999, Chinese Premier Zhu
    Rongji declared that China's family planning policies had delayed by four
    years the day on which the world passed the 6 billion threshold. Mary
    Kwang, 'Birth control here to stay, says Zhu', *Straits Times* 14 October 1999,
    p. 16.

42 World Bank projections cited in 'Expanding Horizons: Australia and Indone-
    sia into the 21st Century', East Asia Analytical Unit, Department of Foreign
    Affairs and Trade, Canberra, 1994, p. 23.

43 Patrick Walters, 'Indonesia on the Edge', *Weekend Australian* 8 October 1994,
    p. 4.

44 This is not to suggest that instability in Indonesia was purely the result of ris-
    ing unemployment, but it was a significant contributing factor. See Peter
    McCawley, 'Human Dimensions of Indonesia's Economic Crisis And Foreign

Assistance', paper presented at Indonesia Update Conference, University of Queensland, Brisbane, 14 October 1998, pp. 5–6.

45 Walters, 'Indonesia on the Edge'.

46 The Indonesian Government intended to move 1.3 million Javanese to central Kalimantan between 1997 and 2002, a program which if fully implemented would effectively have doubled the province's population. See Deny Hidayati, 'Transmigration Settlement: Development or Destruction?', *Business Times* (Singapore) Trends, 25–26 January 1997, p. 4.

47 Don Greenlees, 'Unwanted arrivals', *Weekend Australian* 27–28 March 1999, p. 27.

48 'Transmigration Program A Victim Of Politics', *Kompas* 7 December 2000, www.kompas.co/kompas-cetak/0012/07/ENGLISH/tran.htm.

49 'Scores die as strife spreads to Borneo', *Canberra Times* 21 March 1999, p. 5.

50 'Problems Along Indonesia's Border With Papua New Guinea Continue', *Asian Defence Journal* February 1996, p. 114.

51 Dan Murphy, 'The Next Headache', *Far Eastern Economic Review* 29 April 1999, p. 21.

52 Michael Leifer, *Dictionary of the Modern Politics of South-East Asia*, (Routledge, London and New York, 1995), p. 96. Under a so-called 'act of free choice' Irian representatives of Irian-Jaya's indigenous population formally voted to become a part of Indonesia in 1969.

53 John McBeth, 'Army Under Fire', *Far Eastern Economic Review* 14 September 1995, p. 31; Rowan Callick, 'Irian Jaya rediscovered', *Australian Financial Review* 18 January, 1996, p. 15; Patrick Walters, 'Troops restore uneasy calm in Irian Jaya', *Australian* 14 March 1996, p. 6; John McBeth, 'Now Hear This: Irian Jaya rebels learn to play hardball', *Far Eastern Economic Review* 18 April 1996, pp. 24–5.

54 See Imanuddin, 'Resentment triggering unrest in Irian: Expert', *Jakarta Post* 8 April, 1996, p. 2.

55 Ian Timberlake, 'Jakarta ends transmigration', *Australian* 8 December 2000, p. 6.

56 Deaths already exceed births in Germany, Italy and Sweden. It is estimated that Europe will need 150 million immigrants by 2025 just to maintain the present ratio between workers and the retired: 'Birth rates plummet in Europe', *Straits Times* 17 January 2000, p. 6.

57 Norman Myers, 'Global Population Growth and Security', paper prepared for the seminar 'Global Security Beyond 2000', pp. 16–17.

58 Jamie Mackie, 'Population control shapes the future', *Australian* 16 August 1996, p. 40. See also Chris Manning, *Indonesian Labour in Transition: An East Asian success story?* (Cambridge University Press, 1998).

59 Tubagus Feridhanusetyawan, 'Social Impact of the Indonesian Economic Crisis', *Indonesian Quarterly* 26(4) 1998, p. 352; Steve Emilia, 'Indonesia may see baby boom', *Jakarta Post* 18 October 1998, p. 1.

60 China aims to stabilise its population at 1.6 billion by the middle of this century. *China's Population and Development in the 21st Century*, Information Office of the State Council of the People's Republic of China, Beijing, December 2000, p. 12.

3 Deforestation, Pollution and Climate Change

1 Chris Bright, 'Environmental Surprises: Planning for the Unexpected', *Futurist* July–August 2000, p. 43.

2 Janet N. Abramovitz and Ashley T. Mattoon, 'Reorienting the Forest Products Economy', *State of the World 1999: A Worldwatch Institute Report on Progress Towards a Sustainable Society* (W. W. Norton & Co., New York and London, 1999), p. 60.

3 For a good analysis of these links, see J. L. Jacobson, *Environmental Refugees: A Yardstick of Habitability* (Worldwatch Institute, Washington, D.C., 1989).

4 Abramovitz and Mattoon, 'Reorienting the Forest Products Economy', pp. 60, 61.

5 Norman Myers, 'The Anatomy of Environmental Action: The Case of Tropical Deforestation', in A. Hurrel and B. Kingsbury, *The International Politics of the Environment* (Clarendon Press, Oxford, 1992), p. 437.

6 Philip Hurst, *Rainforest Politics: Ecological Destruction in Southeast Asia* (S. Abdul Majeed & Co., Kuala Lumpur, 1991), pp. xiii, 5.

7 Myers, 'The Anatomy of Environmental Action', p. 433.

8 Gautam Kaji, 'Challenges to the East Asian Environment', *Pacific Review* 7(2) 1994, p. 212.

9 Hurst, *Rainforest Politics*, p. xiii.

10 Eduardo Tadem, 'Conflict over Land-based Natural Resources in the ASEAN Countries', in Lim Teck Ghee and Mark J. Valencia (eds), *Conflict over Natural Resources in South-East Asia and the Pacific* (Oxford University Press, Singapore and New York, 1990), p. 15.

11 Peter Dauvergne, *Globalisation and Deforestation in the Asia-Pacific*, Working Paper No. 1997/7 (Department of International Relations, Australian National University, 1997), p. 12.

12 Kaji, 'Challenges to the East Asian Environment', p. 211.

13 The Bolisat Phatthana Khet Phoudoi (Mountainous Areas Development Company) is headed by General Cheng Sanyavong: Bertil Lintner, 'Before the Flood', *Far Eastern Economic Review* 13 February 1997, p. 49.

14 Michael Richardson, 'Cambodia's New War', *Australian* 4 February 1999, p. 30.

15 Cited in ibid.

16 ibid.

17 Peter Dauvergne, 'Environmental Insecurity, Forest Management and State Responses', in Alan Dupont (ed.), *The Environment and Security: What Are the Linkages?*, Canberra Papers on Strategy and Defence no. 125 (Strategic and Defence Studies Centre, Australian National University, Canberra, 1998), p. 56.

18 Maddock, 'Environmental Security in East Asia', p. 28.

19 Corruption, illegal logging and mismanagement cost Indonesia about $5.2 billion in lost revenue between 1993 and 1998, according to an audit by the international accountants Ernst & Young: Don Greenlees, '$8.6bn graft cuts Indonesian forests', *Weekend Australian* 22–23 July 2000, p. 13.

20 ibid.

21 Margot Cohen and Pecu Lembang, 'Wood Cuts: Illegal logging could stem the flow of aid to Indonesia', *Far Eastern Economic Review* 27 January 2000, p. 20.

22 *World Resources 1994–95*, p. 73.

23 The Chinese government estimates the losses to have been $15 billion but the Worldwatch Institute argues that they were 50 per cent higher: Peter Alford, 'Flooded Asia counts cost and asks why', *Weekend Australian* 7–8 August 1999, p. 14.

24 Lynne O'Donnell, 'China battles its rivers … and profiteers', *Australian* 20 August 1998, p. 7.

25 Trish Saywell, 'A River Run Wild', *Far Eastern Economic Review* 20 August 1998, pp. 18–19; Lynne O'Donnell, 'Dam builders bank on taming the Yangtze', *Weekend Australian* 19–20 September 1998, p. 11; Abramovitz and Mattoon, 'Reorienting the Forest Products Economy', p. 61.

26 The Yangtse basin has lost 85 per cent of its forest cover: Bright, 'Environmental Surprises', p. 42.

27 O'Donnell, 'Dam builders bank on taming the Yangtze', p. 11.

28 Julian Lee, 'Scientist predicts Chinese disaster', *Australian National University Reporter* 29(16) 1998, p. 3.

29 Bruce Gilley, 'Sticker Shock', *Far Eastern Economic Review* 14 January 1999, p. 20.

30 ibid., p. 22.

31 Dauvergne, 'Environmental Insecurity, Forest Management and State Responses', p. 49.

32 For an analysis of conflicts between government supported loggers and displaced or dispossessed indigenous communities in Southeast Asia see ibid., pp. 57–8.

33 Asian Development Bank, *Asian Development Outlook 2000*, www.adb.org/publications; Louise Williams and Mark Baker, 'South-east Asia's Year of Reckoning', *Sydney Morning Herald*, 6 October 1997, p. 9.

34 One reason is that more than 90 per cent of the region's waste water is discharged directly into streams, rivers, lakes, gutters and coastal waters without treatment: Asian Development Bank, *Asian Development Outlook 2000*, www.adb.org/publications.

35 Kaji, 'Challenges to the East Asian Environment', p. 211.

36 Williams and Baker, 'South-east Asia's Year of Reckoning', p. 9.

37 Whether or not these measures will be effective is a moot point, since much of the pollution comes from industrial and power stations in neighbouring Guandong, which Hong Kong can do little to control: Charles Snyder, 'Air pollution control measures are just not enough', *Hong Kong Standard* 12 May 2000, p. 11; Thom Beal, 'Hong Kong Clears Air On Pollution Measures', *Asian Wall Street Journal* 10 May 2000, p. 3; Mark Mitchell, 'Pungent Harbour', *Far Eastern Economic Review* 11 May 2000, p. 24.

38 Bin Shen, 'Acceleration in pace of life drives demand for faster transportation', *China Business Weekly* 6–12 December 1998, p. 2; Kaji, 'Challenges to the East Asian Environment', p. 211. If state-owned vehicles are added the figure could be as high as 11 million. By 2020, the urban vehicle population will probably be ten times greater: Changhua Wu, 'The price of growth', p. 59.

39 Greenpeace, 'China's Environmental Problems Threaten World's Future', www.greenpeace.org/chinarepexsum.html; World Bank figures cited in Wu, 'The price of growth', p. 60.

40 Maggie Farley, 'Setbacks in Lanzhou, Grittiest Front in China's Clean Air War', *International Herald Tribune* 18 June 1999, p. 7. According to the Chinese National Environmental Protection Agency, air and water pollution was costing the nation 15 per cent of GDP in the early 1990s, but this figure seems excessive. Cited in Maddock, 'Environmental Security in East Asia', p. 29. The original calculations were made by Czech economist Vaclav Smil in 'Environmental Change as a Source of Conflict and Economic Losses in China', Occasional Paper no. 2, Project on Environmental Change and Acute Conflict, 1992.

41 Nick Edwards, 'Huge Clean-up Bill on the Way', *Sydney Morning Herald* 24 November 1997, p. 13.

42 Cited in Gregory D. Foster, 'China's Environmental Threat: Crafting a Strategic Response', *Comparative Strategy* 19(2) 2000, p. 123.
43 Many other regions of the world are also experiencing semi-permanent smog because of increased pollution. Scientists have discovered that a cloud of smog about the size of the United States covers the Indian Ocean during winter, comprised of soot and sulphur droplets blown to sea by the winter monsoon from China, the Indian subcontinent and Southeast Asia: William K. Stevens, 'Haze Over Indian Ocean Casts a Cloud on Climates', *International Herald Tribune* 11 June 1999, www.iht.com.
44 'Catastrophic fires "pose global threat"', *Agence France-Presse* 4 April 1998.
45 John McBeth, 'El Nino Gets Blamed', *Far Eastern Economic Review* 9 October 1997, p. 80. The US Department of Agriculture estimated that production would rise from 6.2 million tonnes in 1999–2000 to as much as 9 million tonnes in 2003: 'Asia 2000 Year Book', *Far Eastern Economic Review* 2000, p. 45.
46 Greg Earl, 'Neighbours Angry about "This Arson Thing"', *Australian Financial Review* 30 September 1994, p. 22.
47 Derwin Pereira, 'Jakarta Spells Out More Measures to Halt Fires in Sumatra, Kalimantan', *Sunday Times* (Malaysia) 14 September 1997, p. 1.
48 'The Haze Worsens', *Straits Times* 15 September 1997, p. 1.
49 'Where There's Smoke There's Serious, Long-term Damage', *Australian* 6 October 1997, p. 7.
50 Murray Hiebert, S. Jayasankaran and John McBeth, 'Fire in the Sky', *Far Eastern Economic Review* 9 October 1997, pp. 74–8.
51 Of this $1.4 billion, a 1998 World Wildlife Fund study estimated that Indonesia lost $1 billion, Malaysia $300 million and Singapore $60 million. See also Nick Edwards, 'More Smog May Wreck $40b Asian Tourism', *Canberra Times* 23 March 1998, p. 5; Margot Cohen, Ben Dolven and Murray Hiebert, 'Yet Again', *Far Eastern Economic Review* 19 March 1998, p. 22.
52 Michael Richardson, 'Fear of Fires Rekindled as Jakarta Is Distracted', *International Herald Tribune* 30 April 1999, www.iht.com.
53 Patrick Walters, 'When an Archipelago isn't an Island Entire of Itself', *Australian* 9 October 1997, p. 13.
54 Patrick Walters, 'Indonesians Blame Killer Smoke Haze on Weather', *Australian* 29 September 1997, p. 6.
55 Michael Richardson, 'Haze Battle a Litmus Test for ASEAN Ties', *Australian* 7 October 1997, p. 8.
56 'Forest Fires an Act of Environmental Terrorism', *Nation* 29 September 1997, p. A4.
57 Richardson, 'Haze Battle a Litmus Test for ASEAN Ties', p. 8.
58 Simon S. C. Tay, 'What Should Be Done About the Haze', *Indonesian Quarterly* 26(2) 1998, p. 102.
59 Simon S. C. Tay, 'Indonesia's Forest Fires Pose an Economic Threat', *International Herald Tribune* 31 August 1999, www.iht.com.
60 Tay, 'What Should Be Done About the Haze', pp. 105, 109–110. A $10 million UN plan to counter the fires also fell short of its goals: Dominic Nathan, 'New Sumatra fires despite rain', *Straits Times* 30 April 1998, p. 37.
61 'Gasp, Choke, Wheeze: Who will stop the slash-and-burn folly?', *Asia Week* 23 August 1999, www.pathfinder.com/asiaweek/current/issue/nat6.html; 'Fears of Asian Haze Hazard', *Canberra Times* 11 March 2000, p. 12.
62 According to a six-year study on pollution in Northeast Asia completed by Iowa State University in 1998, the region produced 14.7 million tons of sulphur diox-

ide emissions, 81 per cent of which originated from China. 'Pollution Study Published on Northeast Asia', *Chosun Ilbo* 30 November 1998, www.nautilus. org.napsnet.

63 Thirty-seven per cent of Japan's acid rain problem is sourced to China, while China is responsible for 34 per cent of North Korea's acid rain and 30 per cent of South Korea's. A significant percentage of the sulphur emissions that cause acid rain fall on the surrounding seas – 15 per cent of China's and 51 per cent and 48 per cent of South Korea's and Japan's respectively: 'Dilemmas of Energy Choice in Northeast Asia', 16 October 1998, www. nautilus.org/esena/choice.html; Robert E. Bedeski, 'Unconventional Security and the Republic of Korea: A Preliminary Assessment', CANCAPS Paper no. 8, August 1995, p. 9. Without effective control measures, SO_2 emissions are expected to triple by the end of the decade: UNEP, *Global Environment Outlook 2000*, Chapter 2, www.grida.no/geo2000/english/0069.htm.

64 See Douglas Murray, 'American Interests in China's Environment', *Pacific Review* 7(2) 1994, p. 216.

65 Between 1990 and 2001, electricity generation in China is expected to double to 300 gigawatts, 80 per cent from coal-fired plants: Kari Huus, 'A Question of Economy', *Far Eastern Economic Review* 17 November 1996, p. 52.

66 Fereidun Fesharaki, Allen Clark and Duangjai Intarapravich, 'Energy Outlook to 2010: Asia-Pacific Demand, Supply and Climate Change Implications', Asia-Pacific Issues no. 19 (East-West Center, Hawaii, April 1995), p. 7; 'Dilemmas of Energy Choice in Northeast Asia', 16 October 1998, www.nautilus.org/esena/choice.html.

67 Kevin Sullivan, 'Japanese Incinerator Fouls Navy Base's Air', *Washington Post* 24 November 1997, p. A18.

68 Coastal marine pollution is caused by a combination of urban sewage, industrial discharges, soil erosion, deforestation, aquaculture and farming: Julian Cribb, 'Toxic red tides choke Asia's seas', *Weekend Australian* 12–13 August 1995, p. 19.

69 Vaclav Smil, 'Environmental Problems in China: Estimates of Economic Costs', East–West Center Special Report no. 5, April 1996, p. 28.

70 Prins and Stamp, *Top Guns and Toxic Whales*, p. 56.

71 Bedeski, 'Unconventional Security And The Republic Of Korea', p. 10; Lui Yinglang, 'Red tide dissolves, drifts from Bohai Sea', *China Daily* 6 October 1998, p. 1.

72 Audrey Parwani, Naomi Lee and Alison Smith, 'Row simmers over algae's spread', *South China Morning Post* 15 April 1998, www.scmp. com/news.

73 The number of people living around the periphery of the Yellow Sea is estimated to be between 250 and 450 million, which is the highest population density for any of the world's major enclosed and semi-enclosed seas. The Yellow Sea rim accounts for more than a quarter of China's gross industrial output: Sang-Gon Lee, 'Transboundary pollution of the Yellow Sea', in H. Edward English and David Runnalls (eds), *Environmental and Development in the Pacific: Problems and Policy Options* (Addison Wesley Longman in association with the Pacific Trade and Development Conference, New York, 1998), p. 118.

74 Cited in Mark Valencia, 'Energy and Insecurity in Asia', *Survival* 39(3) 1997, p. 101.

75 Chris Betros, 'Evasion over Russian tanker angers Tokyo', *South China Morning Post* 22 February 1997, p. 12.

76 S. Jayasankaran, 'Air of Concern', *Far Eastern Economic Review* 17 November 1994, p. 50.

77 Indonesia's once pristine coral ecosystem is rapidly being degraded by blast fishing. See Herman Cesar, *The Economic Value of Indonesian Coral Reefs* (Environment Department, World Bank, Washington, D.C., 1996); and the more comprehensive *Economic Analysis of Indonesian Coral Reefs* (Pollution and Environmental Economics Division, World Bank, 1996).

78 'Drifting Oil Tanker Threatens Spill in Malacca Strait', *Canberra Times*, 22 January 1993, p. 11. On the growing incidence of marine pollution in Southeast Asia, see Joseph Morgan, 'Natural and Human Hazards', in Harold Brookfield and Yvonne Byron (eds), *Southeast Asia's Environmental Future: The Search for Sustainability* (Oxford University Press, Kuala Lumpur, 1993), p. 293.

79 Closure of the Malacca Strait might also have global ramifications, depending on the duration. In addition to preventing and managing oil spills and possible congestion, strategic planners must also worry about providing security for the heavy flow of ships that have to negotiate the Strait: John H. Noer, 'Southeast Asian Chokepoints: Keeping Sea Lines of Communication Open', *Strategic Forum* 98, December 1996 (Instititue for National Strategic Studies, National Defense University). For a breakdown of the value of trade passing through the Malacca Strait and other key Southeast Asian straits see Henry J. Kenny, 'An Analysis of Possible Threats to Shipping in Key Southeast Asian Sea Lanes', Occasional Paper (Center for Naval Analyses, Alexandria, Virginia, February, 1996), p. 17.

80 Fereidun Fesharaki, 'Energy and the Asian Security Nexus', *Journal of International Affairs* 53(1) 1999, p. 91; Noer, 'Southeast Asian Chokepoints', p. 3.

81 Hamidah Atan, Vincent De Paul and Azman Ahmad, 'Order to detain ship served on captain', *New Straits Times* 2 June 1995, pp. 1–2.

82 Speakers at a February 1996 Adelaide conference on soil contamination in East Asia (the first of its kind ever held) identified soil toxicity as 'a major long-term problem for the region': Julian Cribb, 'Scientists warn of toxic time bomb in polluted soil', *Australian* 20 February, 1996, p. 4.

83 Kaji, 'Challenges to the East Asian Environment', p. 210.

84 Jennifer Clapp, 'Hazardous Waste and Human Security: Global-Local Linkages in Southeast Asia', *Publication of the Development and Security in Southeast Asia (DSSEA) Project Update* no. 3, January–April 1999, p. 5.

85 Annie Huang, 'Taiwan In Spotlight After Scandal By Writer', *Associated Press* 5 January 1999; 'Taiwan Enters Cambodia Waste Scam', *Associated Press* 28 December 1998; 'Cambodians Don Chemical Suits To Gather Up Waste', *Reuters* 23 December 1998; 'Cambodian Port Calm After Violent Waste Protests', *Associated Press* 20 December 1998.

86 By about 30 per cent, 145 per cent and 15 per cent respectively, between 1750 and 1992. See the IPCC Report prepared by Working Group I entitled 'Summary for Policymakers: The Science of Climate Change', December 1995, p. 1, www.unep. ch/ipcc/ipcc95.html.

87 One reason for the high level of carbon dioxide emissions is that some ancient peat bogs were set alight and smouldered for many months after the initial fire front had passed: 'Bog fires to release year's worth of greenhouse gas', *Sydney Morning Herald* 17 October 1997, p. 11.

88 *Global Warming*, Nuclear Issues Briefing Paper no. 24, May 1997 (Uranium Information Centre, Melbourne), www. uic.com.au/nip24.htm.

89 Amyn B. Sajoo, 'The Kyoto protocol: climate change antidote or just hot air?', ISEAS Trends, *Singapore Business Times* 27–28 December 1997, p. IV.

90 Julian Lee, 'Study of El Nino in history reveals clues for future', *Australian National University Reporter* 29(9) 1998, p. 7.

91 Scotland's weakened economy persuaded its reluctant leaders to accept union with England, while Sweden was enfeebled strategically by the loss of a third of Finland's population in the famine of 1696: Neville Brown, 'Climate Change: A Threat to Peace', Conflict Studies no. 272, Research Institute for the Study of Conflict and Terrorism, July 1994, pp. 5–9.

92 David Wirth, 'Climate Chaos', *Foreign Policy* 74, Spring 1989, pp. 12–13.

93 Richard Ophuls, *Ecology and the Politics of Scarcity* (W. H. Freeman & Co., San Francisco, 1977), pp. 214–16.

94 Wirth, 'Climate Chaos', p. 10.

95 On civilisational change see Alvin Toffler, *Future Shock* (Pan Books, London, 1971) and *The Third Wave* (William Morrow & Co., New York, 1980).

96 Stephen Lonergan, *Climate Warming, Water Resources and Geopolitical Conflict: A Study of Nations Dependent on the Nile, Litani and Jordan River Systems*, ORAE Extra Mural Paper no. 55 (Operational Research and Analysis Establishment, Canadian Department of National Defence, Ottawa, 1991).

97 Scientists speculate that the Pacific Ocean switches every 20–40 years between warm and cold phases because of the PDO which significantly affects temperatures and rainfall around the Pacific rim. The PDO is thought to be moving to a cooler phase which could have its greatest influence at middle latitudes in the Northern hemisphere, especially in the United States and Northeast Asia: Curt Suplee, 'World Climate: Poised for a Big Shift', *International Herald Tribune* 21 January 2000, p. 1.

98 An argument advanced by a prominent US atmospheric physicist, Fred Singer: Andrew Heasley, 'Heat rises as debate rages over alleged global warming', *Canberra Times* 9 January 1999, p. C.4.

99 Sea-level rise is caused by thermal expansion of the sea due to increases in temperature from higher levels of greenhouse gases. The low end of these estimates corresponds to the known rate of sea-level rise over the past century while the high end represents an acceleration of sea-level rise based on plausible forecasts of global warming in the next century: David Schneider, 'The Rising Seas', *Scientific American* March 1997, pp. 96, 101.

100 This summary draws on the findings of the report of the IPCC: *Climate Change: The IPCC, Scientific Assessment* (Cambridge University Press, 1990); the IPCC Report prepared by Working Group I entitled 'Summary for Policymakers: The Science of Climate Change', December 1995; and a supplementary report of the IPCC Working Group on Ecological Systems and Human Health, www.unep.ch/ipcc/ipcc95.html. Climatologists have gradually become much more confident about the accuracy of their forecasts. Compare, for example, the discussions and assessments made at a major conference on climate change in 1991 at Los Alamos, New Mexico, with the 1995 IPCC Review. On the former, see Louis Rosen and Robert Glasser (eds), *Climate Change and Energy Policy* (American Institute of Physics, New York, 1992), especially pp. 17–31.

101 Fred Pearce, 'Greenhouse wars', *New Scientist* 19 July 1997, pp. 38-43.

102 Sajoo, 'The Kyoto protocol', p. IV.

103 By contrast, dissidents were able to muster only about a hundred climate scientists who were prepared to sign the opposing Leipzig Declaration which maintains that the IPCC conclusions are 'flawed': Heasley, 'Heat rises as debate rages over alleged global warming', p. C.4.

104 'Warming to Reality', *International Herald Tribune* 10 January 2000, www.iht.com; 'Definitely Warmer', *International Herald Tribune* 18 January 2000, p. 6. See also James Woodford, 'World climate: experts predict a grim future', *Sydney Morning Herald* 30 September, 1996, p. 1. A more controversial and pessimistic report looking at the effect of climate change on the United States predicts significantly higher temperature increases than the IPCC and drastic changes in the climate of the United States. It anticipates more severe droughts, increased risk of flooding, mass migrations of species, substantial shifts in agriculture and widespread erosion of coastal zones: Curt Suplee, 'Ominous Outlook for the Climate', *International Herald Tribune* 13 June 2000, p. 3.

105 Christopher Flavin, 'Global Temperature Goes Off the Chart', in Linda Starke (ed.), *Vital Signs 1999: The Environmental Trends That Are Shaping Our Future* (W.W. Norton & Co., New York and London, 1999), www.worldwatch.org. Arctic Sea Ice has shrunk by 6 per cent since 1978: 'Weather and security: Climate change and South Asia', *Strategic Comments* 6(1) 2000. Significantly, the US National Oceanic and Atmospheric Administration announced that global ocean temperatures are also rising, which may be a more reliable indicator of global warming: Greg Easterbrook, 'The Facts of Global Warming Don't Need to Be Fudged', *International Herald Tribune* 15 June 2000, p. 9.

106 Presentation by Robert T. Watson, chair, IPCC, at the Sixth Conference of Parties to the UN Framework Convention on Climate Change, 13 November 2000, www.ipcc.ch/press/sp-cop6.htm. At the time of writing, these findings were still awaiting final endorsement by the United Nations, but they were expected to be approved without significant change.

107 Leigh Dayton, 'Science's climate of doubt is over', *Sydney Morning Herald* 24 November 1997, p. 4.

108 The summit agreed to reduce the global level of greenhouse gas emissions to 1990 levels by 2010.

109 Natasha Bit, 'Global Storming', *Australian*, 20 November, 1995, p. 10; Stephen Lonergan, *Environmental Change and Regional Security in Southeast Asia*, Operational Research and Analysis Directorate of Strategic Analysis Project Report No. PR 659 (Department of National Defence, Ottawa, 1994), p. 64. See also IPCC Working Group I, 'Summary for Policymakers: The Science of Climate Change', December 1995; Peter H. Gleick, 'Water and Conflict: Fresh Water Resources and International Security', *International Security* 18(1) 1991, p. 98.

110 Paul Handley, 'Before the flood', *Far Eastern Economic Review* 16 April 1992; p. 65; 'USA: Climate Change Would Damage South Asia', *Reuters* 9 August 1994; and Morgan, 'Natural and Human Hazards', p. 291.

111 'Cities in danger as warming raises sea levels', *Australian* 31 March 1995, p. 9; and Hu Angang, 'China's Environmental Issues', pp. 333–4.

112 Dauvergne, 'Environmental Insecurity, Forest Management and State Responses', pp. 55, 58 details a number of instances of violent clashes between logging companies and indigenous people that have resulted in multiple deaths and injuries.

113 Transnational pollution has also prompted closer cooperation. For example, in April 1998, Asean Environment Ministers agreed to set up a fund to assist fire-fighting in Indonesia and to 'control and channel additional and complementary resources from the region and internationally'; 'ASEAN Pools Fire-fighting Efforts', *Australian* 6 April 1998, p. 8.

114 Sajoo, 'The Kyoto protocol', p. IV.

115 Peter H. Gleick, 'How Will Climatic Changes and Strategies for the Control of Greenhouse-Gas Emissions Influence International Peace and Global Security?', in G. I. Pearman (ed.), *Limiting Greenhouse Effects: Controlling Carbon Dioxide Emission: report of the Dahlem Workshop on Limiting the Greenhouse Effect: Options for Controlling Atmospheric Carbon Dioxide Accumulation* (John Wiley & Sons, Chichester, West Sussex, England, 1992), p. 565.

4 Will There Be an Energy 'Gap'?

1 On the links between resource competition and conflict, see Hanns W. Maull, 'Energy and Resources: The Strategic Dimension', *Survival* 31(6) 1989, pp. 500–18 ; Ronnie D. Lipschutz, *When Nations Clash: Raw Materials, Ideology and Foreign Policy* (Ballinger, Cambridge, Mass., 1989): Paul Kennedy, *The Rise and Fall of the Great Powers: Economic Change and Military Conflict from 1500 to 2000* (Fontana, London, 1988); Jonathan Marshall, *To Have and Have Not: Southeast Asian Raw Materials and the Origins of the Pacific War* (University of California Press, Berkeley, Calif., 1995).

2 Christopher Flavin and Seth Dunn, 'Reinventing the Energy System', *State of the World 1999: A Worldwatch Institute Report on Progress Towards a Sustainable Society* (W.W. Norton & Co., New York and London, 1999), p. 22.

3 Colin J. Campbell, 'Running Out of Gas', *The National Interest*, Spring 1998, p. 52.

4 Public opposition to nuclear power is also increasing its economic costs because of planning and approval delays and the pressure for more stringent safety regimes.

5 Asia is defined here as Northeast Asia plus Australia and South Asia: Fereidun Fesharaki, 'Energy and the Asian Security Nexus', *Journal of International Affairs* 53(1) 1999, p. 89.

6 Maddock, 'Environmental Security in East Asia', p. 27.

7 Even assuming that the rate of growth in the demand for oil drops from 5.2 per cent (the 1990–95 average) to 1 per cent between 1998 and 2000, and averages only 4 per cent a year thereafter, by 2010 the regional demand for oil would still be 9 million barrels a day higher than in 1996: Daniel Yergin, Dennis Eklof and Jefferson Edwards, 'Fuelling Asia's Recovery', *Foreign Affairs* 77(2) 1998, pp. 35, 38. See also Robert A. Manning, 'The Asian Energy Predicament', *Survival* 42(3) 2000, p. 76. Manning concludes that the Asian economic crisis only marginally alters the region's energy picture.

8 By the end of 1999, oil demand had picked up in Japan by 4.8 per cent, 11.1 per cent in South Korea and 3 per cent in China, and stockbrokers Merrill Lynch were predicting that Asian oil consumption would be back to pre-crisis levels by the end of 2001: *Asia 2000 Yearbook* (Far Eastern Economic Review, Hong Kong, 1999), p. 48; Manning, 'The Asian Energy Predicament', p. 75; 'Asian oil demand rally seen beginning in 1999', *Jakarta Post* 7 October 1998, p. 11.

9 See UNEP, *Global Environment Outlook 2000*, Chapter 2, www.grida.no/geo2000/english/0069.htm; Kent E. Calder, 'Policy Forum: Energy Futures', *Washington Quarterly* 19(4) 1996, p. 91; Ji Guoxing, 'East Asia's Energy Security', paper presented at the conference Asia-Pacific Security for the 21st Century, Honolulu, 3–6 November 1997, p. 3; Daniel Yergin, Dennis Eklof and Jefferson Edwards, 'Energy Security in the Asia-Pacific Region', paper presented at the IISS Annual Conference in Singapore, 11–14 September 1997, p. 3.

10 Kent E. Calder, *Asia's Deadly Triangle* (Nicholas Brealey, London, 1996), p. 50.

11 Cambridge Energy Research Associates, *Asia-Pacific Energy Watch* Winter–Spring 1997, p. 15.
12 By one estimate, if China were to achieve a per capita output of electricity comparable to Europe, it would need to double per capita power generation by 2020, requiring roughly 200 new 1000-megawatt power plants: Changhua Wu, 'The price of growth', *Bulletin of the Atomic Scientists* 55(5) 1999, p. 62.
13 *Asia-Pacific Energy Watch*, p. 31.
14 Yergin, Eklof and Edwards, 'Fuelling Asia's Recovery', p. 38.
15 Oil provides 51 per cent of total regional energy consumption compared to the global ration of only 40 per cent: Calder, *Asia's Deadly Triangle*, p. 54.
16 See Burnett, *The Western Pacific*, p. 116; Calder, 'Policy Forum: Energy Futures', p. 92; Guoxing, 'East Asia's Energy Security', p. 3.
17 *Asia 1995 Yearbook* (Far Eastern Economic Review, Hong Kong, 1994), p. 51; *Asia 1997 Yearbook* (Far Eastern Economic Review, Hong Kong, 1996), p. 54. The region is likely to have to import more than 20 million bpd of oil by 2010, compared with 11 million bpd in 1997: Yergin, Eklof and Edwards, 'Energy Security in the Asia-Pacific Region', p. 6.
18 In 1996, despite an official policy designed to diversify oil suppliers, over 80 per cent of the country's crude oil came from the Middle East, Japan's highest level of import dependence on the Middle East since the first oil crisis of 1972: 'Japan Becoming More Dependent on Mideast Oil', *Jakarta Post* 14 February 1997, p. 10.
19 Calder, *Asia's Deadly Triangle*, pp. 44–7.
20 Lorien Holland, 'The New Hot Fuel in China', *Far Eastern Economic Review* 14 September 2000, p. 16; *Asia 2000 Yearbook*, p. 49; James P. Dorian, Brett H. Wigdortz and Dru C. Gladney, 'China and Central Asia's Volatile Mix: Energy, Trade and Ethnic Relations', *Asia Pacific Issues*, East–West Center Report no. 31, May 1997, p. 4; *Asia 1997 Yearbook*, pp. 54–5.
21 Gas will continue to increase as a proportion of China's energy usage over the coming decades but from a low base. In 2000 it provided only 2.2 per cent of China's energy needs: Holland, 'The New Hot Fuel in China', p. 16.
22 Ahmed Rashid and Trish Saywell, 'Beijing Gusher', *Far Eastern Economic Review* 26 February 1998, p. 47; Ryukichi Imai, 'Energy issues in Asia for the twenty first century', IIPS Policy Paper 182 E (Institute for International Policy Studies, Tokyo, June 1997), p. 9.
23 Calder, 'Asia's Deadly Triangle', pp. 47–8.
24 *Asia 2000 Yearbook*, p. 49.
25 Campbell, 'Running Out of Gas', p. 50; Colin J. Campbell and Jean H. Laherrerre, 'The End of Cheap Oil', *Scientific American* March 1998, note 10.
26 Michael C. Lynch, 'The Nature of Energy Security', *Breakthroughs* 4(1) 1997, p. 4.
27 *Global Trends 2015: A Dialogue About the Future With Nongovernment Experts*, NIC 2000-02, December 2000, www.cia/gov/cia/publications/globaltrends2015/.
28 John Zaracostas, 'Pacific to be increasingly dependent on Middle East oil', *Australian* 8 February 1996, p. 35; Geoffrey Kemp, 'The Persian Gulf Remains the Strategic Prize', *Survival* 40(4) 1998–99, p. 137.
29 Bob van der Zwaan, 'Nuclear Power and Global Warming', *Survival* 42(3) 2000, p. 62.
30 Campbell, 'Running Out of Gas', p. 52.
31 ibid., p. 53.
32 *Global Trends 2015: A Dialogue About the Future With Nongovernment Experts*, www.cia/gov/cia/publications/globaltrends2015/.

33 Martha M. Hamilton and William Drozdiak, 'OPEC's New Solidarity Pumps Muscle Into Oil Cartel', *International Herald Tribune* 27 March 2000, www.iht. com; Stephen Romei, 'OPEC launches 40th birthday bash', *Australian* 11 September 2000, p. 37.

34 Christopher Flavin, 'It's Time to Quit Our Damaging Addiction to Oil', *International Herald Tribune* 26 September 2000, www.iht.com.

35 Kemp, 'The Persian Gulf Remains the Strategic Prize', p. 135; Lynch, 'The Nature of Energy Security', p. 6.

36 See, for example, the estimates in 'World Bank sounds Asia alarm on oil', *Business South China Morning Post* 19 September 2000, p. 1.

37 Michael J. Economides and Ronald E. Oligney, 'What goes up can go up even further', *Australian* 22 February 2000, p. 13.

38 According to Ken Koyama, Senior Economist at the Institute of Energy Economics in Japan. 'Asia Vulnerable to Oil Supply Disruptions', *Jakarta Post* 31 October 1997, p. 10.

39 Kemp, 'The Persian Gulf Remains the Strategic Prize', p. 137.

40 Paul Horsnell, *Oil in Asia: Markets, Trading, Refining and Deregulation* (Oxford University Press for the Oxford Institute for Energy Studies, Oxford, 1997), p. 26.

41 Mamdouh G. Salameh, 'China, Oil and the Risk of Regional Conflict', *Survival* 37(4) 1995–96, p. 141.

42 Calder, *Asia's Deadly Triangle*, p. 54.

43 They are Russia's Vostok Plan, running from Yakutsk via Seoul to Fukuoka in southern Japan; Japan's Energy Community Plan, involving China, Japan, South Korea, Russia, Taiwan and the United States; and China's Energy Silk Route Plan, linking the gas fields of Central Asia with China, Japan and South Korea: Valencia, 'Energy and Insecurity in East Asia', p. 87. A fourth project, a pipeline from the Siberian town of Irkutsk through the two Koreas to Japan, was approved in October 1997. The project, which will cost $11 billion, will provide China, South Korea and Russia with 20 million tons of natural gas a year from 2006: 'Regional Effort to Tap into Siberian Gas Field', *Korea Herald* 21 October 1997, www.nautilus.org.

44 Lyuba Zarsky, 'Energy and the Environment in Asia Pacific: Regional Cooperation and Market Governance', paper presented at a symposium on the UN system in the twenty-first century (United Nations University, New York, 14–15 November 1997), pp. 5–6.

45 For example, at the end of 1997 there was only one full-scale commercial sulphur scrubber in operation in China: Wu, 'The price of growth', p. 63.

46 Rashid and Saywell, 'Beijing Gusher', p. 47.

47 ibid., p. 48.

48 Bruce and Jean Blanche, 'Oil and Regional Stability in the South China Sea', *Jane's Intelligence Review* November 1995, p. 511.

49 Esmond D. Smith, 'China's Aspirations in the Spratly Islands', *Contemporary Southeast Asia* 16(3) 1994, p. 278.

50 Rigoberto Tiglao, 'Remote Control: China Expands Reefs to Extend Claims', *Far Eastern Economic Review* 1 June 1995, p. 21.

51 Cited in Valencia, 'Energy and Insecurity in Asia', p. 96.

52 *Asia Yearbook 1995*, p. 22.

53 Michael Vatikiotis, Murray Hiebert, Nigel Holloway and Matt Forney, 'Drawn to the Fray', *Far Eastern Economic Review* 3 April 1997, p. 15.

54 'China Warned to Stop Drilling Near Spratlys', *Jakarta Post* 17 March 1997, p. 6.

55 Vatikiotis et al., 'Drawn to the Fray', p. 14.

56 Kenneth L. Whiting, 'Gas-rich Islands Could be Next Point of Conflict', *Sydney Morning Herald* 18 May 1995, p. 14; Donald Emmerson, 'Indonesia, Malaysia, Singapore: a Regional Security Core?', in Richard J. Ellings and Sheldon W. Simon (eds), *Security Challenges in Southeast Asia: Enduring Issues, New Structures* (M. E. Sharpe, Armonk, NY, 1996), p. 13.

57 'Natuna Plan Must Run as Scheduled', *Jakarta Post* 27 July 1995, p. 1; 'RI Set to Start Development of Natuna Project', ibid., 15 March 1996, p. 1.

58 Michael Richardson, 'Natural Gas is Prize in War Games', *Australian* 27 August 1996, p. 23. See also 'Armed Forces to Stage Major Military Exercises', *Jakarta Post* 21 August 1996, p. 2; Patrick Walters, 'Indonesia to Stage Huge Exercise in South China Sea', *Weekend Australian* 24–25 August 1996, p. 16.

59 Discussions with senior Indonesian officials, Jakarta, September 1996.

60 Later estimates put the oil reserves at between one and ten billion barrels: Paik Jin-Hyun, 'Territorial Disputes at Sea: Situation, Possibilities, Prognosis', paper presented to the 10th Asia-Pacific Roundtable, Kuala Lumpur, 5–8 June 1996, p. 3; Mark Valencia, 'China and the Law of the Sea Convention', *Business Times* (Singapore) 29–30 June 1996, p. 4.

61 Paik Jin-Hyun, 'Territorial Disputes at Sea', p. 3.

62 Ji Guoxing, 'The Diaoyudao (Senkaku) Disputes and Prospects for Settlement', *Korean Journal of Defense Analysis* 7(2) 1994, pp. 293, 295.

63 See Clive Schofield, 'Island Disputes in East Asia Escalate', *Jane's Intelligence Review* 8(11) 1996, p. 518.

64 Teruaki Ueno, 'Japanese rightists say lighthouse for safety of ships', *Reuters* 11 September 1996.

65 Mark Valencia, 'Calming the Tokdo/Takeshima Controversy', *Business Times* (Singapore) 30–31 March 1996, p. 1.

66 Paik Jin-Hyun, 'Territorial Disputes at Sea', pp. 7–8.

67 Barry James, 'Nuclear Power is Called Vital to Helping EU Cut Greenhouse Gases', *International Herald Tribune* 15 June 2000, p. 6.

68 Nuclear power contributes virtually none of the carbon dioxide emissions that are a primary cause of greenhouse gases.

69 Another thirty-seven power plants were under construction: 'Nuclear Power Status' (revised 25 April 2000), *International Atomic Energy Agency Press Release*, www.iaea.org/worldatom/press/P_release/2000/prn0900.shtml. According to some estimates, nuclear fission's share of world electricity could fall to less than 10 per cent by 2020. See Steve Fetter, 'Energy 2050', *Bulletin of the Atomic Scientists* 56(4) 2000, p. 28.

70 The German government intends to phase out nuclear power entirely over a thirty-year period by not replacing Germany's nineteen existing reactors. It aims to produce half Germany's electricity from renewable sources by 2050. Nuclear power provides around 23 per cent of the European Union's electricity: James, 'Nuclear Power is Called Vital to Helping EU Cut Greenhouse Gases', p. 6.

71 US Department of Energy forecasts cited in Calder, *Asia's Deadly Triangle*, pp. 63–4.

72 'South Korea to Build 16 New Nuclear Power Plants by 2010', *AP-Dow Jones News Service* 3 September 1997. The figures cited for the number of operational reactors and percentage of electricity generated are for October 1999. See Chester Dawson et al., 'Nuclear Alert for Asia', *Far Eastern Economic Review* 14 October 1999, p. 19.

73 Producing 50 GWe by 2020. 'Nuclear Winter', *Economist* 10 January 1998, p. 60.

74 Barbara Opall, 'S. Korea Vies for Prime Role in Pyongyang Reactor Effort', *Defense News*, 6–12 March 1995, p. 16.

75 Michael Richardson, 'Asian Nations Plan to Expand Horizons of Nuclear Power', *Australian* 16 January 1996, p. 9.

76 Nuclear waste is generally divided into three categories according to the amount and type of radioactivity generated and heat produced. *High-level nuclear waste* may be the spent fuel itself or the principal waste from its reprocessing. The latter comprises only 3 per cent by volume of the spent fuel but contains 95 per cent of the radioactivity, including highly radioactive fission products and some heavy elements with long-lived radioactivity. *Intermediate-level nuclear waste* is far less radioactive although it may require shielding. It typically comprises resins, chemical sludges and reactor components, as well as contaminated materials from reactor decommissioning. Worldwide it makes up 7 per cent of the volume and 4 per cent of the radioactivity of all radioactive waste. *Low-level nuclear waste* is produced during routine reactor operations. Although it usually contains relatively little radioactivity per cubic metre, it is often relatively large in aggregate volume and so is difficult to dispose of. Low-level waste includes machinery, gloves, aprons, paper, resins and other materials contaminated with radioactive materials. 'Radioactive Waste Management' (Uranium Information Centre, Melbourne, Australia, November 1997), www.uic.com.au/waste.htm.

77 There are essentially two methods of dealing with high-level nuclear waste: disposal in long-term, geologically stable repositories or reprocessing for use as a reactor fuel. Highly enriched uranium or plutonium produced from the nuclear power cycle, although technically classified as 'waste', can also be reconstituted for later use either as fuel or for nuclear weapons. Disposal is designed to remove spent fuel and other nuclear waste from the nuclear fuel cycle and to permanently isolate it from the environment. However, low-level waste, while less radioactive, is more voluminous and therefore presents its own storage and disposal problems.

78 One study estimates that cumulative Northeast Asian low-level waste generated between 1990 and 2020 would be sufficient to bury a road 10 metres wide and up to 300 kilometres long (virtually the length of South Korea) to a depth of one metre: David Von Hippel and Peter Hayes, 'Two Scenarios of Nuclear Power and Nuclear Waste Production in Northeast Asia', *Pacific and Asian Journal of Energy* 8(1) 1998, pp. 9–22.

79 'DPRK Begins Construction for Taiwan's N-Waste', *Chosun Ilbo* 23 July 1997, www.nautilus.org; 'Taiwan Waste Shipments to North Korea Approved – Report', *AP-Dow Jones News Service* 13 July 1997.

80 Dennis Engbarth, 'Nuclear Waste Deal Threatens Reactor Plan', *Weekend Australian* 1–2 February 1997, p. 15; Charles S. Lee and Julian Baum, 'Radioactive Ruckus', *Far Eastern Economic Review* 6 February 1997, p. 16. President Kim Young-sam devoted a major part of his keynote address to the UN-sponsored Earth Summit in June 1997 to the nuclear-waste issue. The South Korean delegation succeeded in inserting a clause into the final document of the UN General Assembly's Special Session on the Earth Summit opposing the 'transboundary' transport of radioactive waste: Chon Shi-yong, 'UN Opposes Taiwan's Nuclear Waste Shipment to DPRK', *Korea Herald* 27 June 1997, www.nautilus.org.

81 'Nuclear "Ploy to Undermine Beijing"', *South China Morning Post* 30 May 1997, p. 10; Robert Garran, 'Beijing Friction as US Awaits Reply to Korea Peace Plan', *Australian* 16 April 1997, p. 8.

82 'China Opposes Taiwan's Plans For Nuclear Waste Disposal', *Reuters* 24 July 1998.

83 *East Asian Strategic Review 1996–97* (National Institute for Defense Studies, Tokyo, December 1996), p. 191.

84 'Halt Nuclear Dumping, Japan Tells Russia', *Age* 19 October 1993, p. 8.

85 Jor-Shan Choi, 'A Regional Compact for the Peaceful Use of Nuclear Energy in East Asia', Institute on Global Cooperation and Conflict, March 1998, www.cc.columbia.edu/sec/dlc/ciao/wps/shs02/shs02ac.htr.

86 See Michael Vatikiotis, Suhaini Aznam, Shim Jae Hoon and Lincoln Kaye, 'Stormy Passage: Japan's Plutonium Shipment Scares ASEAN', *Far Eastern Economic Review* 8 October 1992, pp. 12–13; Calder, *Asia's Deadly Triangle*, p. 67. Some of these ships have also begun to transit the Panama Canal under very tight security: 'N-waste ship clears canal safely', *Straits Times* 12 January 2000, p. 15.

87 'UK Ship Carrying Nuclear Waste From France Arrives In Japan', *Associated Press* 15 April 1999.

88 Two ships, the *Pacific Teal* and *Pacific Pintall*, were each fitted with three 30-millimetre DS 30B automatic guns in 1999: Aleksey Baturin, 'Japan Fights Piracy', *Nezavisimoye Voyennoye Obozreniye* 26 November 1999, p. 3.

89 For a comprehensive analysis of North Korea's nuclear program and its purpose see Joseph S. Bermudez Jr, 'Exposing North Korea's nuclear infrastructure', Parts 1 and 2 in *Jane's Intelligence Review* July and August 1999 respectively.

90 Bermudez, 'Exposing North Korea's nuclear infrastructure', Part 2, *Jane's Intelligence Review* August 1999, p. 41.

91 These were to be built and financed by a consortium of Western and Asian nations under the auspices of KEDO, the principal members of which are the United States, Japan and South Korea.

92 Jor-Shan Choi, 'Spent-Fuel and Radioactive-Waste Management in East Asia', presentation to the US Council for Security Cooperation in Asia and the Pacific Task Force on Confidence and Security Building Measures in Asia Pacific, 23 April 1997, CSIS Building, Washington, D.C., p. 5.

93 The government has decided to dismantle part of the reactor and sell some of the assets. Several other Southeast Asian states have considered nuclear power but none has ever proceeded to build commercial reactors: 'Nuclear Winter', p. 60; Adam Easton, 'No power to people after Marcos nuclear debacle', *Australian* 12 July 1999, p. 8.

94 Desmond Ball, 'Building Blocks for Regional Security: An Australian Perspective on Confidence and Security Building Measures (CSBMs) in the Asia/Pacific Region', Canberra Paper on Strategy and Defence no. 83, (Strategic and Defence Studies Centre, Australian National University, Canberra, 1991), p. 78; Dennis Schulz, 'Danger by the Dozen', *Bulletin* 28 September 1993, pp. 16–18.

95 'House Approves Nuclear Power Bill', *Jakarta Post* 27 February 1997, p. 1; 'Indonesia Plays Down Pro-nuclear Power Program Legislation', *Australian* 28 February 1997, p. 1.

96 The plant is already one-third built and has so far cost the government $1.4 billion. Chen's government agreed to allow work to resume in February 2001: 'Work on Taiwan Power Plant Moves Ahead As Opposition Drops', *Associated Press* 9 October 1998; 'Activists hail move to halt nuclear plant', *Hong Kong Mail* 13 November 2000, p. A8; 'Taiwan Protesters Back

Leader's Move to Scrap Plant', *Asian Wall Street Journal* 13 November 2000, p. 4.

97 Few new power plants have been built since the 1980s. The 1998 approval of a commercial power plant at Higashidori was the first for a decade: Peter Landers, 'Nuclear Bombshells', *Far Eastern Economic Review* 8 May 1997, p. 20; Kozo Mizoguchi, 'Japan To Build Nuclear Power Plant', *Associated Press* 4 August 1998. In August 1996, the residents of Maki, a town in northern Japan, rejected a proposal for a nuclear power plant in their municipality and local resistance stalled construction on a site in the southern island of Kyushu: 'Nuclear Winter', p. 60.

98 Before the 1999 Tokaimura accident there had been a sodium leakage from the prototype fast-breeder reactor Monju in December 1995 and an explosion and fire at the Tokaimura reprocessing plant in December 1995: Kumao Kaneko, *Nuclear Energy and Asian Security in the 21st Century: A Proposal for ASIATOM*, Working Paper (Institute on Global Conflict and Cooperation, Columbia University, March 1998), www.cc.columbia.edu/sec/dlc/ciao/wps/shs02/shs02aa.htr.

99 Tokaimura was the first nuclear accident in Asia to reach level 4 on the International Nuclear Event Scale, with 7 being the highest. Chernobyl was rated 7 and Three Mile Island 5. It occurred because of serious infringements by nuclear workers of operational and safety procedures and poor oversight by government regulatory agencies. Employees erred in adding 16 kg of uranium into a settling tank designed to take only 2.4 kg: Michael Millett, 'Chain Reaction', *Sydney Morning Herald* 2 October 1999, pp. 34–5; Andrew Cornell, 'Japan's nuclear fallout spreads', *Australian Financial Review* 2–3 October 1999, p. 8; 'Official Blames Plant Operator For Japanese Nuclear Accident', *Asian Wall Street Journal* 13 October 1999, p. 3; Stephen Lunn, 'Nuclear Death Sentence', *Weekend Australian* 2–3 October 1999, p. 1; Chester Dawson et al., 'Nuclear Alert for Asia', *Far Eastern Economic Review* 14 October 1999, pp. 18–19.

100 Jinzaburo Takagi, 'Japanese Nuclear Industry Aims at Asian Market', *Jakarta Post* 2 December 1997, p. 4.

101 'Japan's Nuclear Power Expansion Delays Target', *China Daily* 1 April 2000, p. 8.

102 Jinzaburo Takagi, 'Japanese Nuclear Industry Aims at Asian Market', p. 4.

103 Robert A. Manning, 'PACATOM: Nuclear Cooperation in Asia', *Washington Quarterly* 20(2) 1997, p. 219.

104 This resulted in the Framework Convention on Climate Change.

105 Charles J. Hanley, 'World Debates Nuclear Power', *Associated Press* 24 November 1997.

106 On this point see Peter C. Evans, 'Japan's Green Aid Plan: The Limits of State-Led Technology Transfer', *Asian Survey* 39(6) 1999, p. 830.

5 Is a Food Crisis Likely?

1 The World Food Program, 'Food Security: sustaining people', *Tackling Hunger in a World Full of Food: Tasks Ahead for Food Aid, 1997*, www.wfp.org/info/POLICY/HUNGER/Pl.html.

2 De Soysa and Gleditsch, *To Cultivate Peace*, pp. 9–10.

3 See, for example, Cheryl Christensen, 'Food and National Security', in Klaus
   Knorr and Frank Traeger (eds), *Economic Issues and National Security* (University of Kansas Press, 1977), pp. 289–92.
4 According to Clive James, founder of the International Service for the Acquisition of Agri-Biotech Applications, quoted in Lorien Holland, 'Leap of Faith',
   Far Eastern Economic Review, 20 April 2000, p. 60. See also UNEP, *Global Environment Outlook 2000*, Chapter 1, www.grida.no/geo2000/english/0069.htm.
5 C. Ford Runge and Benjamin Senauer, 'A Removable Feast', *Foreign Affairs*
   79(3) 2000, p. 40.
6 UNEP, *Global Environment Outlook 2000*, Chapter 1, www.grida.no/geo2000/
   english/0069.htm.
7 Nigel Holloway, 'No Pain, No Grain', *Far Eastern Economic Review* 16 November 1995, p. 89.
8 Lester Brown, *Who Will Feed China?: Wake-up Call for a Small Planet* (Worldwatch Environmental Alert Series, Earthscan Publications, London, 1995), p.
   126; Lester R. Brown, 'Feeding Nine Billion', in *State of the World 1999*, p. 115.
9 *World Resources 1994–95*, p. 107.
10 Kevin Watkins, 'Why more food hasn't helped the world's hungry', *Jakarta
   Post* 26 October 1996, p. 5.
11 A promise made by Henry Kissinger when US Secretary of State: ibid.
12 Paul Holmes, 'Realism to be hallmark of World Food Summit', *Jakarta Post* 9
   November 1996, p. 5.
13 Most beef is grain-fed. As incomes rise people shift their consumption from
   grain to meat, which increases per capita grain consumption.
14 Brown, 'Feeding Nine Billion', p. 118.
15 Runge and Senauer, 'A Removable Feast', p. 41.
16 Paul Ehrlich quoted in David Suzuki, 'Inside Story', documentary, Australian
   Broadcasting Commission, 15 April 1997.
17 Future Harvest, 'Quick Facts', 1 August 2000, www.futureharvest.org/earth/
   quickfacts.shtml.
18 Norman Myers, 'Environment and Security', *Foreign Policy* 74, Spring 1989,
   p. 10.
19 Julian Cribb, 'Grow or Die', *Weekend Australian* 1–2 July 1995, p. 26.
20 Susan George, 'Choosing food security', *Label France*, French Ministry of Foreign Affairs, Paris, no. 38, January 2000, p. 33.
21 Chao Yang Peng, Christopher Findlay and Randy Stringer, 'Food Security in
   Asia', *Asia-Pacific Economic Literature* 2(1) 1997, p. 2.
22 Kunio Takahashi, 'Food Security: Problems and Solutions for the Asia Pacific
   Region', paper presented at the Fourth CSCAP Working Group Meeting,
   Kuala Lumpur, Malaysia, 14–16 September 1997, p. 1.
23 Claro Cortes, 'Rice experts develop new strain of rice', *Jakarta Post* 20 August
   1998, p. 5; *World Resources 1994–95*, p. 108.
24 'Asian food stock faces lean times', *Agence France Presse* 18 February 1999.
25 According to the US Department of Agriculture, the Philippines imported a
   record 1.75 million tonnes in 1998 on top of the 10.3 million it produced:
   Asia 2000 Yearbook (Far Eastern Economic Review, Hong Kong, 1999), p. 45.
   See also 'Philippines places rice orders ahead of El Nino', *Jakarta Post* 11
   November 1997, p. 10.
26 In 1997 Indonesia imported over 3 million tonnes of rice, rising to 6.1 in 1998
   before falling to around 2.6 million tonnes in 1999: John McBeth, 'Monopoly of Virtue', *Far Eastern Economic Review* 30 July 1998, p. 49; *Asia 2000 Yearbook*, p. 45; Michael Richardson, 'Timely Grain', *Australian* 12 July 1996.

27 This is the most likely scenario according to a study of China's grain needs commissioned by the US National Intelligence Council in 1997: MEDEA Group, *China Agriculture: Cultivated Land Area, Grain Projections, and Implications*, Summary Report, prepared for the US National Intelligence Council (Washington, D.C., November 1997).

28 Lester Brown, 'Who will feed China?', pp. 132–3.

29 ibid., p. 134.

30 ibid., p. 32. Brown also argues that global water shortages will contribute to food insecurity. He contends that because grains are water-intensive, water-deficient countries will seek to conserve their water by importing grain, thereby increasing competition for grain on the world market. 'It is the countries that are financially strongest, not those that are militarily the strongest, that are likely to win in this competition.' Worldwatch News Release of 23 September 1999, www.worldwatch.org/alerts/990923.html.

31 Vaclav Smil, 'Environmental Problems in China: Estimates of Economic Costs', East–West Center Special Report no. 5, 1996, p. 36.

32 ibid., pp. 30–1.

33 *Economic Information Daily of China* cited in ibid., p. 55.

34 Jiang Chunyun, quoted in Elizabeth Economy, 'The Case Study of China – Reforms and Resources: The Implications for State Capacity in the PRC', *Project on Environmental Scarcities, State Capacity and Civil Violence* (American Academy of Arts and Sciences and Committee on International Security Studies, University of Toronto, 1997), p. 14.

35 *The Grain Issue in China* (Information Office of the State Council of the People's Republic of China, Beijing, 1996), p. 11.

36 *Asia 2000 Yearbook*, p. 44.

37 *China Daily* cited in Richard McGregor, 'Beijing Propaganda Blast Defends its Growing Appetite', *Australian* 8 May 1996, p. 11.

38 By 2030, Brown believes that grain production in China will be 20 per cent less than the mid-1990s, with cereal production remaining at 1993 levels, because of the loss of arable land from urbanisation, environmental degradation, and water deficiencies: Brown, 'Who Will Feed China?', pp. 96–7.

39 *The Grain Issue in China*, p. 7.

40 Rongrong Le, 'Food Security: Problems and Solutions for the Asia Pacific Region', paper prepared for the Fourth CSCAP Working Group Meeting, Kuala Lumpur, Malaysia, 14–16 September 1997, p. 5; Xu Giang and Wang Kai, 'China: Can the Awakening Giant Feed a Wealthier Population?', *Asian Perspective* 21(3) 1997, p. 124; Peng et al., 'Food Security in Asia', p. 129.

41 See, for example, Nicholas Alexandratos (ed.), *World Agriculture: Towards 2010* (FAO and John Wiley & Sons, New York, 1995); Donald O. Mitchell and Merlinda D. Ingco, 'Global and Regional Food Demand and Supply Prospects', in Nurul Islam (ed.), *Population and Food in the Early Twenty First Century: Meeting Future Food Demand of an Increasing Population* (International Food Policy Research Institute, Washington, D.C., 1995); Mercedita C. Agcaoili and Mark W. Rosegrant, 'Global and regional food supply, demand and trade prospects', in Nurul Islam (ed.), *Population and Food in the Early Twenty First Century*; Johnson D. Gale, 'Does China Have a Grain Problem?', *China Economic Review* 4(1), pp. 1–4; and the comments by food analysts at the World Bank and Washington's International Food Policy Research Institute in 'Will the World Starve?', *Economist* 16 November, 1996, p. 24.

42   Christina David, 'Food: Is a Crisis Looming?', paper presented at Concurrent Session VIII, 10th Asia-Pacific Roundtable, Kuala Lumpur, Malaysia, 5–8 June 1996, p. 11. Cereals include wheat, rice and coarse grains.

43   Peter Hartcher, 'Facts show up flaws in China food crisis theory', *Australian Financial Review* 25 March 1997, p. 9.

44   Nigel Holloway, 'No Pain, No Gain', p. 90.

45   The Chinese Government White Paper points out that the average annual increase in domestic grain production between 1985 and 1996 was 1.2 per cent, and argues that China can reduce the amount of grain lost every year through poor handling (estimated at 45 million tonnes) by improving storage facilities and harvesting techniques: *The Grain Issue in China*, p. 3; Marshall, 'China plans food self-sufficiency', p. 8.

46   Hartcher, 'Facts show up flaws in China food crisis theory', p. 9.

47   Xu Giang and Wang Kai, 'China: Can the Awakening Giant Feed a Wealthier Population?', p. 124; Peng et al., 'Food Security in Asia', p. 10.

48   The study was carried out by the US-based Millennium Institute in conjunction with several Chinese Government agencies, the US Department of Agriculture, the International Food Policy Research Institute and the World Bank. Its findings were published in March 1999: G. Pierre Goad, 'China's Food Needs Loom Large Indeed', *Asian Wall Street Journal* 5–6 March 1999, p. 3.

49   *Asia 2000 Yearbook*, p. 45.

50   Peng et al., 'Food Security in Asia', p. 8. Or, as in the case of Indonesia, it may make the cost of imported fertilisers and pesticides prohibitive: Dini Djalal, 'Old Ways Return to Favour', *Far Eastern Economic Review* 25 May 2000, p. 51.

51   Brian Hunter, 'Looming Environmental Disasters: Where They are Now and How to Check Them', paper presented to the 11th Asia-Pacific Roundtable, Kuala Lumpur, Malaysia, 5–8 June 1997, p. 11.

52   Peng et al., 'Food Security in Asia', p. 6.

53   ibid., p. 1.

54   Le, 'Food Security', p. 7.

55   *The Grain Issue in China*, p. 11.

56   See Comprehensive National Security Study Group, *Report on Comprehensive National Security*, 2 July 1980, especially pp. 60–5.

57   Terry Rambo, 'The Fallacy of Global Sustainable Development', *Asia-Pacific Issues, Analysis from the East–West Center* 30, March 1997, pp. 3–4.

58   'China's Environmental Problems Threaten World's Future', www.greenpeace.org/chinarepexsum.html.

59   S. Chuluunkhuyag, *Status and Cases of Local and National Environmental Conflicts in Mongolia*, presentation to the 'International Workshop on Environmental Peace in East Asia', co-sponsored by the Korean National Committee for UNESCO and UNEP, Seoul, Republic of Korea, 5 July 2000, p. 59.

60   Robert Paarlberg, 'The Global Food Fight', *Foreign Affairs* 79(3) 2000, p. 31.

61   Plants can only convert about 60 per cent of their photosynthate into seed – the remaining 40 per cent is needed to function. Current hybrid wheat varieties already convert 50 per cent of photosynthate into seed: Brown, 'Feeding Nine Billion', pp. 126–7; Cortes, 'Rice experts develop new strain of rice', p. 5.

62   World grain yields rose from 1.06 tons per hectare in 1950 to 2.70 in 1997. Brown, 'Feeding Nine Billion', p. 128;

63   Runge and Senauer, 'A Removable Feast', pp. 42, 47. Their concerns focus on the implications of GMOs for human health as well as the physical envi-

ronment. Some argue that GM seeds resistant to herbicides could possibly interfere with micro-organisms in the soil and create highly resistant weeds through natural selection, although there is no scientific evidence to support this hypothesis: George, 'Choosing food security', p. 33.

64 Leftist groups are finding common cause with environmental groups in the Philippines. They contend that large transnational companies and landlords will monopolise the technology for their own interests, with little benefit flowing through to small peasants. Muslim and Hindu organisations might oppose the use of GMOs fearing that the genes of pigs and cows could be used in genetically altered plants: 'Asians ponder possibilities of GMO', *Korea Herald* 5 July 2000, p. 5. China's leaders, on the other hand, have made biotechnology the nation's top research priority. They hope that 50 per cent of the country's rice fields can be planted with GM crops by 2010, an ambitious undertaking which underlines the importance China attaches to improving rice yields: Lorien Holland, 'Leap of Faith', *Far Eastern Economic Review* 20 April 2000, p. 60.

65 Brown, 'Feeding Nine Billion', p. 123.

66 ibid., p. 124.

67 Lorien Holland, 'Running Dry', *Far Eastern Economic Review* 3 February 2000, p. 18.

68 As Lester Brown argues, the economics of water do not favour agriculture. A thousand tons of water may produce $200 of wheat or $14 000 of expanded industrial output: Brown, 'Feeding Nine Billion', pp. 124–5.

69 See Teresa Watanabe and Hyungwon Kang, 'With a Bit of Ingenuity, North Koreans Find Food', *International Herald Tribune* 10 June 1997, pp. 1, 6.

70 Shim Jae Hoon, 'Welfare State', *Far Eastern Economic Review* 27 May 1999, p. 24.

71 UN World Food Program estimates cited in Scott Snyder, 'A Coming Crisis on the Korean Peninsula?', *United States Institute of Peace Special Report*, 1996, pp. 10–11; 'CIA Warns of North Korean War Threat', *Australian* 7 February 1997, p. 7.

72 Nayan Chanda, Shim Jae Hoon and Peter Landers, 'On Borrowed Time', *Far Eastern Economic Review* 26 June 1997, p. 23.

73 Robert Garran, 'Desperate N. Korea Pleads for Food Aid', *Australian* 4 February 1997, p. 1.

74 Caritas estimates cited in 'Aid Worker: N. Korea Hunger Grows', *Associated Press* 16 July 1997.

75 Shim Jae Hoon, 'Welfare State', p. 24.

76 It is difficult to assess with complete accuracy the number of deaths that occurred as a result of famine but North Korea estimates nearly 3 million, a figure supported by several independent observers. Cha Lim Sok, Deputy Director of the Farm Produce Bureau of North Korea's Agricultural Commission, reported in January 1998 that 2.8 million North Koreans had died from 'natural calamities' and that per capita food availability had declined to 180 grams a day: '2.8 Million North Koreans Died from Natural Calamities', *Agence France-Presse* 20 January 1998. See also the estimates by the United Nations, NGOs and US Congressional staffers who visited North Korea in 1998: Marcus Noland, Sherman Robinson and Tao Wang, 'Famine in North Korea: Causes and Cures', www.iie.com/wp992.pdf; 'Curbs eased on famine-hit deserters', *South China Morning Post* 6 March 1999, p. 12.

77 A sharp reduction in Chinese and Russian food aid, equipment and cheap oil in the early 1990s rather than the disastrous floods of 1995 was probably the

actual trigger for the famine, which precipitated 'an agricultural and industrial decline of enormous magnitude': Andrew Natsios, *The Politics of Famine in North Korea* (US Institute of Peace Special Report, Washington, D.C., 2 August 1999), p. 2.

78 Rear-Admiral R. M. Sunardi, Senior Adviser to Indonesia's Minister of Defence, quoted in Alan Dupont, 'Indonesian Defence Strategy and Security: Time for a Rethink?', *Contemporary Southeast Asia* 18(3) 1996, p. 280. The Pacific Ocean provides over 60 per cent of the world's fisheries production.

79 Trish Saywell, 'Fishing for Trouble', *Far Eastern Economic Review* 13 March 1997, pp. 50–1.

80 Asian Development Bank, *Asian Development Outlook 2000*, www.adb.org/publications; *Asia 1997 Yearbook*, p. 56.

81 *Asia 1997 Yearbook*, p. 56. See also Kaji, 'Challenges to the East Asian Environment', p. 217.

82 Since 1994, the global catch has levelled out at around 93–95 million tonnes while per capita catch has remained in the range of 15–17.4 kilograms since 1967. World aquaculture production (finfish, crustaceans and molluscs) has expanded considerably in the same time frame and totalled 29 million tonnes in 1999. Global production is dominated by China, which contributes 83 per cent of world aquaculture. World fish production, including aquaculture, was valued at \$120 billion in 1997: Izzat H. Feidi, 'International Seafood Production and Trade to 2010: Where Are We Headed?', paper presented at the Australian Seafood Industry National Conference, 7–8 October 1999, pp. 16, 41. See also *Human Development Report, 1994* (Oxford University Press for the UNDP, New York, 1994), p. 36; Starke, *Vital Signs 1999*, www.worldwatch.org; Daniel Yarrow Coulter, 'South China Sea Fisheries: Countdown to Calamity', *Contemporary Southeast Asia* 17(4) 1996, p. 372.

83 Eduardo A. Loayza and Lucian M. Sprague, 'A Strategy for Fisheries Development', World Bank Discussion Papers no. 135, 1994, p. 2, cited in Coulter, 'South China Sea Fisheries: Countdown to Calamity', p. 372.

84 FAO, *Review Of The State Of World Fishery Resources: Marine Fisheries*, FAO Fisheries Circular No. 920 (FAO, Rome, 1997), pp. 6, 7.

85 Feidi, 'International Seafood Production and Trade to 2010', p. 1.

86 Saywell, 'Fishing for Trouble', p. 51.

87 Geoffrey Lean, 'World Fisheries Now in a Sea of Trouble', *Canberra Times*, 4 February 1995, p. C6.

88 Between 1991 and 1995, roughly 13 per cent of vessels added to the global fishing fleet were registered in Honduras and Liberia, 'two leading "flag of convenience" nations': Anne Platt McGinn, 'Fisheries Falter', in Starke, *Vital Signs 1999*, www.worldwatch.org.

89 Saywell, 'Fishing for Trouble', p. 51. Between 1981 and 1991, the value of exports from the world's fisheries rose by 260 per cent, from \$15 billion to \$39 billion: *Human Development Report, 1994* (Oxford University Press for the UNDP, New York, 1994), p. 36 and Coulter, 'South China Sea Fisheries: Countdown to Calamity', p. 372.

90 'Nations must unite to save depleting world fish stocks', p. 5.

91 'Protect Marine Resources', *Jakarta Post* 17 January 1997, p. 1.

92 'Fishing War Sows Conflict in Pacific Nations', *Korea Times* 19 December 1989, p. 9.

93 *Asia 1997 Yearbook*, p. 56.

94 Mark Valencia, 'Asia, the Law of the Sea and International Relations', *International Affairs* 73(2) 1997, p. 268.
95 Steve Lonergan, 'Environmental Change and Regional Security in Southeast Asia', *Project Report No. PR659*, Department of National Defence, Ottawa, 1994, p. 38.
96 Gordon Fairclough, 'Floating Flashpoint: Fishing Fleets Aggravate Regional Tensions', *Far Eastern Economic Review* 13 March 1997, p. 54.
97 Peter Alford, 'Talks aim to soothe border tensions', *Australian* 12 February 1999, p. 8.
98 Michael Vatikiotis and Adam Schwarz, 'Crossed Lines: Thailand and Vietnam Clash over Fishing Rights', *Far Eastern Economic Review* 15 June 1995, p. 16.
99 'Govt warns Thai fishermen', *Nation* (Thailand) 16 June 1999, p. 7.
100 Fairclough, 'Floating Flashpoint', p. 50.
101 *Asia 2000 Yearbook*, p. 50.
102 'Philippines Arrests Chinese and Taiwanese Fishermen in Disputed Waters', *Reuters* 18 August 1997.
103 'Fish the Real Booty in Spratlys: Experts', *Jakarta Post* 19 June 1995, p. 7.
104 Juita Ramli, 'Malaysia and the Law of the Sea: A Harvest of Riches', *MIMA Bulletin* 4(1) 1997, p. 3; Shee Poon Kim, 'China's Changing Policies Towards the South China Sea', ibid., p. 26.
105 'RI loses $2bn a Year in Fishing Resources', *Jakarta Post* 8 August 1997, p. 2; 'Steps To Curb Poaching In Philippine Territorial Waters', *Central News Agency* 6 August 1997, www.nautilus.org/trade.
106 'Protect Marine Resources', *Jakarta Post* 17 January 1997, p. 1.
107 Mark V. Erdmann, 'Foreign fishing fleets are depriving locals of food', *Jakarta Post* 9 June 2000, p. 5.
108 Elaine Lies, 'North Korea Says Not Involved In Ships Incident', *Reuters* 26 March 1999.
109 'ROK: DPRK Incursion Possibly Done to Protect Fishing Boats', FBIS-EAS-96-116, 14 June 1996, pp. 31–2. Four hundred and seventy-two incidents of illegal fishing by Chinese ships were recorded in South Korea's 12-mile territorial waters during 1995: 'ROK Plans to File Protest with PRC over 'Piracy' Act', FBIS-EAS-96-110, 6 June 1996, p. 56.
110 ibid.
111 Don Kirk, 'South Korean Warships Sink Northern Patrol Boat', *International Herald Tribune* 16 June 1999, www.iht.com; Yuri Savenkov, 'Koreans Battle in the Yellow Sea', *Izvestia* 15 June 1999.
112 Mark Valencia, 'Asia, the Law of the Sea and International Relations', p. 273.
113 Ji Guoxing, 'The Diaoyudai (Senkaku) Disputes and Prospects for Settlement', p. 286.
114 Bruce Gilley, Sebastian Moffet, Julian Baum and Matt Foley, 'Rocks of Contention', *Far Eastern Economic Review* 19 September 1996, p. 15.
115 Frank Ching, 'A Taiwan Dilemma', *Far Eastern Economic Review* 11 February 1999, p. 35.
116 Geoffrey Till, 'Trouble in Paradise: Maritime Risks and Threats in the Western Pacific', *Jane's Intelligence Review*, Special Report No. 7, 1995, p. 10.
117 Schofield, 'Island Disputes in East Asia Escalate', p. 521; Valencia, 'Asia, the Law of the Sea and International Relations', p. 273.

118 Aleksandr Chudodeyev, 'Octopus Hunt Without Risking One's Life', *Segod-nya*, 2 October 1998; Yuri Golotyuk, 'Japanese Poaching near Kurils', *Izvestia* 3 November 1998.

119 Schofield, 'Island Disputes in East Asia Escalate', p. 518.

120 Robert Garran, 'Japan, South Korea Overlap in Claims for Economic Zones', *Australian* 21 February 1996, p. 9.

121 'Japan Denounced Over Fishing Dispute', *Korea Herald* 15 July 1997, www.nautilus.org/napsnet/dr/index.html; 'S. Korea Parliament Denounces Japan', *United Press International* 24 July 1997.

122 Son Key-young, 'Seoul Warns Tokyo of Grave Consequences in Bilateral Ties Over Fishing Disputes', *Korea Times* 9 July 1997, www.nautilus.org/napsnet/dr/index.html; 'Minister Yoo Rejects Japan's Demands on EEZ', *Chosun Ilbo* 15 July 1997, www.nautilus.org/napsnet/dr/index.html.

123 'Seoul trawlers form armada after Tokyo sinks fish pact', *Agence France Presse* 26 January 1998.

124 'Japan–ROK Fishery Agreement is Approved on December 11: Stock from Water Surrounding Takeshima/Tokdo Remains to be Discussed', *Asahi Shimbun* 11 December 1998, www.nautilus.org/napsnet/dr/index.html; 'GNP Deters ROK-Japan Fisheries Accord', *Korea Times* 15 December 1998, www.nautilus.org/napsnet/dr/index.html; 'Japan, S. Korea Sign Fishing Accord', *Associated Press* 28 November 1998.

125 'Japanese–ROK Fishery Accord To Come Into Effect, But Territorial Dispute Still Remains Hot', *Yomiuri Shimbun* 8 January 1999, www.nautilus.org/napsnet/dr/index.html.

126 'Korea to Consider Temporary Fishery Deal with PRC', *Korea Herald* 8 July 1997, www.nautilus.org/napsnet/dr/index.html; Son Key-young, 'Cabinet Endorses Decree Banning Foreign Boats Fishing in EEZ', *Korea Times* 30 July 1997, www.nautilus.org/napsnet/dr/index.html.

127 'ROK, PRC to Ink Fisheries Pact', *Chosun Ilbo* 9 November 1998, www.nautilus.org/napsnet/dr/index.html.

128 Mohammad A. T. Chowdhury, 'Global Food Security in the 21st Century: A Supply Side Perspective with Reference to Cereal', *Indonesian Quarterly* 28(1) 2000, p. 30.

129 Grain stocks in 1996 fell to 13 per cent of annual consumption: 'Will The World Starve', p. 23; US Department of Agriculture figures cited in Holloway, 'No Pain, No Grain', p. 90; 'UN forecasts cereals shortage and sugar surplus', *Nation* (Thailand) 12 June 1999, p. B4.

130 Even the Chinese government recognises that 'the tense situation between supply and demand will continue to exist for a long time to come': *The Grain Issue in China*, p. 4.

6 Water Wars

1 See, for example, the proliferation of articles dealing with water and conflict in the various publications of Jane's and the IISS, both of which represent mainstream strategic thinking and consciously target the international defence and security establishment.

2 Globally, some 70 per cent of water is used for irrigation, 20 per cent for industry and the remaining 10 per cent for personal consumption: Lester R. Brown, 'The World's Growing Water Deficit Threatens Its Food Supply', *International Herald Tribune* 29 June 2000, p. 12.

3 See Vera Haller, 'Water an Issue at Food Summit', *Jakarta Post* 11 November 1996, p. 5.
4 That is, where water consumption is more than 10 per cent of renewable freshwater supply: UNEP, *Global Environment Outlook 2000*, Chapter 2, www.grida.no/geo2000/english/0069.htm;
5 Anthony Goodman, 'Only 0.007 Percent of World Water Found Usable', *Jakarta Post* 10 March 1997, p. 9.
6 It takes about 1000 tonnes of water to produce 1 tonne of grain: Sandra Postel, quoted in Worldwatch News Release of 23 September 1999, www.worldwatch.org/alerts/990923.html and Worldwatch News Release of 17 July 1999, www.worldwatch.org/alerts/990717.html.
7 Peter Gleick, *The World's Water 1998–1999: The Biennial Report on Freshwater Resources* (Island Press, Washington, D.C., 1998), pp. 40, 47.
8 UNEP, *Freshwater Pollution* (UNEP, Nairobi, 1991), p. 6.
9 *World Resources 1994–95*, p. 182.
10 'Global water shortages', *Strategic Comments* 5(6) 1999, p. 1.
11 In the early 1990s, agriculture accounted for about 65 per cent, and industry nearly 24 per cent, of global water use: Peter Wallensteen and Ashok Swain, *International Fresh Water Resources: Conflict or Cooperation?*, Stockholm Environment Institute, Stockholm, June 1997, p. 4.
12 UNEP, *Global Environment Outlook 2000*, Chapter 2, www.grida.no/geo2000/english/0069.htm.
13 Wallensteen and Swain, *International Fresh Water Resources: Conflict or Cooperation?*, pp. 2–3; Peter Gleick, 'Water and Conflict in the Middle East', *Environment* 36(3) 1994, p. 6.
14 Peter H. Gleick, 'An Introduction to Global Fresh Water Issues', in Peter H. Gleick (ed.), *Water in Crisis: A Guide to the World's Fresh Water Resources* (Oxford University Press for the Stockholm Environment Institute, New York, 1993), p. 6.
15 International Water Management Institute, 'Water Scarcity in the Twenty First Century', *International Journal of Water Resources Development* March 1999, www.futureharvest.org/news/03171999.shtml.
16 Brown, 'Climate, Ecology and International Security', p. 124; Wallensteen and Swain, *International Fresh Water Resources*, p. 4; UN Population Fund, *Population, Resources and the Environment* (UN, New York, 1991), p. 47; Julian Cribb, 'Water Wars', *Australian* 15 January 1996, p. 12; 'Finding ways to conserve the world's fresh water', *Jakarta Post* 30 April 1999, p. 14.
17 *Joint UN Environment Program and UN University News Release*, 18 March 1999, www.unep. org/unep/per/ipa/pressrel/r03-1799.001.
18 Gleick, *The World's Water*, pp. 69–70.
19 Gleick, 'Water and Conflict in the Middle East', p. 38.
20 Gleick, *The World's Water*, pp. 20–1.
21 Withdrawal refers to the act of taking water from a source for storage or use. It may not necessarily be consumed. ibid., p. 12.
22 See Miriam R. Lowi, *Water and Power: The Politics of a Scarce Resource in the Jordan River Basin* (Cambridge University Press, 1993), p. 1.
23 Gleick, 'Water and Conflict in the Middle East', p. 8.
24 Cited in Peter H. Gleick, 'Water and Conflict: Fresh Water Resources and International Security', *International Security* 18(1) 1991, p. 86. See also Joyce Starr, 'Water Wars', *Foreign Policy* 82, Spring 1991, p. 17.
25 The population of the Middle East and North Africa has doubled in the last thirty years to 290 million and can be expected to double again in the next

thirty, which largely explains the pessimistic assessment of the UN Economic and Social Commission for Western Asia that water conflicts are more likely in the future among the region's riparian states: Ed Blanche, 'Mid-East water woe can only get worse', *Jane's Intelligence Review* November 1999, pp. 26–7.

26 Natasha Beschorner, *Water and Instability in the Middle East*, Adelphi Paper no. 273 (London, Brassey's for the IISS, 1992), p. 3.

27 'Global water shortages', p. 1.

28 Beschorner, *Water and Instability in the Middle East*, p. 6.

29 *Water: Asia's Environmental Imperative* (Asian Media Information and Communication Centre, Singapore, 1997), p. 23.

30 Cribb, 'Water Wars', p. 12; Juergen Dauth, 'WB Forecasts Water Crisis in Asian Countries', *Jakarta Post* 2 January 1997, p. 4.

31 BGS/ODA/UNEP/WHO, *Characterisation and Assessment of Groundwater Quality Concerns in Asia-Pacific Region*, Environment Assessment Report UNEP/DEIA/AR.96-1, Division of Environment Information and Assessment (UNEP, Nairobi, Kenya, 1996), p. 3.

32 Ian Stewart, 'Anger floods Malaysia', *Weekend Australian* 18–19 April 1998, p. 12.

33 An estimate made by Malaysian Primary Industries Minister, Lim Keng Yaik: Murray Hiebert, 'Water Woes', *Far Eastern Economic Review* 25 June 1998, pp. 52–3 and S. Jayasankaran, 'Liquidity Crunch', *Far Eastern Economic Review* 16 April 1998, p. 53.

34 Murray Hiebert, 'Damned If You Do ...', *Far Eastern Economic Review* 8 April 1999, p. 45.

35 Jayasankaran, 'Liquidity Crunch', p. 53.

36 *Characterisation and Assessment of Groundwater Quality Concerns in Asia-Pacific Region*, p. 19; Lonergan, 'Environmental Change and Regional Security in Southeast Asia', p. 63.

37 ibid.; Dauth, 'WB Forecasts Water Crisis in Asian Countries', p. 4.

38 'Water Crisis in 2005 Predicted', *Jakarta Post* 1 November 1995, p. 3.

39 *Characterisation and Assessment of Groundwater Quality Concerns in Asia-Pacific Region*, p. 20.

40 'Water Crisis in 2005 Predicted', p. 3.

41 'Puncak Not Only Cause of Massive Floods', *Jakarta Post* 31 October 1996, p. 3.

42 Adam Schwarz, 'Looking Back at Rio', *Far Eastern Economic Review* 28 October 1993, p. 48.

43 'Puncak Not Only Cause of Massive Floods', p. 3.

44 Burnett, *The Western Pacific*, pp. 155–6.

45 Lester R. Brown and Brian Halweil, 'China's Water Shortage Could Shake World Food Security', *World Watch Magazine* July–August 1998, www.worldwatch.org/mag/1998/98-4a.html.

46 Gavan McCormack, *Water Margins: Development and Sustainability in China*, Australian Mekong Resource Working Paper No. 2 (University of Sydney, 2000), p. 3; Changhua Wu, 'The price of growth', *Bulletin of the Atomic Scientists* 55(5) 1999, p. 65.

47 Smil, 'Environmental Problems in China', p. 51.

48 Holland, 'Running Dry', *Far Eastern Economic Review* 3 February 2000, p. 18. Water tables are falling rapidly right across the whole North China plain and those parts of China which are flat. Worldwatch News Release of 23 September 1999, www.worldwatch.org/alerts/990923.html.

49 'Cities hit by drought', *Hong Kong Standard* 12 May 2000, p. 5.

50 A country is generally considered to be experiencing a water crisis when it exceeds 20 per cent of usable water reserves: Holland, 'Running Dry', p. 18.

51 'India and Bangladesh: Sweeter Waters', *Economist* 16 November 1996, p. 26. Forty-five per cent of China's arable land is irrigated, producing 74 per cent of its grain, 60 per cent of its cash crops and 80 per cent of its vegetables: Xi Mi, 'Water can bring bonanza or disaster', *China Daily* 29 October 1996, p. 4.

52 Cribb, 'Water Wars', p. 12.

53 Brown and Halweil, 'China's Water Shortage Could Shake World Food Security', www.worldwatch.org/mag/1998/98-4a.html.

54 Cited in Elizabeth Economy, 'The Case Study of China ...', p. 6.

55 W. Harriet Critchley and Terry Terriff, 'Environment and Security', in Schultz, Godson and Greenwood (eds), *Security Studies for the 1990s*, p. 334.

56 See Hurst, *Rainforest Politics*, pp. 197–200; Lim Teck Ghee and Mark J. Valencia (eds), *Conflict over Natural Resources in South-East Asia and the Pacific* (Oxford University Press, Singapore 1990), pp. 44–5.

57 Gleick, *The World's Water*, pp. 69–70.

58 Hiebert, 'Damned If You Do ...', pp. 44–5.

59 For an analysis of the conflict over the Tong River Dam, see Lee See Jae, 'Movement against Damming the Tong River – A Model of Solution for Environmental Conflict', proceedings of the *International Workshop on Environmental Peace in Asia*, Seoul and Wonju, 5–7 July 2000, pp. 71–82.

60 'Faults spark fears of dam disaster', *Australian* 25 March 1999, p. 9.

61 Gleick, *The World's Water*, p. 78.

62 The Yangtse basin is home to 400 million people and produces much of China's food. China is also building a major dam on the Yellow River which is near completion: '159,000 flee Yangtze floodwaters', *Australian* 6 July 1999, p. 8.

63 Trish Saywell, 'Dangerous Waters', *Far Eastern Economic Review* 1 April 1999, p. 38.

64 Seth Faison, 'A Show of Power on Yangtze', *International Herald Tribune* 10 November 1997, p. 1; Liang Chao, 'Blocking Yangtze: "No Problem"', *China Daily* 8 November 1997, p. 1; 'Closing the Last Gap, China Gives the Yangtze a New Course', *International Herald Tribune* 8–9 November 1997, p. 1.

65 Karby Leggett, 'Three Gorges Dam Plan Stirs Mounting Criticism', *Asian Wall Street Journal* 10 May 2000, p. 1.

66 These are not implausible scenarios. Even Chinese officials concede that one billion tons of sewage will flow into the reservoir each year and that silting will be a problem: 'Three Gorges dam, eco-boon or curse?', *Jakarta Post* 4 November 1997, p. 9.

67 David Nelson, *Toxic Waste: Hazardous to Asia's Health*, Asia-Pacific Issues Paper no. 34 (East–West Center, Honolulu, November 1997), p. 2.

68 Significant reservoir-induced seismic activity has been recorded after the construction of large dams: Gleick, *The World's Water*, p. 77.

69 Leggett, 'Three Gorges Dam Plan Stirs Mounting Criticism', p. 1.

70 Gleick, *The World's Water*, p. 87; Crocker Snow Jr, 'Three Gorges holds back flood of criticism', *The World Paper* 18(11) 1996, p. 5; and Erling Hoh, 'Yangtse Guardian', *Far Eastern Economic Review* 20 February 1997, pp. 46–8.

71 'Faults spark fears of dam disaster'. Some Chinese analysts are concerned that the dam's construction could threaten the social stability of the entire Yangtse basin, although these fears seem exaggerated: Lynne O'Donnell, 'Human Flood Damns Yangtse Work', *Australian* 17 August 1999, p. 8.

72 Singapore has abundant rainfall but it lacks the storage capacity and underground aquifers to be self sufficient in water without desalination: Adriel Yap Lian Ho, *Water for Singapore: Management of a Resource in a Subregional Economic Zone* (National University of Singapore, Singapore, 1995), pp. 14, 51.

73 Irene Ng, 'Piping Up on Water Issues', *New Paper* 5 June 1997, p. 14.

74 ibid.; 'Singapore eyes 100-year water deal with Indonesia', *Jakarta Post* 17 January 1999, p. 2.

75 Ng, 'Piping Up on Water Issues', p. 14; Jaqueline Lee, 'KL Uses Water as Political Tool', *Jakarta Post* 7 July 1997, p. 4.

76 Kevin Hamlin, 'Singapore Seeks a Solution to Dependence on Imported Water', *Asia Times* 11 June 1997, p. 3. According to officials of the PUB, desalinated water is around 7–8 times more expensive than normal water.

77 'Two States Likely to Exhaust Water Resources', *Straits Times* 11 November 1997, p. 25.

78 Lee Kuan Yew, *The Singapore Story: Memoirs of Lee Kuan Yew* (Prentice Hall, Singapore, 1998), p. 663.

79 ibid.

80 Ben Dolven and Murray Hiebert, 'Ties That Bind', *Far Eastern Economic Review* 24 September 1998, p. 13.

81 Ian Stewart, 'Apology Fails to Pacify Malaysia', *Australian* 17 March 1997, p. 7.

82 Lee, 'KL Uses Water as Political Tool', p. 4.

83 S. Jayasankaran and Murray Hiebert, 'Snipe, Snipe: Malaysia–Singapore Spat Reflects Growing Economic Rivalry', *Far Eastern Economic Review* 5 June 1997, p. 24.

84 'PM Goh's Speech in Parliament: I Shall Work for a New Era of Cooperation', *Straits Times* 6 June 1997, p. 45.

85 Hamlin, 'Singapore Seeks a Solution'. If Malaysia were to cut off Singapore's water the island state would only be able to provide water from its own resources for about ten days of normal usage, giving it little scope for ameliorative action: 'Water needs: Can Singapore ever be self-sufficient', *Straits Times* 28 June 1997, p. 3.

86 Dolven and Hiebert, 'Ties That Bind', p. 13.

87 Data extracted from Table B.3, 'Lengths and Basin Countries of Selected Major Rivers, Four Estimates', in Gleick (ed.), *Water in Crisis*, pp. 151–2.

88 The wider Mekong region is estimated to have a population of around 330 million and its combined GDP in 1995 was around $200 billion: Nguyen Thi Dieu, 'Whose River, Whose Rights? Mekong Projects and their Environmental Impacts', proceedings of the *International Workshop on Environmental Peace in Asia*, Seoul and Wonju, 5–7 July 2000, p. 104.

89 Cengiz Ertuna and Le Huu Ti, 'Towards Sustainable Development of the Lower Mekong Basin: Recent Developments in Water Resources Management', paper presented at the international conference on 'Perspectives for the Mekong Region – After the Crisis', Canberra, 22–23 February 1999, p. 3.

90 Michael Richardson, 'Cambodia's New War', *Australian* 4 February 1999, p. 30.

91 Tony Gillotte, 'The Heart of the Mekong Threatened by Cambodia's Economic Surgery', *World Paper* 23 November 1997, p. 1.

92 Paul Gonsalves, 'Water security and the Mekong', *Jane's Intelligence Review* June 2000, p. 34.

93 Hoang Anh Tuan, 'Mekong Water Resource Management: Diminishing Possible Conflicts and Enhancing Cooperation', paper presented at the 14th

Asia-Pacific Roundtable Conference, 3–7 June 2000, Kuala Lumpur, Malaysia, p. 3; Cisca Spencer, 'Challenge is to Tap Mekong without Being Damned', *Australian* 6 September 1996, p. 18.

94 Bertil Lintner, 'Before the Flood', *Far Eastern Economic Review* 13 February 1997, p. 49. Laos intends to construct twenty-three dams altogether, four of which had been completed by 2000: Tuan, 'Mekong Water Resource Management: Diminishing Possible Conflicts and Enhancing Cooperation', p. 8.

95 ADB figures cited in Michael Richardson, 'Harnessing the Mighty Mekong', *Australian* 28 April 1997, p. 24. For details on the existing and proposed dams see Milton Osborne, 'The Strategic Significance of the Mekong', *Contemporary Southeast Asia* 22(3) 2000, pp. 435–41.

96 For an illuminating account of the Mekong's development historically see Nguyen Thi Dieu, *The Mekong River and the Struggle for Indochina: Water, War and Peace* (Praeger, Westport, 1998).

97 Bertil Lintner, 'Cold-War Legacy', *Far Eastern Economic Review* 10 August 1995, p. 30.

98 Patrick Lescott, 'Asian Nations Sign Deal to Preserve Mekong', *Australian* 7 April 1995, p. 8.

99 Richardson, 'Harnessing the Mighty Mekong', p. 24.

100 Janne Jokinen, 'The Lancang-Mekong River as Link between the Yunnan Province of the People's Republic of China, the Lao People's Democratic Republic and Thailand', paper presented at the international conference 'Perspectives for the Mekong Region – After the Crisis', Canberra, 22–23 February 1999, pp. 4–5.

101 Burnett, *The Western Pacific*, p. 148.

102 Richardson, 'Cambodia's New War', p. 30.

103 Cisca Spencer, 'Financial Benefits to Flow from River Region Development', *Australian* 5 December 1996, p. 18.

104 There has already been a marked drop in fisheries production because of deforestation, dam construction and the conversion of 1000 square kilometres of mangrove swamps into rice paddies and fish ponds: Nguyen, 'Whose River, Whose Rights?', p. 86.

105 William Barnes, 'Bonanza Dam Plan Threatens Mekong', *Australian* 15 December 1994, p. 4. Fish output in the Tonle Sap has already fallen by 50 per cent and salt water has intruded up to 70 kilometres inland from the sea: Tuan, 'Mekong Water Resource Management: Diminishing Possible Conflicts and Enhancing Cooperation', p. 9.

106 A paradigm inherited from the West but which ironically is now largely discredited in the West: Gavan McCormack, *Water Margins: Development and Sustainability in China*, p. 15.

107 In Gleick's view vulnerability increases when states or regions already use a significant fraction of their total fresh water resources: Gleick, 'Water and Conflict: Fresh Water Resources and International Security', pp. 84–5, 111.

7 Unregulated Population Movements, Ethnic Conflict and the State

1 UNHCR, *The State of the World's Refugees 1995: In Search of Solutions* (Oxford University Press, New York, 1995), p. 11.

2 Gil Loescher, 'Refugee Movements and International Security', Adelphi Paper no. 268 (Brassey's for the IISS, London, Summer 1992), p. 3.

3 UNHCR, *The State of the Word's Refugees 1997-98: A Humanitarian Agenda*, www.unhcr.ch/refworld/pub/state/97/ch3.htm.

4 Jonas Widgren, 'International migration and regional stability', *International Affairs* 66(4) 1990, p. 752.

5 Crosby, *Ecological Imperialism*, p. 5.

6 Peter Nyers, 'Emergency or Emerging Identities? Refugees and Transformations in World Order, *Millennium: Journal of International Studies* 28(1) 1999, pp. 11-12.

7 Michael Marrus, *The Unwanted European Refugees in the Twentieth Century* (Oxford University Press, New York, 1985), p. 15.

8 Nyers, 'Emergency or Emerging Identities? Refugees and Transformations in World Order', pp. 12-13.

9 Charles Ingrao, 'Are we condemned to repeat history?', *Indonesian Observer* 16 October 1999, p. 5.

10 Sadako Ogata, 'An Era of Mass Migrations Needs Updated Rules', *International Herald Tribune* 23 August 2000, www.iht.com.

11 Teitelbaum, 'Immigration, refugees, and foreign policy', p. 431.

12 The balance of 4 million was made up of refugees who had been repatriated but still required UNHCR assistance: UNHCR, *The State of the World's Refugees 1995*, pp. 19-20.

13 There were 21.5 million people of concern to the UNHCR in 1998 and 22.3 million in 1999: *Refugees and Others of Concern to the UNHCR: Statistical Overview*, www.unhcr.ch/statist/98oview/ch1.htm; *UNHCR Global Report 1999: An Overview*, www.unhcr.ch/fdrs/gr99/toc.htm.

14 The UNHCR's mandate and resources only allow it to care for a small proportion of internally displaced people: UNHCR, *The State of the World's Refugees 1997-98: A Humanitarian Agenda*, www.unhcr.ch/refworld/pub/state/97/ch3.htm; 'UN slates wealthy west on refugee intake', *Australian* 10 December 1997, p. 14.

15 This is a 1999 estimate made by the director of the Australian Institute of Criminology, Adam Graycar. See Sally Jackson, 'Army of misery conscripts 30m', *Australian* 8 July 1999, p. 3. In 1993, the United Nations calculated that there were 20-40 million illegal labour migrants globally while the International Labor Organization estimated the figure to be a much higher 80 million: UNHCR, *The State of the World's Refugees 1993: The Challenge of Protection* (UNHCR, Penguin Books, New York), pp. 1, 24-5; ILO figures cited in 'Migrant workers in vicious circle', *Jakarta Post* 30 October 1996, p. 2.

16 Press Release, USCR, 13 June 2000, www.refugees.org/news/press_releases/2000/061300g.htm; USCR, *World Refugee Survey 2000*, www.refugees.org/world/statistics/wrs00_tableindex.htm.

17 UNHCR, *The State of the Word's Refugees 1997-98: A Humanitarian Agenda*, www.unhcr.ch/refworld/pub/state/97/ch3.htm.

18 The Rwandan emergency in 1994, which led to an exodus of over 1 million people, and the displacement of East Timor's entire population of 830 000 in September 1999, are two prominent examples.

19 See foreword to UNHCR, *The State of the World's Refugees 1997-98: A Humanitarian Agenda*, www.unhcr.ch/refworld/pub/state/97/ch3.htm. By the end of the 1990s, 21 million people were internally displaced globally compared with fewer than 12 million refugees: Press Release, USCR, 13 June 2000, www.refugees,org/news/press_releases/2000/061300g.htm.

20 'German Right wrong on race', *Australian* 13 January 1999, p. 9.

21 In early 2001, British Home Secretary, Jack Straw, called for a greater distinction between genuine asylum-seekers and economic migrants: 'UN commissioner warns against "Fortress Europe" laws', *Agence France Presse* 7 February 2001. See also Barry James, 'EU Confronts Illegal Immigration', *International Herald Tribune* 16–17 October 1999, p. 8.

22 Under 'the safe third country rule' adopted by the European Union in 1992, any person seeking asylum in one EU member state 'after passing through another country considered safe, is deemed ineligible for asylum': 'Europe in Harmony Against Asylum Seekers', *Australian* 16 January 1995, p. 7.

23 'Migration Prevention, Control and Management', *Short Report on Wilton Park Conference 497*, Wilton House, United Kingdom, April 1997.

24 Rashna Writer, 'Refugees Become a Strategic Factor', *Defense, Foreign Affairs, Strategic Policy* 24(7)1997, p. 32.

25 There were 4.7 million refugees and 2 million internally displaced persons out of the 7.4 million people of concern to the UNHCR in Asia at the end of 1998: *Refugees and Others of Concern to the UNHCR: Statistical Overview*, www.unhcr.ch/statist/98oview/ch1.htm. It is difficult to provide an accurate breakdown of UPMs in East Asia because of unreliable data, the imprecise use of terminology and different interpretations of who is a refugee. The UNHCR's adoption of the more inclusive term 'persons of concern', while reflecting the growing complexity of humanitarian emergencies, complicates comparisons with earlier periods when more restricted definitions were used. The figures provided for East Asia are drawn from USCR, *World Refugee Survey 2000*, www.refugees.org/world/countryrpt/easia_pacific/htm.

26 See, for example, the proceedings of the Tenth Asia Pacific Roundtable in 1996: Mohamed Jawhar Hassan and Sheik Ahmad Raffie (eds), *Bringing Peace to the Pacific* (ISIS Malaysia, Kuala Lumpur, 1996), pp. 621–50 and the agendas of the Roundtables since.

27 Alan Dupont, 'Unregulated Population Flows in East Asia: A New Security Dilemma?', *Pacifica Review* 9(1) 1997, p. 18.

28 Goldstone, 'A Tsunami on the Horizon?', p. 49.

29 Nicholas D. Kristof, 'Chinese Outcompete Locals in Tokyo's Sex District', *International Herald Tribune* 18 June 1999, p. 1.

30 'Chinese Influx into Russian far east worries leaders', *Straits Times* 26 August 1995, p. 10; Boris Reznik, 'Chinese Tourists Would Like To Stay In Russia', *Izvestia* 3 April 1999.

31 Louise do Rosario, 'Toilers of the East', *Far Eastern Economic Review* 2 April 1992, pp. 20–1.

32 As long ago as 1989, Australian Foreign Minister, Gareth Evans, declared UPMs to be a 'potential, non-military security' threat to East Asia. See *Australia's Regional Security*, Ministerial Statement by Senator Gareth Evans, Minister for Foreign Affairs and Trade, December 1989, p. 35.

33 'Curbs eased on famine-hit deserters', *South China Morning Post* 6 March 1999, p. 12. There are also around 20 000 North Koreans working in forestry, construction and agriculture in the Russian Far East under a visa agreement renegotiated between Moscow and Pyongyang in January 1997: Sophie Quinn-Judge, 'Fancy Footwork', *Far Eastern Economic Review* 27 February 1997, p. 23.

34 UNHCR, *The State of the World's Refugees 1995*, p. 208.

35 *UNHCR Public Information Section Country Profiles*, Hong Kong, May 1999 update, www.unhcr.ch/refworld/country/menus/asia.htm.

36 UNHCR, *The State of the World's Refugees 1995*, p. 208.

37 'KL forcibly repatriates Vietnamese boat people', *Jakarta Post* 3 May 1996, p. 6.

38 David Lamb, 'The "Leftovers" of the Vietnam War', *International Herald Tribune* 6–7 June 1998, p. 11.

39 For a country-by-country breakdown of refugees, asylum-seekers and internally displaced people in East Asia at the end of the 1990s, see USCR, *World Refugee Survey 2000*, www.refugees.org/world/countryrpt/easia_pacific/htm.

40 USCR, *World Refugee Survey 1995*, p. 94; UNHCR, *Public Information Section Country Profiles, Thailand*, May 1999 update, www.unhcr.ch/refworld/country/menus/asia.htm. The last remaining 47 000 Cambodian refugees were repatriated in March 1999: *UNHCR Global Report 1999: An Overview*, www.unhcr.ch/fdrs/gr99/toc.htm.

41 These figures were obtained from senior Thai officials and NGO representatives during private discussions in June 1999. See also Sufi Yusof, 'Thailand renews pledge to check entry of illegals', *New Straits Times* 6 June 1997; *Asian Defence Journal* July 1997, p. 48.

42 In February 1999 there were 19 000 Cambodian refugees in Thailand awaiting repatriation. They were the remnants of two separate refugee outflows. The first followed the ousting of Prince Norodom Sihanouk's FUNCINPEC Party from the government, in 1997, while the second accompanied the death throes of the Khmer Rouge in 1998: 'Refugee rush in aid race', *Australian* 17 February 1999, p. 9.

43 *Overseas Chinese Business Networks in Asia* (East Asia Analytical Unit, Australian Department of Foreign Affairs and Trade, Canberra, 1995), p. 1.

44 Astri Suhrke, 'The "High Politics" of Population Movements: Migration, State and Civil Society in Southeast Asia', in Myron Weiner (ed.), *International Migration and Security* (Westview, Boulder, Colo., 1993), pp. 179–80.

45 Ted Robert Gurr, 'People Against States: Ethnopolitical Conflict and the Changing World System', *International Studies Quarterly* 28(3) 1994, p. 350. See also Gareth Evans, 'Cooperative Security and Intra-State Conflict', *Foreign Policy* 96, Fall 1994; David Welsh, 'Domestic Politics and Ethnic Conflict', *Survival* 35(1) 1983, p. 63.

46 Ted Gurr argues that there is evidence of a strategic shift away from ethnic confrontation towards accommodation. According to Gurr, the number of ethnic groups using violent tactics fell from 115 to 95 during the 1990s but, more importantly, many more conflicts were 'de-escalating' rather than escalating. These figures must be treated with caution, however, as the review period is too short to extrapolate long-term trends and, as ethnic tensions in East Asia, Fiji and the Solomon Islands demonstrate, global trends do not necessarily reflect regional realities. For an elaboration of Gurr's thesis, see Ted Robert Gurr, 'Ethnic Warfare on the Wane', *Foreign Affairs* May–June 2000, pp. 52–64.

47 Gurr, 'People Against States ...', pp. 352–3 and data extracted from appendix.

48 For a good summary of Khmer Rouge attempts to inflame latent anti-Vietnamese sentiment among Cambodians, see Zachary Abuza, 'The Khmer Rouge and the Crisis of Vietnamese Settlers in Cambodia', *Contemporary Southeast Asia* 16(4) 1995, pp. 443–5.

49 FBIS, Daily Report East Asia (FBIS-EAS) 95-091, 11 May 1995. The ethnic hostilities between the Khmer and Vietnamese are of long standing. For a useful account of the origins of these historical antagonisms, see Milton Osborne, 'Kampuchea and Vietnam: A Historical Perspective', *Pacific Community* 9(3) 1978; David Chandler, *Cambodia before the French: Politics in a Tributary Kingdom, 1794–1848* (University of Michigan Press, 1973).

50 Kathleen Newland, 'Ethnic Conflict and Refugees', *Survival* 351(1) 1993, p. 87.

51 Syed Aziz-Al Ahsan, 'Burma's Iron Hands Towards Ethnic Minorities: The Rohingya Plight', *Asian Profile* 21(4) 1993, pp. 311–16.

52 The United Revolutionary National Front, a Uighur separatist movement, is based in Almaty, Kazakhstan: Andre Grabot, 'Ethnic Violence leaves 80 dead in China', *Age* 13 February 1997, p. A13.

53 About 7 million Uighurs live in Xinjiang province, making them the second largest of China's Muslim minorities. In 1950, the PLA crushed the short-lived East Turkestan Republic declared by Uighurs in Western Xinjiang: Matt Forney, 'Uighur Fire', *Far Eastern Economic Review* 27 February 1997, pp. 17, 20.

54 Lynne O'Donnell, 'China executes ethnic separatists', *Australian* 21 June 2000, p. 8.

55 Don Greenlees, 'Spectre of Vietnam over riot-torn nation', *Weekend Australian* 20–21 March 1999, p. 12.

56 The Madurese comprised less than 8 per cent of West Kalimantan's population of 3.5 million in 1997 compared with the Dayak who made up 40 percent: John McBeth and Margot Cohen, 'Murder and Mayhem', *Far Eastern Economic Review* 20 February 1997, p. 28.

57 Patrick Walters, 'Headhunting Dayaks bring ethnic cleansing to Indonesia', *Australian* 18 February 1997, p. 1; McBeth and Cohen, 'Murder and Mayhem', pp. 26–8.

58 'RI understands border closure', *Jakarta Post* 5 February 1997, p. 1.

59 'Resettlement plan an "insult" to Madurese', *Jakarta Post* 27 April 1999, p. 2.

60 John McBeth and Dini Djalal, 'Tragic Island', *Far Eastern Economic Review* 25 March 1999, pp. 28–30; Margot Cohen and Dan Murphy, 'Swept Away', *Far Eastern Economic Review* 8 April 1999, pp. 26–9.

61 Seth Mydans, 'Moluccas Violence Poses Serious Threat to Wahid', *International Herald Tribune* 29 June 2000, p. 1; 'RI rules out foreign troops for Maluku', *Jakarta Post* 18 July 2000, www.TheJakartaPost.com; Paul Dillon, 'Christians ready to flee Ambon', *Australian* 28 July 2000, p. 8; and John McBeth and Dan Murphy, 'Bloodbath', *Far Eastern Economic Review* 6 July 2000, pp. 20–2.

62 '353 Bugis migrants leave East Timor', *Jakarta Post* 27 February 1997, p. 1.

63 Patrick Walters, 'Bishops seek help for E. Timorese', *Australian* 28 September 1995, p. 8.

64 For example, the Philippine government's inability to control the activities of the Abu Sayyaf separatist group in southern Mindanao contributed to a well-publicised kidnapping of Western and Asian tourists from the nearby Malaysian resort island of Sipadan by Abu Sayyaf militants in mid-2000. Kuala Lumpur feared that a Philippines military strike against the Abu Sayyaf would cause thousands of refugees to cross the Sulu Sea to avoid the fighting and seek refuge in Sabah; which is already home to half a million Filipinos: Ian Stewart, 'Malaysia braces for IIs fleeing assault', *South China Morning Post* 18 September 2000, p. 9.

65 Stateless people and long-term refugee communities have proved fertile recruiting grounds for 'freedom fighters' and terrorist groups, which is why international refugee assistance is often seen as aiding groups that are intent on destabilising or overthrowing incumbent governments and regimes: Loescher, 'Refugee Movements and International Security', p. 5.

66 William Pfaff, 'Indonesia Should Not Be Allowed to Thwart the Will of the UN', *International Herald Tribune* 11–12 September 1999, p. 6.

67 Briefing by Sadako Ogata to the UN Security Council, 5 May 1999, www.unhcr.ch/refworld/unhcr/hcspeech/990505.htm; 'Yugoslavia opens door to Kosovo aid convoys', *Australian* 4 June 1999, p. 9.

68 Sam Kiley and Matthew Steven, 'Human Shield of Refugees', *Australian* 9 April 1999, p. 1. Kosovo Albanians exacted retribution on Serbs and gypsies when they returned to Kosovo at the end of the war. As many as 150 000 of Kosovo's 200 000 Serbs were driven out of Kosovo between June and August 1999, while more than 10 000 gypsies were displaced: Matt Spetalnik, 'Kosovo gypsies fleeing in third wave of refugees', *Canberra Times* 27 June 1999, p. 1; *Kosovo Crisis Update* 1 August 1999, www.unhcr.ch/news/media/kosovo.htm.

69 Mark Dodd, 'UN chief finds cache of illegal militia weapons', *Sydney Morning Herald* 18 June 1999, p. 7; John Zubrzycki, 'Food used as a poll sweetener', *Australian* 27 May 1999, p. 7; 'Resettlement plan an "insult" to Madurese', *Jakarta Post* 27 April 1999, p. 2.

70 Seth Mydans, 'What Do Militias Want?', *International Herald Tribune* 8 September 1999, p. 1; Michael Richardson, 'Peacekeeping Wrangle', *International Herald Tribune* 14 September 1999, p. 1; and *East Timor*, Interim Report of the Senate Foreign Affairs, Defence and Trade References Committee, Parliament of the Commonwealth of Australia, September 1999, pp. 11, 18.

71 Some 200 000 are estimated to have departed Vietnam by boat in 1979: Ronald Skeldon, 'International Migration Within and From the East and Southeast Asian Region: A Review Essay', *Asian and Pacific Migration Journal* 1(1) 1992, p. 50; Teitelbaum, 'Immigration, refugees, and foreign policy', p. 437.

72 Jacqueline Desbarats, 'Institutional and Policy Interactions among Countries and Refugee Flows', in Mary M. Kritz, Lin Lean Lim and Hania Zlotnik (eds), *International Migration Systems: A Global Approach* (Clarendon Press, Oxford, 1992), pp. 294–5.

73 Loescher, 'Refugee Movements and International Security', p. 33.

74 See *The Nation*, FBIS-EAS-95-094, 16 May 1995 and FBIS-EAS-95-099, 23 May 1995.

75 Bertil Lintner, 'Burning Ultimatum', *Far Eastern Economic Review* 13 February 1997; 'Karen rebels' HQ falls', *Weekend Australian* 15–16 February 1997, p. 15; Thomas Fox, 'Karen refugee exodus grows', *South China Morning Post* 26 February 1997, p. 14; Michael Vatikiotis, 'Border Burdens', *Far Eastern Economic Review* 6 March 1997, p. 34; 'US Condemns Thai Role in Karen repatriation', *Weekend Australian* 1–2 March 1997, p. 15; Map of Refugee Camps in Thailand, *UNHCR Environmental Database*, 31 March 1999, www.unhcr.ch/refworld/maps/pacific/thai_myan31mar99.htm.

76 Thailand and Vietnam have for centuries competed for strategic influence over Cambodia. See David Chandler, *Cambodia before the French*, p. 60.

77 William Shawcross, *The Quality of Mercy: Cambodia, to Holocaust and Modern Conscience* (Simon & Schuster, New York, 1984) provides a provocative analysis of the dynamics of this conflict.

78 Supang Chantavanich and Gary Risser, 'National Policy and Cross-Border Migration in the Asia-Pacific: Security and Social Implications', paper presented at the Ninth Asia-Pacific Roundtable, Kuala Lumpur, 5–8 June 1995, p. 3.

79 Anthony Davis, 'Burma casts a wary eye on China', *Jane's Intelligence Review* June 1999, p. 40.

80 Bertil Lintner, 'The Third Wave', *Far Eastern Economic Review* 24 June 1999, p. 28.

81 Cited in Paul Smith, 'The Strategic Implications of Chinese Emigration', *Survival* 36(2) 1994, p. 71.
82 Ian Stewart, 'Mahathir warns of migrant flood', *Australian* 7 May 1997, p. 10.
83 'Laos To Resettle One Third Of Its Population', *South China Morning Post* 9 July 1997, p. 5.
84 USCR, *World Refugee Survey 1995*, p. 87.
85 William E. Willmott, *The Chinese in Cambodia* (Publications Center, University of British Columbia, Vancouver, 1967), p. 100.
86 Lonergan, *Environmental Change and Regional Security in Southeast Asia*, p. 88.
87 François Ponchaud, *Cambodia, Year Zero* (Allen Lane, London, 1978), provides a moving account of the massive population displacements and suffering of the early years of the Khmer Rouge regime.
88 'N. Korea Relocating 2 Million People', *Associated Press* 4 February 1999.
89 On this point see David Welsh, 'Domestic Politics and Ethnic Conflict', *Survival* 35(1) 1983, p. 64; Rita Jalali and Seymour Martin Lipset, 'Racial and Ethnic Conflicts: A Global Perspective', *Political Science Quarterly* 107(4) 1992–93, p. 585.
90 Myron Weiner, 'Security, Stability and International Migration', p. 96. See also Judy A. Mayotte, *Disposable People? The Plight of Refugees* (Orbis Books, Maryknoll, New York, 1992), p. 7.

8 People-smuggling, Undocumented Labour Migration and Environmental Refugees

1 Writer, 'Refugees Become a Strategic Factor', p. 32.
2 Jonathan Power, 'Refugee numbers grow as world conflicts subside', *Jakarta Post* 16 January 1997, p. 5.
3 Gerald E. Dirks, 'International migration in the nineties: causes and consequences', *International Journal* 48, Spring 1993, p. 195.
4 There is a clear legal distinction between people-smuggling and human trafficking although in practical terms there is often little difference. In 1999, the Ad Hoc Committee on the Elaboration of a Convention against Transnational Crime defined trafficking in people as 'the recruitment, transportation, transfer, harbouring or receipt of persons, either by the threat or use of abduction, force, fraud, deception or coercion, or by the giving or receiving of unlawful payments or benefits to achieve the consent of a person having the control over another person'. The committee defined smuggling of migrants to mean: 'the intentional procurement for profit for illegal entry of a person into and/or illegal residence in a State of which the person is not a national or a permanent resident'. Unless otherwise specified, this is the definition of people-smuggling used in this book. For a more comprehensive discussion of these definitions, see John Morrison, *The Trafficking and Smuggling of Refugees: The end game in European asylum policy?*, pre-publication edition, July 2000, originally commissioned by the UNHCR's Policy Research Unit, Centre for Documentation and Research, www.unhcr.ch/evaluate/reports/traffick.pdf.
5 Tim Reid, Stewart Tendler, David Lister and Daniel McGrory, '58 die in lorry ride to hope', *The Times* 20 June 2000, www.times-archive.co.uk/news/pages/tim/2000/06/20/timnwsnws03029.html; and Flora Lewis, 'After Dover: People Ever Moving and Not Always Welcome', *International Herald Tribune* 22 June 2000, www.iht.com/IHT/TODAY/THU/ED/edflora.html. The death and apprehension of smuggled Chinese is becoming an all too frequent

occurrence elsewhere in the world. Three Chinese nationals died wedged inside shipping containers and thirty-four were arrested aboard two ships from Hong Kong that berthed in Seattle in January 2000. Fifty-four were arrested in Australia after they were found wandering around a small town on the northern coast of the Australian state of New South Wales in April 1999. Many of these Chinese, who arrived aboard an Indonesian crewed vessel, were dressed in suits and produced brand-new A\$50 and A\$100 notes when they tried to buy bread and milk from a local bakery: Mark Riley, 'Death ships ride on desperate tide', *Sydney Morning Herald* 13 January 2000, p. 9; Jennifer Sexton and John Stapleton, 'Fears some illegals slipped police net', *Australian* 12 April 1999, p. 2.

6 An admission by the head of Britain's immigration service to a joint parliamentary committee in the aftermath of the deaths of the Chinese illegal migrants. The British Government has deployed both its internal and external intelligence services (MI5 and MI6) in the fight against people-smugglers. 'The Last Frontier', *Economist* 26 June 2000, www.economist.com/editorial/freeforall/current/br5088.html.

7 Three hundred thousand 'unauthorised foreigners' are believed to enter the United States annually: James, 'EU Confronts Illegal Immigration', p. 8; 'The Last Frontier', *Economist* 26 June 2000, www.economist.com/editorial/freeforall/current/br5088.html.

8 These figures are based on estimates by the International Organisation of Migration, Europol and the British Home Office's Immigration and Nationality Directorate and are at the conservative end of the spectrum. 'The Last Frontier', *Economist* 26 June 2000, www.economist.com/editorial/freeforall/current/br5088.html; Sally Jackson, 'Army of misery conscripts 30m', *Australian* 8 July 1999, p. 3.

9 Bertil Lintner, 'World Wide Web: The Tangled Trail of Illicit Chinese Immigration', *Far Eastern Economic Review* 14 May 1998, p. 34.

10 Bertil Lintner, 'The Third Wave', *Far Eastern Economic Review* 24 June 1999, p. 29.

11 Smith, 'The Strategic Implications of Chinese Emigration', p. 69.

12 Access to international television programs has sensitised Chinese to the outside world and also conjured up an idealised image of life in the West.

13 Between 1987 and 1995, over half a million illegal Chinese migrants were transported by people-smugglers into the United States, while in East Asia, around 180 000 Chinese immigrants illegally entered Thailand, Hong Kong, Japan and Taiwan between 1992 and 1994: 'Dragons of Crime: Climbing the Golden Mountain', Australian Special Broadcasting Service documentary, 19 April 1996. Although Beijing does not publish official figures, one Chinese political leader admitted in 1994 that 700 000 Chinese had left the country illegally of whom 200 000 went to Asia, 200 000 to the United States, 150 000 to Russia and another 100 000 to Europe. See comments of Zhi Gong Dang, deputy secretary-general of the non-Communist political party Wu Haode, cited in Paul Smith (ed.), *Human Smuggling, Chinese Migrant Trafficking and the Challenge to America's Immigration Tradition*, Significant Issues Series, 19(2) (Center for Strategic and International Studies, Washington, D.C., 1997), p. x.

14 Jeff Wise, 'A New Breed', *Far Eastern Economic Review* 14 August 1997, p. 37. Seventy-four survivors from the *Golden Venture* were eventually returned to China, while others were resettled in Latin America. A further fifty-three were placed in the custody of the US Immigration and Naturalisation Service for

nearly four years: 'Golden Venture kingpin jailed', *South China Morning Post* 3 December 1998, p. 17.

15 Smith, 'The Strategic Implications of Chinese Emigration', pp. 65–6; Smith, *Human Smuggling*, pp. 1–3.

16 Lintner, 'World Wide Web', p. 34.

17 Onnucha Hutasingh, 'Studies show who benefits from alien workers here', *Bangkok Post* 25 May 1997, p. 2.

18 Approximately $3000 for carriage to Taiwan and up to $35 000 to the United States: Smith, 'The Strategic Implications of Chinese Emigration', p. 62.

19 *Thailand Times, FBIS-EAS-95-072*, 14 April 1995.

20 Harold Lierly, 'The Golden Triangle', paper presented at the Multinational Asian Organised Crime Conference, sponsored by the Australian Federal Police and the National Crime Authority, 1–3 November 1994, Sydney, pp. 3–4.

21 Official US estimates cited in Sheldon X. Zhang and Mark S. Gaylord, 'Bound for the Golden Mountain: The social organization of Chinese alien smuggling', *Crime, Law and Social Change* 25, 1996, p. 5.

22 Chu Yiu-kong, 'International Triad Movements: The Threat of Chinese Organised Crime', *International Triad Movements*, Research Institute for the Study of Conflict and Terrorism, July–August 1996, pp. 18–19.

23 Smith, 'The Strategic Implications of Chinese Emigration', p. 66.

24 Lynne O'Donnell and Sally Jackson, 'From the point of no return, to hell and back, for $20,000', *Australian* 19 May 1999, p. 4; Lintner, 'World Wide Web', p. 35.

25 Tom Buerkle, 'A Deadly Traffic in Humans', *International Herald Tribune* 21 June 2000, www.iht.com/IHT/TODAY/WED/FPAGE/dover.2.html.

26 'Organized Crime Moves Into Migrant Trafficking', *Trafficking In Migrants* 11, June 1996, www.iom.ch.

27 Smith, *Human Smuggling*, p. 8.

28 'Tokyo to Send Mission to China Over Illegal Migrants', Tokyo Kyodo in English, *FBIS-EAS-97-072*, 14 March 1997. In the four months prior to the mission's departure, 833 of the 894 illegals apprehended in Japan were from China: 'Tokyo Urges Beijing to Stop Illegal Migrants', Tokyo Kyodo in English, *FBIS-EAS-97-040*, 28 February 1997.

29 Fewer than a hundred were arrested in 1991. By the end of the decade around 1300 were being arrested every year, but the real number of illegal migrants from China was probably in the order of 7–10 000, since Japanese police estimate that only about 20 per cent are caught: Yoshiko Matsushita, 'Japan fights immigrant wave', *Asia Times* 25 April 1997, p. 5; 'Government Seeks China's Help To Reduce Smuggling', *Daily Yomiuri* 20 June, 1999, www.nautilus.org/napsnet/dr/index.html.

30 'Ethnic Koreans from PRC Attempt to Enter', Seoul KBS-1 Radio Network in Korean, *FBIS-EAS-96-139*, 13 July 1996; 'Migrant Route', *Australian* 18 February 1998, p. 10.

31 Raj Rajendran, 'Singapore steps up blitz on illegal workers', *Jakarta Post* 26 March 1998, p. 5.

32 'Final 1,810 RI workers homebound', *Jakarta Post* 10 November 1997, p. 1.

33 Chantavanich and Risser, 'National Policy and Cross-Border Migration in the Asia-Pacific', p. 3.

34 *World Population Monitoring 1997: International Migration and Development* (Department of Economic and Social Affairs, Population Division, United

Nations, New York, 1998), p. 138. According to unofficial estimates by Interpol, 2 million women from Eastern Europe alone may have been sold as 'white slaves' in the late 1990s: Sonya Yee, 'Two million women sold as sex slaves', *South China Morning Post* 17 June 1999, p. 12.

35	Gustavo Capdevila, 'Migrant workers powerless in face of rights violations', *Jakarta Post* 6 April 1996, p. 5.

36	According to the Thai Ministry of Foreign Affairs, in 1994 between 40 000 and 50 000 Thai women were working illegally in Japan. Cited in Chantavanich and Risser, 'National Policy and Cross-Border Migration in the Asia-Pacific', p. 4. See also Andrew Sherry, Matthew Lee and Michael Vatikiotis, 'For Lust or Money', *Far Eastern Economic Review* 14 December 1995, pp. 22–3.

37	Hutasingh, 'Studies show who benefits from alien workers here', p. 2.

38	Pasuk Phongpaichit, 'Trafficking in People in Thailand' *Transnational Organized Crime* 3, Winter 1997, p. 97.

39	*Human Development Report 1999*, Overview, www.undp.org/hdro/.

40	Based on statistics from the United Nations, US Bureau of the Census and the World Bank: Tony Clifton, 'Perish the Baby Girls', *Newsweek* 28 August 1995, p. 13.

41	Thousands of ethnic Chinese women from the poorer provinces of northern Vietnam have been smuggled into southern China since 1992: ibid., p. 14.

42	*World Population Monitoring 1997: International Migration and Development*, p. 139.

43	Maolo Abella, 'Asian Labour Migration: Past, Present, and Future', *ASEAN Economic Bulletin* 12(2) 1995, p. 125.

44	Author's estimate and Jon Greenaway, 'Expendable labour with no strings attached', *Canberra Times* 12 April 1998, p. 20. See also Philip Martin, 'Migrants on the Move in Asia', *Asia-Pacific Issues* No. 29 (East–West Centre, Honolulu, December 1996), p. 1. The comparable figures for Western Europe and the United States are of a similar order. In 1991, the International Labor Organisation calculated that there were about 2.6 million undocumented foreigners in Western Europe, while 4.6 million undocumented migrants were thought to be in the United States in 1996: *World Population Monitoring 1997: International Migration and Development*, p. 121.

45	Tarling, *The Cambridge History of Southeast Asia* vol.1, pp. 366–72.

46	Pasuk Phongpaichit, 'Trafficking in People in Thailand', p. 75.

47	Reginald T. Appleyard, *International Migration: Challenge For The Nineties* (International Organization for Migration, Geneva, 1991), p. 36; Dean T. Alegado, 'The Growth in International Migration and Trade in Services in Southeast Asia: Social and National Security Implications', paper presented at the 9th Asia-Pacific Roundtable, Kuala Lumpur, 5–8 June 1995, p. 3.

48	A useful summary of the economic literature on labour migration can be found in *World Population Monitoring 1997: International Migration and Development*, pp. 142–4.

49	Graeme Hugo, 'Labour Migration in Southeast Asia: The Impact (Political, Economic, Social, Security)', paper presented at the 11th Asia-Pacific Roundtable, Kuala Lumpur, 5–8 June 1997, pp. 1–2.

50	Conversely, as states develop, they become net recipients of foreign workers. Overseas remittances may then become a drain on revenue and lead to complaints about the sums of money sent out of the country by foreign workers: Kalinga Seneviratne, 'Booming Malaysia a magnet for migrants', *Jakarta Post* 22 February 1996, p. 5.

51 Remittances in 1990 were more than $70 billion while Overseas Develop-
   ment Assistance (ODA) was around $54 billion: World Bank Development
   Report 1995 cited in *World Population Monitoring 1997: International Migration
   and Development*, pp. 154–6. See also George Joffe, 'The Impact on Security of
   Demographic and Environmental Change', in G. A. S. C. Wilson (ed.), *British
   Security 2010*, proceedings of a conference held at Church House, Westminster, November 1995.
52 Hugo, 'Labour Migration in Southeast Asia', p. 13.
53 Penchan Charoensuthipan, 'Labour export target for next year set at
   210,000', *Bangkok Post* 14 April 1998, www.bangkokpost.com/today/140498_
   News04.html; 'Thai Prime Minister Views Problems of Overseas Workers',
   Nation (Thailand) 1 June 1996, p. A2; '2.5m Indonesians set to work abroad
   by 2000', *Jakarta Post* 27 July 1996, p. 2.
54 Philipp L. Martin, Andrew Mason and Ching-lung Tsay, 'Overview', *ASEAN
   Economic Bulletin* 12(2) 1995, p. 123; Loescher, 'Refugee Movements and
   International Security', p. 33.
55 Significant numbers of Vietnamese are working illegally in Cambodia: Chan-
   tanavich and Risser, 'National Policy and Cross-Border Migration', p. 7;
   Graeme Hugo, 'Labour Migration in Southeast Asia', paper presented at the
   11th Asia-Pacific Roundtable, Kuala Lumpur, 5–8 June 1997, pp. 1–2; Charles
   N. Myers, 'Labour migration in S-E Asia: analysis, cooperation needed',
   'Trends', *Business Times* (Singapore) 27–28 September 1997, p. IV.
56 *Saigon Times* 10 April 1996, p. 4.
57 Bruce Gilley, 'Irresistible Force: Migrant workers are part of a solution, not a
   problem', *Far Eastern Economic Review* 4 April 1996, p. 18.
58 Pang Eng Fong, 'Labour migration, economic development and regionalisa-
   tion in the Pacific Asian Region', in *Migration and Development: New Partnerships for Cooperation* (OECD, Paris, 1994), p. 251.
59 See UNHCR, *State of the World's Refugees 1993*, pp. 145–6.
60 Khadijah Muhamed, 'Malaysia's Migrant Labour and the Asian Crisis: What
   next?', *Asia-Pacific Magazine* 13, 13 December 1998, p. 25. Most illegals work
   in the manufacturing, plantation and construction sectors. Six hundred
   thousand were from Indonesia, while Bangladesh, India and China were also
   important sending countries. These figures do not include up to 500 000 illegal migrants who were legalised by a Malaysian government amnesty in 1995,
   and another 700 000 who took the opportunity to register in January 1997:
   'Malaysia deports illegal RI workers', *Jakarta Post* 4 January 1997, p. 2; Ridwin
   M. Sijabat, 'Malaysia needs more skilled workers from RI', *Jakarta Post* 18 May
   1995, p. 2; Firdaus Haji Abdullah, 'The Phenomenon of Illegal Immigrants',
   Indonesian Quarterly 21(2) 1993, p. 186.
61 Ignatius Stephen, 'Brunei On Alert As Sabah Targets Illegal Immigrants',
   Straits Times 6 April 1997, p. 9.
62 Martin, Mason and Tsay, 'Overview', p. 12.
63 Graziano Battistella, 'Philippine Overseas Labour: From Export to Management', *ASEAN Economic Bulletin* 12(2) 1995, p. 266.
64 This figure is based on discussion with officials from the Thai Ministry of
   Labour and Social Welfare and the National Security Council in June 1999.
   See also Hutasingh, 'Studies show who benefits from alien workers here', p. 2
   and 'Thailand: Illegal Labour – How to Stem the Flow', *Bangkok Post* 8 February 1997, p. 8. There are so many Burmese illegal workers in the coastal
   province of Ranong that they make up between one-fifth and one-third of the

local population: Tina Gill, 'Thai workers find it's their paychecks that are remitted by economic migrants', *World Paper* (in association with *Jakarta Post* 5 January 1997), p. 5; Hutasingh, 'Studies show who benefits from alien workers here', p. 2. Nearly a million Thais were employed overseas in 1997; 379 500 of them were registered to work in other parts of East Asia while an unknown number were working without permits, many of them in the entertainment trade. The majority of the 40 000 Thai illegals in Japan, for example, are women who are employed as prostitutes and night club workers: '40,000 Thais work illegally in Japan', *Jakarta Post* 4 February 1997, p. 11. Sixteen thousand Thais were repatriated from Singapore in 1989 for working without permits: Prasai, 'Intra-Asian Labor Migration – Redefining the Implications', p. 1062. Figures compiled for 1992 by the Thai Ministry of Labor show about 200 000 Thais working legally in East Asia: Chalongphob Sussangkarn, 'Labor Market Adjustments and Migration in Thailand', *ASEAN Economic Bulletin* 12(2) 1995, p. 249.

65 Private discussions with Cambodian government officials in June 1999.

66 In 1992, there were around 160 000 legal workers and 333 000 illegal migrants – a fourfold increase from 1987: Prasai, 'Intra-Asian Labor Migration', p. 1059.

67 The number of illegal labour migrants doubled between 1989 and 1995 from 50 000 to 100 000: Ching-lung Tsay, 'Taiwan', *ASEAN Economic Bulletin* 12(2) 1995, pp. 180–1.

68 According to the South Korean Ministry of Justice, in 1993 there were approximately 85 000 mainly Chinese and Filipino undocumented workers in South Korea and their numbers increased substantially before falling away briefly during the economic crisis: Young-bum Park, 'Korea', ibid., p. 165.

69 'Severe labour pains grip Asian countries', *New Straits Times* 28 August 1995, p. 14.

70 The majority are from Bangladesh but Malaysian government records show that workers from at least twenty-eight different countries have tried to enter Malaysia illegally: 'Malaysia: Armed Forces to Detain Illegal Immigrants', *Straits Times* 27 October 1996, p. 7.

71 'Malaysia moves to arrest illegal foreign workers', *Jakarta Post* 2 February 1997, p. 1.

72 'Malaysia Labour – Illegal Immigrants Sent Packing', *Economist Intelligence Unit* 8 February 1997. The fence created suspicions among the Thais that it was part of a Malaysian strategy to reinforce Kuala Lumpur's claims to the adjacent sea boundary that was thought to be rich in oil and natural gas: Michael Vatikiotis, 'Back Yard Bickering', *Far Eastern Economic Review* 7 March 1996, p. 22.

73 'Thailand: Labour – Drastic Measures to Push Back Illegals', *Bangkok Post* 6 February 1997, p. 3.

74 *Jakarta Post* 18 May 1995, p. 5.

75 Lincoln Kaye, 'Well-matched economies but competition looms', *Far Eastern Economic Review* 18 April 1985, p. 29.

76 Prasai, 'Intra-Asian Labor Migration', p. 1057.

77 'Malaysia deports illegal RI workers', *Jakarta Post* 4 January 1997, p. 2.

78 'Malaysia sends illegals packing', *Straits Times* 13 January 1997, p. 12.

79 Louise Williams, 'Deportation from Malaysia a double blow for many Indonesians', *Sydney Morning Herald* 31 March 1998, p. 8. Malaysia had established

detention camps well before the economic crisis. There were 7658 illegal Indonesian immigrants housed in eight detention camps throughout Malaysia in April 1996. A Malaysian NGO, Tenaganita, stated that many of these workers had been badly mistreated, a claim denied by the Malaysian Government. 'RI workers in Malaysia not abused: Activists', *Jakarta Post* 26 August 1995, p. 5. See also Abdullah, 'The Phenomenon of Illegal Immigrants', pp. 171–86.

80 Margot Cohen, 'Deport and Deter', *Far Eastern Economic Review* 23 April 1998, p. 16.
81 'Govt to bring illegals home', *Jakarta Post* 27 March 1998, p. 1.
82 'Trade ministry joins illegal migrant crackdown', *Straits Times* 11 January 1997, p. 10.
83 'Malaysia says illegal immigrants pose threat', *Jakarta Post* 16 March 1998, p. 1.
84 This analysis of the Contemplacion issue draws on Brenda Yeoh, 'Labour Migration in Southeast Asia: The Impact (Political, Economic, Social, Security)', paper presented at the 11th Asia-Pacific Roundtable, Kuala Lumpur, 5–8 June 1997, pp. 4, 13–14. See also Al Albita, 'Migrant Workers create domestic dilemma', *Australian* 18 August 1995, p. 17.
85 See, for example, Widgren, 'International migration and regional stability', p. 759; Jodi Jacobson, 'Environmental Refugees: A Yardstick of Habitability', World Watch Paper No. 86 (World Watch Institute, Washington D.C., 1988).
86 According to Norman Myers there were 25 million environmental refugees around the world in 1995 compared with 23 million 'traditional refugees': 'Global Population Growth', paper prepared for the Seminar on Global Security Beyond 2000 (University of Pittsburgh, 2 November 1995), pp. 17–18. The United Nations similarly calculates that there are 25 million 'water refugees' around the world compared with 22 million war refugees: 'Global water shortages', *Strategic Comments* 5(6) 1999, p. 1. See also Jacobson, *Environmental Refugees: A Yardstick of Habitability*, pp. 6, 38.
87 Essam El-Hinnawi, quoted in Lonergan, *Environmental Change and Regional Security in Southeast Asia*, p. 82.
88 ibid., p. 81.
89 *World Population Monitoring 1997: International Migration and Development*, ST/ESA/SER.A/169 (Department of Economic and Social Affairs Population Division, United Nations, New York, 1998), p. 149. See also the study conducted by thirty scholars under the Environmental Change and Acute Conflict Project, the results of which were published in Thomas F. Homer-Dixon, Jeffrey H. Boutwell and George W. Rathjens, 'Environmental Scarcity and Violent Conflict', *Scientific American* 268(2) 1993.
90 At the end of 1992, Africa accounted for only 10 per cent of the world's population but 29 per cent of its refugees: UNCHR, *State of the World's Refugees 1993*, p. 18. About 13.7 million Africans were refugees or internally displaced in 1999: Press Release, USCR, 13 June 2000, www.refugees.org/news/press_releases/2000/061300g.htm.
91 The Study found that 5000 square kilometres of land would be inundated in Thailand and Malaysia and 10 000 in Indonesia: Paul Handley, 'Before the flood', *Far Eastern Economic Review* 16 April 1992, p. 65.
92 'Cities in danger as warming raises sea levels', *Australian* 31 March 1995, p. 9.
93 Harvey Stockwin, 'Famine Struck Refugees Flee North Korea', *Jakarta Post* 13 February 1996, p. 4.
94 Dupont, 'Unregulated Population Flows in East Asia', pp. 15–16.

95 Estimates of the number of North Koreans in China range from 50 000 to 300 000: 'Life is Hard for DPRK People in Yenji', *Chosun Ilbo* 8 January 1999, www.nautilus.org/napsnet/dr/index.html; John Pomfret, 'Portrait of a Famine', *Washington Post* 12 February 1999, p. 1. The absence of reliable data and the constant movement of North Koreans back and forth over the mountainous border area makes it difficult to estimate precise numbers at any given time. A figure of 200 000 is most often mentioned by North Korean officials but NGOs and refugee reports suggest that the aggregate figure for 1998 was probably higher. See Andrew Natsios, 'The Politics of Famine in North Korea', *United States Institute of Peace Special Report*, Washington. D.C., 2 August 1999, p. 11.

96 Shim Jae Hoon, 'A Crack in The Wall', *Far Eastern Economic Review* 29 April, 1999, pp. 10–12.

97 ibid., p. 10.

98 'Politics Silences N. Korean Refugees' Plight', *Dow Jones Newservice* 20 October 1999.

99 Hungary's decision to allow East Germans to travel to the West without visas on 10 September 1989 led to a massive outflow of people from East Germany and signalled the end of the Honecker regime: 'Hole in the Iron Curtain: 3 Nations Mark Anniversary', *International Herald Tribune* 11–12 September 1999, p. 2.

100 UNHCR, *The State of the World's Refugees 1997–98: A Humanitarian Agenda*, www.unhcr.ch/refworld/pub/state/97/ch1.htm.

101 A point that US Ambassador Richard Holbrooke made during an open debate on the subject in the UN Security Council at the beginning of 2000. Holbrooke went on to assert that the distinction between refugees and internally displaced people ought to be 'eroded if not erased'. Defenders of the status quo, fearful that such a move could be used as a pretext for interference in their internal affairs, countered that erasing the distinction would be impossible because of complex legal and sovereignty issues: 'Who's a refugee?', *Straits Times* 16 January 2000, p. 12.

9 Transnational Crime

1 Martin van Creveld, quoted in Alice Hills, 'Criminality and Policing in Stability and Support Operations', *Military Review* 79(6) 1999, p. 18.

2 The principle of non-interference in the internal affairs of member states has long been enshrined in ASEAN's declaratory policy.

3 Transnational crime first gained recognition as an emerging threat to US national security in 1986 after the release of a presidential report. See Report by the President's Commission on Organized Crime, *America's Habit: Drug Abuse, Drug Trafficking and Organized Crime* (The White House, Washington, D.C., March 1986).

4 James Woolsey, 'Globalised Organized Crime: Threats to U.S. and International Security', in Linnea P. Raine and Frank J. Cilluffo, *Global Organized Crime: The New Empire of Evil* (Center for Strategic and International Studies, Washington, D.C., 1994), p. 137.

5 Cited in Roy Godson and William J. Olson, 'International Organized Crime', *Society*, January–February, 1995, p. 19. For a fuller exposition of Kerry's arguments see John Kerry, *The New War: The Web of Crime That Threatens America's Security* (Simon & Schuster, New York, 1997).

6 Mark Galeotti, 'Cross-Border Crime in the Former Soviet Union', *Boundary and Territory Briefing* 1(5) (International Boundaries Research Unit, Department of Geography, University of Durham, UK, 1995), p. 3; Robert S. Gelbard, 'US Policy to Combat International Narcotics Trafficking and International Crime', Statement before the House International Relations Committee, Washington, D.C., 31 October 1995, reprinted in *Strategic Digest* 26(3) 1996, p. 329. At the time, Robert Gelbard was the US Assistant Secretary of State for International Narcotics and Law Enforcement Affairs.

7 Samuel D. Porteous, 'The Threat from Transnational Crime: An Intelligence Perspective', *Commentary* 70, Winter 1996, p. 1.

8 Declaration of the Birmingham G-8 Summit, 16 May 1998.

9 See Alan Dupont, 'Transnational Crime, Drugs and Security in East Asia', *Asian Survey* 39(3) 1999, p. 433 and 'US anti-narcotics strategy: At war with reality?', *Strategic Comments* 6(2) 2000.

10 'US anti-narcotics strategy: At war with reality?'

11 The five-point proposal was enunciated by Clinton in a speech to a special session of the UN General Assembly on 22 October 1995 to mark the body's 50th anniversary: *Clinton Proposes New U.N. Agenda For The 21st Century*, EPF 103, 23 October 1995.

12 *International Crime Control Strategy* (The White House, Washington, D.C., May 1998), p. 4. This shift in US national security perceptions is clearly evident in Presidential Decision Directive 42 (PDD-42) of 21 October 1995.

13 Comments by Peter Grinenko, a former New York detective and expert on the Russian mafiya in Raine and Cilluffo, *Global Organized Crime*, p. 121.

14 Phil Williams, 'Transnational Organized Crime: Threat Assessment and Strategic Response', presentation to the 12th Asia-Pacific Roundtable, Kuala Lumpur, Malaysia, 31 May–4 June, 1998, pp. 5–6.

15 Carol Jones, 'Capitalism, Globalization and Rule of Law: An Alternative Trajectory of Legal Change in China', *Social and Legal Studies* 3, 1994, p. 201.

16 When police successfully disrupted the heroin flow from Turkey to Europe and the United States in the late 1980s, growers and distributors demonstrated their newfound agility by simply switching their efforts to Southeast Asia, South Asia and Mexico: Godson and Olson, 'International Organized Crime', p. 23.

17 Scott McDonald, 'The New 'Bad Guys': Exploring the Parameters of the Violent New World Order', in Max G. Manwaring (ed.), *Gray Area Phenomena: Confronting the New World Disorder* (Westview, Boulder, Colo., 1993), p. 36.

18 'International Crime', in *Strategic Assessment 1997: Flashpoints and Force Structure* (Institute for Strategic Studies, National Defense University, 1997), p. 201.

19 Bertil Lintner, 'Organised Crime: A Worldwide Web?', *Global Dialogue* Summer 1999, p. 117.

20 Sheldon X. Zhang and Mark S. Gaylord, 'Bound for the Golden Mountain: The social organization of Chinese alien smuggling', *Crime, Law and Social Change* 25, 1996, p. 11.

21 There were probably 12–15 major mafiya groups at the beginning of the decade: Mark Galeotti, 'Inside the Russian Mafiya', *Jane's Intelligence Review* March 2000, p. 80; Mark Galeotti, 'Russia's criminals go global', *Jane's Intelligence Review* March 2000, p. 10.

22 Yuriy A. Voronin, 'The Emerging Criminal State: Economic and Political Aspects of Organized Crime in Russia', *Transnational Organized Crime* Special Issue, 2(2–3) 1996, p. 52.

23 Arnaud de Borchgrave in Raine and Cilluffo, *Global Organized Crime*, p. 106; Lintner, 'Organised Crime: A Worldwide Web?', p. 116; 'Mafia uses Cold War end to threaten world economy', *Australian* 21 February 1995, p. 12.

24 These are 1999 estimates: Galeotti, 'Inside the Russian Mafiya', p. 8. See also Guy Dunn, 'Major Mafia Gangs in Russia', *Transnational Organized Crime* Special Issue, 2(2–3) 1996, p. 62.

25 Mark Galeotti, 'Russia's bleeding wounds', *Jane's Intelligence Review* November 1999, pp. 8–9.

26 David Hoffman, 'In Post-Soviet Russia, Law Enforcement Takes a Holiday', *International Herald Tribune* 10 September 1999, p. 2.

27 Galeotti, 'Inside the Russian Mafiya', p. 9.

28 Godson and Olson, 'International Organized Crime', p. 23. The power of the Medellin Cartel was effectively broken in December 1993 after the death of its leader, Pablo Escovar Gaviria. The successor Cali Cartel had ceased to exist as a single entity by 1995. However, most of their drug operations have been 'atomised' and taken over by smaller splinter groups or *cartelitos*. 'US anti-narcotics strategy: At war with reality?', *Strategic Comments* 6(2) 2000; Steve Salisbury, 'Millennium chaos for drug cartels', *Jane's Intelligence Review* December 1999, p. 46.

29 Jasjit Singh, 'Strategic Impact of Transnational Crime', in Carolina G. Hernandez and Gina R. Pattugalan (eds), *Transnational Crime and Regional Security in the Asia Pacific* (Council for Security Cooperation in the Asia-Pacific and the Institute for Strategic and Development Studies, Inc., Manila, 1999), p. 64.

30 Cited in Dupont, 'New Dimensions of Security', p. 40.

31 Thomas A. Constantine, 'International Organised Crime – Today's Primary Law Enforcement Challenge', *Police Chief* August 1997, p. 8.

32 According to the 2000 edition of *Forbes* magazine: 'Gates still the world's richest man, says "Forbes"', *Jakarta Post* 17 June 2000, p. 8.

33 Although these are only estimates they probably err on the conservative side. See the UN International Drug Control Program, *World Drug Report* (Oxford University Press, 1997), p. 31; *UN Human Development Report 1999*, Overview, www.undp. org./hdro/; Jessica T. Mathews, 'Power Shift', *Foreign Affairs* 76(1) 1997, pp. 57–8; Nigel Morris-Cotterill, 'Funking the Fight in War on Dirty Money', *The European* 25 April–1 May 1996, pp. 6–7; *The Military Balance 1999–2000* (Oxford University Press for the International Institute for Strategic Studies, London, October 1999), pp. 183–209.

34 On this theme, see Jim Rohwer, *Asia Rising: How History's Biggest Middle Class Will Change The World* (Butterworth-Heinemann Asia, Singapore, 1995).

35 Bruce Gilley and Shawn W. Crispin, 'A New Game of Cops and Robbers', *Far Eastern Economic Review* 20 April 2000, pp. 50–2.

36 Robert S. Leiken, 'Controlling the Global Corruption Epidemic', *Foreign Policy* 105, Winter 1996–97, p. 60.

37 Louis B. Freeh, *Speech at the 17th Annual International Asian Organized Crime Conference* (Boston, 3 June 1995), p. 1.

38 For a useful compilation of the cooperative measures adopted and instruments used in the regional fight against transnational crime see Captain Porfiro A. Calagan, 'Combating Transnational Crime: The Way Forward', paper presented at the 14th Asia-Pacific Roundtable, 3–7 June 2000, Kuala Lumpur, Malaysia, pp. 5–8.

39 Chairman's Statement, para 18, ARF 3, Jakarta, July 1996.

40 Report to the Australian CSCAP Meeting on the Working Group on Transnational Crime, Annex B, 5 February 1998. See also the reports on the estab-

lishment of the Transnational Crime Study Group and Working Group in the Australian CSCAP Newsletters nos 4 and 5 of March and October 1997 respectively.

41 See John McFarlane, *Containing Transnational Crime in the Asia-Pacific: Defining the Issues,* presentation to the 12th Asia-Pacific Roundtable, 31 May–4 June 1998, Kuala Lumpur, Malaysia, pp. 3–4.

42 Denis Engbarth, 'Crime wave fuels Taiwanese anger', *Weekend Australian* 10–11 May 1997, p. 18. China's crime wave is largely attributable to widespread official corruption, escalating unemployment, a dramatic rise in the number of itinerant workers and the widening gap between rich and poor.

43 Richard McGregor, 'Elite not spared in Beijing crime wave', *Australian* 7 February 1996, p. 13.

44 Suharto placed transnational crime on the national agenda during a 1996 speech marking the 50th anniversary of the Indonesian police: 'RI to build stronger police force', *Jakarta Post* 2 July 1996, p. 1 and editorial in *Jakarta Post* 3 July 1996. See also 'Organized crime syndicates here: Criminologist', *Jakarta Post* 27 December 1995, p. 3.

45 Two Citibank buildings and the Philippines headquarters of the Shell oil company were damaged when grenades were thrown into the buildings, injuring several people: 'Philippine govt pledges to curb rising crime', *Jakarta Post* 3 January 1996, p. 11; Florence Chong, 'Philippines achilles heel threatens its economic prosperity', *Australian* 20 February 1996, p. 63. Ramos's successor, President Estrada, faced impeachment proceedings in the Philippines Senate at the end of 2000 over allegations of corruption and involvement in illicit gaming.

46 Abu Sayyaf, which has an estimated 200 combatants, has specialised in high-profile kidnappings and extortion including, in one particular case, the abduction of twenty-one foreign tourists from the Malaysian resort island of Sipadan in April 2000: Anthony Davis, 'Philippines set for wider conflict', *Jane's Intelligence Review* June 2000, p. 3; 'Separatist rebellion in the southern Philippines', *Strategic Comments* 6(4) 2000.

47 Anthony Davis, 'Thailand tackles border security', *Jane's Intelligence Review* March 2000, p. 31.

48 ibid., pp. 30–1; Stefan Leader and David Wiencek, 'Drug money: the fuel for global terrorism', *Jane's Intelligence Review* February 2000, p. 53.

49 There were also doubts about the reliability of some of the reports, particularly those sourced to South Korea's intelligence agencies which have a vested interest in portraying the North as a criminal state.

50 Raphael Perl, *North Korean Drug Trafficking: Allegations and Issues for Congress,* CRS Report for Congress (US Congress, Washington, D.C., 8 February 1999), p. 5; Douglas Farah and Thomas W. Lippman, 'The North Korean Connection', *Washington Post* 26 March 1999, p. A21; discussions with Japanese police officials and Western intelligence analysts.

51 'NK Selling to Drug Rings', *Chosun Ilbo* 11 April 1999, www.nautilus.org/napsnet/dr/index.html citing a document published by South Korea's National Intelligence Service.

52 Perl, *North Korean Drug Trafficking,* p. 5.

53 Robert Harnischmacher, 'Chinese Triads and Japanese Yakuza – How Dangerous is the Asian Mafia?', *Australian Police Journal* June 1996, p. 88.

54 Much of the Western literature about the triads before the 1990s subscribes to this historical explanation, drawing on the writings of W. P. Morgan, in particular his 1960 thesis, *Triad Societies in Hong Kong* (Hong Kong Government

Printer, Hong Kong, 1960). However, Dian Murray argues that the Shaolin monastery probably did not exist. See Dian H. Murray in collaboration with Qin Baoqi, *The Origins of the Tiandihui: The Chinese Triads in Legend and History* (Stanford University Press, 1994). Other Western accounts of the triads include Fenton Bresler, *The Trail of the Triads* (Weidenfeld & Nicolson, London, 1980); Gerald Posner, *Warlords of Crime* (McGraw Hill, New York, 1988); James Dubro, *Dragons of Crime* (Butterworth, Markham, Ontario, 1992); Martin Booth, *The Dragon Syndicates: The Global Phenomenon of the Triads* (Doubleday-Transworld, London, forthcoming).

55 Chu Yiu-kong, 'International Triad Movements: The Threat of Chinese Organised Crime', *International Triad Movements*, Research Institute for the Study of Conflict and Terrorism, July–August 1996, p. 2.

56 Both Sun Yat-sen, the founding father of the Kuomintang, and his successor, Chiang Kai-shek, were initially triad members: Lintner, *Organised Crime: A Worldwide Web?*, p. 120.

57 Mark Craig, 'Chinese Underworld', *Australian* 11 December 1998, p. 34.

58 Wu Han, 'Comparison of China's Group Crime to the West's Organized Crime', in Ann Lodl and Zhang Longguan (eds), *Enterprise Crime: Asian and Global Perspectives* (Office of International Criminal Justice with Shanghai Bureau of Justice and East China Institute of Politics and Law, University of Illinois, Chicago, 1992), p. 107.

59 Wu Han, 'Comparison of China's Group Crime to the West's Organized Crime', p. 107.

60 These figures are based on a leaked 1998 Hong Kong anti-corruption commission report: Stephen Vines, 'Triads enjoy increasing political protection', *Canberra Times* 23 March 1998, p. 1.

61 Mike Chinoy, 'Crime gangs fight Macau turf war', *CNN Interactive*, 16 May 1997, www.cnn.com.

62 Cited in Chu Yiu-kong, 'The Triad threat to Europe', *Policing* 10(3) 1994, p. 205.

63 ibid.

64 *Hong Kong Standard* 9 April 1993, p. 5.

65 ibid.

66 'Dragons of Crime: Climbing the Golden Mountain', SBS Documentary, *The Cutting Edge*, 19 April 1996.

67 Chu Yiu-kong, 'The Triad threat to Europe', p. 207.

68 David Hodson, 'Chinese Criminal Groups: Criminal Implications for the Asia/Pacific Region Including Reversion of Sovereignty of Hong Kong to China in 1997', paper presented at the Multinational Asian Organised Crime Conference, sponsored by the Australian Federal Police and the National Crime Authority, Sydney, 1–3 November 1994, p. 4. This assessment is supported among others by Harry Blud, a former chief superintendent of the Hong Kong Police. See Tom Mintier, 'Hong Kong gangs may not thrive under Beijing rule', *CNN Interactive* 28 June 1997, www.cnn.com.

69 For example, according to Hong Kong police intelligence reports two prominent members of the Chinese-appointed legislature are triad members or have close ties to them: Vines, 'Triads enjoy increasing political protection', p. 1.

70 The major Macau triads at the time of the island's handover to China were the 14K, Shui Fong, Wo Shing Yee, Dai Huen Jai and the Sun Yee On. The Wo Shing Yee may have been forced out of business and the 14K suffered a setback when its leader, Wan Kuok-koi ('Broken Tooth Koi'), was arrested and sentenced to fifteen years' gaol by the Chinese authorities. He was mainly

responsible for the gang warfare of the late 1990s: Bertil Lintner, 'Macau: Triad war, Triad peace', *Jane's Intelligence Review* March 2000, pp. 26–9.

71 Cathy Hilborn, 'Making a Killing', *Far Eastern Economic Review* 12 March 1998, pp. 26–9.

72 Wang Yong, 'Ho committed to Macao's security, attack on crime', *China Daily (Business Weekly)* 12–18 September 1999, p. 1. See also 'Mean Macau Streets', *Asiaweek* 4 June 1999, www.pathfinder.com/asiaweek/99/0604/ed3.html; Peter Lim, 'Macau's new leader vows to target crime', 16 May 1999, p. 4.

73 'Executions clear way for Macau handover', *Australian* 25 November 1999, p. 7; Lintner, 'Macau: Triad war, Triad peace', p. 26.

74 Allen T. Cheng, 'Taiwan's Dirty Business', *Asia Inc.* April 1997, pp. 19–20.

75 Xu Qing Zhang, 'Enterprise Crime and Public Order', in Lodl and Zhang Longguan, *Enterprise Crime*, p. 16.

76 Julian Baum, 'Perilous Politics', *Far Eastern Economic Review* 1 May 1997, p. 18.

77 Allen T. Cheng, 'Taiwan's Dirty Business', *Asia, Inc.* April 1997, p. 20.

78 'Taiwan general held on graft charges', *Singapore Times* 29 April 1998, p. 17.

79 Cheng, 'Taiwan's Dirty Business', pp. 18 and 23.

80 Ian Dobinson, 'Pinning a Tail on the Dragon: The Chinese and the International Heroin Trade', *Crime and Delinquency* 39(3) 1993, p. 374.

81 Chu Yiu-kong, 'International Triad Movements: The Threat of Chinese Organised Crime', p. 3. For other estimates of Triad membership see Brian Sullivan, 'International Organized Crime: A Growing National Security Threat', Strategic Forum, No. 74, Institute for National Strategic Studies, May 1996, p. 3; Harnischmacher, 'Chinese Triads and Japanese Yakuza', p. 89.

82 Zhang and Gaylord, 'Bound for the Golden Mountain', p. 4.

83 Chu Yiu-kong, 'International Triad Movements', pp. 4–5.

84 Godson and Olson, 'International Organized Crime', p. 27; Zhang and Gaylord, 'Bound for the Golden Mountain', p. 4.

85 Chu Yiu-kong, 'International Triad Movements', p. 4.

86 Stephen E. Flynn, 'Asian Drugs, Crime, and Control: Rethinking the war'. In James Shinn (ed.), *Fires Across the Water: Transnational problems in Asia*, Council on Foreign Relations, New York, 1998, p. 26.

87 Vietnamese gangs have been particularly active in the United States since the end of the Vietnam War in 1975, but they are not as powerful or as organised as the triads. See Paul Coffey, 'Current and Future Trends in Vietnamese Crime: A US Perspective', paper presented at the Multinational Asian Organised Crime Conference, sponsored by the Australian Federal Police and the National Crime Authority, Sydney, 1–3 November 1994, pp. 8, 16.

88 John McFarlane, 'Transnational Crime as a Security Issue', in Hernandez and Pattugalan, *Transnational Crime and Regional Security in the Asia-Pacific*, pp. 50–1; Flynn, 'Asian Drugs, Crime, and Control', p. 26; Faith Keenan, 'Hanoi's new scourge: Growing heroin trade reaches high level of government', *Far Eastern Economic Review* 6 February 1997, p. 26.

89 Harnischmacher, 'Chinese Triads and Japanese Yakuza', p. 90.

90 Bakuto was an organisation of gamblers, labour contractors and lower-class criminal elements whose main activity was gambling: Masayuki Tamura, 'The Yakuza and Amphetamine Abuse in Japan', in Harold H. Traver and Mark S. Gaylord (eds), *Drugs, Law and the State* (Transaction, New Brunswick, 1992), p. 100.

91 ibid.

92 Harnischmacher, 'Chinese Triads and Japanese Yakuza', p. 90.

93 Shoichiro Ishikawa, 'The Criminal Characteristics of the Yakuza', paper presented at the Multinational Asian Organised Crime Conference, sponsored by the Australian Federal Police and the National Crime Authority, 1–3 November 1994, Sydney, p. 2.

94 Flynn, 'Asian Drugs, Crime, and Control', p. 24.

95 Godson and Olson, 'International Organized Crime', p. 28.

96 Brian Bremner, 'Yakuza and the banks', *Australian Financial Review* 26 January 1996.

97 Michael Hirsh, 'Tokyo's Dirty Secret: Banks and the Mob', *Bulletin* 19 December 1995, pp. 60–1.

98 Harnischmacher, 'Chinese Triads and Japanese Yakuza', p. 91.

99 See for example the revelations of the yakuza involvement in Japanese politics in David E. Kaplan and Alec Dubro, *Yakuza* (Addison-Wesley Publishing Company, Inc., Reading, Mass., 1986), pp. 119–23, 282.

100 Sullivan, 'International Organized Crime', p. 3.

101 Flynn, 'Asian Drugs, Crime, and Control', p. 24.

102 Nicholas D. Kristof, 'Chinese Outcompete Locals in Tokyo's Sex District', *International Herald Tribune* 18 June 1999, p. 4.

103 'International Crime', in *Strategic Assessment 1997: Flashpoints and Force Structure* (Institute for Strategic Studies, National Defense University, 1997), p. 199.

104 Phil Williams and C. Florez, 'Transnational criminal organizations and drug trafficking', *Bulletin on Narcotics* 46(2) 1994, p. 12.

105 Zhang and Gaylord, 'Bound for the Golden Mountain', p. 4.

10 Drug-trafficking – An Emerging Threat

1 Rensselaer W. Lee III and Scott B. McDonald, 'Drugs in the East', *Foreign Policy* 105, Winter 1996–97, p. 89.

2 Stefan Leader and David Wiencek, 'Drug money: the fuel for global terrorism', *Jane's Intelligence Review* February 2000, p. 49.

3 Giacomelli's foreword in UN International Drug Control Program, *World Drug Report* (Oxford University Press, 1997), p. 7.

4 The classic account of the Golden Triangle's drug politics is Bertil Lintner's *Burma in Revolt: Opium and Insurgency Since 1948* (Westview, Boulder, Colo., 1994).

5 At the 6th Steering Committee meeting of CSCAP a decision was taken in Canberra on 10 December 1996, to establish a Study Group on Transnational Crime to consider the security implications for the region of transnational crime, including drug-trafficking. The Study Group was elevated to the status of a full Working Group in December 1997.

6 China, of course, has a long history of opium addiction but opium-smoking was proscribed by the Chinese Communist Party after 1949.

7 The trade in illicit drugs has traditionally focused on cannabis, cocaine and heroin but is increasingly shifting to synthetic stimulants often grouped as ATS. ATS can be subdivided into two subgroups – amphetamines and ecstasy (MDMA), which are closely related but have slightly different pharmacological effects. Ecstasy is not a pure stimulant and is sometimes classed as a euphoric drug having both stimulant and hallucinogenic effects: *Australian Illicit Drug Report 1996–97* (Australian Bureau of Criminal Intelligence, Canberra, December 1997), p. 51; *World Drug Report*, p. 39.

8   *World Drug Report*, p. 31.

9   ibid.

10 'New Trends in the international drugs trade: The rise of synthetic ampheta-mines', *Strategic Comments* 4(7) 1998.

11 'US anti-narcotics strategy: At war with reality?'; Tamara Makarenko, 'Crime and terrorism in Central Asia', *Jane's Intelligence Review* July 2000, p. 16.

12 'Transnational Crime: A New Security Threat', *Strategic Survey 1994–1995* (Oxford University Press for the IISS, London, 1995), pp. 29–30.

13 Rensselaer W. Lee III, 'Global Reach: The Threat of International Drug Traf-ficking', *Current History*, May 1995, p. 208; *Strategic Assessment 1997: Flashpoints and Force Structure* (Institute for Strategic Studies, National Defense Univer-sity, 1997), p. 202.

14 *UN General Assembly Special Session on the World Drug Problem*, New York, 8–10 June, 1998, www.un.org/ga/20special/presskit/pubinfo/info2.htm.

15 Salisbury, 'Millennium chaos for drug cartels', p. 46.

16 Even President Samper, who was defeated in the 1998 election, seems to have been on the payroll of the Medellin cartel: 'Cocaine Cops', *The Cutting Edge*, SBS documentary shown on Australian television, 27 February 1999.

17 Drug money is used to pay the FARC's soldiers and to finance its operations. In exchange the rebels protect the cartel's coca and opium plantations. The result is that FARC and the smaller National Liberation Army have extended their control over 40 per cent of the country, while cocaine production has risen steadily: Bryan Bender, '2 Fronts, 1 War', *Jane's Defence Weekly* 27 January 1999, pp. 25–7.

18 In 1996, the arms trade was valued at US39.9 billion: *The Military Balance* (Oxford University Press for the IISS, London, 1997–98), p. 264.

19 *UN General Assembly Special Session on the World Drug Problem*, New York, 8–10 June, 1998, www.un.org/ga/20special/presskit/pubinfo/info2.htm; *World Drug Report*, pp. 18, 24–8. In 1999 there were 89 500 hectares under opium cultivation in Burma, down 31 per cent from the previous year. The SPDC's attempts to eradicate some areas of poppy cultivation may have contributed to the fall: *International Narcotics Control Strategy Report, 1999* (Bureau for Inter-national Narcotics and Law Enforcement Affairs, US Department of State, Washington, D.C., March 2000), www.state.gov/www/global/narcotics_law/1999_narc_report/policy99.html.

20 *International Narcotics Control Strategy Report, 1999.*

21 'Burmese Opium Aplenty', *Far Eastern Economic Review* 27 July 2000, p. 12.

22 Edward, J. Kelly, 'Cooperative Efforts in Combating Drug Trafficking', in Lodl and Zhang Longguan, *Enterprise Crime: Asian and Global Perspectives*, p. 151.

23 Bertil Lintner, 'The Dream Merchants', *Far Eastern Economic Review* 16 April 1998, p. 27.

24 Barbara Remberg, 'Stimulant Abuse: From amphetamine to ecstasy', in *World Drug Report*, pp. 39–43.

25 In that year seizures reached 14.6 tonnes: *UN General Assembly Special Session on the World Drug Problem*, www.un.org/ga/20special/presskit/pubinfo/info2.html.

26 *International Narcotics Control Strategy Report, 1997* (Bureau for International Narcotics and Law Enforcement Affairs, US Department of State, Washing-ton, D.C., March 1998), www.state.gov/www/global/narcotics_law/1997_narc_report/index.html. The President is required by US law to identify and

notify those countries which he has determined are major illicit drug producers and/or transit countries. Burma was one of four states singled out in 1998 as not doing enough to eradicate drug-trafficking.

27 The BCP split into four main groups. The largest was the UWSA, which numbered about 8000–10 000 armed men at the time of the break-up. The others were the Myanmar National Democratic Alliance Army (MNDAA), more commonly known as the Eastern Shan State Army (ESSA); the National Democratic Alliance Army (NMAA); and the New Democratic Army (NDA): Bertil Lintner, 'The Drug Trade in Southeast Asia', *Jane's Intelligence Review*, Special Report No. 5, April 1995, pp. 6–7.

28 In 1988, before the BCP's fragmentation, Burma produced 1280 tonnes of opium. By 1996, opium production had more than doubled to 2560 tonnes out of the 4000 tonnes produced globally – enough to make 250 tonnes of refined heroin: 'No end to Burma heroin flow', *Australian* 11 June 1997, p. 7; Stephen Brookes, 'SLORC fired up over drug issue', *Asia Times* 31 January 1997, p. 2.

29 Senior Thai military officers believe that the first secretary of the SPDC, Lieutenant General Khin Nyunt, has close links to the Wa and treats the UWSA as his own private army: Rodney Tasker and Shawn W. Crispin, 'Flash Point', *Far Eastern Economic Review* 1 June 2000, p. 25.

30 'No end to Burma heroin flow', *Australian* 11 June 1997, p. 7.

31 Khun Sa's Chinese name is Chang Qifu: Bertil Lintner, 'Drug Asian Crisis', *Asia-Pacific Magazine* 13, December 1998, p. 5.

32 Micool Brooke, '"Drug Invasion" Fuels Thai Force Modernisation Programme', *Asian Defence Journal* May 2000, p. 10. The Burmese Army is not allowed to enter the territory of the UWSA without permission from the Wa: Burma section, *International Narcotics Control Strategy Report, 1999*, www.state.gov/www/global/narcotics_law/1999_narc_report/policy99.htm. Burmese troops stationed along Thailand's border were instructed to 'live off the land' in mid-2000, a command interpreted by Thai intelligence officials as giving permission to become involved in the drug trade: 'Burmese Troops "Live Off The Land"', *Far Eastern Economic Review* 18 May 2000, p. 10.

33 Bruce Hawke, 'Burma's military implicated', *Pointer* October 1998, p. 10. Many heroin refineries are located close to Burmese Army garrisons, and families with known drug connections have been provided with official security passes and are involved in joint ventures with the government: William Barnes, 'Junta in league with drug barons', *South China Morning Post* 3 October 1998, p. 9. See also Desmond Ball, 'Burma and Drugs: The Regime's Complicity in the Global Drug Trade', Strategic and Defence Studies Centre Working Paper No. 335 (Strategic and Defence Studies Centre, Research School of Pacific and Asian Studies, Australian National University, Canberra, 1999), pp. 1–14, which documents the military regime's involvement in drug-trafficking.

34 Shi Huanzhang, 'China's Approach to Drug Offences', in Lodl and Zhang Longguan, *Enterprise Crime: Asian and Global Perspectives*, p. 69.

35 Yuan Yougen, 'Shanghai's Transient Crime and Its Countermeasures', in ibid., p. 45.

36 Shi Huanzhang, 'China's Approach to Drug Offences', in ibid., p. 71.

37 Thomas Fuller and Dan Eaton, 'Even the heroin trade has been affected by globalization', *Asia Times* 27 May 1997, p. 1.

38 *Narcotics Control in China* (Information Office of the State Council of the People's Republic of China, Beijing, 2000), p. 1.

39	China section, *International Narcotics Control Strategy Report, 1999*, www.state. gov/www/global/narcotics_law/1999_narc_report/policy99.html.

40	Several of these laboratories were located and seized by the Philippines police in 1999: The Philippines section, ibid.

41	Cecilia Quiambao, 'Dirty Harry vs RP drug dealers', *Jakarta Post* 28 July 1997, p. 4. West African groups are increasingly involved in the transshipment of heroin through the Philippines to the United States.

42	'RP senator warns of narco-state', *Jakarta Post* 11 August 1997, p. 6.

43	An allegation which was made by an admitted drug-trafficker and has not been substantiated: Rigoberto Tiglao, 'Explosive Mix', *Far Eastern Economic Review* 14 August 1997, p. 16.

44	Joe Cochrane, 'Thai drug lords get hooks into Cambodia', *Australian* 20 October 1999, p. 13.

45	Among the 34 charged with drug-related offences, twelve were police officers and four were members of the border police tasked with responsibility for guarding Vietnam's northwestern border with Laos. They included the police captain in charge of the Lai Chau border crossing, the head of the Interior Ministry's Economic Investigation Section, and the deputy head of the Ministry's Anti-Narcotics Bureau: Andy Soloman, 'Drugs scandal puts Vietnam on trial', *Asia Times* 11 April 1997, p. 1.

46	The public security officials were sentenced to death: Vietnam section, *International Narcotics Control Strategy Report, 1999*, www.state.gov/www/global/ narcotics_law/1999_narc_report/policy99.html.

47	'Police captain nabbed for involvement in drug syndicates', *Jakarta Post* 14 June 1997, p. 5; Cecilia Quiambao, 'Dirty Harry vs RP drug dealers', *Jakarta Post* 28 July 1997, p. 4.

48	Robert Scalapino, *Asia: The Past Fifty Years And The Next Fifty Years*, Commemorative Address on the Silver Anniversary of the Centre for Strategic and International Studies, Jakarta, 18 September 1996, p. 7.

49	Members of the Chiu Chao gang control much of the heroin transshipped through Bangkok, while the 14K triad dominates the heroin trade between Hong Kong and the Netherlands: Phil Williams and C. Florez, 'Transnational criminal organizations and drug trafficking', *Bulletin on Narcotics* 46(2) 1994, p. 16.

50	'Slump accelerates speed trade', *Sydney Morning Herald* 2 December 1997, p. 11.

51	Lintner, 'The Dream Merchants', p. 26.

52	Craig Skehan, 'Drug dealers recruit foreign chemists', *Sydney Morning Herald* 27 February 1998, p. 13.

53	James Mills, *The Underground Empire* (Doubleday, New York, 1986), p. 3.

54	Phil Williams, 'Transnational Criminal Organizations: Strategic Alliances', *Washington Quarterly* 18(10) 1995, p. 67.

55	Thomas Fuller and Dan Eaton, 'Even the heroin trade has been affected by globalization', *Asia Times* 27 May 1997, p. 1.

56	Richard Shaffer, 'The International Characteristics of AOC Groups which Distinguish them from Other Criminal Groups', paper presented at the Multinational Asian Organised Crime Conference, p. 10.

57	Zainuddin Bin Abdul Bahari, 'Non Conventional Threats to Security in the Region – Narcotics', paper presented at the 8th Asia-Pacific Roundtable, ISIS Malaysia, Kuala Lumpur, 5–8 June 1994, p. 2.

58	David Hodson, 'Drug Trafficking and Abuse in Hong Kong: A Situation Report', in Lodl and Zhang Longguan, p. 90. See also Ian Dobinson,

'Pinning a Tail on the Dragon: The Chinese and the International Heroin Trade', *Crime and Delinquency* 39(3) 1993, p. 375.

59 Burma section in *International Narcotics Control Strategy Report, 1997*, www.state.gov/www/global/narcotics_law/1997_narc_report/index.html.

60 Lintner, 'The Dream Merchants', p. 27.

61 William Simpson, 'Worldwide Networking is the most important factor in containing narcotic supply in the Asian Pacific region', paper presented at the 10th Asia Pacific Roundtable, Kuala Lumpur, 5–8 June 1996, p. 12.

62 Peter Chalk, 'The Golden Triangle And Heroin: A Growing Challenge', *CAN-CAPS Bulletin* 14, August 1997, p. 7.

63 Cambodian police arrested a Buddhist monk from the Langka pagoda in Phnom Penh, when he was found with 5 kilograms of heroin which he intended to smuggle out of the country: 'Buddhist holy man busted', *Australian* 13 February 1998, p. 10.

64 Cochrane, 'Thai drug lords get hooks into Cambodia', p. 13.

65 The first documented case of Burmese heroin turning up in Laos occurred in August, 1991: Lintner, 'The Drug Trade in Southeast Asia', pp. 17–18. See also Simpson, 'Worldwide Networking is the most important factor in containing narcotic supply in the Asian Pacific region', p. 11.

66 'Vietnam, Laos meet to plug illegal drug flow', *Nation* (Thailand) 16 June 1999, p. 2.

67 Singapore section in *International Narcotics Control Strategy Report, 1997*, www.state.gov/www/global/narcotics_law/1997_narc_report/index .html.

68 Yaman Mohamed Ismail Mohamed, 'Supply and trade in narcotics: checking sources and distribution – the Malaysian experience', paper presented at the 9th Asia Pacific Roundtable, Kuala Lumpur, 5–8 June 1995, pp. 4, 14.

69 Lynne O'Donnell, 'Drugs trail from poppy soup to Australian addicts', *Australian* 5 May 1999, p. 8.

70 Indonesia section, *International Narcotics Control Strategy Report, 1999*, Bureau for International Narcotics and Law Enforcement Affairs, US Department of State, Washington, D.C., March 2000, www.state.gov/www/global/narcotics_law/1999_narc_report/policy99.html.

71 'Ecstasy abuse "a global epidemic"', *Jakarta Post* 27 June 1997, p. 16; 'Illicit drugs trade worth $400b a year', *Jakarta Post* 26 June 1997, p. 16.

72 These estimates are cited in the Burma and Thailand sections of the *International Narcotics Control Strategy Report, 1997*, www.state.gov/www/global/narcotics_law/1997_narc_report/index.html. If other drugs are added, such as opium, marijuana and stimulants, the number of Thai addicts rises to 1.27 million.

73 Thomas Fuller and Dan Eaton, 'Even the heroin trade has been affected by globalization', *Asia Times* 27 May 1997, p. 1; Yaman, 'Supply and trade in narcotics: checking sources and distribution – the Malaysian experience', p. 2; Andy Soloman, 'Drugs scandal puts Vietnam on trial', *Asia Times* 11 April 1997, p. 1. These figures almost certainly understate the true dimensions of drug addiction in the region. In Malaysia, for example, some experts believe that the level of drug addiction is four to five times the official figure. 'Ten Deadly Years of Dadah: why Kuala Lumpur hasn't won the war on narcotics', *Asiaweek* 8 June 1994, p. 29.

74 Andy Soloman, 'Drugs scandal puts Vietnam on trial', *Asia Times* 11 April 1997, p. 1; Vietnam section, *International Narcotics Control Strategy Report, 1999* (Bureau for International Narcotics and Law Enforcement Affairs, US Department of State, Washington, D.C., March 2000), www.state.gov/ www/global/narcotics_law/1999_narc_report/policy99.html.

75 Vietnam section in *International Narcotics Control Strategy Report, 1997*, www.state.gov/www/global/narcotics_law/1997_narc_report/index.html.

76 More than 79 per cent were under the age of 35: *Narcotics Control in China*, p. 2. See also Yang Chunya, 'Anti-drug education called for', *China Daily* 6 June 1998, p. 2.

77 In 1999, Japanese police made record seizures of methamphetamines, surpassing the total of the previous five years. Most of it is sourced to China but some has been linked to North Korea. There are over 2 million methamphetamine users in Japan: Japan section, *International Narcotics Control Strategy Report, 1999* (Bureau for International Narcotics and Law Enforcement Affairs, US Department of State, Washington, D.C., March 2000), www.state. gov/www/global/narcotics_law/1999_narc_report/policy99.html.

78 'New Trends in the international drugs trade: The rise of synthetic amphetamines', p. 1.

79 Thailand section, *International Narcotics Control Strategy Report, 1999*, www. state.gov/www/global/narcotics_law/1999_narc_report/policy99.html.

80 The Thai Development Research Institute estimated in 1998 that there were 257 000 methamphetamine-users in Thailand compared with 214 000 heroin-users: Lintner, 'Drug Asian Crisis', pp. 3–4. See also Lintner, 'Speed Demons', p. 28.

81 This was the Bangkok street price in 2000. These same tablets cost only 8 cents to produce, making the traffickers a handsome 800–900 per cent profit: Anthony Davis, 'Thailand tackles border security', *Jane's Intelligence Review* March 2000, p. 31.

82 Ampa Santimatanedol, 'Amphetamines claim more teenagers', *Bangkok Post* 4 August 1998, www.bangkokpost.com; 'Jurin: San Ma Ket crossing to remain shut despite pressure', *Bangkok Post* 10 August 1999, www.bangkokpost.com; Rodney Tasker and Shawn W. Crispin, 'Flash Point', *Far Eastern Economic Review* 1 June 2000, p. 24; Gretchen Peters, 'Bangkok hardens stance on junta', *South China Morning Post* 2 July 2000, p. 7; Rodney Tasker and Bertil Lintner, 'Danger: Road Works Ahead', *Far Eastern Economic Review* 21 December 2000, p. 26.

83 Jason Sherman, 'Thai, U.S. Leaders Join To Battle Drug Trade', *Defense News* 16 October 2000, p. 24; 'Thailand–Myanmar tensions: Bangkok loses patience', *Strategic Comments* 6(9) 2000, p. 2.

84 Lintner, 'Speed Demons', p. 28.

85 Piyanart Srivalo, 'Most amphetamine addicts are youths, study reveals', *Nation* (Thailand) 14 June 1999, p. A3.

86 Craig Skehan, 'Drug dealers recruit foreign chemists', *Sydney Morning Herald* 27 February 1998, p. 13; *Australian Illicit Drug Report 1996–97*, p. 54.

87 *Australian Illicit Drug Report 1996–97*, p. 54.

88 China section in *International Narcotics Control Strategy Report, 1999*, www.state.gov/www/global/narcotics_law/1999_narc_report/policy99.html.

89 'Drug networks fan out to Central, E. Java', *Indonesian Observer* 16 October 1999, p. 4.

90 'Military denies rampant drug use among members', *Jakarta Post* 19 November 1999, www.thejakartapost.com and discussions with Australian intelligence officials. See also Indonesia section, *International Narcotics Control Strategy Report, 1999*, www.state.gov/www/global/narcotics_law/1999_narc_report/policy99.html.

91 Estimated at 4400 tons in 1999: 'The Fergana Valley: A magnet for conflict in Central Asia', *Strategic Comments* 6(6) 2000.

92 Ahmad Rashid, 'Taliban Temptation', *Far Eastern Economic Review* 11 March 1999, p. 21; 'Heart of Darkness', *Far Eastern Economic Review* 5 August 1999, pp. 8–11.

93 Why Burma would want to do this is not clear, but the reemergence of historical antipathies and Burmese suspicion that Thailand is supporting the Karen and other anti-government insurgent groups are likely factors: Brooke, '"Drug Invasion" Fuels Thai Force Modernisation Programme', p. 10.

94 Shawn W. Crispin, Santi Suk and Bertil Lintner, 'Drug Tide Strains Ties, *Far Eastern Economic Review* 9 September 1999, p. 26.

95 Julian Gearing and Ban Huai San, 'Thailand's Battle For Its Soul', *Asiaweek* 10 August 1999, www.pathfinder.com/asiaweek/current/issue/nat9.html.

96 'Thailand–Myanmar tensions: Bangkok loses patience', p. 2.

97 Tasker and Crispin, 'Flash Point', *Far Eastern Economic Review*, p. 26.

98 Gearing and Ban Huai San, 'Thailand's Battle For Its Soul', www.pathfinder.com/asiaweek/current/issue/nat9.html.

99 Crispin, Suk and Lintner, 'Drug Tide Strains Ties', p. 27. There is some evidence that Thailand is running clandestine operations into Burma aimed at disrupting UWSA narcotics-trafficking: Crispin, 'Flash Point', *Far Eastern Economic Review*, p. 25.

100 Brooke, '"Drug Invasion" Fuels Thai Force Modernisation Programme', p. 11.

101 Lintner, 'The Drug Trade in Southeast Asia', p. 21.

102 'NK Diplomat Arrested for Opium Deal', *Chosun Ilbo* 13 February 1999, www.nautilus.org/napsnet/dr/index.html.

103 Raphael Perl, *North Korean Drug Trafficking: Allegations and Issues for Congress*, CRS Report for Congress (US Congress, Washington, D.C., 8 February 1999), p. 4.

104 'Interpol: Korean Diplomats Smuggled Cocaine', *Reuters* 18 February 1998.

105 Kim Song-Yong, 'North Korean Threats of Opium Smuggling and Terrorism Are Increasing', *Chosun Ilbo* 16 September 1996, p. 5.

106 Galeotti, 'Cross-Border Crime and the Former Soviet Union', p. 15.

107 Perl, 'North Korean Drug Trafficking', p. 5. Japanese police discovered 60 kilograms of methamphetamine in jars of honey aboard a North Korean freighter in 1997. See also Leader and Wiencek, 'Drug money: the fuel for global terrorism', p. 54. North Korea is strongly suspected of complicity in the shipment of 600 kilograms of methamphetamines seized by Japan in October 1999: North Korea section, *International Narcotics Control Strategy Report, 1999*, www.state.gov/www/global/narcotics_law/1999_narc_report/policy99.html.

108 Jooan Kang, 'NK Becomes One of the Largest Narcotics Producers', *Joongang Ilbo* 7 May 1999; Bang Seong-su, 'NK Suspected Philopon Seized', *Chosun Ilbo* 10 May 1999, www.nautilus.org/napsnet/dr/index.html.

109 'Illegal Drugs Confiscated in Kochi Prefecture Found to be of DPRK Product', *Yomiuri Shimbun* 7 January 1999, www.nautilus.org/napsnet/dr/index.html.

110 The North Korean diplomat was attempting to smuggle 500 000 tablets of rohypnol when arrested by Egyptian police: North Korea section, *Interna-*

tional Narcotics Control Strategy Report, 1999, www.state.gov/www/global/narcotics_law/1999_narc_ report/policy99.html.

111 As evidenced by the convening, at Japan's instigation, of the first ever official Japan–China dialogue on drugs held during former Japanese Home Minister Mitsuhiro Uesugi's visit to Beijing in May 1998: 'Government Seeks China's Help to Reduce Smuggling', *Daily Yomiuri* 20 June 1999, napsnet://www.nautilus.org/napsnet/dr/index.html.

11 The AIDS 'Pandemic'

1 More than 95 per cent of all HIV infected people are in the developing world: *AIDS epidemic update: December 1998*, UNAIDS Joint United Nations Program on HIV/AIDS, www.unaids.org.

2 Needle-sharing among heroin users is common. If one user has been infected with HIV, then the disease spreads rapidly among IDUs, many of whom work in the sex industry. They, in turn, facilitate HIV's transmission to their customers through unprotected sex.

3 An epidemic is defined as an outbreak of a disease that infects many individuals in a population, and can be difficult or impossible to contain. A pandemic is an epidemic that occurs in many regions of the world: 'Emerging and Re-emerging Infectious Diseases', *UN Chronicle* 1, 1999, p. 11.

4 *Report on the Global Aids Epidemic-Update-June 2000*, UNAIDS, www.unaids.org/epidemic_update/index.html

5 In 1998, 200 000 people died from war and internal conflict but AIDS accounted for 2.2 million, ten times that number: UNAIDS Statement to the UN Security Council, 10 January 2000, www.un.org/News/dh/latest/piotaids.htm.

6 Mieko Nishimizu, 'Time for Asians to Wake Up to the AIDS Menace', *International Herald Tribune* 26 October 1999, www.iht.com.

7 The Asian victims were mainly from India, China, Bangladesh, Pakistan, Indonesia and the Philippines. Cambodia and Thailand also have a significant TB problem: Peter Alford, 'Age-old killer rises again to stalk Asia', *Australian* 24 November 1998, p. 10.

8 Justine Ferrari, 'AIDS epicentre moving from Africa to Asia', *Australian* 19 September 1995, p. 7.

9 There are different variants of HIV-1 which are classified into distinct genetic subtypes, numbered from A to O. B is most common in the West, and E in Southeast Asia: 'An ounce of prevention ...', *Economist* 3 July 1999, www.economist.com/editorial/freeforall/current/st4573.html.

10 *World Drug Report*, pp. 88–9.

11 Denis Pirages, 'Microsecurity: Disease Organisms and Human Well-Being', *Washington Quarterly* 18(4) 1995, p. 8.

12 *AIDS epidemic update: December 1998*, www.unaids.org.

13 People whose immune systems are weakened by AIDS become more susceptible to other microbes including the tuberculosis bacillus. Approximately 30 per cent of all AIDS deaths are from tuberculosis: ibid.

14 Brian Halweil, 'HIV/AIDS Pandemic Decimates', excerpted from Linda Starke (ed.), *Vital Signs 1999* (W. W. Norton & Co., New York and London, 1999), p. 102, www.worldwatch.org.

15 Ann Hwang, 'AIDS Has Arrived in India and China', January–February 2001, www.worldwatch.org.

16 According to Lester Brown and Brian Halweil. In Zimbabwe, life expectancy has fallen from 60 years in 1990 to 44 in 1999. It is projected to fall to 39 by 2010. See *Worldwatch News Brief*, 'HIV Epidemic Slowing Population Growth', released on 28 September 1999, www.worldwatch.org/alerts/990928.html.

17 'AIDS Orphans to Increase Five-Fold by 2010', *The State of World Population 1998*, Box 5, p. 18.

18 For a revealing insight into the reluctance of medical authorities and national security officials in the West to recognise the full import of AIDS, see Barton Gellman, 'West Refused to Heed Early Warnings of Pandemic', *International Herald Tribune* 6 July 2000, pp. 1–2.

19 Cameron Forbes, 'US alarm at spread of AIDS', *Australian* 2 May 2000, p. 11.

20 Cited in Roxanne Bazergan, 'HIV/AIDS and the military', *Conflict, Security & Development Group Bulletin* 7, August–September 2000, p. 2.

21 Chris Beyrer quoted in Bertil Lintner, 'Condoms or Landmines', *Far Eastern Economic Review* 9 April 1998, p. 50.

22 Norman Davies, *Europe: A History* (Oxford University Press, Oxford and New York, 1996), pp. 409–12, 777. See also the *Encyclopaedia Britannica*, vols 3 and 12 (William Benton, Chicago, 1968), pp. 742 and 242 respectively.

23 Author's estimate of the number of deaths from AIDS at the end of 2000 extrapolating from UN statistics.

24 Alan Whiteside and David FitzSimons, 'The AIDS Epidemic: Economic, Political and Security Implications', *Conflict Studies* 251, May 1992, p. 1.

25 UN Development Program, *Human Development Report 1994* (Oxford University Press, Oxford, 1994), p. 28.

26 Nishimizu, 'Time for Asians to Wake Up to the AIDS Menace', www.iht.com.

27 Chris Beyrer, *War in the Blood: Sex, politics and AIDS in Southeast Asia* (White Lotus, Bangkok, 1998), p. 150. See also 'The Status and Trends of the Global HIV/AIDS Pandemic Final Report', *Report on the global HIV/AIDS epidemic, June 1998*, the Joint United Nations Program on HIV/AIDS and the World Health Organisation, reservoir.fhi.org/aids/aidscap/aidspubs/special/statustrends/vanpan.html.

28 Harold Lierly, 'The Golden Triangle', paper presented at the Multinational Asian Organised Crime Conference, sponsored by the Australian Federal Police and the National Crime Authority, 1–3 November 1994, Sydney, p. 4.

29 'The Status and Trends of the Global HIV/AIDS Pandemic Final Report', *Report on the global HIV/AIDS epidemic, June 1998*, reservoir.fhi.org/aids/aidscap/aidspubs/special/statustrends/vanpan.html.

30 Forty-five per cent of Dutch peacekeepers in Cambodia during the run-up to the UN supervised elections in 1992 were found to have sexual contact with sex workers or other local members of the population during a five-month tour of duty. UNAIDS figures cited in Bazergan, 'HIV/AIDS and the military', p. 4.

31 ibid., p. 2.

32 Jack Chow, 'Health and International Security', *Washington Quarterly* 19(2) 1996, p. 65.

33 This assessment was made to the US Senate Select Committee on Intelligence in 1995 by the head of the US Defense Intelligence Agency, Lieutenant General James Clapper: Karen Lowe, 'AIDS poses a threat to armies', *Jakarta Post* 11 May 1995, p. 5.

34 Not only are they young, sometimes no more than 15, but they are also generally poorly educated and away from their homes and families for the first time, making them more susceptible to the attractions of casual sex.

35 Lowe, 'AIDS poses a threat to armies', p. 5.
36 Helmoed-Romer Heitman, 'AIDS: a time bomb of security issues', *Jane's Intelligence Review* November 1997, p. 12.
37 Halweil, 'HIV/AIDS Pandemic Decimates', p. 102.
38 According to Gilles Poumerol, regional adviser in sexually transmitted diseases and AIDS for the WHO in the Western Pacific: Johanna Son, 'AIDS plateaus in Thailand, but dangerous hotspots remain', *Jakarta Post* 10 April 1997, p. 5. See also 'The Status and Trends of the Global HIV/AIDS Pandemic Final Report', *Report on the global HIV/AIDS epidemic, June 1998*, reservoir.fhi.org/aids/aidscap/aidspubs/special/statustrends/vanpan.html.
39 '278,000 infected with HIV in E.Asia, Pacific: WHO', *Jakarta Post* 18 November 1996, p. 6.
40 Beyrer, *War in the Blood*, p. 28. This means that over one in sixty Thais is HIV-positive but only about 5 per cent of those with AIDS can afford drug therapy: 'Cheap Aids drugs "must be for all"', *South China Morning Post* 13 May 2000, p. 13.
41 In 1991, over 10 per cent of new recruits from this area were HIV-infected compared with 2 per cent of draftees from Bangkok. In the November 1993 draft, 1001 out of 28 787 Thai conscripts tested HIV-positive: Jonathan Ken Stier, 'Marching Orders: Infection rate among Thai army recruits is rising', *Far Eastern Economic Review* 29 July 1993, p. 46; Beyrer, *War in the Blood*, p. 20.
42 Johanna Son, 'AIDS plateaus in Thailand, but dangerous hotspots remain', *Jakarta Post* 10 April 1997, p. 5.
43 In 1999, the percentage of recruits in northern Thailand who tested HIV-positive was less than 3 per cent compared with 12.5 per cent in 1993 because of an effective public education program and a vigorous condom-use campaign: Chris Beyrer, 'AIDS In Asia and America: Is the War Being Won or Lost?', paper presented to 14th Asia-Pacific Roundtable, Kuala Lumpur, 3–7 June 2000, p. 4.
44 Frank Ching, 'Thai Army Winning Aids Battle', *Far Eastern Economic Review* 30 April 1998, p. 36.
45 Charles Bickers, 'Asia Sets Its Sights On an Aids Breakthrough', *Far Eastern Economic Review* 7 December 2000, p. 38.
46 'Aids rate rising fast', *Bangkok Post* 30 September 1998, p. 5; Huw Watkins, 'Flower of Cambodia's people cut down in another killing field', *Australian* 2 March 1998, p. 7; 'AIDS Cambodia's new killing field', *Weekend Australian* 28 February–1 March, 1998, p. 11.
47 The estimate of 500 000 infections by 2006 is probably conservative and may be as high as 1 million: 'Anti-AIDS campaign struggling in Asia', *Jakarta Post* 2 December 1997, p. 7.
48 *The Military Balance 1999–2000*, p. 185; 'UN warns Asia-Pacific of AIDS cost blow-out', *Australian* 27 October 1997, p. 6.
49 Son, 'AIDS plateaus in Thailand, but dangerous hotspots remain', p. 5.
50 Katya Robinson, 'Few Cambodians fully understand consequences of AIDS', *Jakarta Post* 12 March 1997, p. 7.
51 Joe Cochrane, 'Forces not armed to fight deadliest enemy', *Australian* 31 March 1999, p. 8.
52 A 1995 survey of military personnel in Koh Kong province found that 30 per cent were HIV-positive, as were over 10 per cent of the police: Leo Dobbs, 'AIDS looms large over Cambodian military, police', *Reuters* 10 May 1995.
53 Cochrane, 'Forces not armed to fight deadliest enemy', p. 8.
54 Dobbs, 'AIDS looms large over Cambodian military, police'.

55 John Dempsey, 'Burma's New Nightlife', *Far Eastern Economic Review* 13 January 2000, p. 58.

56 Bertil and Hseng Noung Lintner, 'Blind in Rangoon', *Far Eastern Economic Review* 1 August 1996, p. 21.

57 These figures are for 1997: 'Epidemiological Fact Sheet on HIV/AIDS and sexually transmitted diseases – Myanmar', *Report on the global HIV/AIDS epidemic, June 1998*, www.us.unaids.org/highband/document/epidemio/June98/global_report/data/globrep_e.pdf.

58 Author's estimates, extrapolating from UNAIDS preliminary data available in mid 2000.

59 Beyrer, *AIDS In Asia and America*, p. 3.

60 Nancy Hudson-Rodd, 'Sex, Drugs and Border Patrol', *Asia-Pacific Magazine* 13, December 1998, p. 10. The booming night club scene in Rangoon and the city's reputation as Southeast Asia's newest sex-tourist destination is likely to accelerate infection rates. See John Dempsey, 'Burma's New Nightlife', *Far Eastern Economic Review* 13 January 2000, pp. 56–8.

61 David I. Steinberg, 'AIDS in Burma: A Growing Disaster', 30 September 2000, *International Herald Tribune*, www.iht.com/IHT/TODAY/SAT/ED/edstein.html. Tests of military recruits in Rangoon and Mandalay in 1996 showed an infection rate of 0.9 per cent. 'Epidemiological Fact Sheet on HIV/AIDS and sexually transmitted diseases – Myanmar', *Report on the global HIV/AIDS epidemic, June 1998*, http://www.us.unaids.org/highband/document/epidemio/June98/global_report/data/globrep_e.pdf.

62 Lynne O'Donnell, 'A million at risk but China ignores AIDS', *Australian* 2 December 1999, p. 9.

63 'Country's first AIDS clinic to open', *South China Morning Post* 27 November 1996, p. 1; Bickers, 'Asia Sets Its Sights On an Aids Breakthrough', p. 38.

64 'Confirmed cases of HIV', *Far Eastern Economic Review* 19 November 1998, p. 17. See also 'Epidemiological Fact Sheet on HIV/AIDS and sexually transmitted diseases – China', *Report on the global HIV/AIDS epidemic, June 1998*, www.us.unaids.org/highband/document/epidemio/June98/global_report/data/globrep_e.pdf.

65 The government has decreed that by 2002, 40 per cent of rural residents and 70 per cent of urban dwellers should have some knowledge of AIDS prevention: Ma Guihua, 'Battle against Aids moves to rural schools', *South China Morning Post* 2 July 2000, p. 9.

66 'China's new focus on AIDS hailed', *Jakarta Post* 8 May 1996, p. 1. See also 'UN warns Beijing to move on AIDS', *Australian* 12 January 1998, p. 1.

67 Cited in Hwang, 'AIDS Has Arrived in India and China'. See also 'Millions of lonely migrant workers feed AIDS fears', *Australian* 29 October 1997, p. 9.

68 Gordon Fairclough, 'A Gathering Storm', *Far Eastern Economic Review* 21 September 1999, p. 27; Son, 'AIDS plateaus in Thailand, but dangerous hotspots remain', p. 5; Information Office of the State Council of the People's Republic of China, *Narcotics Control in China*, p. 2.

69 He Aifang, 'Revealing the "Blood Wound" of the spread of HIV AIDS in Henan Province', 28 November 2000, www.usembassy-china.org.cn/english/sandt/henan-hiv.htm.

70 Beyrer, *War in the Blood*, p. 98.

71 'Epidemiological Fact Sheet on HIV/AIDS and sexually transmitted diseases – Vietnam', *Report on the global HIV/AIDS epidemic, June 1998*, www.us.unaids.org/highband/document/epidemio/June98/global_report/data/globrep_e.pdf; *Australian* 16 April 1998, p. 6.

72 Steve Dow, 'Asian governments "in denial" on HIV', *Indonesia Daily News Online*, www.uni-stuttgart.de/indonesia/news/95/9725/Monday/1.html.

73 Although AIDS was first detected in April 1995, official figures recorded only 218 HIV-positive people. But Minister of Health Sujudi conceded that for every reported case there were probably a hundred unreported. The true number of people with HIV was probably around 300 000 in 1996: 'Condoms alone will not stop AIDS, minister says', *Jakarta Post* 21 April 1995, p. 3.

74 For example, the Ministry of Health admitted to only 769 cases of HIV and 274 with AIDS in 1999 compared with the UNAIDS estimate of 52 000 HIV/AIDS cases: 'HIV/AIDS cases reach 200 in 1999', *Jakarta Post* 5 January 2000, www.thejakartapost.com. *Report on the Global AIDS Epidemic-Update-June 2000*, UNAIDS, www.unaids.org/epidemic_update/index.html.

75 *Projection of HIV/AIDS in Indonesia 1990–2005*, Working Group on AIDS Control, National AIDS Commission 1994, pp. 6–9.

76 'Indonesia and Vietnam said to face AIDS epidemic', *Jakarta Post* 10 October 1996, p. 2. AIDS is not confined to big cities like Jakarta and Surabaya but is also present in outlying provinces. For example, Irian Jaya, which is adjacent to AIDS-racked Papua New Guinea, has a significant and growing rate of HIV infection probably introduced by itinerant workers from PNG and foreign fishermen: Patrick Walters, 'Indonesia AIDS toll vast: new estimates', *Australian* 30 October 1996, p. 7.

77 Sixty-eight thousand compared with 52 000: 'Epidemiological Fact Sheet on HIV/AIDS and sexually transmitted diseases – Malaysia and Indonesia', *Report on the global HIV/AIDS epidemic, June 1998*, www.us.unaids.org/highband/document/epidemio/June98/global_report/data/globrep_e.pdf.

78 This charge has been levelled by Asian as well as Western critics. Former Thai Prime Minister Anand Panyarachun castigated his fellow leaders for 'not taking AIDS seriously enough' at a 1995 conference on AIDS: 'Asia at edge of AIDS abyss', *Canberra Times* 24 September 1995, p. 7.

79 Lintner, 'Condoms or Landmines', p. 51.

80 Cited in Tim Brown and Peter Xenos, 'Aids in Asia: The Gathering Storm', *East–West Asia-Pacific* 16, August 1994, p. 11.

81 Dennis Altman, 'AIDS and Questions of Global Governance', *Pacifica Review* 11(2) 1999, p. 198.

82 Dupont, 'Transnational Crime, Drugs and Security in East Asia', p. 435.

83 Jonathan Friedland, 'AIDS: The Coming Holocaust', *Far Eastern Economic Review* 18 August 1994, p. 16. See also the comments of WHO Regional Director Han Sang Tae in '278,000 infected with HIV in E. Asia, Pacific: WHO', *Jakarta Post* 18 November 1996, p. 3.

84 Brown and Xenos, 'Aids in Asia', p. 6; 'AIDS threatens Thai life expectancy', *Weekend Australian* 23–24 September 1995, p. 15.

85 Supang Chantavanich and Gary Risser, 'National Policy and Cross-Border Migration in the Asia-Pacific: Security and Social Implications', paper delivered to the Ninth Asia-Pacific Roundtable, Kuala Lumpur, 5–8 June, 1995, p. 10.

86 Compared with 6 per cent in the UK and 25 per cent in France: *World Drug Report*, Figure 3.3, p. 93.

87 William Barnes, 'HIV exploding on heroin routes', *South China Morning Post* 3 October 1998, p. 9.

88 Chantavanich and Risser, 'National Policy and Cross-Border Migration in the Asia-Pacific', p. 4.

89 Michael Vatikiotis, Sachiko Sakamaki and Gary Silverman, 'On the Margin: Organized crime profits from the flesh trade', *Far Eastern Economic Review* 14 December 1995, p. 26.

90 The author's own estimates extrapolating from UN and WHO data.

91 Whiteside and FitzSimons, 'The AIDS Epidemic', p. 11.

92 Anti-HIV drug cocktails typically cost between $10 000 and $15 000 a year, well outside the means of most sufferers in non-Western countries. Even if the drugs are dramatically reduced in price they may still be beyond the reach of the poor. For details of the agreement reached by the five pharmaceutical companies see 'Africa to get low-cost AIDS drugs', *Hong Kong Standard* 12 May 2000, p. 4.

93 Lawrence Goldyn, 'The Western Way of Fighting AIDS Will Not Work in Africa', *International Herald Tribune* 8–9 July 2000, p. 6.

94 Martha Ainsworth, 'AIDS, Development, and the East Asian Crisis', Plenary Address to the 5th International Conference on AIDS in Asia and the Pacific, 25 October 1999, Kuala Lumpur, Malaysia, p. 3, www.iaen.org/impact/ainspch.pdf.

95 'AIDS endangers Asian economy, warns banker', *South China Morning Post* 3 August 1994, p. 1.

96 'UN warns Asia-Pacific of AIDS cost blow-out', *Australian* 27 October 1997, p. 6.

97 Jonathan Friedland, 'AIDS: The Coming Holocaust', *Far Eastern Economic Review* 18 August 1994, pp. 15–16; Robert Black, Sara Collins and Don Boroughs, 'AIDS', *Sunday Herald-Sun* 23 August 1992, p. 12. Former Thai Prime Minister Anand Panyarachun predicted that the total cost to the Thai economy could be 'around 20 per cent of Thailand's GDP by 2000'. Anand made these comments at the closing session of the Third International Conference on AIDS in Asia and the Pacific held at Chiang Mai in Thailand: 'Asia at edge of AIDS abyss', *Canberra Times* 24 September 1995, p. 7. Some question the accuracy of these estimates. See, for example, Fairclough, 'A Gathering Storm', p. 26.

98 Fairclough, 'A Gathering Storm', p. 27.

99 Rob Moodie and Edith Fry, *HIV-AIDS – a global overview with emphasis on Asia and the Pacific*, draft paper prepared for the Australian Agency for International Development's (AusAID) Advisory Group on Health, 22 November 2000, pp. 9–10.

100 Cited in Hwang, 'AIDS Has Arrived in India and China'. There were 10.4 million fatalities from armed conflict in East Asia during this period. 'The 1999 Chart of Armed Conflict', *The Military Balance 1999–2000*.

Conclusion

1 On this point see Emma Rothschild, 'What Is Human Security?', *Program on Peace and International Cooperation* 3, Fall 1996, p. 4; 'What is Security?', *Daedalus* 124(3) 1995, p. 55.

2 Jeffrey W. Legro and Andrew Moravcsik, 'Is Anybody Still a Realist?', *International Security* 24(2) 1999, p. 6.

3 Kenneth N. Waltz, *Man, The State, And War: A Theoretical Analysis* (Columbia University Press, New York, 1959), p. 6.

4 P. J. Simmons, 'Learning to Live with NGOs', *Foreign Policy* 112, Fall 1998, p. 84. A useful compilation of some of the largest and most influential NGOs can be found on pp. 95–6.
5 Burma's narco-insurgents, for example, command significant military power as well as considerable wealth, patronage and political influence.
6 Matthew and Shambaugh, 'Sex, Drugs and Heavy Metal', p. 164.
7 Fidel Ramos speaking at the annual conference of the International Institute for Strategic Studies in Manila, the Philippines, on 17 September 2000.
8 Richard K. Betts, 'Should Strategic Studies Survive?' *World Politics* 50, October 1997, pp. 8–9.
9 Jack Levy, 'The Causes of War: A Review of Theories and Evidence', in Philip E. Tetlock et al. (eds), *Behavior, Society, and Nuclear War*, vol. 1 (Oxford University Press, 1989), p. 210.
10 Karen A. Tellis, 'Review Essay', *Transnational Organized Crime* 1(1) 1995, p. 107.
11 Norman Myers quoted in Bright, 'Environmental Surprises: Planning for the Unexpected', *Futurist* July–August 2000, p. 43.
12 See Robert Mandel's comments in Shultz, Godson and Greenwood (eds), *Security Studies for the* 1990s, p. 347.
13 Homer-Dixon, 'On the Threshold: Environmental Changes as Causes of Acute Conflict', p. 106.
14 See, for example, Shi Chunlai, 'Speech at the ARF Working Group Meeting on Preventive Diplomacy', *ARF Track Two Conference on Preventive Diplomacy*, 9–10 September, 1997, Singapore, co-sponsored by the Institute of Defence and Strategic Studies, Singapore and the International Institute for Strategic Studies, London, p. 9.
15 Mark Sommer, 'Non-military factors bring new meaning to art of spying', *Jakarta Post* 15 January 1996, p. 5.
16 Dalby, 'Security, Intelligence, the National Interest and the Global Environment', p. 191.
17 Paul Mann, 'Fathoming A Strategic World Of "No Bear, But Many Snakes"', *Aviation Week and Space Technology*, 6 December 1999, p. 61.
18 There is a growing literature on this subject. See, for example, Michael Harbottle, 'New Roles for the Military: Humanitarian and Environmental Conflict', Conflict Studies no. 285 (Research Institute for the Study of Conflict and Terrorism, London, 1995); Graham Turbiville, 'Operations Other Than War: Organised Crime Dimension', *Military Review* 74(1) 1994; Jennifer Morrison Taw, 'Planning for Military Operations Other Than War: Lessons From US Army Efforts', in Desmond Ball (ed.), *Maintaining The Strategic Edge: The Defence of Australia in 2015*, Canberra Papers on Strategy and Defence no. 133 (Strategic and Defence Studies Centre, Canberra, 1999), pp. 207–28.
19 Kaplan, '*The Coming Anarchy* ...,' p. 46.

Index

5T gang 189
14K triad 179t, 185

Abdullah, Firdaus Haji 297n60, 299n79
Abella, Maolo 296n43
Abramovitz, Janet N. 47n, 48n, 262n2, n4, 263n25
Abu Sayyaf group 183
Abuza, Zachary 290n48
Acharya, Amitav 248n30
acid rain 55, 65–6, 69, 233, 241
actors, non-state: criminal groups 7, 30; emergence of 5, 194, 228, 230, 242; and population movements 168–9; and national sovereignty 211
Afghanistan 207; narcotics trade 196
Africa: AIDS 213–14; refugees 165
Agcaoili, Mercedita C. 277n41
Agency for International Development, US 220
Agreement on Cooperation for the Sustainable Development of the Mekong River 128–9
agriculture 39, 48, 90, 114, 239; China 42; North Korea 191, 166; water 117, 123
Ahmad, Azman 58n, 266n82
Ahsan, Syed Aziz-Al 144n, 291n51
AIDS 173, 212–27; in Africa 213–14; and armed forces 217–18; ASEAN task force 222; Burma 220–21; Cambodia 219–20; characteristics of 213–14, 216, 225; China 221–2; and crime 212, 236; and demographic imbalance 216, 226; impact in East Asia 37, 213f, 216, 218–25, 230; Indonesia 222; Laos 222; Malaysia 222–3; public education programs 219–24, 226, 237; reasons for epidemic 223–5; and security 6, 11–12, 214–18; 236, 237, 239, 241; Thailand 218–19; therapies 223; Vietnam 222, 225
Ainsworth, Martha 226n, 318n94
air pollution 52, 54, 59, 66, 88
Akatsuki Maru, nuclear waste shipment 84
Akkadian empire 60
Alagappa, Muthiah 7, 248n31, n33, 253n29
Albanese, Jay S. 24n, 25n, 256n60, n65
Alegado, Dean T. 296n47
Alexandratos, Nicholas 277n41
Alford, Peter 105n, 262n23, 281n97, 313n7
Alptekin, Erkin 145
Altman, Dennis 317n81
Ambon, ethnic conflict in 145–6
amphetamine-type stimulants (ATS) 195, 198, 201, 205–7, 210, 236; North Korea 209; profitibility of trade 206; Philippines 201
amphetamines 190, 195
Andaman Sea, fishing disputes 103, 105
Anwar, Dewi Fortuna 145
Appleyard, Reginald T. 159n, 296n47
armed forces and AIDS 217–18; Cambodia 220
arms trade, clandestine 29, 175, 183, 190
Arroyo, Gloria Macapagal 201
ASEAN: Burma 148, 208; non-intervention policy 1, 7, 53, 55; and pollution 1, 288n113; and refugees 148–9; Regional Forum 140, 182, 240; task force on AIDS 222–3; Vietnam 77; and water disputes 131
Asian Development Bank 49, 52, 129, 226, 263n33, n34, 280n80
asylum-seekers 138, 140; *see also* refugees

320

21, 155n46, n51; and ethnic cleansing 147; Karen refugees 149; Vietnamese boat people 142, 289n34, n35, n36
UN International Atomic Energy Agency 87
UN International Drug Control Program 194
UN projections of population 36–8; projections on water 113–14, 131
UN Security Council 10
UN World Food Programme 89, 100
UNAIDS 220, 223
unemployment 39, 45–6, 132, 202, 232; China 140; Indonesia 43, 50
United Bamboo Gang 179t, 188
United Malays National Organisation 126; Youth Wing 126
United Wa State Army 184, 207
unregulated population movements 12, 13, 18–23, 31, 135–6, 228–9; in East Asia 140–43, 235; environmental refugees 164–7; and extended security 231, 240–41; global nature of 138–40, 169; reasons for 136, 137–8, 168–9
Uruguay Round 96
urbanisation: and conflict 36–8, 232; and crime 176; in China 42, 120; in East Asia 41t, 45, 165; and water 114, 117
US Committee for Refugees 290n40, 293n84
US Department of Agriculture 95
US Drug Enforcement Agency 178
US-KPRK (North Korea) Agreed Framework 84–5

Valencia, Mark 75n, 80n, 104n, 106n, 107n, 271n43, 272n65, 281n94, n112, n117, 285n56
Vatikiotis, Michael 76n, 77n, 105n, 149n, 225n, 271n53, n55, 274n86, 281n98, 292n75, 298n72, 318n89
Veng Bun Lay, General 220
Ver, General Fabian 51
Vietnam 19, 72, 92, 161; AIDS 222, 226; boat people 21, 142–3, 148; displaced persons 150; ethnic conflict 144, 149; ethnic gangs 189, 193; fishing disputes 105; heroin addiction 205; and labour migration 160; and Mekong River Basin 128, 130; sea-level rises 65; Spratly Islands 76–7
Vietnamese New Agency 76
Viking community in Greenland 60
Vines, 304n69
violence 30, 139, 144
Vision 2020, Malaysia 163
Viviani, Nancy 14n, 252n10

Voronin, Yuriy 301n22
Vostok Plan, Russia 271n43

Wa ethnic minority 1, 149, 184, 207
Waever, Ole 20n, 254n38
Wahid, Abdurrahman 106, 146; Wahid Government 44, 55, 144
Wallensteen, Peter 113n, 283n11, n13
Walters, Patrick, 145n, 147n, 261n53, 291n57, n63; Indonesia 43n, 54n, 77n, 260n43, 261n45, 264n53, n54, 272n58
Waltz, Kenneth 230, 245n4, n9, 318n3
Wang Jingong 185
Wang Kai 95n, 96n, 277n40, 278n47
Wang Yong 187n, 305n72
war 153, 167, 230, 232; criminalisation of 173, 183, 236
Wasserman, Beno 247n21
Watanabe, Teresa 279n69
water 112–32; availability of 64, 94, 234–5; and climate change 60, 67; and conflict 116–17, 124–6; deforestation and 48, 113, 117–18; demand for 39, 115, 121, 238; forecasts 112–14, 117–18, 131; irrigation 92, 98–9, 131, 235; management 113–14, 121, 131; Mekong River Basin 126–30; pollution 69, 117, 120; scarcity 35, 112–24, 234; and security 112, 120–24, 124–6, 131, 239; water-sharing agreements 124–5, 128–9
Watkins, Huw 315n46
Watkins, Kevin 276n10
Watson, Robert T. 63, 268n106
weather patterns 62, 67, 110; see also drought, El Niño, floods
Weiner, Myron 22n, 151n, 256n55, 293n90
Welsh, David 293n89
Wendt, Alexander 248n32
Western Pacific Naval Symposium Workshop 241
White, James 24, 24n, 256n61
Whiteside, Alan 216, 216n, 225n, 318n91
Whiting, Kenneth L. 77n, 272n56
Widgren, Jonas 137n, 288n4, 299n85
Wiencek, David 29n, 194n, 257n88, 303n48, 306n2
Wigdortz, Brett H. 270n20
Williams, Louise 52n, 164n, 263n33, n36, 298n79
Williams, Phil 28, 29n, 31n, 176n, 193n, 203, 256n62;, 257n77, n79, n83;, 258n91, 260n36, 301n14, 306n104, 309n49, n54
Willmott, William E. 151n, 293n85
Wirth, David 61, 267n92
Wise, Jeff 155n, 294n14